The Asbury Theological Seminary Series in Christian Revitalization Studies

This volume is published in collaboration with the Center for the Study of World Christian Revitalization Movements, a cooperative initiative of Asbury Theological Seminary faculty. Building on the work of the previous Wesleyan/Holiness Studies Center at the Seminary, the Center provides a focus for research in the Wesleyan Holiness and other related Christian renewal movements, including Pietism and Pentecostal movements, which have had a world impact. The research seeks to develop analytical models of these movements, including their biblical and theological assessment. Using an interdisciplinary approach, the Center bridges relevant discourses in several areas in order to gain insights for effective Christian mission globally. It recognizes the need for conducting research that combines insights from the history of evangelical renewal and revival movements with anthropological and religious studies literature on revitalization movements. It also networks with similar or related research and study centers around the world, in addition to sponsoring its own research projects.

In a timely study, Professor William Payne here offers in intensive study of the factors responsible for the explosive growth in early American Methodism, propelling it to become the largest American religious denomination in the nineteenth century. He engages relevant sociological models in evaluating the data, demonstrating the usefulness of the Hartford typology, with the intention of explicating Methodism's missionary character, organizational strengths, and historical and social dynamics which functioned to facilitate its global evangelistic mission. This study, grounding revitalization research in socio-demographic realities, is included in the Pietist and Wesleyan Studies sub series of the Revitalization Studies Series.

J. Steven O'Malley
Director, Center for the Study of World Christian Revitalization Movements,
General Editor, The Asbury Theological Seminary Series
in Christian Revitalization Studies

AMERICAN METHODISM: PAST AND FUTURE GROWTH

William P. Payne

Asbury Theological Seminary Series:
The Study of World Christian Revitalization Movements in
Pietist/Wesleyan Studies, No.10

EMETH PRESS
www.emethpress.com

American Methodism: Past and Future Growth

Copyright © 2013 William P. Payne
Printed in the United States of America on acid-free paper

All rights reserved. No part of this book may be reproduced, or stored in a retrieval system or transmitted in any form or by any means, electronic, mechanical, photocopying, recording, scanning or otherwise, except as permitted by the 1976 United States Copyright Act, or with the prior written permission of Emeth Press. Requests for permission should be addressed to: Emeth Press, P. O. Box 23961, Lexington, KY 40523-3961.   http://www.emethpress.com.

Library of Congress Cataloging-in-Publication Data

Payne, William P.
  American Methodism : past and future growth / William P. Payne.
      pages cm. -- (The study of world Christian revitalization movements in Pietist/Wesleyan studies ; no.10)
   ISBN 978-1-60947-047-0 (alk. paper)
   1. Methodist Church--United States--History. 2. United States--Church history. I. Title.
   BX8235.P39 2012
   287.0973--dc23
                                                2012039539

Front Cover
Bishop Francis Asbury on the circuit. This painting by Kenneth Wyatt is located at Asbury Theological Seminary. Photograph by seminary staff. Used by persmission.

TABLE OF CONTENTS

Foreword / vii
Preface / ix

1. The Case for EAM and Church Growth Research / 1
2. Counting the Converts: Making Disciples of All Nations / 13
3. Looking at the Numbers / 21
4. How EAM Proliferated the Circuit / 51
5. The Beginnings of EAM / 59
6. The Progress of EAM from 1766 through 1784 / 77
7. Special Issues in EAM from 1766 through 1784 / 91
8. The Sectional Crisis at Fluvanna and Its Consequences / 101
9. The Christmas Conference and Beyond, 1785 through 1800 / 109
10. Demographics, Economy, and Politics: How these Contextual Factors Shaped EAM from 1785 through 1800 / 117
11. Revivals and Decline in Southern Methodism from 1785 through 1800 / 137
12. Republicanism and the Rejection of Wesley / 147
13. The Rise of O'Kelly and His Defection / 157
14. Slavery and Other Contributing Factors to the Southern Decline / 175
15. Methodism in New England from 1789 through 1800 / 199
16. Understanding the Data in Terms of Sociological Theory / 221
17. Looking Backward to Look Forward / 239

Appendix – State Membership Totals from 1770 through 1812 / 257
Chapter Notes / 305
Bibliography / 341
Index / 353

FOREWORD

The amazing and unprecedented growth of American Methodism from to 1850 is well known. What is much less understood is that the growth patterns were uneven. Methodism was not always growing everywhere. In fact, even in periods of rapid expansion Methodism was declining in some areas.

Why? Bill Payne provides some very insightful answers. By taking a close-up look at particular regions during specific time periods, the author shows how complex Methodism growth-and-decline patterns really were. This ground-level analysis holds insights for the church today—for United Methodism certainly, but also more broadly.

A tremendous amount of careful research and analysis has gone into this significant book, as readers will readily see. The book provides important insights into the dynamics of early American Methodism that illuminate much of Methodism's later growth and then decline.

Bill Payne is a scholar; a missiologist with a pastor's heart. He has served churches and seen people transformed by God's grace. He has a passion for the kind of evangelism that leads to genuine discipleship. He notes in his introduction that in conducting the research that lies behind this book, "A protracted encounter with the early apostles of Methodism ignited a fire in my soul." Having been both a successful Methodism pastor in multicultural contexts and a seminary professor, Payne sees things and makes connections that may easily escape ivory-tower academics.

Payne's research and his own ministry experience, he says, "combined to validate a core truth: God wants the church to make disciples." Early Methodists understood this, and knew how to do it. Payne shows that early American Methodist growth wasn't primarily about making converts; it was about forming communities of faithful disciples.

The book investigates these dynamics, finding patterns in complex data. Payne examines the role of "strictness" and analyses the James O'Kelly defection as well as the complex issue of slavery and slaveholding. This is all part of the story, and a full understanding of the growth and impact of Methodism in America requires grasping all these relevant factors.

A final word of advice to readers: If you don't read anything else, be sure to read the last chapter, "Looking Back to Look Forward."

--Howard A. Snyder
Professor of Wesley Studies
Tyndale Seminary, Toronto

PREFACE

On a crisp February morning in 1998, I called my district superintendent (D.S.) to inform him of my intention to return to the conference for a pastoral appointment in June. I did not want a run-of-the-mill appointment. I asked him to send me to a congregation that would test my new degree in the crucible of apostolic ministry. In March, I received notice of my appointment. I undulated with excitement when I imagined the divine plan behind the assignment.[1] By this time, most of my peers had already completed their studies and had taken teaching positions in various parts of the world. I determined to take a different route to the academy.

In the years preceding my return to the full-time pastorate, two occurrences radically changed my ministry mindset. First, I embarked on a research project that examined the growth and decline of early American Methodism (EAM). A protracted encounter with the early apostles of Methodism ignited a fire in my soul. Because I spent so much time in their journals and other writings, I felt like I knew them. The research gave me a vision for the essence of Methodism; a movement that evangelized people and formed them into an army of itinerants, local preachers, and energized laity that transformed early America. Second, I served as the pastor of evangelism and church growth ministries at a large United Methodist Church (UMC). The ministry setting taught me how to release the potential of a United Methodist congregation by making strategic interventions in the corporate culture. When I arrived, the senior pastor told me that I had to make a minimum of 200 new members each year in order to keep the church from declining. Through the work of a process action team and a lot of coaching, the church leadership stopped focusing on membership and started to focus on disciple making. The new goal shifted the emphasis to assimilation. Assimilation included a robust stress on evangelism, spiritual formation, and the ministry of the laity. Afterward, an intractable pattern of decline gave way to a 475 person increase in average Sunday attendance in one year. The research project and the ministry experience combined to validate a core truth: God wants the church to make disciples. Both also made me excited about my pending transition to the pastorate.

In early April, my children and I flew to Orlando. Excitedly, we packed into my mother's car and headed to spy out our new appointment. During the trip, two of the tires on the low mileage older car blew due to dry rot. I changed the first but did not have a second spare. To make matters worse, we found ourselves in an endless sea of tomato fields and orange groves. After an eternity of driving 20 miles per hour, we finally arrived at a flashing light that signaled the heart of the community where I would serve. The good folks at the only gas station directed us to the only garage in town. The garage boasted a bucolic look replete with sleeping dogs, dirt floors, and a tin shed roof. It reminded me of a scene from Mayberry in The Andy Griffith Show. I would discover that the people who worked there were great mechanics and some of the finest people on God's green earth.

After buying used tires, we explored the town. Soon, we got lost in a maze of dirt roads. Cows and horses were as ubiquitous as trees. Houses were sparse. As the comedy of the situation settled upon us, my mother began to laugh uproariously. For my part, excitement pulsated within me. If I could grow a church in this town, I could teach others how to grow churches.

When I assumed pastoral leadership, the church averaged 430 active participants in the winter months and 180 during summer. Previously, the congregation had built a new sanctuary that seated 250 to accommodate the influx of winter visitors. Attendance grew as the population of winter visitors increased. The core congregation consisted of Florida natives and Northern transplants. The children's and youth ministries were meager. Adult Sunday school consisted of two classes. Morning worship included a traditional service and a blended service.

Most of the winter visitors lived in gated communities that segregated them from the general population. Deed restrictions excluded young families. Florida natives remained in their own homes and had little social interaction with the Northern visitors. Most of the winter visitors were middle to upper class white retirees from Illinois to Upstate New York. Church growth literature would classify them as a homogenous population. To be honest, an Ohio State fan may not feel an "Our Kind of People" sensation toward University of Michigan fans, especially during college football season![2] Still, in terms of experience, worldview, and values, the various mid-west populations shared a common set of cultural traits that extends to ecclesial preferences.

Over time, the in-gathering of winter visitors changed the internal dynamics of the congregation. First, in order to facilitate the winter surge, the church expanded programming, staff, and facilities. However, the vast majority of the winter visitors tithed to a church in another state. Second, most didn't participate in local ministry even though they had been choir members, Sunday school teachers, trustees, and church secretaries before coming south. Third, 70 volunteered to work in a highly organized thrift cottage that made money to pay off the church mortgage. The cottage leadership did not view the thrift cottage as a ministry to the community or as a way to make disciples. In fact, most of the volunteers had a negative view of the migrants who frequented the shop. This engendered conflict when the church attempted to utilize the cottage as an outreach ministry. Also, since the effective outreach of a church depends on the mobilization of its people for that purpose, the thrift cottage hindered outreach because it monopolized a huge percentage of the available pool of volunteers to work in a money-making enterprise. Fourth, over time, the style of the worship services morphed to accommodate the preferences of the winter visitors. Fifth, when the church focused its outreach on the winter visitors, it ignored outreach to the pre-Christian populations that dominated the social landscape. The unchurched included Hispanics, young families who had recently relocated from surrounding metropolitan areas, a working class drawn to the new job market that the retirees generated, those who worked on Sunday morning, and young people. In sum, the presence of the winter visitors and the sensation of growth that accompanied their attendance anesthetized the core congregation to the masses of unchurched people who surrounded them.

During the next few years, the congregation attempted to grow with each of the unreached populations without abandoning its commitment to Northern visitors. The shift met with stiff opposition. The following comment from a member who had permanently relocated to a gated complex, managed the thrift cottage, and served in other leadership positions illustrates the point: "Pastor, why do you waste your time reaching out to Hispanics? Don't you realize that one couple from [a particular well-to-do community] is worth more than 40 Hispanics?" From his perspective, one should prioritize the evangelization of the wealthy because they will give large sums of money to the church. Others complained that I did not spend enough time doing visitation with older members. To satisfy this expectation, the church hired a recent seminary graduate to serve as the assistant pastor of membership care. It became clear that the congregation needed to be converted to the ideals of early Methodism before the various populations that surrounded the church would be converted to Christ.

Shortly after I arrived, the church approached a vivacious member and asked her to serve as the director of youth and children's ministries. She had no training or experience. Yet, she demonstrated a hunger for God, a dynamic personality, the sincerity of new faith, a teachable spirit, and openness to the movement of God. After acquiescing, she took her cheerleader enthusiasm and began to connect with the youth. As the youth became excited about church and their faith, their unchurched friends began to participate in youth programming. As a response to a see-you-at-the-pole event, the youth organized a student club at the local high school.[3] Musicians from the high school band started to attend youth programs at church so they could rap with the youth band. Soon, the youth began a Sunday morning worship service that paralleled the traditional service. It featured culturally relevant music, a youth speaker, opportunities for youth to participate, and an altar call. Afterward, attendance skyrocketed. In an effort to go deeper and to evangelize more participants, the youth formed themselves into home prayer groups. In time, the program resembled a revival in terms of spontaneous growth, the work of the Holy Spirit, regular conversions, and a deep burden for God.

During the same time period, the church began a Wednesday evening program that targeted working families. A retired physician who always wanted to be a professional cook prepared gourmet meals so families could come directly from work. His wife, children, and grandchildren assisted him. The Wednesday night program grew out of a Vacation Bible School that attracted over 200 children. The Wednesday night program sought to assimilate the families that had participated in the VBS. During the Wednesday night program, children attended an alternate Sunday school and parents went to adult classes related to parenting, spiritual disciplines, and financial management. In time, the parents and their children migrated to the Sunday program. Because the parents did not feel comfortable in the traditional services, we started a contemporary service during the Sunday school hour. Within six months, 89 adults worshipped in this service. None of them had previous connections with the church. By this time, the director of youth and children's ministry guided a large team of volunteers that coordinated an expanding program of outreach ministry to unchurched people.

Most surprisingly, the church reached a group of African American youth who lived on the other side of town. Ministry to the African American youth began by accident. One day as I jogged past a school bus, a large group of boys followed me on their bikes. We sang running songs as I jogged about. When we got back to the parsonage, we did calisthenics. In time, they began to come to the parsonage and my office to ask me to play with them. I tried to meet them for basketball in the afternoons. Finally, I persuaded some local boys from the youth group to play basketball with them. A friend and I organized a Boy Scout troop in the church. Afterward, we went to the African America neighborhood and asked the parents if the boys could join. Soon, 12 of them united with our Boy Scout troop.[4] The same twelve went through confirmation class because I combined it with a scout religious award. Through participation in the confirmation class, the boys were evangelized. At the same time, they attended youth group and Sunday school.

Within the first month of moving to the community, a Hispanic couple asked if the church wanted to have a Hispanic ministry. After a long conversation and some prayer, we created an ad hoc Hispanic ministry team. By Christmas, 35 Hispanics participated in weekend programming. All came from a distant metropolitan area. In order to build the ministry around the local community, we relocated the Hispanic leader and his family to the old parsonage. Soon, the church became a center for Hispanic outreach. Migrants began to show up after work. Those who had gone to bars now congregated at the church for meals, Bible studies, and additional worship services. The programming included a heavy emphasis on Christian community and the Holy Spirit.

After a few months, eager participants took the worship services to off-campus locations including migrant camps and the sprawling barrios by the bodegas (tomato canning factories). On Sunday mornings, while new converts and children attended Sunday school, Hispanic members canvassed flea markets and Hispanic neighborhoods seeking to evangelize the unchurched. In time, the Hispanic ministry boasted a youth program, a large Sunday school program, five weekly services, an excellent praise and worship band, and an evangelism team. The historic chapel in which the Hispanics worshipped held 125 people. Over 170 crammed into the building during weekend services. Often, we went to the ocean or to a local park to baptize converts. During a three year period, we estimated that 900 migrants filtered through the ministry. Many remained in contact with us as they followed the crops to North Carolina. More importantly, they continued to lead Bible studies and to engage in ministry. We looked upon them as our missionaries.

The Hispanic ministry benefitted from the church's relationship with the Methodist Church in Cuba. It hosted the D.S. from the Camaguey District. Experience made him an expert at running revivals and in working with young leaders. His lay pastors resembled our Hispanic leaders and the itinerants of EAM. They lacked formal education, evidenced a sound conversion, had a great testimony, did evangelism with zeal, relied upon spiritual gifting, and were young. More importantly, the Cuban D.S. brought the Cuban revival to us when we arranged for him to preach in the church and to lead open air services in the Hispanic barrios.

During a typical open air evangelism event, the Hispanic ministry used cross-over music to gather a crowd. As the praise and worship team set up in a vacant lot, others would canvass the community to invite residents to attend a free concert at 8:00 pm. After a large crowd assembled, people from the ministry would give moving testimonies about their conversations and the transformation that Christ brought to their lives. Throughout the event, other members circulated among the people and engaged them in conversations as they sought evidence of receptivity to God. They gathered personal information on those who appeared interested. In the following days, lay ministers conducted follow-up. Because most migrants lacked access to transportation, the Hispanic ministry began local meetings in homes and in other available facilities close to the barrios and in the migrant camps.

At the request of my D.S., I developed a district Hispanic ministry plan that combined the insights from my church's Hispanic ministry with insights from EAM. The following excerpt illustrates how the plan drew upon both sources:

Vision: Disciple 5,000 Hispanics into new or existing ministries by the 2007 Annual Conference.
Mission: To establish viable and indigenous Hispanic ministries throughout the district so local churches and the district can partner with Hispanic ministries to evangelize, assimilate, and disciple Hispanic people.
Goals:
- Cover the district with a web of interconnecting Hispanic ministries. Establish Hispanic ministry hubs around existing Anglo churches. Spokes from hubs should reach out until a web of Hispanic ministries covers the entire district. As the hubs expand, establish more hubs.
- Recruit, train, and equip a cadre of Hispanic leaders from existing works to be hub preachers. Certify them as lay missioners, local pastors, missionaries, lay speakers, or any combination of the above.
- Assign a full-time Hispanic to each hub as the hub preacher (circuit rider) over the work in that area.
- Partner Hispanic ministries with local United Methodist churches so there is mutual accountability and a shared ministry.
- Establish a district Hispanic ministry team to organize and coordinate the Hispanic ministry initiative. The team will include the district coordinator, hub preachers, non-Hispanic hub-church pastors, selected lay people, and district representatives. The D.S. or a person appointed by him or her will lead the team.
- Through the partners in mission program, raise enough money to support the hub preachers and the District Coordinator of Hispanic Ministries. Supplement this fund with grants, offerings, Hispanic tithes, and special gifts. Ask each church in the district to support the Hispanic ministry in some

significant way. Some churches will be partnering churches. Others will be supporting churches.

The plan includes a detailed analysis of Hispanic demographics with an assessment of receptivity; a review of the organizational genius of EAM; and an application section that lays out the district Hispanic ministry plan based on the model of EAM, the success at the church I served, and the opportunity in the field. In short, the district Hispanic ministry plan treats EAM as a church growth case study, argues that EAM represents a rediscovery of apostolic Christianity, and opines that EAM can serve as a model for the evangelization of Hispanic populations. Like the church in Acts, contagious evangelism, numerical increase, enthusiastic worship, manifestation of spiritual gifts, rampant growth in grace, lay ministry, and a passion for discipleship dominated our Hispanic ministry and EAM.

Clearly, the example of EAM is still viable. It is normative in parts of Africa and in other parts of the globe. It also works with immigrant populations in America. If adjusted, it could be applied to the larger connection. Church growth is in the genes of Methodism. The numerical decline of modern United Methodism reflects the extent to which American Methodism has drifted from its origins and the ideal of apostolic Christianity. I hope that this book will inspire Methodist clergy and laity to rediscover the vision and passion of EAM as they consider the possibility of a radical faith that is combined with church growth know-how.

I would be extremely remiss if I did not acknowledge those who have helped to make this book possible. George Hunter III has served as a mentor for the last 20 years. Not only are we members of the Florida Annual Conference of the UMC, we also graduated from Florida Southern College and Emory University. Additionally, both of us ministered in England. His wife, Ella, served as my wife's nursing professor. During a very cold Thanksgiving break in 1988, Dr. Hunter met with me in the cafeteria at Asbury Theological Seminary. At that meeting, he opined that God wanted me to earn my doctorate in missiology. Not only did he read this manuscript, he also gave encouragement and inspiration. I count him a giant in the field of Church Growth and a true friend. His stories and numerous books have helped to shape my passion for evangelism and Church Growth.

I also want to extend my gratitude to Dr. John Shultz, President of Ashland Theological Seminary, for giving me a study leave to complete this work. My teaching assistant Esther Sim edited the original manuscript. Currently, she is working on a Ph.D. in Intercultural Studies at Trinity Evangelical Divinity School.

Finally, I want to give thanks to my wife, Ann. Not only has she traveled the world with me and patiently endured 26 years of sermons, she has given me space to complete this work. Without her divine patience and steadfast love, this book would not have been completed.

CHAPTER ONE

THE CASE FOR EARLY AMERICAN METHODISM AND CHURCH GROWTH RESEARCH

In the annals of American history, no religious organization has soared from virtual insignificance to the domination of the religious landscape as quickly as EAM. During its centennial celebration in 1884, Methodist Episcopal Church (MEC) leaders ruminated on past glories like aged veterans reminisce about the exploits of old battles. In the Preface to *Why the Marvelous (Former) Success of Methodism,* the Rev. J. L. Sooy[1] details the extraordinary significance of the Methodist story:

> The history of American Methodism is without a parallel in modern times. Not only is she the leading Protestant Church in numerical strength; not only do the figures show that, while the population of the United States has increased during the last century [1784-1884] about sixteen-fold, Methodism has increased her numerical strength more than five-hundred-fold but "virtue has gone out" of her to every Christian sect that has "touched the hem of her garment." Therefore, at the end of this her first century of organized ecclesiastical life, no question assumes such importance as this: *What are the causes of this phenomenal progress and success?*[2]

Table 1-1. Comparison of American Methodism and the U.S. population between 1770 and 1840

Year	Methodist Membership	Percent Increase	U.S. Population	Percent Increase
1770	361		2,205,000	
1780	8,264	2,267	2,781,000	26
1790	57,621	577	3,929,214	41
1800	65,883	13	5,808,483	46
1810	172,034	168	7,239,881	25
1820	257,736	50	9,638,020	33
1830	483,053	87	12,866,020	33
1840	883,709	83	17,069,453	33

Sources: Data from U.S. Bureau of the Census, *Historical Statistics of the United States, 1789–1945* (Washington, DC, 1949); Methodist Church Council on World Service and Finance Department of Research, *The Methodist Fact Book* (Evanston, IN, 1960).

Table 1-1 validates Sooy's exuberance. Numerical growth exceeded that of the general population in all but one decade, 1790-1800. In 1770, Methodism was so infinitesimal that it did not compare to the American population. By 1790, Methodist membership equaled 1.48 percent of the total population. By 1820, the percentage increased to 2.7. By 1843, it reached the high-water mark of 6.49 percent. The percentage of the American population that belonged to the MEC in 1843 was larger than the percentage of the American population that participated in all churches in 1800.[3]

In 1791, Bishop Thomas Coke wrote a personal letter to Bishop William White of the newly formed Protestant Episcopal Church in America. The missive looked beyond the printed membership summaries in order to reveal the actual numerical vitality of American Methodism:

> If we number the Methodists as most people number the members of their church, viz., by the families which constantly attend the divine ordinances in the places of worship, they will make a larger body than you possibly conceive.... The adults which form our congregations in these states amount to 750,000. About one-fifth of these being black.[4]

In 1791, the actual membership of the MEC equaled 61,082. If 750,000 adults formed the congregations, the ratio between members and participating non-members would have been 1:12. If Coke factored the children of the participating adults into his estimate, the total would have exceeded a million. Coke may have exaggerated the size of the congregations in order to sway Bishop White in terms of his scheme to merge the MEC into the Protestant Episcopal Church. However, this is unlikely since Coke's estimations mirror those of Bishop Francis Asbury.[5]

As the father of American Methodism, Asbury knew Methodist attendance patterns because he itinerated throughout the entire connection on a regular basis. In 1797, he wrote, "Altho [sic] we do not number yet, we may calculate upon one hundred thousand that stand in the above states in friendship and are in some degree of fellowship with us and perhaps ten hundred thousand [1,000,000] that are our regular hearers."[6] After five years of southern membership decline, Asbury opined a modest 1:10 ratio of membership to regular hearers.[7]

If Asbury's "regular hearers" and Coke's attendees represent the same group of people, approximately 18.5 percent of the U.S. population in the 1790s related to the MEC. This extraordinary percentage accentuates EAM's meteoric growth from its inception in the late 1760s, points to its vast influence in the 1790s, and shows why the annual membership summaries belie Methodism's numerical influence.

According to Robert Coleman, within 30 years of its founding in 1784, the MEC was the largest denomination in America. It had 20 percent more members than the Baptists, and it was larger than the Episcopalian, Congregational, and Presbyterian churches combined. Within 50 years of the arrival of the first Methodist missionaries to America in 1769, more than one quarter of all the professing Christians in America, both Protestants and Roman Catholics, claimed to be Methodists. The growth rate was so hyperbolic, every American would have been won to Christ and an overwhelming majority would have been called Methodists if it had continued for a few more generations.[8]

Table 1-2 shows the projected growth rate of Methodist participants to the U.S. population from 1770 through 1840 based on a 1:11 membership to participant ratio. The data in this table presupposes that the averaged 1:11 ratio that Coke and Asbury noted in the 1790s held true for the entire period.[9]

Table 1-2. Projected Methodist participants to U.S. population based on a 1:11 ratio

Year	Methodist Membership	Methodist Participants	U.S. Population	Participants as Percent of Population
1770	361	3,971	2,205,000	1.8
1780	8,264	90,904	2,781,000	3.3
1790	57,621	633,831	3,929,214	16.7
1800	65,883	724,713	5,808,483	12.5
1810	172,034	1,892,373	7,239,881	26.1
1820	257,736	2,835,096	9,638,020	29.4
1830	483,053	5,313,583	12,866,020	41.3
1840	883,709	9,720,799	17,069,453	56.9

Source: Data from U.S. Bureau of the Census, *Historical Statistics of the United States, 1789–1945* (Washington, DC, 1949); Methodist Church Council on World Service and Finance Department of Research, *The Methodist Fact Book* (Evanston, IN, 1960).

Assuming that Methodist birthrates were the same as those of the general population (biological growth), that Methodist immigrants did not add significant numbers to American Methodist rolls (transfer growth from European

Methodism),[10] and that a low percentage of Americans attended church during the era of the Early Republic, one can suppose that EAM increased in relationship to the total population primarily by means of conversion growth.[11] Conversion growth refers to the evangelization, assimilation, and discipling of unchurched people. It must be conceded that EAM grew in some areas in which the population was nominally associated with another Christian tradition by baptism, heritage, or establishment laws. Still, Finke and Stark have shown that the population of early America, regardless of religious affiliation, was almost completely unchurched.[12] The evangelization of nominal Christians falls under the category of conversion growth.

Some would argue that the numerical strength of EAM was of little importance. After all, what difference did it make if a person belonged to an Episcopal, Presbyterian, Congregational, Roman Catholic, or Methodist congregation? In truth, it made a big difference. In EAM, affiliation led to spiritual maturity and right living. The discipleship process included a deep conviction of sin, awakening, repentance, personal faith in Christ, participation in a local class, keeping the discipline, accountability, and the regular use of the various means of grace. As Methodists "moved toward perfection," they underwent a radical change. Furthermore, as the membership increased, the social sway of EAM on the emerging American ethos also increased. By 1810, the transforming influence from Methodism's growing tentacles reached deep into the political and cultural arenas of American life.[13]

The question that Sooy asked at the time of the centennial celebration of the MEC remains a compelling question. What are the causes of its phenomenal progress and success? The answer looms with tremendous implications. If one could offer a conclusive response to Sooy's question and attach reproducible principles to it, one could suggest ways to reignite the flames that burned EAM into a raging fire. Granted, numerical growth for the sake of more people in the pews is of little value unless the growth is related to a larger process of salvation, discipleship, and transformation. If American Methodism were reinvigorated so that it took on the character and soul of EAM, it would become a potent force for spiritual vitality, social holiness, and apostolic faith.

A Re-examination of the Growth Data

From its origins in America to 1844, EAM sustained exceptional progress in terms of numerical growth and social influence. This fact has been trumpeted by historians and denominational officials. Typically, consolidated national growth statistics undergird the explanations for the numerical growth. The following word picture characterizes the institutional hagiography that has dominated many Methodist writers: Like an ecclesiastical giant, American Methodism slowly rose out of a sea of competing denominations so that it towered over the other churches. The giant was buoyed by some or all of the following institutional factors: the itinerancy, the work of local preachers, the lifestyles of the circuit riders, the circuit system, evangelical preaching, camp meetings, constant evangelism, democratic theology, Arminianism, the doctrine of sanctification, episcopal leadership, Methodist discipline, local organization, revivalism, the hymnody, the Book Concern, and the Americanization of Methodism. In the mind of the denominational apologist, these institutional factors represent independent principles that derive from the success story and are assumed to be causes for numerical growth.

Yet, Methodism's success story contains a striking inconsistency. Based on the institutional growth factors, the uniformity of the Methodist system, and the phenomenal expansion of the denomination, one should expect uniform and consistent growth in all the geographical regions in which Methodism labored if the institutional growth factors represent independent variables that caused the explosive growth.[14] In other words, the institutional factors that caused growth in one area should have caused similar growth in every area. However, the growth data do not bear this out. In fact, regions within EAM experienced periods of significant decline during time-frames of denominational growth. Additionally, periods of decline shifted between the various regions so that no single area had continuous growth or decline.

The 1790s illustrate this point. Despite the general slump that EAM sustained in 1795 and 1796, Figure 1 shows that Northern Methodism increased in membership during a decade in which Southern Methodism declined.[15] In fact, each of the various regions followed a unique membership pattern.

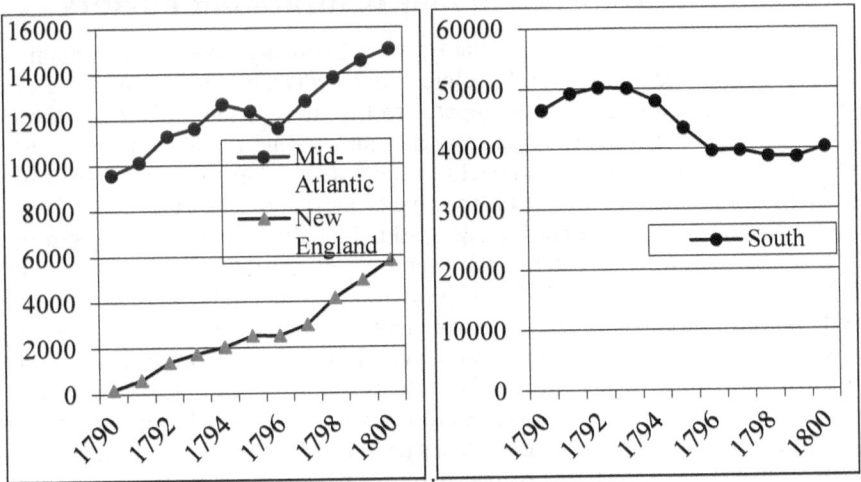

Figure 1. Regional line-graphs of Methodist membership between 1790 and 1800.

During the 1790s, New England Methodism burgeoned from 181 to 7,236 members and expanded into every New England state. Mid-Atlantic Methodism grew from 3,624 to 15,065 members. Frontier membership grew from 1,372 to 2,318. The combined memberships of New England, the Mid-Atlantic, and the frontier increased by 19,623 (379 percent) in the 1790s. Conversely, southern membership plummeted by 7,894 (17 percent) in the 1790s. After increasing by 34,727 members from 1786 through 1792, Southern Methodism lost 11,602 members (22.3 percent) from 1792 through 1799. Following 1799, membership rebounded quickly. Even still, the aggregate did not surpass the 1792 membership zenith until 1803.[16] The southern slump during the 1790s stands in stark contrast to Methodism's impulses in the Mid-Atlantic and New England regions. During previous periods, Northern Methodism declined or crept along while Southern Methodism grew at a rapid rate. Between 1800 and 1812, all the regions in EAM experienced exceptionally strong growth.

By concentrating on the national consolidated growth data and the institutional growth factors derived from them, the regional pattern of growth and decline has been ignored. More importantly, factors that caused regional declines have remained invisible. Consequently, a significant and important aspect of the Methodist story has been neglected. Furthermore, because the assumed growth factors were derived from national statistics that glossed over periods of regional decline, the conclusions associated with them are misleading. Growth and decline do not happen within a vacuum. They are related to the interfacing of contextual and institutional factors. As such, one must understand how contextual and institutional factors combine to affect membership totals in order to answer Sooy's question.

A Brief Review of Church Growth Theory as It Relates to Contextual and Institutional Factors

In the mid-1970s, researchers from the Hartford Seminary Foundation examined the causes for church growth and decline. Unprecedented membership losses in the mainline denominations gave impetus to the study.[17] The task force developed a useful framework for organizing and interpreting a wide variety of factors that contribute to growth and decline. Specifically, they analyzed contextual and institutional factors from the perspective of local and national settings.[18]

The Hartford group did not include spiritual factors because they used a social science approach. C. Peter Wagner and others argued for the inclusion of spiritual factors. They contended that spiritual forces should be measured if they exert an influence that shapes the environment and sways receptivity. According to Wagner, at its core evangelism and conversation are spiritual processes. One cannot ignore spiritual factors and hope to account for the totality of church growth and decline. For example, some practitioners have demonstrated that concerted prayer evangelism that precedes an outreach event increases the effectiveness of that event in terms of decisions for Christ and the manifestation of God.[19] Still, even though one can affirm the correlation, one cannot define and measure the exact causations for it. Because spiritual factors have defied quantification, most social scientists do not attempt to account for them. More research should be directed at this important topic.

Contextual factors relate to the external environment. They vary from place to place. They include anything that affects the demographic and ethnographic milieu in which a church or denomination exists. Common examples include changes in birthrates, movements of people in or out of a particular area, patterns of immigration, the availability of transportation, a natural disaster, a change in economic conditions, shifting levels of education, war, the building of a highway that cuts a parish in half, or an epidemic. Contextual factors shape a church's future.[20] By definition, a church may respond to contextual factors but it does not control them.[21] Even though contextual factors greatly influence church growth and decline, they do not determine them. A church's response to a given contextual factor will determine how the contextual factor affects church health.

Institutional factors are forces internal to the church. They include patterns of organization and structure, evangelism methods, the strictness of a group's religious beliefs, church programs, and other characteristics and orientations.[22] They also relate to the corporate culture, patterns of leadership, the pastor, commitment to outreach, worship styles, signage, marketing, location, denominational affiliation, the building, accessibility, parking availability, theology, and attitudes. According to the Hartford study, institutional factors interact with contextual factors to determine church growth or decline within a given environment.

The same contextual factor may cause growth or decline. For example, when hurricane Katrina precipitated a large exodus of people from lower Louisiana, church attendance declined. Destroyed church buildings, disrupted congregational life, limited mobility, and the absence of established leaders abetted the decline. At the same time, many of the people who remained were open to God. Those who ministered in the aftermath spoke of high receptivity and effective evangelism. In some cases, new churches were planted. The churches that met physical needs, gave spiritual encouragement, shared the plight of the residents, and did evangelism reaped a harvest. The diminished population was a negative contextual factor that adversely affected church attendance. Incarnational outreach that built on high levels of receptivity was a positive institutional factor in response to the negative contextual factor.

Additionally, hurricane Katrina positively influenced numerical increases in the areas where the evacuees moved because churched migrants looked for a new church home. Additionally, unchurched migrants had special needs that predisposed them to turn to the church. All the churches in the areas to which the people spread could have leveraged this opportunity for numerical growth. Unsurprisingly, churches that prioritized outreach to the newcomers grew at a faster rate than those that did not. This is especially true for churches that formed "New Orleans" congregations and did evangelistic outreach to the unchurched among the evacuees. In general, a growing population is a positive contextual factor. How a church responds to the growing population is an institutional quality that will determine rates of growth.

The same fact holds true for a church in a changing neighborhood. A homogeneous congregation built around an aging population in a transitional community will decline and eventually die if the members believe that the church and the pastoral leadership exist to meet their needs. Nevertheless, the declining church can stave off death and find growth by targeting one or more of the new populations. In many cases, aging churches resist evangelism because outreach to a new population may lead to an influx of new participants who will radically change the internal dynamics of the church. In order to grow with a new population, an aging church has to focus on the unchurched and seek to lose itself in ministry to them. George Hunter calls this apostolic ministry.[23] Growth comes with a price. A congregation that is not willing to pay the price will not reap a large harvest.

This book distinguishes between national, regional, and local institutional factors. A denomination is a national factor that has a life of its own. A national institution determines polities, standard theology, bylaws, and practices. Denominations raise money and spend money. They hire staff, appoint leaders, equip pastors, found seminaries, and promote programs. They project a corporate personality that "brands" local congregations. To an extent, be they connectional or congregational, they tell local churches what to do and how to do it. Yet, denominations do not make disciples; local churches do that. From an institutional perspective, however, a denomination influences the growth or decline of its congregations.

National denominations may become fractured when competing groups within a denomination push ideas, programs, and theologies that cater to one segment and estrange other segments. Such activities may reflect the influence of regional contextual factors like political affiliations and the desires of regional bodies to contextualize the church to their setting. For example, to the extent that institutional United Methodism in New England adjusts to its ideological setting, it may push a social agenda in the denomination that Southern United Methodists find unacceptable. If New England Methodism positively moves the denomination in its direction, southern members may leave their local churches out of protest or a sense of disaffection. Even worse, potential affiliates in the South may become resistant to United Methodist outreach because of its perceived branding. In this way, a national institutional factor that positively influences numerical growth in one region may induce decline in another region.

In the above illustration, New England could be replaced with Africa. In that case, one would approach United Methodism as a global institution that is composed of global constituencies that function like independent regions. In fact, the African connection has asserted a huge influence in the branding and shaping of United Methodism. African leaders know that certain social positions are not tenable within their context. As such, they have successfully resisted attempts to change portions of the social principles much to the chagrin of many United Methodist leaders in New England and other parts of the connection.

The existence of a regional pattern requires that the majority of the congregations in a given region share a cluster of characteristics that distinguish them from congregations in other regions. Even still, local congregations within a region will evidence diversity because the regional character does not imply homogeneity. For example, some United Methodist churches in the South are largely composed of northern transplants. Others are composed of academics and social liberals. These churches may affirm the social and theological perspective of New England Methodism. In fact, these churches could grow by targeting likeminded unchurched populations who live in the South if they discovered an effective way to evangelize them. Certainly, migration patterns have landed large numbers of New Englanders in the South who could be evangelized by churches who reach out to them.

Sadly, it has been shown that high incidences of secularism and affinity to progressive ideology predispose a congregation or denomination to numerical decline. The same factors predisposed academics and the liberal elite to resist evangelical outreach. Two generalized reasons stand out. First, liberal churches do not emphasize personal evangelism. It may seem axiomatic, but churches that do not do evangelism do not grow as well as those that do. This point is lost on many who will do everything but evangelism and then wonder why their church does not grow.[24] Second, the local church may not be as important to a liberal Christian as it is to a conservative one. Liberals can find common cause with a number of likeminded voluntary organizations that provide fellowship and promote an agenda that meshes with their values to include a heavy emphasis on social justice, advocacy for the poor, prophetic outreach, intellectual stimulation, aesthetic inspiration, and identity formation. In general, church participation is not as important to the liberal minded Christian as it is to the evangelical in that the liberal does not depend on the church to satisfy an equivalent set of needs.[25]

Interestingly, even though the mainline traditions champion the cause of the poor and disenfranchised, overwhelmingly, the poor attend socially conservative churches that promote tight community and experiential religion. This becomes a glaring exclamation mark when one examines the current social demographics of the mainline churches. During its formative years, EAM promoted tight community, exuded experiential religion, and recruited its members and leaders from the ranks of the poor and middling folks. Wesley and EAM leaders resisted respectable religion and outreach to the wealthy because they feared that the inclusion of those people would corrupt the movement. In fact, the official rhetoric toward wealth and the gentry seems harsh and antagonistic. Strategic alliances between EAM and wealthy benefactors existed only because Methodism desperately needed a constant infusion of capital in order to pay the itinerants, expand the circuits, grow the Book concern, and build preaching houses.[26]

In the 1980s, the Hartford Seminary Foundation overemphasized the deleterious effects of negative contextual factors when it suggested that contextual factors account for 70 percent of growth of decline in order to excuse the alarming numerical decline of mainline churches.[27] By implication, since the church has little or no control over them, the mainline denominations should not be overly concerned with church growth in a contextually hostile environment. Blaming numerical decline on the determinative nature of negative contextual factors appealed to the leadership of the declining denominations because it buffered them against criticism and allowed them to maintain their course.[28]

Dean Kelley, a United Methodist member of the Hartford Foundation, challenged their assumptions in a pioneering book, *Why Conservative Churches Are Growing*.[29] If negative contextual factors doomed American Christianity to decline, why were the conservative churches reaping a huge harvest that outpaced the growth of the U.S. population? In fact, during the period of greatest mainline decline, Pentecostals, Southern Baptists, the Church of Christ, Mormons, and non-denominational evangelical churches registered tremendous growth. Additionally, many conservative congregations within the mainline denominations also grew.

Unlike the Hartford Group, Kelley realized that a local church can grow in a seemingly hostile contextual environment if the church adjusts its institution to take advantage of growth opportunities. Like Kelley, C. Peter Wagner emphasized institutional factors. Since denominational growth happens as individuals affiliate with local congregations, denominations should emphasize local institutional factors. He stated, "The majority of church growth problems can be corrected by appropriate decisions and action on the part of the congregation."[30] Donald McGavran, the father of the church growth movement, shared this opinion. Even though negative contextual factors seem insurmountable, in most cases, decline can be minimized or reversed when institutional factors are positively adjusted to compensate for negative contextual factors.

Pragmatism, the Church Growth Movement, and Early Methodism

According to Wagner, "Church growth is that discipline which investigates the nature, expansion, planting, multiplication, function, and health of Christian churches as they relate to the effective implementation of God's commission to 'make disciples of all peoples.'"[31] Church growth is a theological conviction based on the belief that God wants his lost children found. Numerical growth is important because lost people matter to God. In order to measure how effectively the church is actualizing the goal of world evangelization, one must amass accurate data related to those who are reached and those who are not reached, what methods work and what methods do not work. The researcher must cut through the "fog" of inaccurate information resulting from a lack of rigorous investigation.[32] In regard to this, church growth is a research based social science that collects data, interprets data, and tests hypotheses in terms of a scientifically informed protocol.[33] It strives to determine exact causes for growth and decline. It also strives to establish church growth principles that derive from field research. These principles can be used to assist the church in its task of world evangelization.

For the purposes of this book, one should note three additional points about church growth. First, it emphasizes the evangelization of all the "people groups" in the world (cf. Matt. 28:19). A people group is a large grouping of individuals or families who perceive that they are connected to each other by means of social relationships or a common affinity of some sort. Examples from EAM include poor farmers in eastern North Carolina, African slaves, and settlers on the frontier. Typically, a local church that succeeds in evangelizing one people group will not succeed with other people groups. The homogeneous unit principle attempts to explicate this fact in terms of social factors.[34] It shows that most people come to Christ through their participation in a social web movement. A friend, relative, neighbor, or associate may be the one who most influences a person's decision. In EAM slaves evangelized each other, women evangelized their husbands, and neighbors evangelized neighbors. Socially similar people grouped themselves together as they formed classes and preaching points. Still, a growing movement like EAM had to reach many people groups simultaneously in order to evangelize the nation. For this reason, EAM adapted to the various social contexts and geographic regions in which it ministered. Even so, the need to hold many people groups together in the same organization caused institutional stress. The great conflicts and splits in EAM evidence this.

Second, church growth advocates for the making of responsible church members. A responsible church member is a disciple. A responsible church member has repented, received Christ, been assimilated into a believing community, and is maturing in the faith as he or she lives out the gospel. Wesley's order of salvation and his emphasis on the means of grace assume responsible participation in the Body of Christ. The Methodist "discipline" required responsible church membership.[35] Simply stated, early Methodism transformed sinners into saints. Preachers awakened sinners, initiated them into the fellowship of a class, and managed a process by which they were spiritually matured. In other words, the local class became a nursery in which Jesus was planted in the heart of an individual. As the person grew into the image of Christ, the person bore the fruit of discipleship. Methodist wisdom dictated that it was best not to awaken lost people if there was no means by which to form them into classes. Otherwise, the awakened people would quickly fall away and be much harder to win back at a later date.[36]

In EAM, the evangelism process did not exist to make church members who did nothing more than fill pews on Sunday. Itinerants counted membership because it equated to discipleship. Through participation in the class and local society one gained access to the numerous means of grace that helped to form the person into the image of Christ. As such, a person could not become a Methodist or remain a Methodist without actively participating in the life and ministry of the local church. In this regard, the practice of early Methodism and the goals of church growth mesh. Discipleship requires active participation in a faith community in which one accepts Christ, receives baptism, and learns to become a follower of Christ.

Third, church growth is pragmatic. The spirit of pragmatism runs deep in early Methodism. Luke Keefer touches on this point. He states that Wesley's study of Acts led him to a dynamic concept of ecclesiology. This opened him to pragmatic innovations and discoveries. From Acts, Wesley discovered that "the Spirit providentially led the church to forms of government and ministry that enhanced the spread of the gospel."[37] Based on this he determined that the true church was a missionary church and that the form of church government and practice were purely functional issues. Keefer states, "The determinative question regarding ecclesiastical practices was the degree to which they contributed to or detracted from the missionary task of the church."[38]

Wesley was a pragmatist with an "of necessity" disposition. In "A Plain Account of the People Called Methodists," Wesley documents the various aspects of Methodism that he discovered and determined to use because they produced tangible results in accordance with his goals.[39] They include the society, classes, bands, the select society, special classes for penitent people, love feasts, watch-night services, the Poor House, and readings of the work of God in other denominations and the world to encourage faith and fight a partisan spirit. One should add that exhorters, lay preaching, the circuit system, field preaching, conferences, and the like were also discovered and utilized because they were used by God to produce good results. Ultimately, despite great criticism, Wesley justified the ordination of American preachers on pragmatic grounds.

Wesley adopted a practice if it worked, if God blessed it, and if it was not against the clear teaching of Scripture. Wesleyan pragmatism calls for experimentation and observation. It also requires an open mind. Conversely, if something does not work in the field, a new approach must be found even if the old method is tried and true in another context. Wesley wanted to see results. He was not against bending the rules or being irregular for the sake of achieving his ministry objectives and the advancing of the kingdom of God. This point presaged the pragmatic emphasis of the church growth movement. For this reason, there is no conflict between pristine Methodism and the church growth emphasis on pragmatism.

This chapter demonstrates that EAM can be studied as a church growth case study based on its extraordinary growth. It also shows that Methodism did not have uniformed growth since discrete regional growth patterns existed. For that reason, the growth cannot be fully attributed to national institutional growth factors. Rather, regional growth or decline happened as national, regional, and local institutional and contextual factors interacted with each other.

The chapter also demonstrates the striking similarities between the church growth movement and the actual practice of Wesley and EAM. Both emphasize evangelism. Both demonstrate a pragmatic approach that adopts innovations that work. Both seek to make disciples and emphasize the importance of participation in a community of believers where one will be nurtured into a disciple. Finally, both understand the need to adapt to the social context as one contextualizes the faith to a particular people or region.

CHAPTER TWO

COUNTING THE CONVERTS: MAKING DISCIPLES OF ALL NATIONS

The phrase "counting the converts" appears frequently in the literature on EAM. Bishops Asbury and Coke counted the converts. In fact, every circuit rider counted the converts. Not only did the preachers count the converts, they also counted those who were being converted. For example, those who kept journals often recorded the number of members and nonmembers who attended their preaching as they worked their circuits. Not surprisingly, EAM measured clergy effectiveness in terms of a preacher's fruit. Did people respond to his preaching? Were people joining the classes and societies over which he gave leadership? Did he grow his circuit by adding preaching points, classes, and societies? Officially, the Methodist *Minutes* counted the number of circuits, the number of preachers, and the number of members. One could say that early Methodist preachers obsessed on counting. Certainly, if one aspired to be a Methodist preacher, he had to be good at arithmetic.

In modern American Methodism, counting the converts causes some to wince. They opine that it reflects a very non-spiritual approach to kingdom based ministry. They argue that it is nothing more than the institutional church reducing people to giving units. In this guise, converts are a means to a not-so-holy end. Furthermore, they contend that counting churches are dominated by a marketing mentality that is contrary to the spirit of the missional church movement. The criticisms reflect the reality of modern Methodism and show how far the modern church has drifted from its apostolic roots. Additionally, the critique does not reflect the reality of EAM and it may impede the apostolic rebirth of modern American Methodism.

Some who oppose church growth have used II Samuel 24 as a justification for not counting the converts. In that passage, David counted the valiant men in Israel and Judah. The parallel passage in I Chronicles 21:1 says that Satan prompted David to enumerate the people. For it, God sent a pestilence upon the people. Ironically, the chapter counts the number of Israelites who died at the hand of the Lord's angel (cf. II Sam. 24:15).

If counting is wrong, why did God direct Moses to count the people in Israel in Numbers 1:1-4?

> [1]The LORD spoke to Moses. . . . He said: [2]"Take a census of the whole Israelite community by their clans and families, listing every man by name, one by one.[3] You and Aaron are to count according to their divisions all the men in Israel who are twenty years old or more and able to serve in the army.[4] One man from each tribe, each of them the head of his family, is to help you" (Num. 1:1-4 NIV).

David counted the troops in order to gauge the strength of his army. He sinned when he counted the valiant men for one of several possible reasons. First, he may have been motivated by prideful arrogance. Second, counting may have symbolized a lack of faith in God. God gave the victory. Past experiences should have taught David this lesson. Certainly, the Exodus and the story of Gideon exemplify this truth. Third, God may have directed David not to count the valiant men. Regardless, counting the converts as a percentage of the potential harvest for a given location so that the church can become more effective in winning receptive people to Christ is not sinful. Ignoring the harvest potential by becoming a hired chaplain to a cloistered community of xenophobic believers who have domesticated the gospel and live for themselves is wrong because it ignores the evangelistic mandate and shows a striking lack of love for the unchurched. God loves the perishing. He sends the church into the world to bid the perishing to believe in Christ and be reconciled to God in the context of a worshipping community of faithful saints. A declining church that ignores the harvest does not have the mind of Christ or the heart of the Father.

I once attended a district pastor's meeting in which my DS wanted to empathize with the pastors who were not growing their churches. He told us that Jesus did not count the sheep; rather, he fed them. According to my former DS, pastors would be less stressed and more effective if they focused on feeding more than on counting. I chuckled to myself. Jesus tells the parable of the shepherd who left the 99 sheep and went to find the lost sheep (cf. Luke 15:1-7). A woman counted her coins; realized that one was missing; and searched all over her home until she found the lost one (cf. Luke 15: 8-10). Both of these stories demonstrate the implicit evangelistic mandate that characterized the ministry of Jesus and the early church. Additionally, the gospels tell us how many people attended to the ministry of Jesus. For example, he healed ten lepers (cf. Luke 17:11-19) and fed over 5,000 men (cf. John 6:1-15). Jesus chose 12 apostles (cf.

Matt. 10:1-4) and sent out 72 disciples to go before him as they prepared the people to receive his ministry (cf. Luke 10:1).

In Matthew, the word "crowd" is used to describe the throngs of people to whom Jesus ministered 38 times. Often, the term is preceded by "large." Throughout the book of Acts, Luke tells the readers that converts were added to the church on a repeating basis. For example, about 3,000 were added on the Day of Pentecost (cf. Acts 2:41). Daily, the Lord added to the number of converts who were being saved (cf. Acts 2:47). The number of disciples increased on a regular basis (cf. Acts 6:1 and 7). Often, Acts uses quantitative phrases like "great number" to describe new converts and those who received ministry (e.g., Acts 5:12-16). When Paul returned to Jerusalem to tell of God's work with the Gentiles, the Jerusalem Church countered that many thousand Jews had believed and become followers of the Way (cf. Acts 21:20). The early church attracted crowds, counted the converts, and celebrated the results because feeding and counting are not mutually exclusive activities. A good shepherd does both.

Pastors who de-emphasize counting the converts tend to lack external standards by which they measure effectiveness or the extent to which the kingdom of God is advancing through their ministries. The absence of an objective standard also allows them to avoid accountability. In the context of the mainline malaise that features a sustained membership loss and an accompanying mitigation of social influence, this has become a problem. In preparation for the 2012 General Conference of the UMC, the Ministry Study Commission proposed new rules that target unproductive pastors. Specifically, one rule will abolish guaranteed appoints for ministers who show a pattern of ineffectiveness. United Methodism is at a critical crossroads. As an aging denomination, it will cease to exist if it does not reverse the annual membership bleed. Other mainline churches attempt to diminish the reality of annual membership declines by merging with other shrinking churches. Mergers give a sense of renewed vitality because they artificially inflate membership. In reality, most mergers postpone the inevitable because the merged church does not address the reasons that caused the decline.

Recently, some conservative churches within the Evangelical Lutheran Church in America and the Episcopal Church separated from the mother denominations. Hopefully, the separating churches will grow by means of conversion growth as they recapture and repackage the essence of their traditions in light of the growing secularism that dominates the landscape of unchurched America. In fact, denominational splits may be the means by which God grows the declining traditions. Microbiologists who study cells speak of multiplication by division when an organism grows by means of cell division (mitosis). From an ecclesial perspective, multiplication by division occurs when a breakaway church and the old church both grow by recruiting new members. One wants to grow to compose a new congregation. The other wants to grow to compensate for its membership loss. The same phenomenon can occur when a mother church plants a daughter church. Both church planting and the dividing of existing congregations may spur church growth.

The Great Commission, Church Growth, and the Example of EAM

> Then Jesus came to them and said, "All authority in heaven and on earth has been given to me. [19] Therefore go and make disciples of all nations, baptizing them in the name of the Father and of the Son and of the Holy Spirit, [20] and teaching them to obey everything I have commanded you. And surely I am with you always, to the very end of the age" (Matt. 28:18-20 NIV).

The Great Commission calls the church to make disciples of all nations. "All" is a quantifiable term that begs to be measured. The "go" or "having gone" in verse 19 directs the apostles to move out from Jerusalem. It assumes that they and those who follow after them will take the gospel to all nations. In the common parlance of that time, a nation was a group of people who had a shared identity. Often, it is translated "people group" (cf. page 11). According to Matthew 24:14, the gospel of the kingdom will be preached to the *whole world* as a testimony to *all nations*. Mark 16:15-16 calls the church to preach the Gospel to all creation. Those who repent and believe are to be baptized. The commission in Acts 1:8 emphasizes witnessing from Jerusalem to the ends of the earth. As the church moved out from Jerusalem following the stoning of Stephen (cf. Acts 8*ff*), it crossed cultural, linguistic, and geographic boundaries as it evangelized, baptized, and founded communities of faith in the following order: Jerusalem (Acts 2-7), Samaria (Acts 8:4-25), an Ethiopian Jew (Acts 8:26-39), a God-fearing Roman centurion (Acts 10), and pagan gentiles with no affiliation with Judaism (Acts 11:19-21). As the itinerant evangelists and missionaries took the Gospel to the ends of the earth, they planted churches within each people group they encountered. The emerging churches were culturally relevant. As these local churches expanded, they evangelized their own people starting in the city centers and moving out to the surrounding environs.

Making disciples is the main point. In the Great Commission, a disciple is a baptized person who has been taught to obey all that Christ has commanded. An adult convert who received baptism had heard the gospel, repented, and confessed Christ. The Apostle Matthew models repentance when he leaves his tax collector booth and follows Jesus (cf. Luke 5:27-32). The rich young ruler models the failure to repent when he is unable to sell all his possessions and follow Christ (cf. Matt. 19:16-26). Repentance represents a change in orientation. One's allegiance to Christ and the in-breaking kingdom dominates the disciple's life (cf. Matt. 6:33). The parable of the buried treasure illustrates this. The person who discovers a buried treasure in a field sells all she has so she can purchase the field and possess the treasure (cf. Matt. 13:44). In Luke 14:25-35, Jesus tells the large crowds of world-be disciples to count the cost of becoming a disciple. In the gospels, becoming a disciple is serious business. In and by itself, raising one's hand in a service and coming down to the altar area to take membership vows does not make one a disciple.

In baptism the believer is assimilated into a community of faith. Before and after baptism, the local church nurtures the seeker into Christian belonging and into Christian maturity. One cannot become a disciple apart from participation in the local church. As such, church planting is a penultimate activity associated with the larger task of making disciples of all nations. Apostolic churches reach the unchurched, assimilate those who respond, and nurture the participants into the image of Christ. Mature Christians bear fruit by living for Christ and by ministering in accordance with their callings and spiritual gifts (see Figure 2-1). Through their location as members of Christ's body, they share in the general calling of the church to make disciples of all nations.

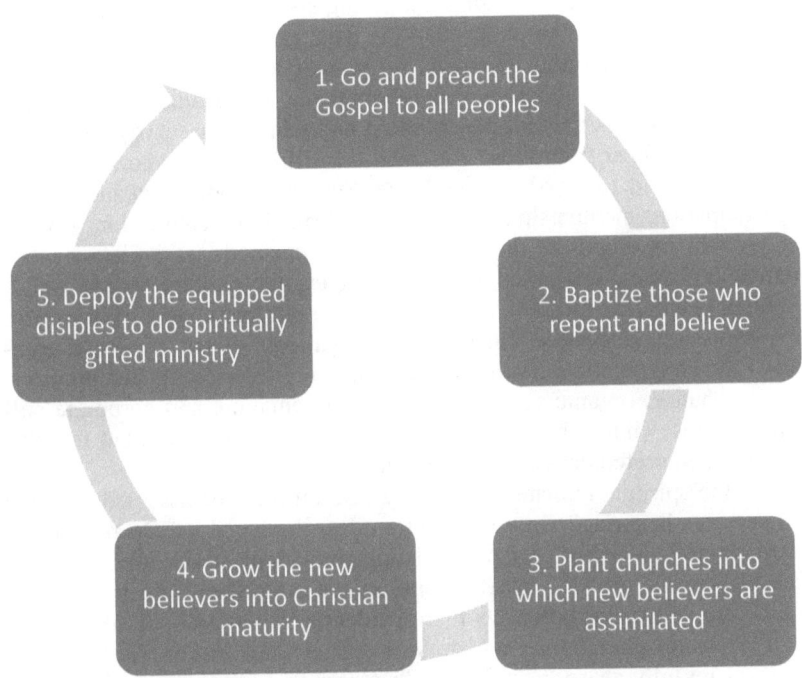

Figure 2-1. The Discipleship cycle based on the Great Commission.

EAM intuitively understood this process because it duplicated it. The following chapters will clearly demonstrate this. In brief, circuit riders followed the example of the great itinerant evangelists of New Testament times. Their lives were severe. Most died young. Still, they championed the cause of Christ everywhere they went. They covered the land from Canada to the Natchez and from Baltimore to the furthest extreme of the frontier as it expanded west. As they went, the circuit riders preached, formed awakened seekers into classes, and gave leadership to organic societies. Seekers became disciples via their participation in a class and through the regular use of spiritual disciplines. As they matured, they learned to minister to others who were passing through the same process. Every Methodist was a witness in word and deed. In essence, EAM was a disciple-making machine that modeled the evangelistic ideal of the New Testament.

Understanding Church Growth Studies and the Case for this Book

When doing a church growth analysis for a local congregation, protocol dictates that numerical data be carefully gathered and clearly presented. Normally, the data are displayed in ten year increments. After decadal growth rates have been determined, the researcher/consultant (r/c) assiduously examines the institutional data for signs of church health or disease, giving special attention to periods of growth or decline. In order to understand the data, assess the congregation, explain the trends, and determine a strategy for growth, the r/c will use a combination of qualitative and quantitative research methods. For example, the r/c may utilize interviews, do participant observation, and administer surveys. It is important that the r/c hear from those who attend and from those who stopped attending. Data related to worship attendance, Sunday school attendance, small group participation, membership, baptisms, confirmations, conversion growth, transfer growth, reversions to the world, outreach methods, assimilation rates, assimilation processes, self-branding, marketing efforts, parking spaces, building layout, accessibility, location, congregational friendliness, needs fulfillment, outreach ministries, leadership, finances, congregational dynamics, social composition of the congregation, pastoral leadership, lay leadership, gifted ministry, openness to change, organic verses institutional orientation, and corporate culture help diagnose church health. The r/c should strive to understand the attitudes, values, and preferences of the congregation.

Second, the spiritual climate of the congregation must be assessed. Are the worship services inspiring? Do people respond to the worship? Do people actively participate in worship? Are people being converted and discipled? Is there evidence of spiritual growth? When people minister, do they minister in areas where they are spiritually gifted? Is there evidence of personal sin and institutional sin? Does the church have a history of dysfunctionalism or repeated sins? Do members joyfully share their faith with others and invite their friends, acquaintances, co-workers, relatives, and neighbors to church. Do people use spiritual disciplines and desire to reach others for Christ? Does the church exist for itself or does it reach out to the community as it interacts with the community in meaningful ways? Are there signs of a revival? Do people hunger for spiritual renewal? Spiritual climate can also be understood in terms of spiritual vitality. As was stated in Chapter One, some use spiritual mapping as a tool to discern the spiritual climate of a local church and the community in which it ministers.

Third, the r/c must study and quantify contextual information, e.g., demographics, marketing research, population movement, unreached peoples in the community that the church serves, and trends. A meticulous consideration of contextual facts sheds light on numerical trends and shows where the harvest is located. What are the attitudes, values, and preferences of the unchurched in the area? What do the people in the community say about the congregation? What are the needs of the community? Where is God at work in the community? In what ways are people receptive to God?

Four, the researcher needs to discern the interplay between institutional and contextual factors in order to explain the numerical data. When the study focuses on a local church, the treatment plan will include a prescription for qualitative and quantitative growth in accordance with church growth's definition of a disciple. A healthy church will make disciples and be composed of disciples as it reaches beyond itself to incarnate Christ in the community it serves.[1] For example, the church may seek to build bridges to the community by means of meeting identified needs. In so doing, the church will attempt to target specific groupings of unreached people with specialized ministries that incarnate Christ in the community. The outreach will focus the church on the community and help it become more organic. A de-centralized church that combines attraction ministries with outreach ministries will grow in qualitative and quantitative ways. Some churches will lose members to new church plants. Others will establish a network of home churches that organically connect to the mother church. Some will be called to prophetic ministry and will act on behalf of the church to combat social evils as they give witness to the lordship of Christ in word, deed, and sign. All ministry must be understood in terms of a strong mission statement that focuses the church on making disciples and being disciples. Growing congregations of kingdom minded disciples who live the gospel will be a means through which the Holy Spirit transforms culture and challenges social injustice. However, if the elimination of social injustice is not tied to a strategy that plants disciple-making churches, the end result will not be the growth of the kingdom of God or world evangelization. The mainline tradition has missed this point.

Larger church growth studies begin with the challenge of a unique church growth case study related to a region, a movement among a particular people group, or the growth of a denomination. For example, Donald McGavran published a church growth study of Jamaica that examined membership patterns, ecclesial history, social customs, impediments to growth, and reasons for growth. In one chapter he discusses how the sex mores of the largest people group kept them from being evangelized until they were able to marry or live a celebrant life.[2] After the data related to growth or decline is gathered and presented, initial explanations are tendered. Those explanations are tested through research. Often the researcher employs a participant observer technique in order to acquire a clearer understanding of the presenting issues. If the explanations are validated or modified, the researcher may offer them as a new church growth principle. Others may test the proposed principle in other contexts.

This book differs from the above types of church growth studies. It presents a historically based church growth study that examines EAM in order to understand reasons for regional growth and decline. In most ways, it follows the protocol of a traditional church growth study. However, instead of doing interviews and using participant observation tools, it refers to journals and other firsthand accounts.

CHAPTER THREE

LOOKING AT THE NUMBERS

The first chapter lays out the case for this study, shows its significance, and discusses the interplay of institutional and contextual factors. The second chapter contends for church growth studies. This chapter examines the numerical data associated with EAM. Numerical data include membership summaries, the number of circuits, and the geographical spread of EAM from 1770 through 1812. These data come from the *Minutes of the Annual Conferences Annually Held in America from 1773 to 1813 Inclusive* (*Minutes*).[1] This study located the circuits on a map, grouped them within the geo-political boundaries of states, and tracked them from 1770 through 1812 (cf. Appendix). The various tables in this chapter give state membership totals.[2] Figures display state membership totals individually and on regional charts. When compared, the various line-graphs show regional patterns. Brief summaries follow the presentation of the data. The summaries interpret the line-graphs, highlight trends, discuss deviations, and reference the number of circuits. Later chapters offer a detailed analysis of the causes for membership growth and decline.

The numerical data are presented in three chronological sections of varying lengths. The periods correspond to defining events. The first section begins with 1770. In that year, the Wesleyan *Minutes* record the American circuit.[3] The section concludes with the Christmas Conference in 1784. At this conference, American Methodism formed itself into the MEC. The second section runs from 1785 through 1799. As the new denomination blossomed, growth ensued from 1785 through 1791. The 1790s are dominated by a growing regionalism, a numerical slump in the South, institutional conflict, growing pains, and contextualizing to the American ethos. The start of the third section in 1800 corresponds with the advent of camp meetings, the Second Great Awakening, and dramatic membership growth in all the regions. The third section concludes in 1812. Afterward, war radically influenced growth and decline.

Section One: 1770 Through 1784

Between 1766 and 1769, immigrant lay preachers from the Wesleyan Connection established Methodism in New York, Maryland, Pennsylvania, and Virginia.[4] Philip Embury formed a society in New York City and built a Methodist chapel in 1768. In a letter to Wesley on October 31, 1769, Joseph Pilmoor wrote that Thomas Webb, a licensed local preacher and British Army Captain, formed a society in Philadelphia that contained about 100 members.[5] Robert Strawbridge, a former preacher from the Irish connection, itinerated in Maryland and Virginia. His society purchased a lot in 1766 and completed a preaching house (chapel) in 1770.[6] By 1770, Methodism stretched from Virginia to New York.

In that year, Wesley appointed Richard Boardman, Joseph Pilmoor, Robert Williams, and John King to the America circuit.[7] These were the first official Methodist preachers in America. Wesley sent Boardman and Pilmoor as missionaries. Williams and King came with Wesley's permission. According to Pilmoor, Wesley gave Williams a license to preach occasionally under the direction of the regular preachers. King was put on trial and given a license to preach by Pilmoor. On November 4, 1769, Pilmoor noted that Webb and Robert Strawbridge started a large work in Baltimore, Maryland.[8] Wesley did not dispatch Strawbridge to America or know of his work at this time.

The above mentioned missionaries left England after the August 1769 conference and arrived in Philadelphia on October 21, 1769.[9] Since every Methodist itinerant turned in an annual membership summary, one wonders why the 1770 Wesleyan *Minutes* omit a numerical summary for America. As previously noted, Pilmoor sent Wesley his summary in October 1769. The Wesleyan *Minutes* contain the following American membership summaries for the years 1771 through 1773: 316, 500, and 1,000.[10] For 1773, the American *Minutes* report 1,160. The American conference convened in June. The English conferences happened in early August. If the American itinerants sent their membership report to Wesley after the American conference in June 1773, it is unlikely that Wesley received it before he published the 1773 Wesleyan *Minutes*. If that is the case, where did the Wesleyan *Minutes* obtain the American membership summary of 1,000 for 1773? Because 1,000 is less than 1,160, it may be assumed that it preceded the 1,160 membership total that was listed in the American *Minutes* in June 1773. The number "1,000" represents an estimate. The membership summaries of the various circuits for the 1773 American conference are more specific. It appears that the American membership summaries in the Wesleyan *Minutes* are off by one year. If true, the American membership totals for 1770 through 1773 should read 316, 500, 1,000, and 1,160.

Table 3-1 displays the number of American Methodists from 1773 to 1784. Figure 3-1 contains a series of line-graphs depicting Methodist membership in six individual states between 1773 and 1784.

Table 3-1. Numbers of Methodists in America between 1773 and 1784

	1773	1774	1775	1776	1777	1778*	1779	1780	1781	1782	1783	1784†
NY	180	222	200	132	96	0	0	0	0	0	0	0
NJ	200	257	300	150	160	130	140	196	512	657	1028	963
PA	180	240	264	236	232	140	179	190	361	517	605	560
DE	0	0	0	0	0	0	795	410	1052	1447	1017	982
MD	500	1063	1429	1737	2101	1987	1873	2129	3382	4294	5122	5308
VA	100	291	955	2456	3449	3693	3937	3928	3839	4082	3699	3449
NC	0	0	0	683	930	1291	1653	1411	1393	1492	2279	3443
SC	0	0	0	0	0	0	0	0	0	0	0	99

Sources: Data from Jesse Lee, *Short History*, 358; MEC, *Minutes* (1813).

* No circuit totals are listed in the *Minutes* for 1778. The circuit memberships for 1778 are estimated so that state totals can be graphed in Figure 2-1. In 1778, the *Minutes* list an incorrect membership total (6,095) because they omit two circuits in southeastern Pennsylvania and one in Maryland. The above estimates for the circuits in 1778 take into consideration troop movements, the date of the conference, and growth patterns. The estimated membership total is 7,241. The Wesleyan *Minutes* listed 6,968 for 1778.

† Robert Coleman locates Wilmington in Delaware for a table that he composed for 1784.[11] During this period, Wilmington appears in the *Minutes* for one year. It is listed in the same district as Roanoak [sic] and Tar River. Thus, the circuit refers to Wilmington, North Carolina, not Delaware.

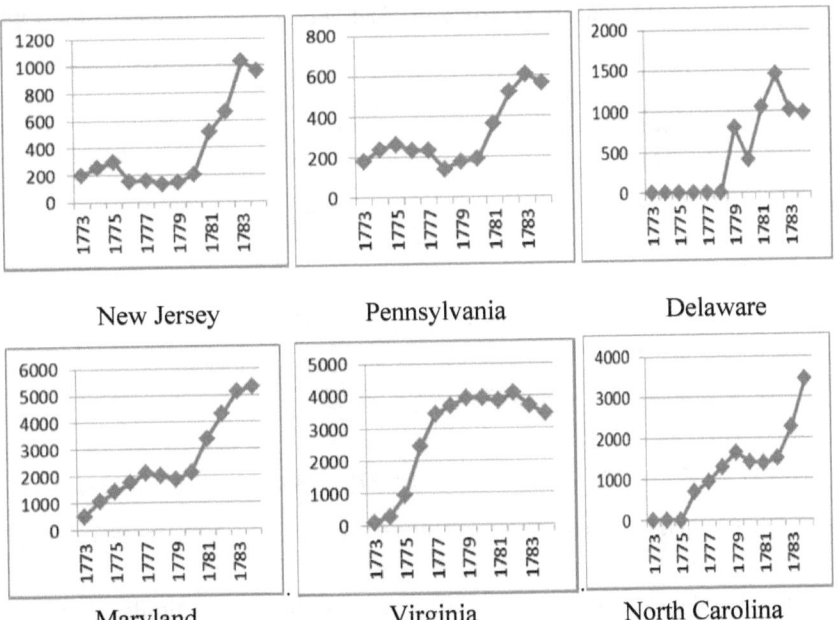

Figure 3-1. Series of line-graphs depicting Methodist membership in America between 1773 and 1784.

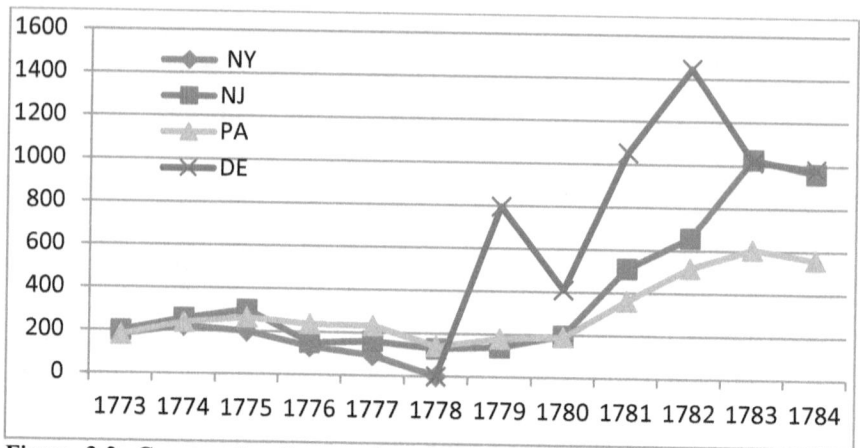

Figure 3-2. Comparative line-graphs of Methodist membership in Mid-Atlantic States between 1773 and 1784.

Figures 3-2 displays line-graphs of membership totals from the various Mid-Atlantic states.[12] New Jersey's and Pennsylvania's line-graphs are very similar. They intersect at several points. The lines split in 1780, but continue to follow the same pattern of incline and decline. In 1784, the membership totals in the various states are within 400 members of each other. At the end of this period, there were two circuits in New Jersey and three in Pennsylvania. Delaware became a circuit in 1779. New York ceased to be a circuit in 1777 because of British occupation. The circuit re-emerged in 1784 and posted a membership of 84 in 1785.

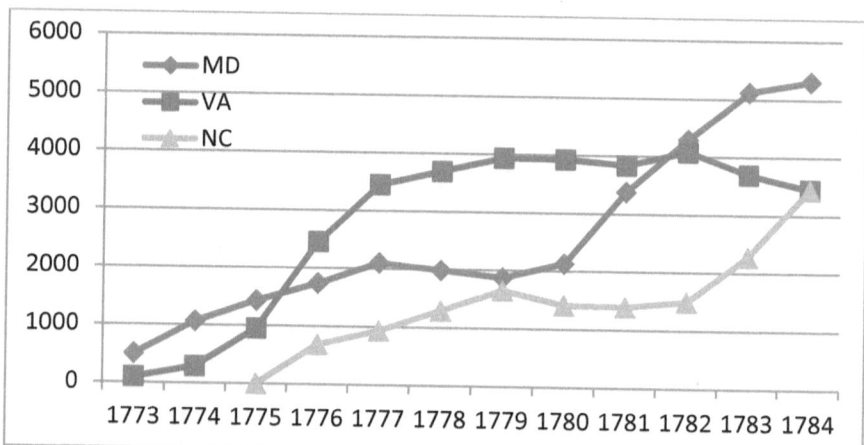

Figure 3-3. Comparative line-graphs of Methodist membership in southern states between 1773 and 1784.

Figure 3-3 shows that Maryland and North Carolina follow similar membership trajectories. The Virginia graph shoots up between 1774 and 1779 due to a great revival in the Brunswick area that spread to other parts of Virginia and into

North Carolina. Revival growth will flag within a few years if the new members are not discipled and if a new revival does not push the membership forward. Revival growth becomes a characteristic of southern Methodism. As such, the trend line for Virginia follows a typical revival pattern.

Jesse Lee reported the following about the 1776 portion of the "Virginia outpouring:"

> Such a work of God as that was, I had never seen, or heard of before. It continued to spread through the south parts of Virginia. . . . When the returns of the members were made to the conference this year, there had been added to the society in Brunswick circuit 811 members. But if we include Hanover circuit, and Carolina, which had been united to Brunswick, there had been added in one year 1800 members.[13]

From the time that the revival started until its zenith in 1779, Virginia Methodism increased by 3,646 members and eight circuits. Afterward, Virginia membership leveled off for four years and declined for the final two years of this period. The number of circuits continued to increase through the plateau and the period of decline. In 1784, 13 circuits existed in Virginia. This positioned Virginia Methodism for growth in the next period.

North Carolina Methodism began in 1776 as an outgrowth of the Brunswick revival. It recorded 1,653 members in 1779. Based on the revival growth pattern, membership slumped after the plateau. It did not recoup its losses until 1783. Unlike Virginia, North Carolina Methodism experienced meteoric growth following 1783. In that year, state membership rebounded sharply because of the addition of five new circuits that extended Methodism into new areas. By 1784, it had expanded to 3,443 members and 11 circuits.

Maryland Methodism realized most of its growth in the Chesapeake Bay area. Substantial growth occurred from 1773 through 1777. For the next three years, growth leveled off. From 1775 through 1780, Maryland Methodism had three circuits that corresponded to three loci of growth. They were Frederick in the west-central area, Baltimore on the northwestern part of the Chesapeake Bay, and Kent on the Delmarva Peninsula. Between 1781 and 1784, the membership increased by 3,179 people and the circuits increased to six. All the new circuits formed around the Chesapeake Bay. Five of the six were on the Delmarva Peninsula. By the end of this period, Maryland Methodist had 1,959 more Methodists than Virginia.

Delaware is a part of the Delmarva Peninsula. Asbury lived with Judge Thomas White in Kent County, Delaware from 1778 through 1780. William Williams calls Delmarva the "Garden of Methodism." Russell Rickey has called it the "Nursery of American Methodism."[14] This area bore much fruit for Methodism. Curiously, the membership summaries from Delaware do not reflect strong growth. For example, in 1780, Lee reports that Eastern Shore had a gracious revival of religion.[15] Consequently, the Kent circuit in the Maryland portion of the peninsula registered a 233 member increase in 1780. However, in the same year, the circuits in Delaware registered a 385 member decrease. In 1783, the Methodist membership in Delaware decreased from 1,447 to 1,017. In that year, the membership in the Maryland portion of the peninsula increased from

2,505 to 3,352. The Maryland portion increased by an incredible 3,129 members between 1779 and 1784. During those same years, the Delaware circuits only increased by 187 members. In the midst of area growth, Methodism in Delaware finished the period with an anemic 982 members and one circuit.

The Delaware conundrum can be explained. Methodist circuits were named after a county, a city, or a topographical feature. For example, the Caroline circuit is named after Caroline County, Maryland. As such, the Caroline circuit is listed on Maryland's table.[16] The county looks like a half-circle. The large part borders Delaware. Since Methodist circuits were not restricted by state boundaries, the Caroline circuit included portions of Delaware. The same can be assumed for other circuits that bordered Delaware. According to Wade Barclay, Methodist societies existed in every county of Maryland and Delaware by 1784.[17] For Delaware, he lists five chapels in Sussex County, three in Thoroughfare Neck, and one in Dover; yet, the *Minutes* only list the Dover circuit in 1784. Two circuits existed in Delaware until the Sussex circuit disappeared from the *Minutes* in 1783. Obviously, the 595 members from the Sussex circuit did not vanish. Most likely one or more of the five new circuits organized on the Maryland portion of the Delmarva Peninsula absorbed them. As such, it is probable that Delaware's losses came as the result of redistributing Delaware Methodists to Maryland circuits that crossed over into Delaware.

In summary, the Pennsylvania and New Jersey trend lines are quite uniform. Methodism in North Carolina, Virginia, and Maryland also demonstrated similar patterns of growth and decline. In all three states, a period of intense growth preceded a slump. Virginia Methodism decreased after its slump. Methodism in Maryland and North Carolina increased after slumping. In the same way that the Mid-Atlantic states are united by small membership totals, the southern states are united by large membership totals. Delaware represents a special case.

Section Two: 1785 Through 1799

Table 3-2 and subsequent line-graphs display Methodist membership between 1786 and 1799. The table begins with 1786 because the statistical data related to circuit membership for 1785 is omitted from the *Minutes*. The table does not estimate the state totals for that year.[18]

Table 3-2. Number of Methodist in various states between 1786 and 1799

	1786	1787	1788	1789	1790	1791	1792	1793	1794	1795	1796	1797	1798	1799
NY	360	442	1114	2125	3366	3421	3883	4390	4581	4542	4259	4850	5326	5957
NJ	1259	1642	2046	1751	2363	2358	2475	2450	2616	2532	2351	2573	2826	2892
PA	1157	1405	1178	1304	1451	1856	2242	2121	2807	2649	2794	3098	3188	3309
DE	848	863	878	798	2414	2505	2698	2674	2682	2646	2228	2284	2490	2415
MD	6040	7735	9951	11127	15407	15281	15552	15193	14701	14164	12406	12078	11335	11647
VA	4434	6389	11642	12395	16522	17283	17699	17777	16466	13758	13878	13530	13408	12832
NC	4275	5061	5615	7662	8803	9737	10458	10063	9958	8996	8380	9100	7821	7551
SC	638	1766	2470	2784	3458	4650	4397	4457	4560	4042	3818	3818	4843	5026
GA	78	450	1227	2011	2294	2250	2086	2151	1832	1564	1174	1170	1310	1534
KY	0	90	480	863	1080	1550	1808	1896	1909	1956	1750	1797	1601	1638
TN	0	0	63	225	282	759	701	674	737	592	548	576	580	631
OH	0	0	0	0	0	0	0	0	0	0	0	0	0	99
CT	0	0	0	0	181	523	986	988	1155	1262	1050	1201	1455	1497
MA	0	0	0	0	0	85	391	677	727	787	824	913	1194	1409
RI	0	0	0	0	0	0	0	74	157	208	220	177	162	196
ME	0	0	0	0	0	0	0	0	0	268	357	616	936	1117
NH	0	0	0	0	0	0	0	0	0	0	68	92	122	131
VT	0	0	0	0	0	0	0	0			0	0	286	604
CN	510	0	0	0	0	730	167	349	1434	633	474	795	809	869

Source: MEC, *Minutes* (1813).

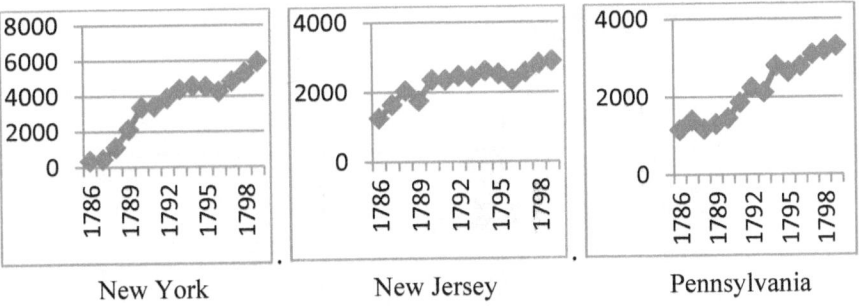

New York   New Jersey   Pennsylvania

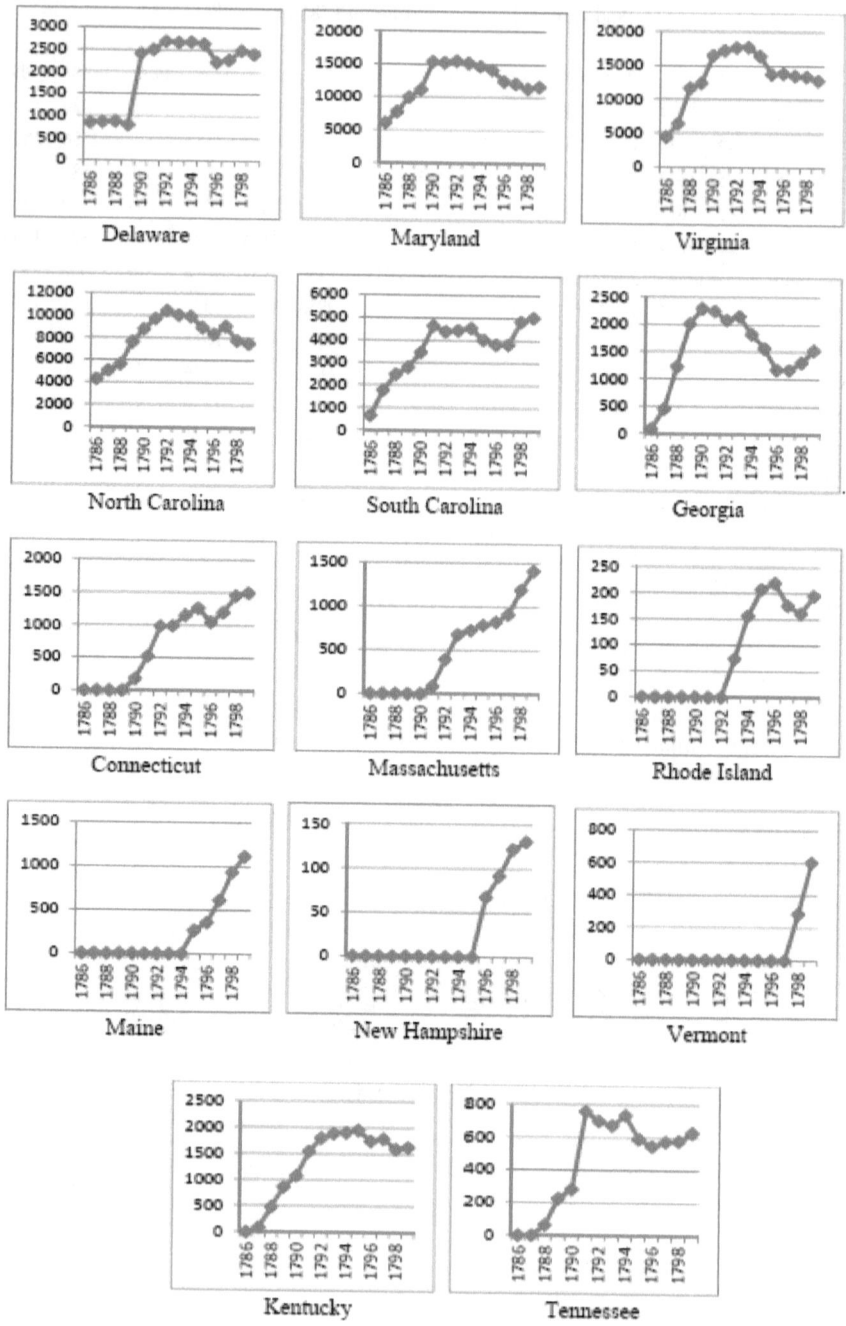

Figure 3-4. Series of line-graphs depicting Methodist membership in America between 1786 and 1799...

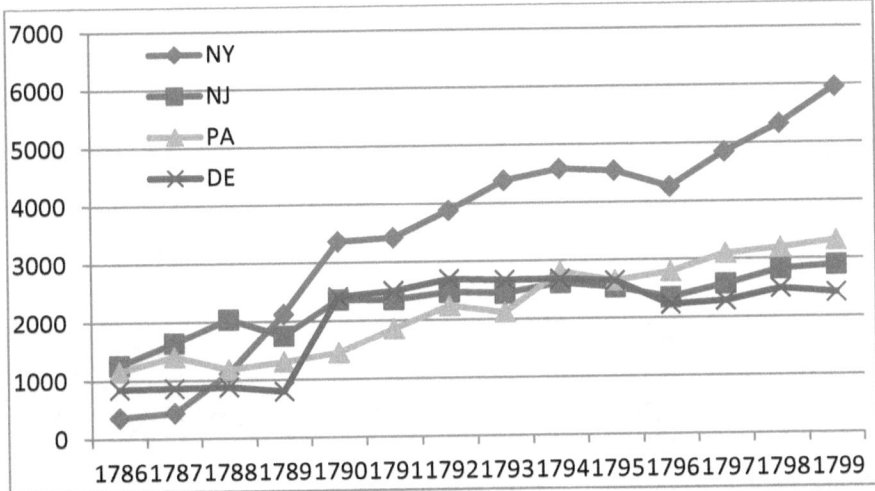

Figure 3-5. Line-graphs of Methodist membership in Mid-Atlantic States between 1786 and 1799.

The Mid-Atlantic Region

A comparison of Figures 3-4 and 3-5 reveals the similar Methodist growth patterns in Pennsylvania, New Jersey, and New York. New Jersey Methodism began this period with three established circuits and a new one called Newark. It expanded to seven circuits in 1794 and remained at that level through the remainder of this period. Pennsylvania Methodism began with three circuits. It increased to 12 in 1794 and finished the period with 11 circuits. During this period, New York Methodism experienced tremendous growth, increasing from 360 members and two circuits in 1786 to 5,957 members and 17 circuits in 1799. The surge slowed in 1791, and it slumped in 1795 through 1796. The line-graphs for New Jersey and Pennsylvania display a similar pattern of decline for these same years. Methodism rebounded in the Mid-Atlantic states during the closing years of this period. For example, New York Methodism increased by 1,698 members from 1796 through 1799. During this same period, Southern Methodism remained mired in a membership downturn.

The Delaware line-graph follows the same basic pattern as Maryland. Between 1786 and 1789, its membership totals remain fairly level. In 1790, Methodism in Delaware expanded by 1,616 members. The number of circuits increased from two to three. The new circuit was not taken from Maryland. The whole Delmarva area experienced strong growth.

The Southern Region

Figures 3-4 and 3-6 illustrate the growth patterns of Methodism in Virginia, Maryland, North Carolina, and South Carolina between 1786 and 1799.

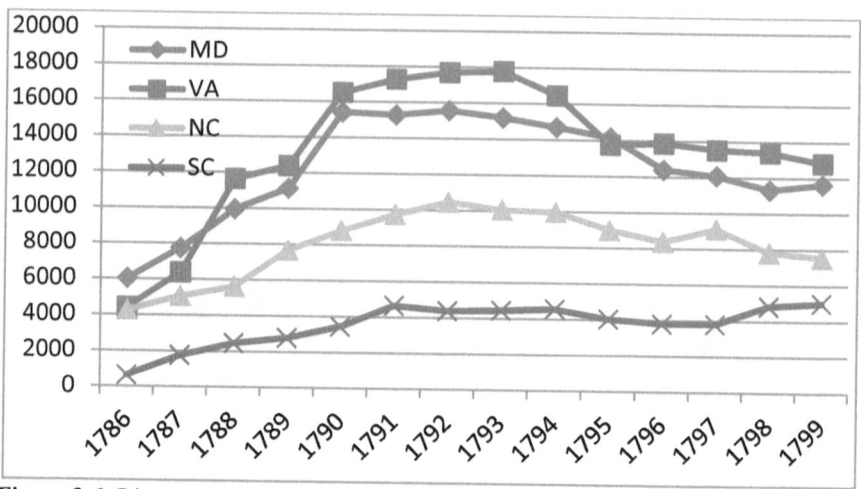

Figure 3-6. Line-graphs of Methodist membership in Southern states between 1786 and 1799.

In the previous period, Southern Methodism grew expeditiously from 1780 through 1785. During those years, Southern Methodism increased from 7,468 to 12,299 without any declines. Explosive growth continued into this period. From 1786 through 1791 Southern Methodism grew from 15,387 to 46,951 members. The growth continued unabated from 1780 to 1791.

Virginia Methodism grew the fasted during the years of the Southern surge. It quadrupled its membership in six years with 17,283 reported members in 1791. In 1784, it had reported 3,449 members. At that time its membership equaled North Carolina's and was 1,859 less than Maryland's. Virginia Methodism began its comeback in 1786, and outpaced Methodism in the other states in 1788. By 1793, Virginia Methodism reported 7,714 more members than North Carolina and 2,225 more members than Maryland. However, South Carolina Methodism had the strongest percent growth. From 1784 to 1791, it grew from 99 to 4,650 members.

Between 1791 and 1794, Southern Methodism stopped growing. Afterward, it began a precipitous membership decline that ensued until the end of the period. During the decline, Southern Methodism lost 4,945 members in Virginia, 4,217 members in Maryland, 2,907 members in North Carolina, and 1,152 in South Carolina. Respectively, that equals 28, 27, 28, and 25 percent of the total membership in the southern states.

Like the other southern states, Methodism in South Carolina reached a membership apex in 1791. Unlike Methodism in the other southern states, it inched up after its decline until 1794. Afterward, it declined dramatically through 1797. However, from 1798 to 1799, its membership added two circuits and 2,208 members. Its mild membership slump and quick recovery stand in contrast to the six year declines in Virginia, Maryland, and North Carolina. Since Georgia Methodism was a geographic extension of South Carolina Methodism during this period, it followed the South Carolina pattern. Partly the South Carolina pattern can be attributed to its expanding nature. It was not well established when the period began and continued to reach into new areas during the decline.

A hidden factor existed during these years. From 1786 through 1799, Virginia Methodism added 1,942 African Americans, North Carolina Methodism added 1,422, Maryland Methodism added 3,418, and South Carolina added 883.[19] In 1799, African Americans accounted for the following percentages of total membership in the southern states: Virginia–18 percent, Maryland–44 percent, North Carolina–22 percent, and South Carolina–25 percent. During this period, Maryland Methodism added 1,229 more blacks than whites.[20]

From 1786 to 1799, the number of circuits in the southern states increased through the early 1790s, and then declined. Virginia's 13 circuits grew to 34 before declining to 32. Maryland Methodism began the period with ten circuits and grew to 20 before it declined to 17. North Carolina circuits grew from 11 to 18 before declining to 16 circuits. Methodism in South Carolina began this period with three circuits, grew to 13 circuits, and ended with ten circuits.

The Frontier Region

The American frontier included northern New England, Georgia, and all of the area west of the Appalachians to the Mississippi River during this time period. New York, Pennsylvania, Maryland, Virginia, North Carolina, and South Carolina contained both populated and unsettled regions (see Table 3-3).[21] During the War of Independence, the American population migrated to frontier areas to escape fighting. After the war, the population pushed out in all directions. Border disputes over European land claims and treaties that recognized Indian land holdings became points of tension.

Table 3-3. Population density per square mile by state in 1790

Dist. of Columbia	156.6	New Hampshire	15.7	Maine	3.2
Rhode Island	64.5	Virginia	11.6	Kentucky	1.8
Connecticut	49.4	Pennsylvania	9.7	Ohio	1.1
Massachusetts	47.1	Vermont	9.4	Tennessee	0.8
Maryland	32.1	South Carolina	8.2	Georgia	0.6
Delaware	30.1	North Carolina	8.1	MS Territory	0.3
New Jersey	24.5	New York	7.1	NW Territory	0.1

Source: U.S. Bureau of the Census. *1970 Census of Population and Housing*. Bureau of the Census. Washington, DC: Government Printing Office, 1987. Also, see http://www.census.gov/prod/www/abs/decennial/1790.html (accessed August 1, 2012).

Even though Georgia was a part of the original colonies and is considered to be a part of the traditional South from a cultural perspective, it groups more naturally with the frontier states in this timeframe because of its demographics and small membership counts. Its population was densest along the South Carolina border and the coastal region down to Florida. Its population density in 1790 was similar to the frontier areas of Kentucky, Ohio, Tennessee, the Mississippi

Territory, and the Northwest Territory. In fact, only the Mississippi and the Northwest Territories show a smaller population density per square mile.

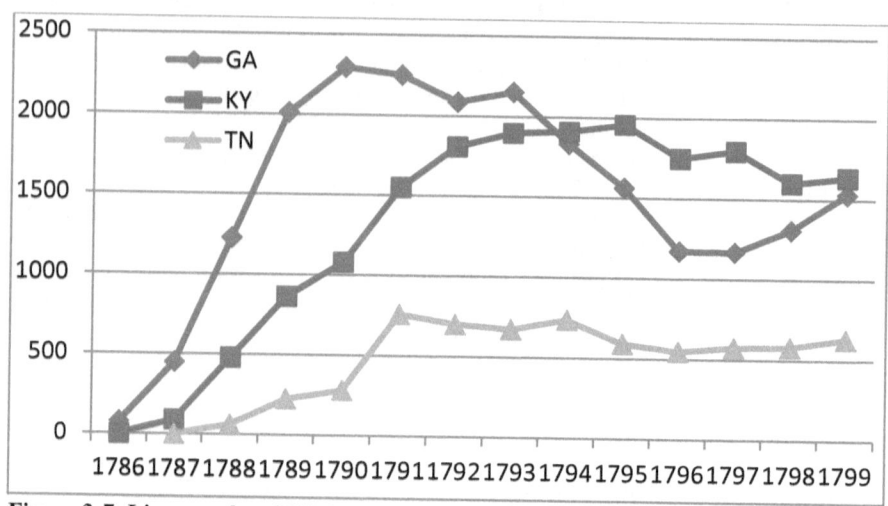

Figure 3-7. Line-graphs of Methodist membership in the frontier between 1786 and 1799.

Figure 3-7 displays divergent line-graphs for Georgia, Kentucky, and Tennessee. The Georgia and Kentucky line-graphs cross each other. Yet, a closer look at Figure 3-4 reveals that Methodism in South Carolina and the frontier states followed the same basic membership pattern; four to six years of sharp increase followed by a decline. The decline is followed by an up-swing that produces a double hump or saddle effect.

Methodism in Georgia began with one circuit, grew to six circuits, and ended with four circuits. The first Kentucky circuit was organized in 1787. By 1797, Kentucky Methodism had grown to six circuits. It concluded the period with four circuits. Tennessee Methodism made its debut in 1788. It grew to two circuits in 1791 and did not change for the remainder of this period.[22]

New England Region

Jesse Lee took Methodism to New England in 1789. Consequently, New England membership totals are small when compared to those in the Mid-Atlantic and South in this period. In fact, New England Methodism resists facile generalizations during this period. When a state has a small number of Methodist adherents, minor membership variations appear as an exaggerated deviation on line-graphs. The Rhode Island graphs in Figures 3-4 and 3-8 demonstrate this.

Figure 3-8 shows that Methodism experienced strong growth in four of the six New England states during this period. It had anemic growth in the other two. Methodism did not decline in Massachusetts,[23] Maine, Vermont, and New Hampshire during the 1790s. In 1799, there were ten circuits in Massachusetts and six circuits in Connecticut. The membership in each state exceeded 1,400. Between 1794 and 1799, Methodist membership skyrocketed in Maine. Maine Methodism finished the period with six circuits and 1,117 members. Even though New Hampshire's trend line appears flat, Figure 3-4 shows that New Hampshire Methodism advanced at a slow but steady rate. Methodism's meteoric debut in Vermont was an omen of things to come.

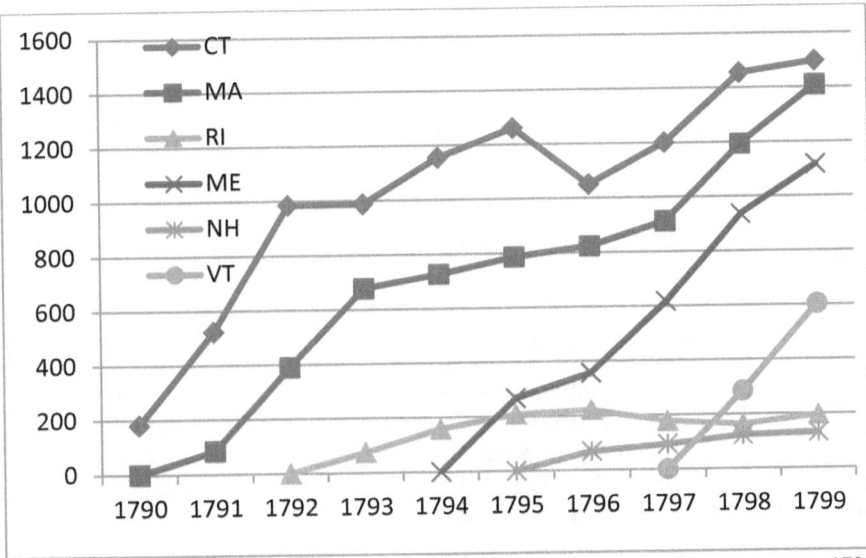

Figure 3-8. Line-graphs of Methodist membership in New England between 1790 and 1799.

Figure 3-9 combines the membership totals of the New England states and graphs them on a single trend line in order to show a regional pattern. According to Figure 3-9, New England Methodism lunged forward in the early and late 1790s. It slowed its rate of growth in 1792 through 1795 and showed a slight decrease in 1796. New England Methodism continued with strong growth from 1797 through 1799.

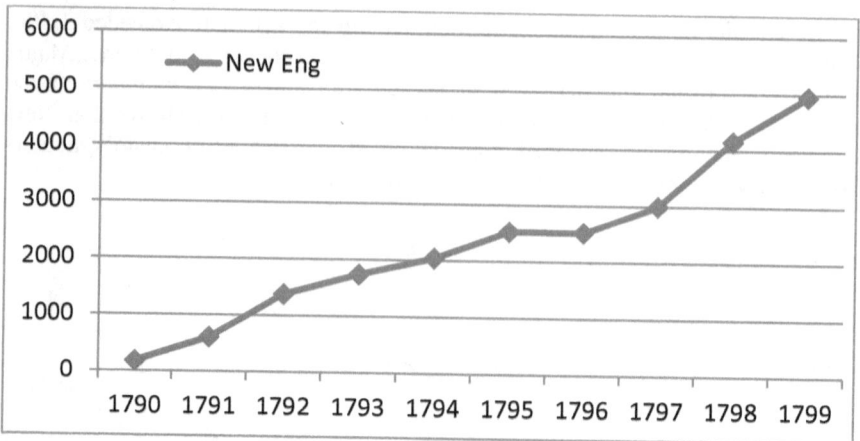

Figure 3-9. Composite line-graph of New England membership between 1790 and 1799.

Section Three: 1800 through 1812

Table 3-4 displays the number of Methodists in America by state between 1800 and 1812. The numerical data for this period shows that EAM built on the momentum of the Second Great Awakening. Each of the regions posted strong growth during these years. Even still, the growth patterns were not the same because EAM in each of the regions interacted with a different set of contextual and institutional factors.

Table 3-4. Number of Methodist in states between 1800 and 1812

	1800	1801	1802	1803	1804	1805	1806	1807	1808	1809	1810	1811	1812
NY	6355	7034	8148	8876	10283	10559	11879	13678	15884	17887	19053	20576	21226
NJ	3030	3159	4165	4463	4562	4528	4544	5098	5701	6232	6839	6979	8091
PA	3187	3829	4785	5304	6822	7453	8327	9428	9940	10090	10523	11214	12500
DE	2493	4123	5289	5993	4926	5065	5932	7108	6425	6117	5674	5298	5457
MD	12046	15594	20253	24055	24822	24548	25981	28307	28643	27520	27802	26946	26536
VA	13390	14047	13761	17141	19687	21644	23157	24712	24695	25434	26074	26725	27443
NC	8003	7556	7918	8910	9683	9899	13094	15434	15925	16256	16378	17577	18459
SC	5151	5232	5565	7318	8953	8656	7812	8529	9360	10378	13168	14491	17165
GA	1655	1639	2455	3702	4271	4887	4811	4906	5704	7052	8090	8510	9227
KY	1741	2165	2619	3518	4431	5671	6077	6438	6740	7660	8449	9414	11156
TN	703	978	1258	2249	2123	2439	2301	2781	3002	3622	4069	4779	4979
OH	257	463	887	1273	1708	2233	2840	3564	4402	5578	6,529	8585	9471
MS	60	80	100	87	102	136	204	358	375	350	330	436	576
IL	0	0	0	0	0	67	120	110	220	275	354	356	482
LA	0	0	0	0	0	0	0	17	40	30	30	73	99
IN	0	0	0	0	0	0	0	67	166	540	762	1160	1121
MO	0	0	0	0	0	0	0	0	106	200	584	528	512
AL	0	0	0	0	0	0	0	0	0	0	265	422	488
MI	0	0	0	0	0	0	0	0	0	0	78	134	134
CT	1571	1567	1658	1759	1825	1853	1946	1980	2125	2517	2734	2886	2884
MA	1577	1665	1907	2439	1610	1516	2169	2672	3008	3318	3307	3550	3643
RI	227	227	312	133	382	425	172	387	406	683	733	579	781
ME	1197	1386	1414	1747	2102	2400	2501	2562	2785	3150	3498	3548	3450
NH	224	524	665	644	635	878	1137	1151	1168	1334	1541	1799	1750
VT	1016	1607	2116	2720	3100	3296	3354	3768	3849	4244	5170	5279	5535

Source, MEC, *Minutes* (1813).

The series of line-graphs in Figure 3-10 illustrate Methodist membership growth patterns in the individual states during this time period.

New York　　　　　New Jersey　　　　　Pennsylvania

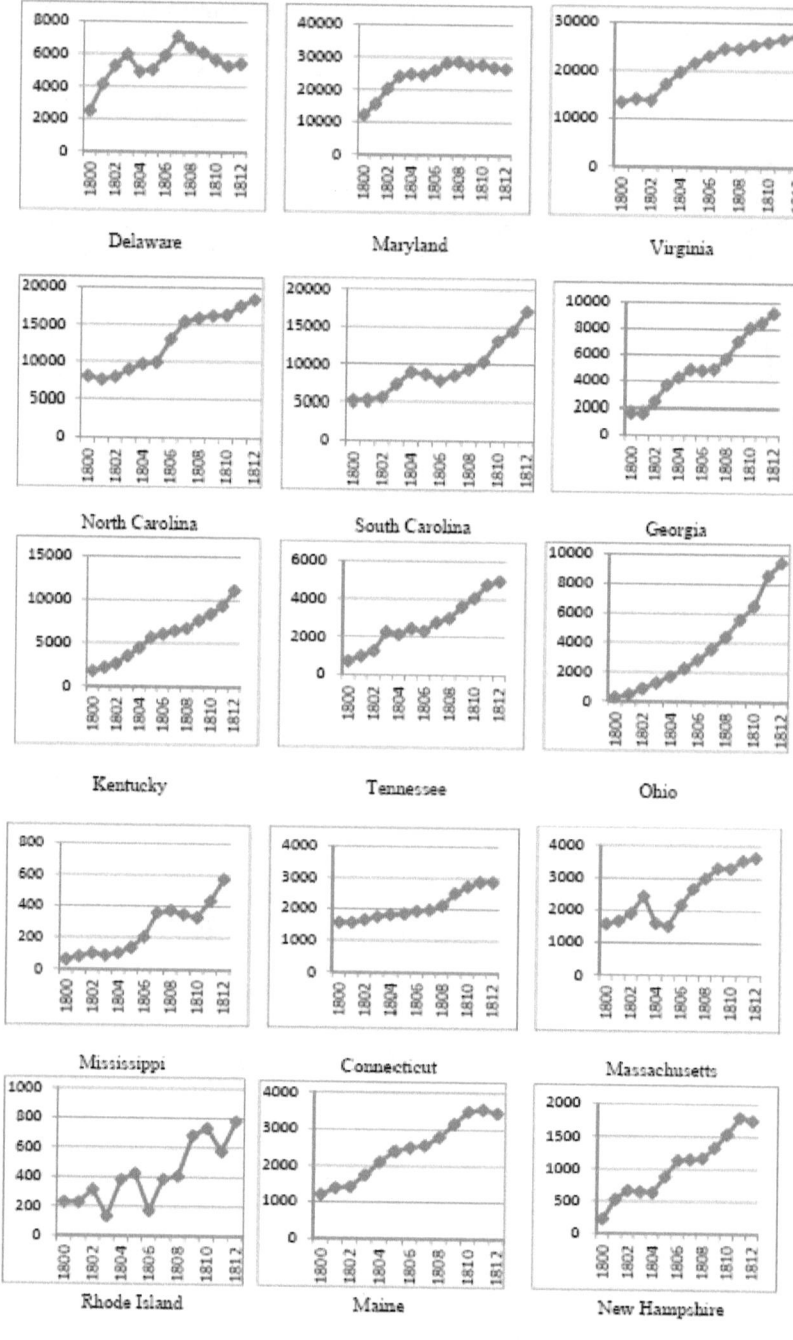

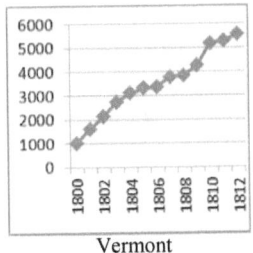
Vermont

Figure 3-10. Series of line-graphs depicting Methodist membership in America between 1800 and 1812.

Like Maryland, Delaware Methodism had a sizable African American membership that equaled 37 percent of its total membership in 1812. As a border state, Delaware appears to be dominated by Maryland. According to Richey, Delaware is an extension of Maryland even though it is not associated with the South.[24]

According to Figure 3-11, Methodism in the Mid-Atlantic region grew by 32,209 members. Delaware Methodism commenced this period with three circuits and grew to five. It registered a membership gain of 2,964. Pennsylvania Methodism began with ten circuits and grew to 24. Membership increased by 9,313. New Jersey Methodism began with seven circuits and increased to 13. Four of those circuits made their debut on the membership returns in 1812. Membership increased by 5,061. New York Methodism demonstrated exceptional growth during this period. It increased from 18 to 43 circuits. Its membership increased by 14,871.

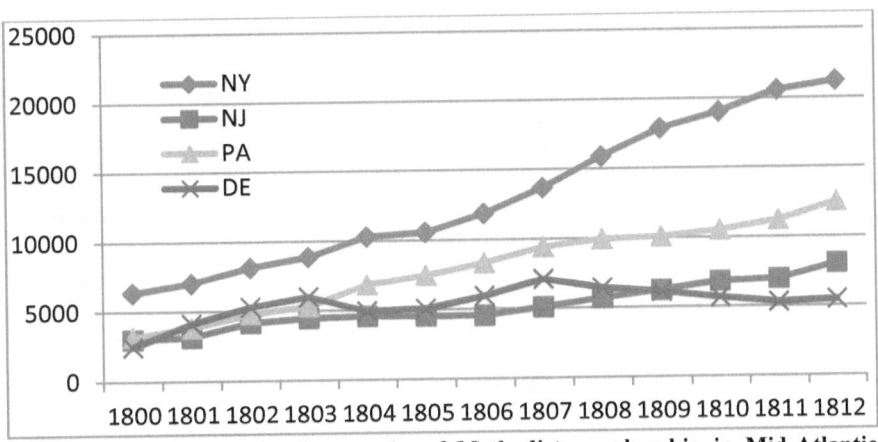

Figure 3-11. Comparative line-graphs of Methodist membership in Mid-Atlantic states between 1800 and 1812.

The Southern Region

Figure 3-12 displays the similarities between Maryland and Virginia. From 1800 through 1802, Virginia Methodism slumped, while Maryland Methodism grew by 8,207 members. At that time, 6,492 more Methodists lived in Maryland than in Virginia. Methodism in these states grew in parallel tracks from 1805 through 1810. During 1811 and 1812, Maryland Methodism declined, while Virginia Methodism experienced moderate growth. Virginia Methodism finished this period with 907 more members than Maryland Methodism.

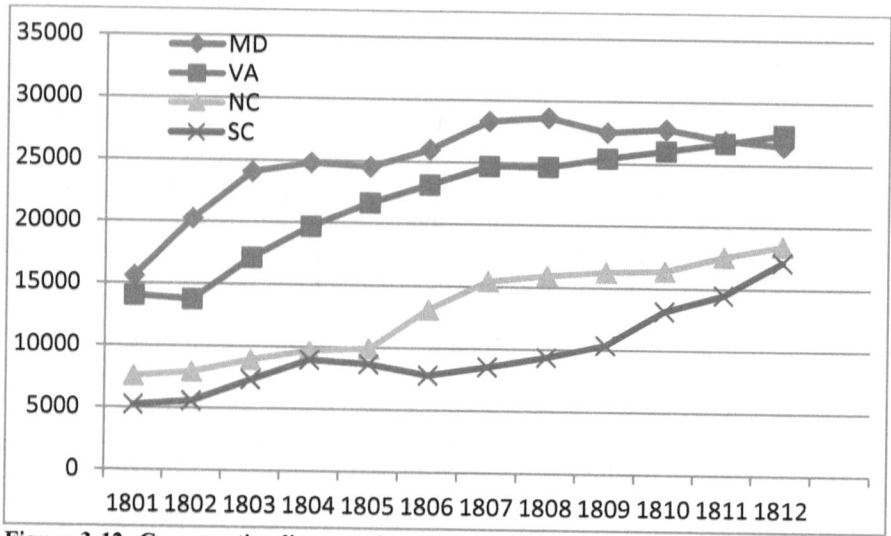

Figure 3-12. Comparative line-graphs of Methodist membership in South between 1800 and 1812.

Figure 3-12 indicates that Methodism in the Carolinas progressed along roughly parallel paths from 1800 through 1805. From 1806 through 1807, North Carolina Methodism grew by 2,340 members. South Carolina Methodism declined by 844 members in 1806. From 1807 through the end of this period, South Carolina Methodism grew at a slightly faster rate than North Carolina Methodism. In 1812, North Carolina Methodism had 1,294 more members than South Carolina Methodism. North Carolina Methodism reached a membership apex of 10,063 in 1792. Following the southern decline of the 1790s, it did not recoup its losses until 1806. By means of comparison, South Carolina recouped its losses in 1798, Maryland recouped its losses in 1801, and Virginia recouped its losses in 1804.

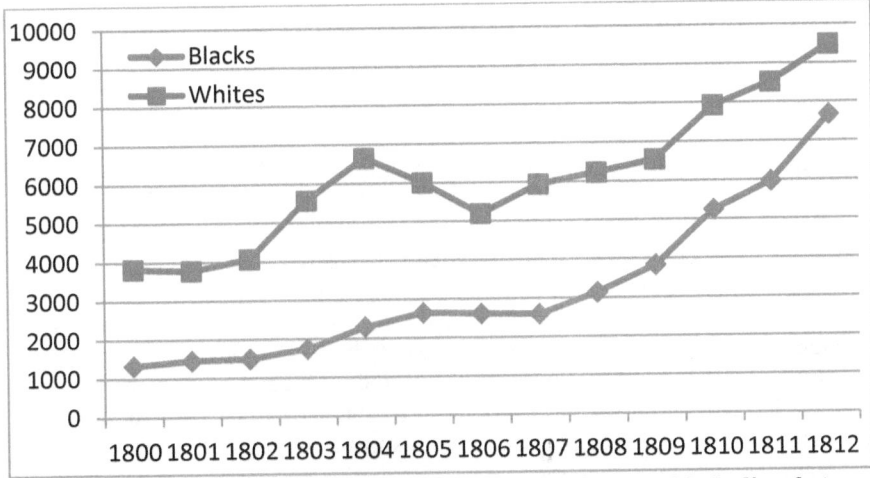

Figure 3-13. White and Black membership of South Carolina Methodism between 1800 and 1812.

During the growth spurt from 1797 to 1804, South Carolina Methodism went from 3,818 to 8,953 members. The ratio of black to white members was 31 percent in 1797 and 34 percent in 1804. According to Figure 3-13, from 1807 to 1812, black membership grew by 5,086 and white membership by 3,550. By 1812, blacks equaled 45 percent of the total membership. By comparison, blacks equaled 43 percent of the South Carolina population in 1800 (149,151) and 47 percent in 1810 (196,365). In 1812, the percentage of blacks in South Carolina Methodism mirrored the percentage of blacks in the total population of South Carolina. Previously, blacks were under-represented in South Carolina Methodism. By 1812, four percent of the black population in South Carolina affiliated with the MEC. Two percent of the white population belonged to the MEC. The growth of black membership depended on the willingness of slave owners to allow itinerants to preach to the slaves and unite them to a society. Due to Methodism's abolitionist rhetoric, the gross racism of slave owners, the fear of slave uprisings, and the social composition of EAM, the planter class who owned most of the slaves felt negatively disposed to the MEC in the 1790s. A church that advocated for the rights and salvation of slaves was not a church that could be trusted with the pastoral care of slaves.

In 1812, the Methodist membership totals in the four southern states remained in the same numeric order as in 1800. Virginia Methodism began this period with 33 circuits and grew to 49 circuits. Virginia Methodism spawned some new circuits in the western parts of the state; however, most of the additions came as a result of dividing larger circuits. Virginia membership grew by 14,053. Maryland Methodism started this period with 18 circuits and finished it with 25 circuits. Membership grew by 14,490. North Carolina Methodism began the period with 17 circuits and finished it with 31 circuits. Membership increased by 10,456. South Carolina Methodism started the period with ten circuits and completed it with 17. Membership grew by 12,014. In 1812, the African American membership equaled 19 percent in Virginia, 45 percent in Maryland, 29 percent in North Carolina, and 45 percent in South Carolina.

The Frontier Region

Figure 3-14 portrays Methodist membership in the frontier states. Methodism in Kentucky and Ohio completed the period without a decline. The graph for Ohio Methodism shows an exceptional rate of growth. During this period, Methodism in Georgia and Tennessee declined for two years. Georgia Methodism began this period with a decline and then rebounded with strong growth through 1805. Its membership leveled off for the next two years. From 1808 through the end of the period, Georgia Methodism rebounded with strong growth. Tennessee Methodism began the period with good growth. Its membership leveled off between 1803 and 1806. Then it grew from 1807 to the end of this period. Methodist membership in Ohio surpassed membership in Tennessee and Georgia during this period.

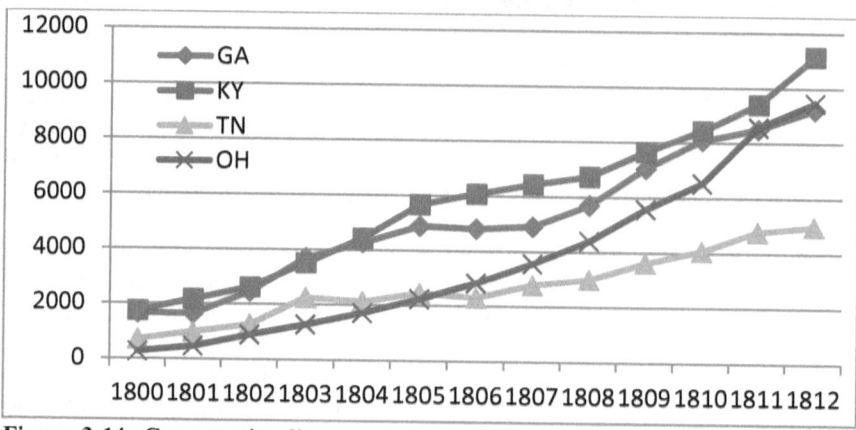

Figure 3-14. Comparative line-graphs of Methodist membership in the Frontier states between 1800 and 1812.

Georgia Methodism began this period with three circuits and ended with 16. It posted a membership gain of 7,572. Kentucky Methodism began this period with six circuits and finished with 20. It posted a membership gain of 9,415. Tennessee Methodism began the period with two circuits and finished it with nine. Its membership increased by 4,276. Ohio Methodism began the period with two circuits and completed the period with 17. Its membership grew by 9,214. Georgia Methodism differed from the other frontier states because it had a sizable black membership. In 1800, its black membership equaled 18 percent. In 1812, it equaled 22 percent. It is grouped with the frontier region in this chapter because of demographics and small membership. With the exception of Savannah, in most ways it was an extension of South Carolina.

The New Frontier

Map 3-1 shows the American frontier in 1800. Figure 3-15 depicts the growth of Methodism on the "new frontier." New frontier designates newly settled areas beyond the old frontier. Following the Revolutionary War, migrating populations converged in Kentucky and southern Ohio. By 1800, a southern and a northern frontier existed.[25]

Map 3-1. Map of the United States and Territories in 1800.
Sources: Public domain map of 1800. Unknown author. Data from Ellsworth D. Foster, ed., *The American Educator,* Vol. 8 (Chicago, IL: Ralph Durham Company, 1921), 3697. Courtesy the private collection of Roy Winkelman. Available at http://etc.usf.edu/maps/pages/11600/11685/11685.htm.

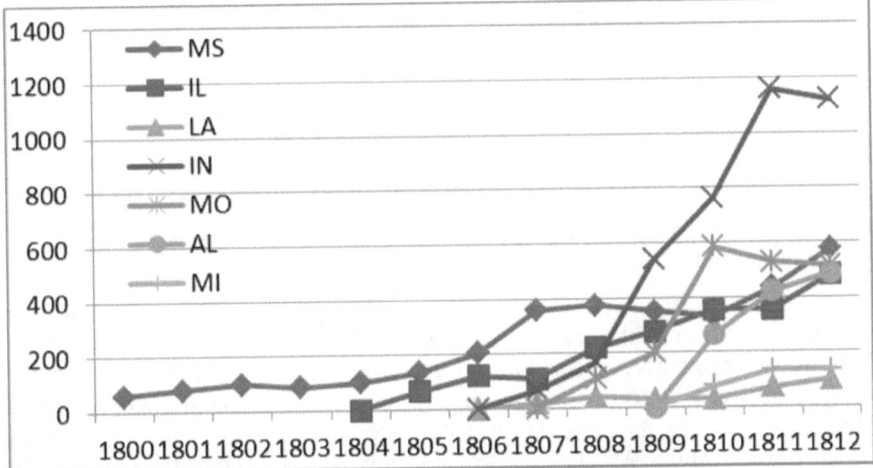

Figure 3-15. Comparative line-graphs of Methodist membership in the New Frontier between 1800 and 1812.

The tables in the Appendix reflect the development and expansion of Methodism in the new frontier. Methodist missionaries infiltrated the Mississippi area in the late 1790s. They worked the area around Natchez, Mississippi and eastern Louisiana. By 1812, they had divided the area into eight circuits. Circuit riders moving west from Kentucky and Ohio worked Illinois, Indiana, and Missouri. The first circuits were located on the southern and eastern border areas of these states. In 1812, the ten circuits in Indiana, Illinois, and Missouri had a combined membership of 2,115. Circuit riders coming down through Canada established Methodism in the Detroit area of Michigan. The 1812 *Minutes* list Detroit in the Upper Canada District with 134 members. The Niagara circuit contained 527 members. In 1812, the Upper Canada District belonged to the MEC and was a frontier area that contained seven circuits. Alabama Methodism had a membership of 488 and two circuits in 1812. One was in the northern part of the state. The other was along the western border. Indian treaties delayed the settlement of Alabama.

New England Region

Vermont was the last New England state to be infiltrated by Methodism. Vermont Methodism did not report a membership until 1798. By 1800, Methodism was firmly planted in all the New England states.

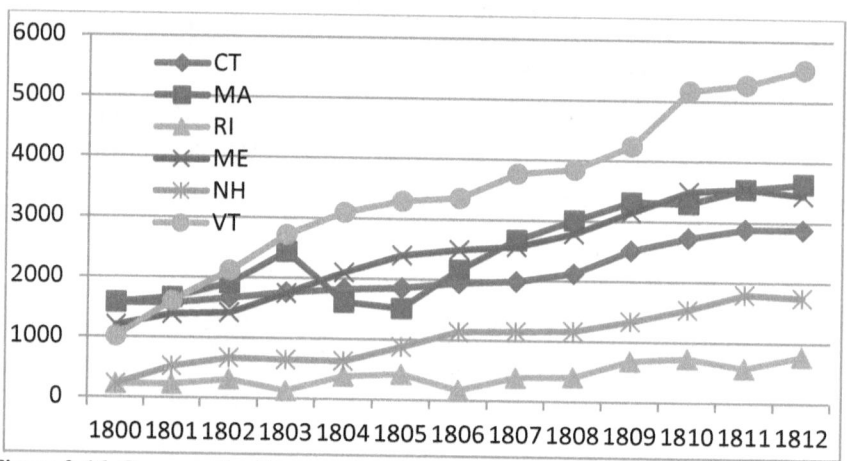

Figure 3-16. Comparative line-graphs of Methodist membership in New England between 1800 and 1812.

According to Figure 3-16, with the exceptions of Massachusetts and Rhode Island, Methodism in the New England states follows comparable membership patterns. Vermont Methodism had no declines in this period. By 1802, more Methodists lived in Vermont than in any other New England state. Vermont Methodism slowed its progress in 1804 through 1806. Afterward, it posted strong growth. Maine Methodism declined only in 1812 due to the onset of the war. The Massachusetts and Maine trend lines crisscrossed four times in this period. In 1804, Massachusetts Methodism posted an 829 member decrease that equaled 34 percent of its total membership. New Hampshire Methodism declined by 30 members between 1802 and 1804. Besides that, it showed steady growth during this period. Connecticut Methodism had a membership loss of six in 1801 and of two in 1812. Overall, its membership increased at a moderate rate during this period.

As the individual graphs on Figure 3-10 show (see page 36), the membership pattern for Rhode Island was erratic. For seven of the 13 years in this period, Rhode Island Methodism grew when Massachusetts Methodism grew. During the other six years, when one declined the other grew. This can be explained in terms of circuit boundaries and groupings. Like the situation with Delaware and Maryland, the states border each other, and some of the circuits in southeast Massachusetts were yoked with Rhode Island circuits from time to time. For example, the Somerset circuit was yoked to various Rhode Island circuits on three different occasions. In two of those cases, it was the junior circuit. Since the *Minutes* only list one membership total for the combined circuit, Somerset's membership was absorbed into Rhode Island's during those years. When Somerset was listed as the senior circuit, the opposite occurred.

In 1800, Connecticut Methodism contained six circuits. It concluded this period with seven circuits and posted a membership gain of 1,313. Massachusetts Methodism began this period with ten circuits and concluded it with 20. Its membership increased by 1,953. Rhode Island Methodism began this period with three circuits and finished it with four. Its membership increased by 554. Maine Methodism began this period with six circuits and ended it with 19. Its membership grew by 2,253. New Hampshire Methodism started this period with three circuits and increased to eight in 1812. It posted a membership gain of 1,526. Vermont Methodism began the period with five circuits and ended it with 16. It grew by 4,519 members. In 1812, New England Methodism had 123 blacks on its membership rolls.

Section Four: Summary

This section shows the comprehensive pattern for the growth and decline of EAM from 1773 through 1812. In the following Figures, the regional nature of early American Methodist membership growth and decline is striking and unambiguous.

The Mid-Atlantic Region

Figure 3-17 establishes the growth pattern of Methodism in the Mid-Atlantic states. The trend lines for New Jersey, Pennsylvania, and Delaware intersect and overlap throughout the majority of this period. Granted, the line-graphs split in the early 1800s; however, New Jersey's, Pennsylvania's, and New York's continue to follow similar growth trajectories. From 1807 to 1812, the rate of growth was the only factor that distinguished the growth patterns of Methodism in New York, Pennsylvania, and New Jersey. Delaware's line-graph follows the same track as Maryland's during the closing years of this period. Certainly, the

Mid-Atlantic states, with the exception of Delaware, show a unique pattern of growth and decline.

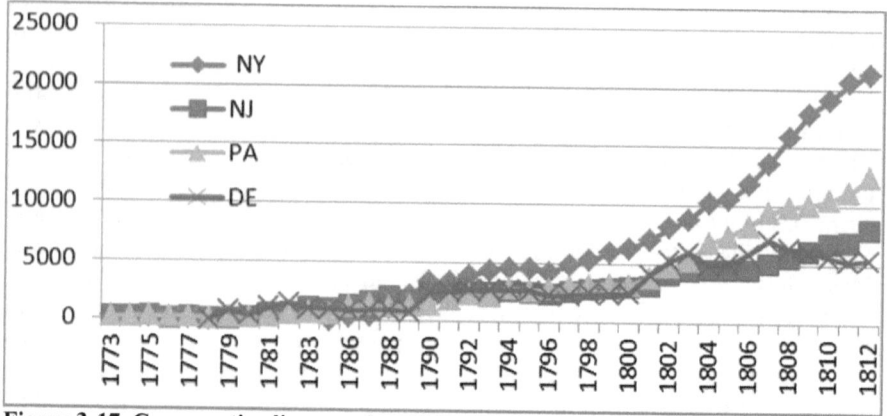

Figure 3-17. Comparative line-graphs of Methodist membership in the Mid-Atlantic States between 1771 and 1812.

The Southern Region

Figure 3-18 depicts a clear membership pattern in the southern states. A hump that is followed by strong growth dominates the individual trend lines. The line-graphs for Maryland and Virginia crisscross seven times. North Carolina's trend line closely follows the pattern of Virginia and Maryland. The trend line for South Carolina Methodism lacks the exaggerated hump because South Carolina Methodism was not firmly established during the numerical impulse in the late 1780s or the decline of the 1790s. However, in most ways, it tracks North Carolina's trend line and follows the same trajectory as Virginia's.

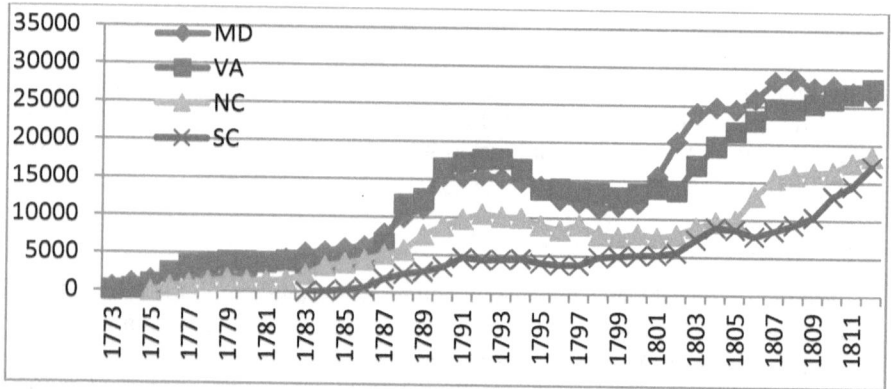

Figure 3-18. Comparative line-graphs of Methodist membership in the Southern States between 1773 and 1812.

The Frontier Region

Figure 3-19 shows that the frontier states followed a distinctive pattern of growth and decline. Tennessee Methodism departs from the dominant pattern from 1804 through 1806. The trend lines for Georgia and Kentucky crisscrosses four times. Georgia membership has the same decline in the 1790s as Maryland, Virginia, and North Carolina. The Ohio trend line appears to be parabolic. It overtakes Georgia's membership in 1812. The rate of membership increase in Georgia, Kentucky, and Ohio is exceptional from the mid-1790s to 1812.

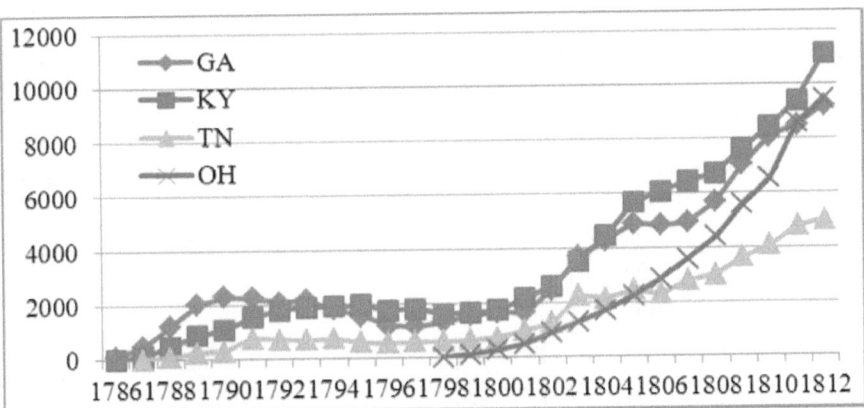

Figure 3-19. Comparative line-graphs of Methodist membership in the Frontier states between 1786 and 1812.

The New England Region

Figure 3-20 covers a 22-year period. It shows that the New England region lacks a definitive pattern. Vermont Methodism blasts off in 1797 and surpasses Rhode Island Methodism in one year. In a five year period, more Methodists lived in Vermont than in any other New England state. At the same time, Rhode Island Methodism lags behind the other states in the region. Its membership spikes at the same time that Massachusetts membership declines because their circuits overlap.

New England displays divergent growth because it consisted of two distinct areas. The actual pattern appears when the consolidated growth of Methodism in Massachusetts, Connecticut, and Rhode Island (Old NE) is compared to the consolidated growth of Methodism in Vermont, New Hampshire, and Maine (Frontier NE). Figure 3-21 depicts that Old NE Methodism grows at a slower rate than Frontier NE Methodism. The frontier membership surpasses Old NE Methodism in 1801 and continues to outpace it through 1812. By 1810, the membership ratio between the two regions is 2:3.

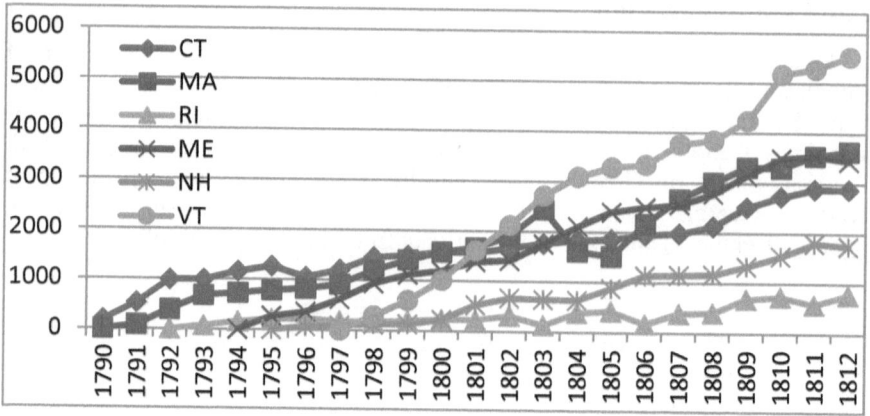

Figure 3-20. Comparative line-graphs of Methodist membership in New England states between 1790 and 1812.

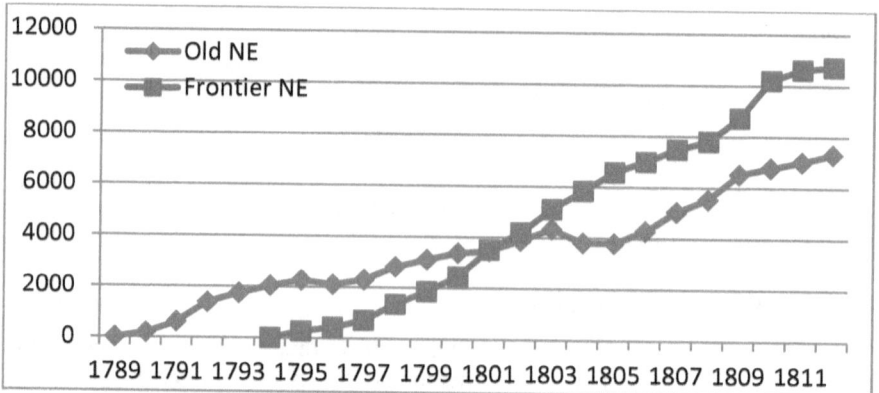

Figure 3-21. Comparative line-graphs of Methodist membership in Old and New NE between 1790 and 1812.

With the exception of Rhode Island, Congregationalism dominated old New England as the state church. Connecticut did not disestablish Congregationalism until 1818 and Massachusetts held out until 1833. Those who felt disenfranchised by the established order in those states turned to Methodism, the Quakers, Universalists, Baptists, Jews, and others. Methodism benefitted from its strong stance against the state church, glebe taxes, clericalism, divine election (Calvinism), and social stratification. In the rhetoric of patriotism and democracy, Methodism argued that Congregationalism belonged to the old world. America broke free from the shackles of ecclesial domination when it won its independence. Methodism identified with the disenfranchised and functioned as a protest movement for them. Methodism never grew well in Rhode Island for the very reasons that it flourished in Massachusetts and Connecticut. Rhode Island was a bastion of religious tolerance and freedom. In that state, the Methodist message fell on deaf ears.

Those who populated the New England frontier fled from the socio-political hegemony of the established order. They were predisposed to the Methodist message and the Methodist style. Plus, the Methodist system of itineration perfectly suited that area. Table 3-3 shows that Connecticut and Massachusetts had a population density of 49 and 47 and New Hampshire, Vermont, and Maine had population densities of 16, 9, and 3 in 1790. Churches that required a populated community to build a church and support a parish pastor could not function well in less populated areas that did not have a critical mass of people. Plus, the Congregational Church was at a disadvantage in a free market religious environment in which it did not receive state aid because its theology and its methods did not encourage popular evangelism with a democratic appeal.

In sum, from 1800 to 1812, Methodism posted tremendous membership increases in all four regions. Between 1800 and 1812, Southern Methodism grew from 38,590 to 89,603 members (132 percent). Mid-Atlantic Methodism grew from 15,065 to 47,281 (214 percent). Frontier Methodism grew from 4,209 to 34,833 (728 percent). New England Methodism grew from 5,812 to 18,043 (210 percent). Even though Southern Methodism and Frontier Methodism followed a similar pattern in terms of percent change in the 1790s, they follow vastly different patterns from 1800 to 1812 in terms of percent increase. Southern Methodism had the slowest rate of growth, and Frontier Methodism had the strongest.

Comparison of Regional Membership Patterns

Figure 3-22 graphs consolidated regional trend lines on the same figure. Regional growth patterns in this figure represent the total membership of the combined states in each region. The regional trend lines in Figures 3-22 and 3-23 reveal the regional nature of EAM growth. Because Figure 3-22 is scaled to Southern Methodism, it suppresses the trend lines of the smaller regions.

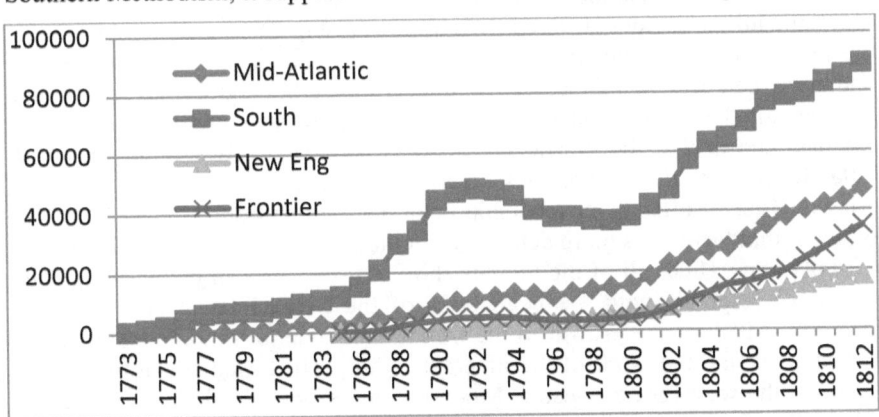

.Figure 3-22. Comparative line-graphs of Methodist regional membership between 1773 and 1812.

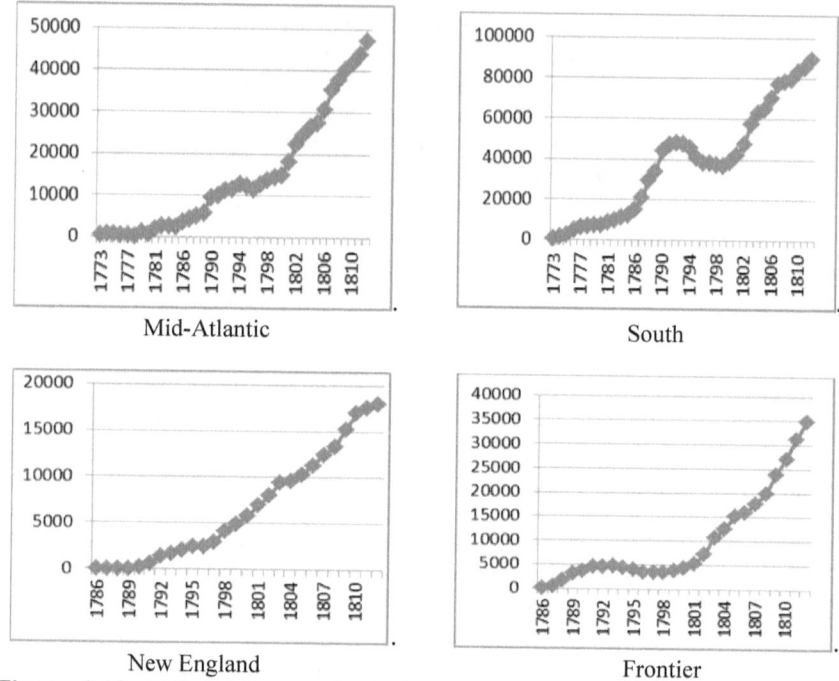

Figures 3-23. Series of line-graphs depicting Methodist membership by region between 1773 and 1812.

The postwar membership surge dominated the growth pattern of EAM from 1781 to 1791. During this time, the great revival in Virginia, Maryland, and North Carolina added multitudes to Southern Methodism. The growth is so intense, that it appears parabolic on the southern trend line in Figure 3-23.

While all the regions suffered from a membership downturn or slowdown in the mid-1790s, the southern decline stands out. Because southern Methodism had more members than the combined totals of the other regions, its exaggerated decline pulled down national membership totals. However, a regional analysis of the data shows that the drastic decline was peculiar to the South. The Mid-Atlantic and New England regions experienced strong growth in the 1790s. Still, a national factor effected membership in all the regions from 1795 to 1796. The effect of that factor was more deleterious in the South and on the frontier.

Following 1800, all of the regions show a strong pike in membership. This period corresponds with the beginnings of the Second Great Awakening in America. Much of the growth in the frontier was due to migration from established areas and the work of the itinerants who pushed Methodism to the vanguard of the westward expansion. Migrating lay leaders also helped to establish Methodism in the most distant parts of the frontier. Despite the loss of membership in the eastern areas due to relocating members, the established regions still showed strong growth. In fact, established Methodism increased its market share in the early 1800s. Growth in terms of percent of total population is shown in Table 3-1.

This chapter reports that the membership patterns for EAM varied by region. Figures 3-17 through 3-20 show the regional membership patterns. Figures 3-22 and 3-23 display the consolidated membership trend lines for each region. The line-graphs make it possible to compare the regional patterns. In other words, Figures 3-15 through 3-19 show that a regional pattern existed, and Figures 3-20 and 3-21 show that the regional patterns were unique. Variation exists within the regions; however, the establishment of a pattern does not require complete homogeneity.

CHAPTER FOUR

HOW EARLY AMERICAN METHODISM PROLIFERATED THE CIRCUIT

Figure 4-1 shows a 1:2:500 ratio between circuits, itinerants, and members. For every circuit, EAM averaged two itinerants and 500 members. During the years of EAM, this remained the optimal growth ratio. Whenever one of the quantities diverged from the others, an exaggerated period of positive or negative numerical change ensued until the optimal ratio was restored. Prolific growth could not be sustained if the number of circuits and itinerates did not increase. For example, if Southern Methodism grew by 5,000 members in a year, it needed to add 20 itinerants and ten circuits in order to preserve the growth and disciple the people. The growth would dissipate if the new members could not be corralled into circuits that were adequately supplied with itinerants in accordance with the optimal ratio. Ultimately, EAM's ability to expand it circuits and grow its membership depended on its ability to recruit, train, sustain, and appoint an adequate number of itinerants. To a lesser extent, local preachers could offset a deficiency in itinerants in places like Virginia. However, in virgin territory or in places not graced with an abundance of local preachers, membership growth depended on the adequate supply of itinerants. The positive relationship between circuits, itinerants, and members remained constant in EAM.

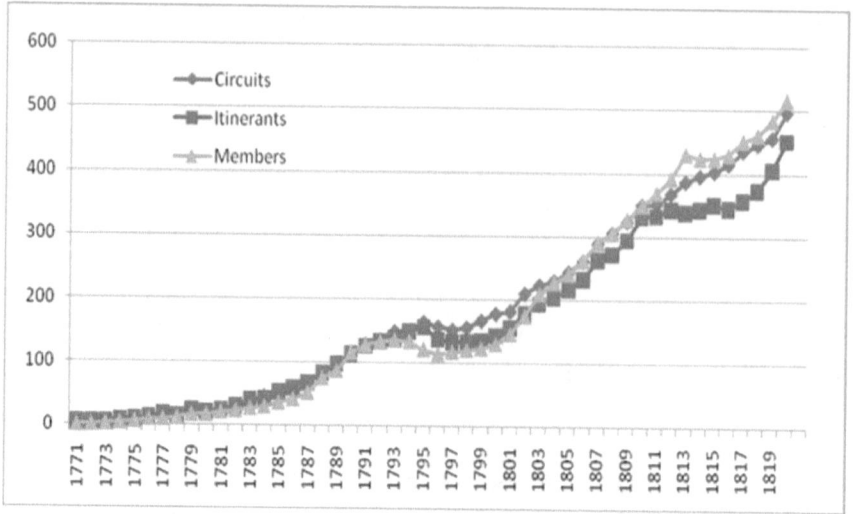

Figure 4-1. Number of circuits, circuit riders, and members between 1770 and 1820.
Note: W. Guy Smeltzer produced a similar graph for 1784 through 1797. See (*Bishop Francis Asbury: Field Marshall of the Lord*, Denver, CO: Eastwood Printing, 1982), 85. His ratio was 1 to 2 to 400. The ratio 1 to 2 to 500 more accurately demonstrates the correlation through 1820.

A Description of the Circuit and the Methods of Its Expansion

The circuit was the basic unit of measurement in EAM. Conference statistics were calculated from circuit membership reports, itinerants were appointed to a circuit, and the *Minutes* list each circuit by name. Three levels of ministry organization existed in a circuit: classes, societies, and bands.[1] The class was the most basic unit of organization in the circuit and the doorway into society membership. EAM enrolled a seeker into a class as soon as he became "awakened" or desired to become a Methodist. A circuit rider appointed a lay person as the class leader. Class meetings were intimate events. Singing, prayer, and Bible reading usually happened at a class meeting during the opening and the closing. However, most of the class time focused on self-examination and accountability.

Classes promoted discipline and growth in grace. For example, to join a class, one needed to evidence a desire to "flee from the wrath to come" and be willing to abide by the Methodist discipline.[2] Discipline existed to facilitate growth in grace and was a means through which one received grace to escape from the wrath to come. The positive relationship between growth in grace and discipline is crucial. Experience proved to Wesley that growth in grace happened as a person kept the discipline. Growth in grace is the key to understanding Wesley's order of salvation. A person moves forward in the salvation continuum as the person grows in grace. That is why Wesley encouraged his preachers not to awaken people through preaching if they did not have the means or time to form the people into classes and societies where they would grow in grace. Discipline and Methodism went hand in glove.[3]

Classes ferreted out from the society those who did not live in accordance with Methodist discipline. People in good standing received a class ticket after they were tested by the circuit rider. The various books of discipline required a three to 12 month trial period before a person received a class ticket. The admittance of undisciplined people to the society meetings hindered the spiritual growth of those who were striving for more grace.

When the New York society purchased a meeting house in 1769, the missionary listed the following rules: it exists for the benefit of all people from all denominations, all duly convinced people who desire to flee from the wrath to come may become probationary members, those who live holy lives after the oracles of God will be admitted into full membership because their fruit bears witness to their faith, a member who does not maintain a holy life will be admonished in an attempt to restore him to God, and if the person does not repent and evidence a godly life, the member will be expelled from the society.[4]

After purging a society, Asbury said, "Disorderly members [are] always a weight and a curse to any religious community. . . . No doubt but this frequently checks the spiritual progress of the righteous; especially if ungodly members are known and not dealt with according to the Gospel."[5] At another time he writes, "There is an evil here: I believe some were improperly taken into the society who never had any deep conviction; I am afraid of them. Some have fallen into sin and others have been on the verge."[6] Some preachers evangelized well but did not enforce the discipline. They received the ire of Asbury. However, the mechanical use of rules without the vision for spiritual growth caused others to fall into cold legalism and spiritual pride.[7]

A seeker could visit a society meeting several times and attend public preaching but could not become a full-member of the society until he or she enrolled in a class and passed a probationary period. Only society members were counted as Methodists. In theory, everyone in a society belonged to a class, but every member of a class was not a full member of a society due to the probationary period. Those in good standing received a class ticket.[8] It allowed class members to participate in restricted society functions. If a person did not maintain the discipline, he or she would be removed from the society or returned to a probationary status. "Testing" the society and "purging" the membership were common practices in EAM.[9] The 1798 *Discipline* explained the process as it had evolved at that time.

> On application for admission into the society, [candidates] must be duly recommended to the preacher who has the oversight of the circuit, by one in whom he can place sufficient confidence, or must have met three or four times in a class, and must be truly awakened to a sense of their fallen condition. Then the preacher who has the oversight of the circuit, gives them notes of admission, and they remain on trial for six months. When the six months are expired, they receive tickets, if recommended by their leader, and become full members of the society.[10]

Originally, classes were distinguished from bands and societies by size and function. Classes were composed of upward to 12 people. As a rule they contained males and females. Bands were composed of mature Christians of the same sex who were moving on to perfection. Usually, they contained four or five people. They focused on strict accountability and the watching over of each other's souls. There were fewer bands than classes.

As one reads Asbury's journal, it is clear that a crisp distinction between classes and bands gradually disappeared in EAM. For example, the word "bands" sometimes described slightly smaller classes or a group having only one gender in attendance. But even this distinction was not absolute, as Asbury often referred to "classes" as single-sex meetings.[11] The ministry function of bands was not as well received or as long-lasting in American Methodism as it was in British Methodism. This accounts for the confusion in the use of their terms.

Since one had to belong to a class in order to be enumerated in the society, more people belonged to the classes than the society. A society contained one or more classes and could contain bands. Large circuits contained many societies. More people participated in Methodist programming than belonged to the official organization.[12] They are represented by "other participants." Many came to public preaching or self-identified with Methodism even though they never went through the official process of becoming a member.

As American Methodism developed, districts evolved. They included the designation of presiding elders and quarterly conferences. The office of presiding elder developed following the Christmas Conference. The newly ordained elders provided the sacraments to a group of circuits. Since an elder was of a higher ecclesiastical order than the preachers or deacons in the area in which he served, he began to take on the leadership role of supervising those circuits. The MEC formalized the office of presiding elder in 1789.

The concept of "general conference" evolved from the need to bring all the preachers together in one place. The Christmas Conference of 1784 is an early example and is considered the first general conference. The term "conference" grew out of Wesley's practice of meeting with chosen preachers for the purpose of discussions. In America, it designated the coming together of the preachers under the leadership of a general assistant or bishop for the purpose of encouragement, preaching, conducting business, and setting appointments.

Types of Church Growth

The church growth movement distinguishes between four types of growth. **Internal growth** refers to a qualitative process by which individuals within a congregation are discipled and formed into the *imago Christi*. As classes and societies in EAM worked to transform awakened people into disciples, they preoccupied themselves with internal growth. The conversion and discipling of the children of members would be included under this category. **Expansion growth** happens as church participation increases through the evangelization of the unchurched. This may include the restoration of lapsed Christians or the assimilation of those who have been cut-off from a church due to relocating. In its most apostolic form, it refers to the conversion of those who have never known Christ. **Extension growth** happens when a church plants daughter churches among those with whom they share cultural similarities. EAM experienced extension growth when a circuit rider started a new society in a new location among a group of relocated Methodists. In turn, this core group expanded by reaching out to neighbors, friends, and relatives. **Bridging growth** happens when a denomination or congregation crosses cultural, class, and/or linguistic barriers to establish a church with a new people group. Methodism's work with African Americans and Native Americans exemplify bridging growth. Because early America was an "immigrant nation," Methodism had to evangelize people from many cultural orientations in order to grow Methodism in all the regions. EAM was not a homogeneous population of likeminded people. For example, the lay preacher who started Methodism in New York was a Palatine German. Even though English served as the *lingua franca* for the hordes of assimilating immigrants, most retained a distinctive cultural heritage.

George Hunter proposed the addition of catalytic growth and proliferation growth to the four-part typology.[13] "**Catalytic Growth** refers to a distinctive, powerful, infectious dynamic that [one] can usually observe when a church is experiencing movemental growth or apostolic growth."[14] In chemistry, a catalyst speeds up a reaction or produces a reaction. In contagious church growth, a converted person or event can serve as a catalyst to dynamic growth. For example, when an unlikely individual or a group of people have a profound conversion, their witness may become contagious. Over a short time, increasing numbers of people may be attracted to Christ through them. The story of EAM bears witness to catalytic growth. The infectious dynamic of revival growth also reflects a catalytic process. EAM realized its greatest harvest through revival growth.

Proliferation growth refers to the way a church makes structural changes in order to grow with new populations or in new ways. For example, instead of adding duplicate services, a church may grow with a new population by adding culturally relevant services. Through proliferation growth, a church may cover a large area in a network of interlinked ministries to distinct populations. In botany, proliferation is a process by which a plant produces others of its kind. It may include enlargement of the existing plant. For example, banyan trees, crab grass, and other plants can extend roots that grow new plants that remain connected to the original plant. Soon, a group of interconnected plants may resemble a single organism while spreading over a large area. In EAM, the adapting tendencies of the movement allowed it to make structural changes that increased its ability to reach and sustain growth with new populations without ceasing to function as a single church. However, even though EAM adapted to reach and assimilate new people, it replicated itself as it grew. Wherever it went, it sent out growth tentacles that enlarged the church and covered the area within its embrace.

The Method of Expanding Circuits

In EAM, bishops appointed itinerants to circuits, not local churches. A circuit was a geographic area that included many preaching points and any number of societies, classes, or chapels. The appointment to a geographic area required the preacher to evangelize the area while giving oversight to the societies. Oversight included preaching, administering the sacraments if ordained, testing the members, appointing local leaders, supervising local preachers, and maintaining the discipline. The reality of itineration meant that the circuit rider could not spend much time in a single location. The need to travel the circuit prevented the circuit rider from being a dedicated pastor. In fact, the term pastor did not exist in the lexicon of early Methodism. Wesley insisted that itinerants were not pastors. That does not mean that members lacked access to pastoral care. Before 1784, pastors from other denominations provided basic support. After 1784, a team of lay leaders, local preachers, and located circuit riders provided pastoral support to societies in the absence of the itinerant.[15] Often, the local preachers conducted funerals, married couples, and baptized children. The itinerants complained about this practice because the local preachers received an honorarium for their services. During a later time, important societies with a parsonage and chapel could lay claim to a stationed itinerant and expect him to act like a pastor. However, during the early years, American Methodism suffered from a shortage of itinerants. Since a wide-open country beckoned to Methodism, the evangelistic mandate and the missionary character of EAM required the bishops to prioritize evangelism. Every circuit rider became a church planting evangelist.

A circuit grew by means of the vanguard method, the missionary method, or the division method.[16] According to the **vanguard method**, a circuit rider geographically enlarged an existing circuit when it bordered an area into which Methodism had not penetrated. He did this by making preaching forays into the new area. In these journeys, he would visit in the homes of the people, stay at taverns, and make acquaintances in any way possible. In the sparsely populated regions, the circuit rider would visit every cabin he came upon. Whenever possible, he would preach to a group of people. Usually, the group would be the friends and neighbors of a family in whose home he stayed.

The following example comes from Garrettson in 1775:

> As I passed through Tuckeyhoe Neck [Tuckahoe Neck is in Caroline County Maryland], I called at a house and asked the woman, if she wanted to hear the word of the Lord preached, if she did, to send and call in her neighbours; she did so, and I found great freedom. I gave out that I would preach again the next day. The man of the house was an officer of rank, and it being a day of general mustering, he marched up all the company, and I spoke to hundreds with freedom; many tears were shed, and several convicted, one of whom has since become a preacher.[17]

At other times, the preacher would announce a preaching time at a given location like a court house, school, or barn and let the people come to him. Occasionally, he would preach to a publicly assembled crowd. Sermons that accompanied public executions exemplify this. Sometimes he would be invited to preach in a local church building.

Preaching served to awaken people or to pique their curiosity, depending on the circumstances. In places where people nursed personal prejudices against Methodism or in locations where an established tradition strove against Methodism, preaching took on an apologetic function. In time, Wesleyan-Arminian sermons became very powerful tools in the battle to sway public opinion in favor of Methodism.[18] After preaching in a new area, the circuit rider would form those who responded into a class and attach them to a society. Afterward, he would add the new outpost to his circuit and seek to expand from it. In essence, each new outpost became a step that took the itinerant deeper into a new area. This is the primary way that Methodism expanded its borders.

Garrettson offers a unique example of the vanguard method. In 1788, he was appointed the presiding elder of the Northern District in New York. He did not have an established district. He had to form it. He states, "I set out to the North with about twelve young preachers to form circuits; and our dear Lord opened our way in a most surprising manner: although much evil was said of us. Many houses, hands, and hearts were opened; and before the commencement of the winter, we had several large circuits formed; and the most of the preachers were comfortably situated."[19]

According to the **missionary method**, a circuit rider was appointed to a distant location that was not adjacent to an existing work. When this occurred, the *Minutes* refer to such circuit riders as missionaries. As Methodism became more prevalent in the Mid-Atlantic and South, some Methodists received appoints to the frontier and others to populated areas into which Methodism had not ventured. Examples of the former are Kentucky, Georgia, Nova Scotia, and the Natchez area of Mississippi.[20] An example of the latter is Massachusetts. Obviously, a person could not win the whole region by himself. The first person appointed would feel out the area in an attempt to find a place of receptivity. Once a work became established, Asbury would send in additional itinerants who would move out from the established beachhead in order to cover the adjacent locations with a light network of circuits. Afterward, the area would be enlarged by the vanguard method until it bumped into the boundaries of another circuit. For example, Asbury appointed Jesse Lee to Boston in 1790. However, Lee abandoned Boston and focused on Lynn because the people there opened themselves to him. As the work grew, Asbury dispatched other circuit riders to the area. Soon, an army of crisscrossing itinerants covered lower New England within a network of circuits. In short order, the New England work connected to an existing work in New York.

The method of evangelizing New England differed from the method used on the western frontier because other churches occupied New England and portions of the region had a dense population. Kentucky presents an interesting example. Often the circuit rider would happen upon or be invited into a new area by transplanted Methodists. At other times, migrant class leaders or lay preachers preceded the circuit rider to the area and formed a nucleus of people into a class or society before the circuit rider arrived. The following illustrates this:

> The Broad River circuit which we took in this year [1785] was partly formed by James Foster, a local preacher. . . . He moved to South Carolina, and there he preached and laboured among the people for a considerable time, before any travelling preachers went into that part of the country. Several Methodist families had removed from Virginia into those parts, and they united and held their class meetings regularly. . . . Then they petitioned our conference to send them some travelling preachers; which at last we did, and by taking in the places where the

local preacher used to preach, and adding a few more new places, there was a good circuit formed at once.[21]

In regards to the work of James Foster, Bishop Coke says that he raised up 110 members in the state of South Carolina before the arrival of circuit riders.[22] In 1781, Asbury commented that local preachers preceded the itinerants across the Allegheny Mountains with the gospel. In Asbury's words, "They prepare the way."[23] In frontier regions, a circuit could cover 200 miles. Usually, in remote areas, the circuit rider only visited the society or class once a month.[24] Such a circuit would be called a "four-week circuit." As the number and density of Methodists increased within the geographic bounds of the circuit, a junior circuit rider could be added. The circuit was still a four-week circuit because it took four weeks for the circuit riders to make one complete tour. However, after the apprentice had some training, the circuit riders split up so that one of the circuit riders visited every two weeks. Eventually, the junior circuit rider would receive his own circuit.

The **division method** evolved as a consequence of growth. In time, the circuit membership became large enough to be divided. For example, in 1787, the Georgia circuit was divided to form the Burk and Augusta circuits. In the next year, the Augusta circuit divided again.[25] According to Lee, "Some of these circuits had been taken off from old circuits, which had been enlarged till there was room for more preachers, and then dividing them we made two circuits out of one."[26] This allowed one circuit rider to work a part of the original circuit more intentionally. A four-week circuit could become a two-week circuit, and a two-week circuit could be turned into a weekly circuit. Eventually, a chapel would be built. In time, the society could expect regular services similar to a modern Methodist church on a multi-point charge.

In EAM, circuit riders always attempted to "grow" their circuits by expanding the borders or by dividing existing circuits. Both methods equally added to numerical growth. Following 1784, South Carolina Methodism exploded with vanguard growth as it pushed out in all directions to cover the state within a light web of circuits. Virginia had already been blanketed with circuits. From 1786 to 1792, both states showed the same growth in terms of raw numbers. Virginia achieved its growth by dividing existing circuits and working the area more carefully. South Carolina achieved its growth by taking Methodism to new locations. Regardless of the method, EAM increased its presence in an area through the multiplication of new societies, classes, and preaching points.

In sum, the following pattern emerges. EAM sought to get a foothold in an area. Then it expanded from that foothold in an effort to cover the area with a light network of circuits. Afterward, it increased its presence in the area by concentrating on local growth, which necessitated dividing growing circuits and adding more circuit riders. Within the area, it worked the places that were most receptive first. Even though one can isolate and describe how each area grew in accordance with this observation, all phases of the process occurred simultaneously from the perspective of the larger church. EAM sent circuit riders (missionaries) to new areas, expanded its borders, and divided circuits continuously.

CHAPTER FIVE

THE BEGINNING OF EARLY AMERICAN METHODISM

The period from 1766 through 1784 represents a transitional moment in American history and in EAM. The years can be divided into three phases. In American history, the phases correspond to the ending of the colonial era with its tensions and preparations for conflict, the Revolutionary War, and the birthing of a new nation. For EAM, the phases correspond to its taking root in American soil, the domination of British missionaries, and the emergence of a sectional crisis that signaled a movement away from British Methodism. The ratification of the American Constitution in 1787 and the organizing of the MEC in 1784 reflect similar national movements. One hailed the birth of a free nation; the other hailed the birth of the first independent American church.

Growth, turmoil, and critical self-evaluation characterized the early years of American Methodism. In the period from 1766 to 1770, Strawbridge, Embury, and Webb organized societies that determined patterns and character. In the period from 1770 to 1778, Wesley's missionaries commanded EAM as they reorganized American Methodism in accordance with the British design. The period witnessed the emergence of many native preachers in the South. Remarkable growth in numbers and geographic expansion distinguished the southern revival belt. During the war years, disruptive persecution, armed conflict, and troop movements negatively impacted membership and ministry. Additionally, the independent spirit that gave birth to Maryland Methodism re-emerged. The ensuing conflict pitted the British model against the American model. Ultimately, diplomacy and the spirit of connectionalism caused Southern Methodism to submit to Asbury's rule.[1]

As EAM adapted to the American scene, it experienced incremental change. For this reason, one cannot talk about its structure in normative terms. The established model that Wesley developed in his context represents pristine Methodism. Wesley was the force and inspiration behind that movement. Others influenced him and worked with him, but Wesley remained the undisputed father-in-residence of British Methodism. As long as he lived, he pressed his imprimatur into every aspect of the organization. However, Wesley never enjoyed the same respect or allegiance with the American Methodists. The questioning of his rule caused institutional stress during this period and in the subsequent period.

Two factors relate to this. First, the American context differed from the British context because of its frontiers, polyglot populations, lack of a rigid social structure, the strong influence of other denominations, tensions from colonialism, and the precursors of war. Second, an indigenizing force worked in American Methodism from its inception. EAM needed to be "Methodized" and "Americanized." The missionaries Methodized EAM and the native preachers pushed to Americanize EAM. Ultimately, Asbury combined both of these processes in one movement. Even though the conference structure made Asbury amenable to the preachers in ways that differed from Wesley's autocratic stance, by 1784, he had the same force of presence in America that Wesley had in England. From the perspective of strategy and presence, Asbury emerged as the Wesley of American Methodism.

Population Distribution

On the verge of the Revolution in 1775, the American population stood at 2,600,000.[2] By 1770, Savannah, Charleston, Norfolk, Baltimore, Philadelphia, Albany, and New York City boasted populations that exceeded 3,000 residents.[3] According to Map 5.1, in 1775, a heavily populated swath of area ran from Baltimore to Boston.[4] A less population area surrounded the denser population. A separate population zone ballooned around Charleston and Savannah. Between 1760 and 1775, American immigration can be summarized as follows: more than 55,000 Protestant Irish; 40,000 Scots; and 30,000 Englishmen came to America from the British Isles. An additional 84,500 African slaves were brought to the southern colonies. That equaled 209,500 new immigrants or about 14,000 immigrants each year.[5]

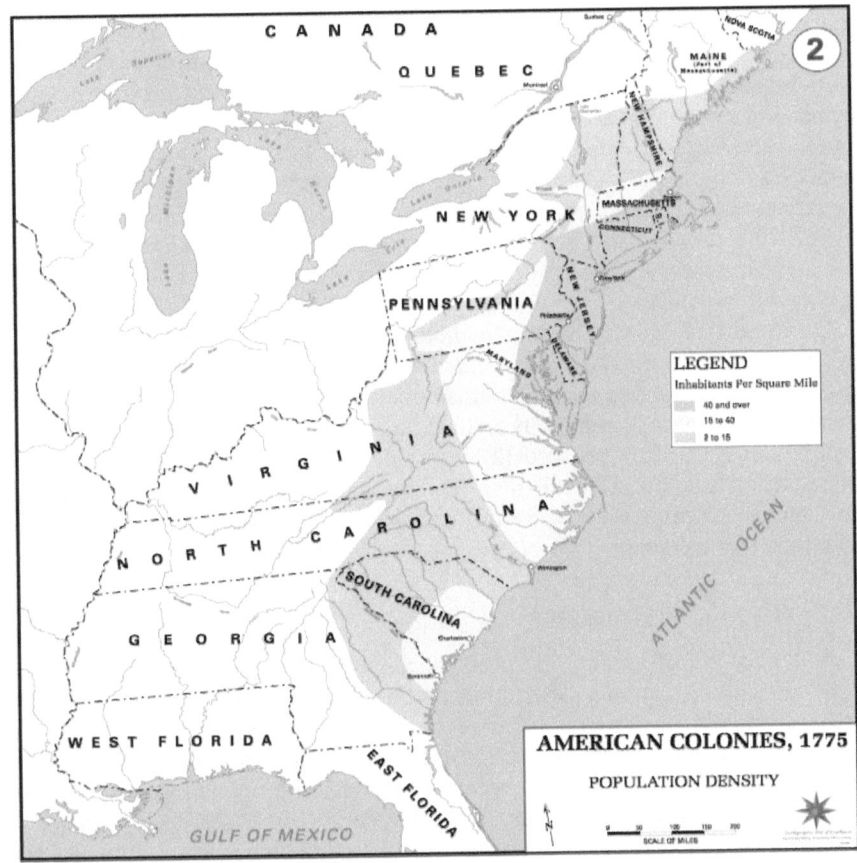

Map 5-1. Population density of American colonies in 1775.
Source: http://www.emersonkent.com/map_archive/american_colonies_population.htm (accessed August 1, 2012). Used with permission. Courtesy of the United States Military Academy Department of History.

English-speaking immigrants proved to be very receptive to the preaching of the Methodists. The overwhelming majority were unchurched because they lived in areas that lacked organized churches.[6] American Methodism was planted in immigrant communities and it continued to have great success in these communities during its formative years as it fought to carve out a foothold in the terrain of American religious tradition. It did not grow with German speaking populations. If Asbury would have had German speaking itinerants, he would have established a parallel work with the German immigrants.

Institutional Factors during the Missionary Years

Because American Methodism came into being through the work of immigrant preachers that did not have an appointment from Wesley (Strawbridge in Maryland and Virginia, Embury in New York, and Webb in New York, Trenton, Philadelphia and Delaware), irregularities attended to their ministries. The peculiarities caused institutional stress when Wesley began to oversee American Methodism through appointed missionary preachers in the Mid-Atlantic and the South. The ensuing tension is a major institutional factor in the first chronological period (1770-1784). Conflict between the missionaries and the other preachers deflected Methodism from its evangelistic mission and hurt morale. Conflict between the missionaries and the established societies engendered resistance, hindered growth, and caused localized declines. Some people left out of anger; others were expelled.

During the missionary years, Methodism struggled in New York, New Jersey, and Pennsylvania. Methodist membership in the Mid-Atlantic vacillated. After five years, the number of circuits remained unchanged. New Jersey Methodism showed some increases. It divided into two circuits before the war. Philadelphia and New York showed little growth. Internal conflicts and contextual constraints adversely affected them. On the other hand, Southern Methodism grew rapidly. It registered seven full circuits by 1775. Two of them contained more than 800 members.

Mid-Atlantic Methodism

In the late 1760s, the New York society functioned like an independent Methodist church. Embury never itinerated because he was a local preacher; not a circuit rider. In most ways, he acted like a hired pastor. This example established expectations in the New York society. In Philadelphia, Webb did not give careful attention to his society because he itinerated up and down the East Coast.[7] Consequently, the Methodists in the New York and Philadelphia societies had grown accustomed to having a say in every issue. When Pilmoor and Boardman arrived, the people assumed that they would be stationed pastors. The English missionaries bought into this deal. The following quotation from Daniels illustrates the problem and the reason for the clash:

> Captain Webb, who was on shore to greet [the first missionaries on their arrival from England], put into their hands a plan of the first American circuit, which, with the help of himself, Williams, and King, they were to travel. New York, however, desired the full service of Boardman, while Philadelphia wished to monopolize Pilmoor, and thus at the outset the itinerant system, so vital to the success of Methodism in America, was in danger of being replaced by a settled ministry.[8]

Wesley appointed Boardman to act as his assistant in America. Because he did not pay strict attention to Methodist order, he overlooked certain points of discipline. Consequently, Wesley made Asbury his assistant in October, 1772.[9] In December 1772, Asbury told the New York society that he would not give into their demands. He insisted that the people abide by Wesley's rules. He mused, "Mr. Boardman had given them their way at the quarterly meeting held here before, and I was obliged to connive at some things for the sake of peace."[10] In 1774 he wrote, "I saw a letter from Mr. Pilmoor, filled with his usual softness."[11] "Softness" refers to pastoral demeanor and a spirit of compromise.

Asbury's dedication to Wesley's model brought him into conflict with the missionaries and the American societies. In both cases, Wesley sided with Asbury. In the meantime, in order to avoid favoritism and long tenures, Asbury made the missionaries switch circuits on a regular basis. This kept the societies from co-opting the missionaries. It also kept the missionaries from building a power base around a local society. Tensions increased when Thomas Rankin arrived in 1773 and took over as Wesley's general assistant in America. His unyielding demeanor and his punctilious dedication to discipline made him appear antagonistic and arrogant.[12]

In 1773, American Methodism held its first conference in Philadelphia. The conference actions illustrate the tensions that existed in the Mid-Atlantic area at this time.[13] First, only Wesley's appointed missionaries participated in the conference. They established that Wesley's rule extended to America. Before the arrival of the missionaries, American Methodists were nominally aligned with Wesley. A strong lay leadership that wanted to participate in the decision-making process resisted Rankin's leadership style. In fact, two days after the Conference, people in the New York society wanted to expel him.[14] In British Methodism, an itinerant could expunge members from a society but the society could not fire the preacher. The New York society had leverage because the members owned the chapel. Repeatedly, Pilmoor's journal calls New York's St. George Chapel a church. This reflects the society's self-understanding. In the tradition of the Methodist movement at that time, he should have called it a meeting house, a preaching house, or a chapel. Unlike other missionaries, Pilmoor was very attached to the building and to the congregation that assembled in it.

Second, the conference affirmed that the doctrine and discipline as contained in the British and American *Minutes* would serve as the sole rule for the conduct of those who labor in America.[15] This aligned American Methodism with British Methodism and gave the missionaries a pattern for organization and administration. However, this measure had an unintentional consequence in that it advanced the American conference to a new level of authority. In British Methodism, the conference gave advice to Wesley. The rise of the American conference made it possible for EAM to make decisions in the absence of Wesley.

Third, the conference determined that no one could attend the love feasts more than two or three times until he or she became a member of the society, and no one would be admitted to a society meeting more than three times without submitting to its rules. The absence of this regulation threatened American Methodism because it undermined the sociological and salvific function of strict discipline. This rule reiterated a standard rule in British Methodism. The reaffirmation of the rule checked the soft discipline of the Mid-Atlantic societies and the lack of discipline in the Southern societies. Both allowed non-members to attend as often as they wanted. Rankin dispatched Asbury to fix the problems in the Baltimore area. The situation in the Mid-Atlantic area required more finesse.

Pilmoor illustrates the issue. He conducted "general" love feasts after he arrived due to the established pattern that existed in the Mid-Atlantic societies. Asbury complained to Wesley about this irregularity.[16] According to Thomas Taylor, "[Embury] had formed two classes, one of men, and the other of women, but he had never met the society apart from the congregation.... Great numbers of serious persons came to hear God's word as for their lives; and their numbers increased so fast that our house for six weeks past could not contain half the people."[17] On September 5, 1772, Asbury queried the New York Society with the following question: "Shall we have the Society meetings in private? This was doubted by some; but I insisted on it, from our rules and Mr. Wesley's last letter."[18]

When Asbury and Rankin pushed for strong adherence to the rules, the people in the Mid-Atlantic area recoiled. Asbury's *Journal* contains 14 entries from 1772 through 1775 that highlight how the administration of strict discipline caused numerical decline in EAM.[19] The following is a typical illustration: "Some slight me in this place [Philadelphia] on account of my attention to discipline; and some drop off."[20] "Many were offended at my shutting them out of society meeting.... An elderly Friend [Quaker] told me very gravely, that 'the opinion of the people was much changed ... about Methodism: and that the Quakers and other dissenters had laxed [sic] their discipline.'"[21] "We had collected twenty-seven persons in our little society here, when I first came; but I have been obliged to reduce them to fourteen; and this day I put out a women for excessive drinking. Here we see the necessity and advantage of discipline."[22]

Quotations from Asbury's *Journal* also highlight conflict between Wesley's assistants and the Mid-Atlantic societies: "I understand that some dissatisfied persons in New York, threaten to shut the church door against Mr. Rankin. If they should be bold enough to take this step, we shall see what the consequences shall be."[23] "Mr. Rankin keeps driving away at the people, telling them how bad they are, with the wonders which he has done and intends to do. It is surprising that the people are not out of patience with him. If they did not like his friends better than him, we should soon be welcome to take a final leave."[24] Asbury had his own problems. Those accustomed to lax discipline did not take to his firm deportment. This caused complaints and infighting. "Heard that many were offended at my shutting them out of society meeting, as they had been greatly indulged before. But this does not trouble me. While I stay, the rules must be attended to."[25] "Mr. Lupton was pleased to say, 'He did not know but the church door would be shut against me;' and that 'some persons would not suffer matters to go on so.'"[26]

If Embury would have established New York Methodism after the British model, the conflict between the missionaries and the society would not have happened or it would not have been as severe. After the missionaries established the rule in the Mid-Atlantic area, much of the internal opposition lessened.[27]

Southern Methodism

In the mid-1760s, Strawbridge formed a class in his home, built a preaching house, and organized a society.[28] From his base in Frederick, Maryland, he began to itinerate without the benefit of an appointment. The location gave him easy access to northern Virginia and southern Pennsylvania. By 1769, he mapped out a wide circuit and supervised a far-reaching ministry that included other preachers.[29] Three facts associated with Strawbridge presage institutional conflict and point to the indigenizing process associated with the emergence of Southern Methodism.

First, the ministry over which Strawbridge presided produced the first substantial Methodist harvest in America. Many influential itinerants and local preachers came to faith under his ministry. He discipled, mentored, and deployed them in ministry. He also made his influence felt among the Methodist people. The southern laity held him in high esteem. This provided a check against Wesley's assistants when they wanted to minimize him because of his irregularities.

When Wesley's missionaries ventured to Maryland, they encountered a functioning system of itineration under the charge of Strawbridge. His previous association with British Methodism influenced him and determined many aspects of his ministry. As one who had served under Wesley's charge in Ireland, he appreciated British Methodism. However, in America, he did not become a slave to it or allow it to prevent him from taking liberties. In fact, he did not attempt to align himself with Wesley when he began his ministry in Maryland. He did his own thing in the way that seemed right to him. For example, in the absence of Wesley's rules, he formed a Methodist church complete with sacraments, itineration, and preachers. Daniels captures this point. He calls Strawbridge's meeting house "the cathedral church of Strawbridge's little diocese . . . over which he presided in true episcopal fashion."[30]

> It is evident that the Lord was with this little church in the wilderness in spite of its alleged irregularities, for its numbers increased in an encouraging manner, and in the log chapel on Sam's Creek as many as four or five preachers were raised up [William Watters, Philip Gatch, Richard Owings, Freeborn Garrettson, and John Hagerty], who, under the direction of Strawbridge, traveled little circuits on Sabbath, and worked for their daily bread on the other days of the week.[31]

Second, Strawbridge and his preachers lacked the training or vision to organize new converts into societies and classes. This undermined their ability to assimilate the people into Methodism or to maintain Methodist discipline. Arthur Moss opines the following:

> A serious organizational problem appeared. Despite his zeal for souls and his gift of drawing people to the Savior, Strawbridge seems to have possessed only a modicum of ability in organizing them beyond the casual or local congregation. He established many societies, but the accepted tests for membership were not strictly followed by all of his helpers, and frequently the organization of classes was not observed.[32]

In 1773, Rankin appointed Asbury to the Baltimore circuit for the purpose of fixing irregularities. The circuit included all the societies in Maryland and nearly half the Methodists in America. Strawbridge and two junior preachers received appointments to the same circuit. The circuit encompassed Strawbridge's base. In essence, Rankin put Asbury in charge of Strawbridge's extended congregation. According to Daniels, "These Societies had been formed in a very unmethodical manner; indeed, the whole body was thought, by Rankin and Asbury, to be sadly wanting in order and discipline; and one of the first cares of the new preacher was to organize the Societies into classes . . . on the Wesleyan plan."[33] Asbury took it upon himself to re-examine each society in order to determine the seriousness of the membership and to assign the participants to classes. He expelled many of the lukewarm and undisciplined members. His journal makes copious references to this process between 1772 and 1773.

This situation highlights a fundamental issue. An incredible evangelist who lacks the time, energy, or gifts necessary to form large numbers of converts into disciplined units will not maintain his converts or established a longstanding work. George Whitfield made this mistake. Like a shooting star that burns brilliantly in the sky before disappearing with no residue, Whitfield left no evidence of his ministry when he died because he did not organize his converts into classes and societies. Strawbridge's desire to reach as many people as possible with the Methodist message collided with the organizational demand of forming the people into classes and structured societies. Evangelism that does not shape converts into disciples will not produce Methodists. This became a recurring problem in Southern Methodism. As Southern Methodism grew large and became more popular, it waxed increasingly more difficult for the itinerants to adhere to Wesley's design for societies and classes.

Third, the 1773 conference fixed rules that reflected Strawbridge's irregularities:

> 1. Every preacher . . . is strictly to avoid administering the ordinances of baptism and the Lord's Supper. 2. All the people among whom we labour to be earnestly exhorted to attend the church, and to receive the ordinances there; but in a particular manner, to press the people in Maryland and Virginia, to the observance of this minute.[34]

Asbury recounted a slightly different version of these rules: "No preacher in our connection shall be permitted to administer the ordinances at this time; except Mr. Strawbridge, and he under the particular direction of the assistant."[35] He made no mention of the second rule.[36] It is possible that some of the preachers that helped Strawbridge also administered the sacraments. In December 1772, while at a quarterly meeting in Maryland, Asbury asked, "Will the people be content without us administering the sacrament? . . . Brother Strawbridge pleaded much for the ordinances; and so did the people who appeared to be much biased by him."[37]

The fact that the conference allowed Strawbridge to continue administering the sacraments shows his popular appeal and his institutional clout. Conversely, it shows the vulnerability of EAM. The newly formed connection needed Strawbridge's converts. Even though Asbury itinerated in Maryland, the people remained Strawbridge's devotees. The 1773 conference compromised out of need when it permitted Strawbridge to continue his administration of the sacraments. Failure to compromise would have caused a split in American Methodism. At the same time, Strawbridge's ministry created an untenable problem. As long as he administered the sacraments while itinerating as a Methodist circuit rider, the members, the local preachers, and the other itinerants would be influenced by it. Also, the symbiotic relationship with the Episcopal Church would be jeopardized. In fact, it would threaten a theological imperative of the Methodist movement

Wesley published *The Ministerial Office* in 1789.[38] It served as an apology for the "old" Methodist way and shows Wesley's original plan for the American connection before he ordained preachers for it. In it, he declares that Methodist preachers do not compete with priests in that they are not called to serve the sacraments. Methodist preachers lead people to the church. They do not take members from the church. The ideas contained in the sermon hearken back to 1744 and were common knowledge to the British missionaries and the American itinerants.

In the sermon, Wesley declares that the New Testament office of pastor differs from the office of evangelist in the same way as the Old Testament office of priest differs from the office of prophet. The history of the early church demonstrates that the pastor served the sacraments; the evangelist did not.[39] The evangelist worked in support of the church but was not subjugated to the rule of the pastor because the itinerant evangelist exercised an extraordinary calling to preach in the highways and byways. Methodism represents a rediscovery of the apostolic model of itinerant evangelism. They complemented the ministry of the pastor as they convicted people of sin and formed them into groups whereby they might become better members of the church. Methodist itinerants would blur their calling and compromise the New Testament order if they took up the sacraments. For this reason, the British missionaries struggled with Strawbridge's sacramental ministry. Wesley did not allow any of his preachers to serve the sacraments except those who were ordained priests.

Strawbridge's name does not appear in the *Minutes* after 1775. Most likely, he located because he did not want to leave his wife. Once he and his helpers became itinerants, they had to serve the entire connection at the direction of the general assistant. For example, Daniel Ruff, one of his disciples, was appointed to Philadelphia and New Jersey from 1775 through 1779. It is doubtful that Strawbridge would have taken an appointment to New Jersey. Possibly, Strawbridge stopped cooperating with the connection so he could continue to do his own thing without the supervision of the missionaries. From 1776-1781, Strawbridge ministered at his original Log Meeting House on Sam's Creek and to the society at Bush Chapel. Possibly, he itinerated up to the society at Shirleysburg, Pennsylvania. It cannot be determined if he ministered as a local preacher or as an independent preacher with a nominal connection to Methodism.

Abel Stevens offers the following details concerning his last days:

> We trace him at last to the upper part of Long Green, Baltimore county, where an opulent and generous public citizen, who admired his character and sympathized

with his poverty, gave him a farm, free of rent, for life. It was while residing here, "under the shadow of Hampton," his benefactor's mansion, that, in one of his visiting rounds to his spiritual children, he was taken sick at the house of Joseph Wheeler, and died in great peace.[40]

Strawbridge courted controversy in that he was an independent person who chafed at being under someone's authority. In fact, Barclay intimated that Strawbridge had problems with Wesley's authority before he immigrated to America.[41] His independent thinking and irregularities did a great deal to influence the ethos of Southern Methodism and the indigenization of American Methodism. "For him it was enough that crowds waited upon his ministry, that many burdened souls sought and found to their satisfaction the forgiveness of their sins and came into the fellowship of the Society he had formed."[42] Asbury struggled with the Strawbridge ethos and his popularity.

In sum, Strawbridge's organizational precedent and independent spirit brought him into conflict with Wesley's missionary preachers and presaged the Southern mutiny in 1779 that divided EAM between North and South. As long as the English preachers directed the show, Strawbridge was minimized and Southern Methodism acquiesced. However, as soon as they left in 1778, the Strawbridge ethos of EAM re-emerged with a vengeance.

Comparison of Mid-Atlantic and Southern Methodism

During this period, Mid-Atlantic and Southern Methodism differed from each other in specific ways. First, Mid-Atlantic Methodism began in the cities and focused on urbanites until Asbury determined to take the message to the backcountry. The following quotations from Asbury's journal demonstrate the urban nature of Mid-Atlantic Methodism:

> I remain in New York, though unsatisfied with our being both [Boardman] in town together. I have not yet the thing which I seek–a circulation of preachers, to avoid partiality and popularity. However, I am fixed to the Methodist plan [of itinerating and strict discipline], and do what I do faithfully as to God. I expect trouble is at hand.[43]

> At present I am dissatisfied. I judge we are to be shut up in the cities this winter. My brethren seem unwilling to leave the cities, but I think I shall show them the way. I am in trouble, and more trouble is at hand, for I am determined to make a stand against all partiality.[44]

> I find that the preachers have their friends in the cities and care not to leave them. There is a strange party-spirit. For my part I desire to be faithful to God and man. . . . I have found many trials in my own mind, but feel determined to resist. I see traps set for my feet.[45]

> 'Tis one great disadvantage to me I am not polite enough for the people. They deem me fit for the country, but not for the cities; and it is my greater misfortune I cannot, or will not, learn, and they cannot teach me. . . . I was not born so, nor educated after this sort, I cannot help it.[46]

By comparison, Strawbridge began his work in the backcountry. In today's vernacular, Strawbridge was an unsophisticated country boy with leadership abilities, a deep faith, and strong opinions. In this regard, he resembled Asbury. He created a legacy through the native born preachers that he recruited and trained for the ministry. They continued his influence long after he located and died.

Second, Mid-Atlantic Methodism consciously aligned itself with Wesley when it sought his help and requested that he send them preachers. A letter written by Thomas Taylor to Wesley on April 11, 1768, shows this.[47]

> You will not wonder at my being agreeably surprised in meeting a few here who have a desire again to be in connection with you. . . . I was determined that the house [Wesley Chapel in New York] should be on the same footing as the orphan house at Newcastle, and others in England; but as we were ignorant how to draw the deeds, we purchased for us and our heirs, until a copy of the writing is sent us from England. . . . There is another point far more material, and in which I must importune your assistance, not only in my own name, but also in the name of the whole society [in New York]. We want an able and experienced preacher; one who has both gifts and grace necessary for the work. . . . In regard to a preacher, if possible we must have a man of wisdom, of sound faith, and a good disciplinarian. . . . We may make many shifts to evade temporal inconveniences, but we cannot *purchase* such a preacher as I have described.[48]

Wesley took their missive seriously. It laid the foundation for the sending of the first missionaries:

> On Thursday, August 1, 1769, our Conference began at Leeds. On Thursday I mentioned the case of our brethren in New-York. For some years past, several of our brethren from England and Ireland, (and some of them preachers), had settled in North America, and had in various places formed societies, particularly in Philadelphia and New-York. The society at New-York had lately built a commodious preaching-house; and now desired our help, being in great want of money, but much more of preachers.[49]

One wonders why Embury did not write the letter to Wesley since he founded the New York society and served as the lead preacher. The letter indicates that Taylor wrote on behalf of the congregation. He had a working knowledge of British Methodism and knew Wesley. The request asks Wesley to supply a preacher, not an itinerant who would nurture a budding Methodist movement in America. For whatever reason, Taylor does not suggest that Embury stay on as the main preacher.[50] After the missionaries began to arrive, Embury and other native leaders of the early movement in New York relocated.[51] The absence of native leaders gave the missionaries *carte blanche* to take control of the Mid-Atlantic societies. Captain Webb remained for a season.

On the other hand, the southern converts had no prior connection with Wesley. Plus, the southern movement produced native preachers who gave leadership to the work. Before the war, the native preachers worked side-by-side with the missionaries as appointed preachers. By means of this on-the-job-training, they learned how to work a circuit. After the war caused the British missionaries to leave, the native leaders continued to work their home terrain. Also, Southern

Methodism did not request help from Wesley or the missionary preachers. It appears that they yielded to them. Finally, southern Methodists already expected itinerating preachers when the missionaries incorporated them into the larger connection. They did not anticipate settled preachers.

In summary, between 1770 and 1775, Strawbridge and his band of preachers were the primary institutional factor for the tremendous growth of Southern Methodism. They had plowed the soil and reaped a large harvest before Wesley's preachers came to oversee the work. Many other institutional factors relate to this. The preachers were home-grown, demonstrated natural abilities, and had a tremendous evangelistic zeal. As a group, they were well organized. At the same time, conflict between the missionaries and preachers, reaction to strict discipline, and the inability of the preachers to assimilate the new converts into classes and societies militated against growth.[52] The administration of the sacraments was a neutral factor.

It should be noted that the British preachers helped Southern Methodism. In the *Minutes* for 1775, fourteen itinerants worked the southern states. Five of those were missionaries. Early in the 1770s, English preachers John King, Robert Williams, Captain Webb, Pilmoor, and Asbury made preaching forays to the South. Pilmoor went as far as Savannah, Georgia and established societies in Norfolk and Portsmouth. Other missionaries tended to the societies while Pilmoor continued his southward sojourn. The British preachers advanced the work in areas where Strawbridge and his preachers had not ventured.[53]

By 1775, only five preachers itinerated in the Mid-Atlantic area. Three of those worked New Jersey. The New York work seemed small in comparison to the growing work in Southern Methodism. Soon the New York Society would cease to be listed in the *Minutes*.

1770 Through 1775, Contextual Factors

The first section gives a general overview of American Methodism through 1775 with a comparison of Southern and Mid-Atlantic Methodism. It focuses on institutional factors that show the sectional nature of Methodism. This section examines the contextual factors associated with New Jersey and Virginia that affected Methodist growth and development. These colonies typify their regions.

Mid-Atlantic -- New Jersey

Methodism in New Jersey grew faster than Methodism in the other Mid-Atlantic states during this period. After 1775, it participated in the northern declension. By 1776, barely 500 Methodists remained on the rolls in the Mid-Atlantic states. Problems related to the pending war most influenced the membership decline in New Jersey.

In 1770, New York and Philadelphia boasted large societies. Since New Jersey lay between them, the itinerants passed through it often. Webb preached in Burlington in 1770. Others preceded him.[54] As they traveled through New Jersey, they preached and set up societies. Also, New Jersey Methodism benefited from the burgeoning work in the bordering societies because the work overflowed into it.[55] By 1773, New Jersey Methodism reported twenty more members than New York and Philadelphia. It continued to lead the Mid-Atlantic region in membership until 1776. At that time the membership in Pennsylvania surpassed it because the Philadelphia society declined at a slower rate than the one in New Jersey.

In 1774, New Jersey included the Trenton and Greenwich circuits. In 1776, the conference consolidated them into the New Jersey circuit.[56] Asbury's *Journal* describes a Methodist work between Staten Island and Philadelphia down to southern New Jersey, and along the Hudson River to Wilmington, Delaware. Significant New Jersey works centered around Burlington, Amboy, Greenwich, Glouster, and New Mill (later called Pemberton).

Asbury made a series of references to his itineration in New Jersey during a two week period in 1772. The journal entries give insight into the contextual factors that influenced ministry in this area. "Went to Trenton, but as the court was sitting, I was obliged to preach in a school house to but few people; and as there were soldiers in the town, I could hardly procure lodging."[57] Afterward, he preached on "the other side of the river" in Pennsylvania to a small group. Then he went down to Burlington and preached to a few people. He blamed the slack attendance on competition from a fair. Following this, he traveled to Greenwich on the Delaware River in the southern part of the state where he preached to 300 people. Afterward, he rode to Glouster where he preached to 200 people before returning to Philadelphia. The next day, he went back to Burlington where he preached and ministered to a prisoner. On May 27, he preached in New Mills, which is located in the center of the state approximately 25 miles east of Philadelphia. By May 29, he returned to Burlington where he attended the prisoner to his execution. There he preached to the attending crowd and warned them to "flee from the wrath to come."[58] He returned to Philadelphia on the same day. From Saturday through Monday, he stayed in Philadelphia. On June 2, he went back to New Jersey, passed through Haddonfield and preached to a large congregation along the Maunta Creek at 5:00am the following morning. After the service, a crowd of 150 followed him to a Mr. Taper's for more preaching. On the third, he preached to 200 people at Greenwich. During the previous week, his audience was 300. Later, he returned to Glouster where the crowd had dwindled since his last stop.

The number of those who attended Asbury's preaching in 1772 exceeded the Methodist membership for New Jersey. On the New Jersey portion of his circuit, at least 650 different people came out to his preaching during the two-week period. Asbury listed only the rounds that he made in southwest New Jersey. Others worked the area around Staten Island. All totaled, more than 1,000 people attended Methodist preaching in New Jersey in 1772. The 1773 *Minutes* only enumerate 200 members. The same phenomenon happened in New York. On November 14, 1774, Asbury reported, "Many people attended at our church in the morning; and in the evening there were about a thousand who seriously listened."[59] The New York membership numbered 222.

Asbury refers to two contextual issues. One relates to soldiers in town and the other to a fair. The problem with soldiers increased as the war drew near. Early in 1776, while in Philadelphia, Asbury reported that the preachers in Trenton neglected their societies because of war tensions.⁶⁰ Asbury said, "Rode to Burlington [and] found to my grief, that many had so imbibed a martial spirit that they had lost the spirit of pure and undefiled religion."⁶¹ The preachers to whom he referred were local preachers. Throughout the Methodist work in New Jersey, lay preachers helped the circuit riders. When they neglected their duties, the work suffered.

Second, races and fairs annoyed Asbury because they appealed to the carnal and kept people from attending Methodist meetings. In December 1772, a church parson accused Asbury of distracting the people from their work with all of his preaching. Asbury replied by asking whether fairs and horse races did not also hinder the people. In 1772, quarterly meetings had to be moved to Saturdays and Sundays because slaves and working people could not come to the preaching on any day but the Sabbath.⁶² On those same days fairs, horse races, and other types of diversion provided competition and kept people from participating in Methodist meetings. Thus, one can appreciate Methodism's negative appraisal of these events. When one became a Methodist, discipline required that one avoid trifling amusements.

EAM had 19 preachers appointed to ten circuits with a total of 3,148 members in 1775. Rankin traveled at large. This means that there was one preacher for every 166 members. Mid-Atlantic Methodism had five preachers and 618 members. That equals one preacher for every 123 members. This shows that Mid-Atlantic declines did not occur because of an absence of itinerants.

Emigration from the Mid-Atlantic area did cause numerical decline. Lee said that people fled areas in which there were troop activities and other preparations for war. Specifically, many people in the Mid-Atlantic moved to the frontier and to the South.⁶³ Also, as one of the first areas of hard combat, clashes between Loyalists and Patriots tore at the Mid-Atlantic. In this area, Methodism appealed to Loyalists because of its strong affirmation of the English Church, the Tory sentiments of Wesley, and the outspoken patriotism of some English missionaries. A society that appealed to Tories would not attract Patriots. When the Tory population diminished, the Methodist work in that area would also diminish. Even worse, after the Loyalist population left, Americans would still not want to attend a church that had a previous association with them. Tensions related to the pending war and demographic shifts are the primary contextual factors that caused slow growth in the Mid-Atlantic area from 1770 through 1775.

Southern -- Virginia

In 1773, Virginia Methodism only had 100 members. By 1775, the membership increased to 955. A general revival of religion that began around 1765 and lasted until the late 1770s greatly influenced Methodist growth in Virginia.⁶⁴ For the purposes of this study, revival is considered a contextual factor. Iain Murray referred to this period as "Glory in Virginia." The transdenominational movement benefited evangelical Anglicans, New Light Presbyterians, Separatist Baptists, and Methodists. The Separatist Baptists reaped a large harvest before the Methodist became involved. After 1770, revival growth in Virginia among the Baptist increased greatly through 1773. By 1773, they grew to 4,004 members and from seven to 54 churches.[65] In speaking of the Baptist surge in Virginia in the late 1760s, Murray stated:

> These Baptist preachers were unconnected with Jarratt or the Presbyterians. . . . Their evangelistic preaching was the same in content to that of Whitefield. . . . One writer estimates that in 1772 "as many as forty thousand Virginians may have heard the gospel from the Baptists."[66] The growth in the Separate Baptist churches bears out the effects of this evangelism. . . . The dates of the revival of which Jarratt wrote when compared with the period of the surprising Baptist advance, can be seen to be the same.[67]

As noted in the above quotation, the Anglican priest, Devereux Jarratt, began establishing Methodist-style societies in 1770 all over his parish in south-central Virginia.[68] Another priest, Archibald McRoberts did the same thing. It is possible that the priests learned of this form of local organization from Strawbridge, though he is not mentioned by them in this regard. Since the priests spoke of Wesley in their letters and since Jarratt saw Wesley in London when he went to be ordained, it is likely that the inspiration for their organization came from Wesley.

Jarratt gave a splendid account of the revival in his autobiography and in a letter reproduced in Asbury's journal.[69] For the sake of brevity, portions of Jarratt's account are quoted from his letter:

> But in the year 1765, the power of God was more sensibly felt by a few. . . . The next year I became acquainted with Mr. M'Roberts, rector of a neighboring parish; and we joined hand in hand in the great work. . . . A remarkable power attended his preaching . . . not only in his parish, but in other parts. In the years 1770 and 1771, we had a more considerable outpouring of the Spirit, at a place in my parish called White Oak. It was here first I formed the people into a society that they might assist and strengthen each other. . . . In the year 1772, the revival was more considerable, and extended itself in some places, for fifty or sixty miles round. It increased still more in the following year. . . . In spring, 1774, it was more remarkable than ever. . . . A goodly number were gathered in this year, both in my parish and in many of the neighboring counties. I formed several societies out of those which were convinced or converted.[70]
>
> In the counties of Sussex and Brunswick, the work, from the year 1773, was chiefly carried on by the labours of the people called Methodists. The first of them who appeared in these parts was Mr. Robert Williams. . . . The next year others of his brethren came, who gathered many societies both in this neighborhood, and in other places, as far as North Carolina. They now began to ride the circuit, and to take care of the societies already formed.[71]

Williams stayed at the home of Jarratt for a week in March 1773 and preached in his church many times. He found favor with Jarratt because of his animated preaching. Since his doctrines agreed with Jarratt's, he was alive to God, and he was completely dedicated to the Church of England, Jarratt formed a partnership with him and the other Methodist preachers who followed him.[72] In fact, he combined his work with the Methodists in 1773.

The revival continued to expand. In the latter part of 1775 and early 1776, a most remarkable outpouring spontaneously fell on three chapels in or near Jarratt's parish. Jarratt called it the greatest ever in a country place. He credited the divine deluge to the preaching of George Shadford, one of Wesley's missionaries. In response to the heightened receptivity, a platoon of Methodist preachers descended on the revival area and spread it as they worked their circuits.

Asbury's journal contains fifteen pages of letters describing the general revival through 1776.[73] When one reads these letters, one is struck by three facts: the Methodists found a transdenominational revival that was localized, they regularized it, and they reproduced it. Word of mouth, news accounts, testimonies from converted sinners, changed lives, and other people movement dynamics spread the revival flame. The following quotation illustrates this:

> The multitudes . . . returning home all alive to God, spread the flame through their respective neighborhoods, which ran from family to family: so that within four weeks, several hundreds [sic] found the peace of God. And scarce any conversation was to be heard . . . but concerning the things of God. . . . The unhappy disputes between England and her colonies, which just before had engrossed all our conversation, seemed now in most companies to be forgot.[74]

The Methodists influenced other denominations during the general meetings and revival services. Letters and journal entries from non-Methodists contain phrases that indicate Methodist influence. Love feasts, quarterly meetings, experiencing perfect love, circuit riding, and the like punctuate the primary sources. Methodists had the experience and the organization to disciple the converts and to "Methodize" the movement. The "Methodizing" of the general revival of religion represents the confluence of contextual and institutional factors. In reality, one of the geniuses of EAM was its ability to take advantage of positive contextual factors and to minimize negative contextual factors. Later, the Methodizing of revivals would give way to Methodist revivalism. A non-Methodist by the name of Charles Finney would champion revivalism.

The pugnacious relationship between the colonies and England shadowed Methodism during this time. Most of the problems associated with the war happened after 1776. However, the pending war posed a tension and a distraction before 1776. In most areas, it consumed the media and public discourse. Asbury said that the general revival took people's minds off the pending war. Perhaps the stress of war positively influenced people's receptivity to revival. The emotional, spiritual, and physical release associated with the revival may have served as a psychological vent. However, one does not need to assume a cause-and-effect relationship or limit oneself to psycho-social interpretations. The fact that the revival dominated some parts of the South and not others bears witness to this. Interestingly, a great revival returned to the same areas in the mid-1780s after the stress of war had passed. Also, it should be noted that the general revival happened in a region of great population flux. In fact, the rural populations of Virginia and North Carolina grew at a tremendous rate during the time of the general revival. According to *The American Heritage Pictorial Atlas of United States*:

> The filling up of the Shenandoah Valley made Virginia the most populous colony; by 1770 it had more whites (260,000) than Pennsylvania (240,000) or Massachusetts (235,000), and more Negroes (187,000) than South Carolina (75,000). In North Carolina, where back-country settlers received their first 50 acres free, the population during the Revolution was larger (270,000) than New York's (270,000).[75]

In an article titled "Religious Community in a Cuban Refugee Camp: Bringing Order Out of Chaos," I show how religious community and revival served as ordering devices for Cubans who left one social structure and were not incorporated into a new one. "Religious community countered the destructive aspects of the liminal experience by giving participating refugees an informal social structure and a sense of hope."[76] The same concept can be applied to Virginia and North Carolina during the 1770s. War and mass migration disrupted the social structure of the established order and produced a liminal effect for a large number of migrants.[77] This increased the peoples' receptivity to revivalism and to the social ordering that comes from participation in a religious community. It may be the primary contextual cause for the increase in religious participation.[78]

CHAPTER SIX

THE PROGRESS OF EARLY AMERICAN METHODISM FROM 1766 THROUGH 1784

During its nascent phase from 1766 to 1776, Southern Methodism organized itself around three discrete growth centers that did not adhere to state boundaries. The unique characteristics associated with each of the centers show that they responded to a different set of institutional factors. Two growth centers sprung up in Maryland. Originally, Maryland Methodism included three circuits that stretched from Frederick to Kent. Baltimore lay between the two. Strawbridge started his ministry in Frederick. It was the farthest west and it reached down to an area north of Richmond, Virginia. The **Maryland growth center** developed around Frederick and Baltimore. The **Delmarva growth center** grew out of the Kent circuit. The **Virginia growth center** grew out of the general revival that swept south-central Virginia and northern North Carolina. Brunswick, Virginia seems to be the epicenter of the revivals. In terms of numbers and influence, the growth center dominated EAM. The **Mid-Atlantic growth center** refers to the work in Pennsylvania, New York, and New Jersey.

The terminology can be a bit confusing. During the early years, the *Minutes*, Asbury, and Jesse Lee all use the designation "South" when referring to the Virginia growth center. The same primary texts group the Maryland and Delmarva growth centers with the Mid-Atlantic growth center. Collectively, the sources referred to these areas as "the North." By 1763, Charles Mason and Jeremiah Dixon had surveyed the Mason-Dixon Line to separate the Maryland and Pennsylvania border. Gradually, the line took on a symbolic meaning. By the time of the Missouri Compromise in 1820, it demarcated the North from the South. The line placed Delaware in the North. It placed Maryland in the South. EAM identified Maryland and the Delmarva circuits with the North because they aligned with the Mid-Atlantic preachers during internal controversies.[1] Those controversies pitted Virginia Methodism (southern) against the northern preachers. As America matured, Maryland and Delmarva became a border zone between the North and the South. From a contextual perspective, Maryland belongs with the South during this era. From an institutional perspective, Maryland and Delmarva aligned with the Northern Methodism.

Asbury exerted more influence over Northern Methodism than he did over Southern Methodism. Even though Strawbridge operated in Maryland, he bequeathed his ethos upon Southern Methodism, i.e., an indigenizing spirit, an independent demeanor, and a cadre of homegrown preachers who replicated his ways. Because Asbury's presence dominated Delmarva Methodism during most of the war years, he kept the area aligned with Mid-Atlantic Methodism. For example, in 1780, Asbury stated, "If I cannot keep old Methodism in any other place, I can in the peninsula [Eastern Shore]: that must be my last retreat."[2]

Development of Growth Centers

In 1775, the Mid-Atlantic growth center contained five circuits that had a membership of 764. The growth center declined to one appointed preacher and about 150 members in and around New Jersey in 1778.[3] By 1784, the Mid-Atlantic membership recouped its losses and swelled to 1,626 members and 14 circuits that stretched 300 miles from the eastern tip of Long Island to the western tip of Juniata. That work expanded through Chester, Little York, and Lancaster. At that time, Pennsylvania had five itinerants and New Jersey had six.

Early Methodists distinguished Maryland Methodism from Eastern Shore Methodism because of its geography and character. The Chesapeake Bay separated them from each other. Because of its geographical isolation and its dense Methodist population, Eastern Shore Methodism withstood negative contextual factors better than Methodism in Maryland. However, the geographic isolation, dense Methodist population, and stable demographics also throttled the growth of Eastern Shore Methodism after 1784.

From 1781 to 1784, the Eastern Shore growth center expanded to six circuits and 17 itinerants. Membership grew from 486 in 1776 to 4,604 in 1784. From 1776 to 1784, the membership of the Maryland growth center grew from 1,289 to 2,119 members.[4] The 1784 *Minutes* report five circuits in the Maryland growth center to include two in northeastern Virginia. From 1776 to 1784, the Virginia growth center had exceptional growth. It grew from 2,789 to 6,459 members and from five to 22 circuits (cf. Table 6-1).

The great revival that began in 1775 birthed the Brunswick circuit in Virginia. By 1779, 14 circuits had expanded from it. Ten were in Virginia and four in North Carolina. In regards to the 1776 revival, Lee states, "The out-pouring of the spirit [sic] extended itself, more or less, through most of the circuits, which takes in a circumference of between four and five hundred miles."[5] From 1774 to 1779, the combined membership of the revival circuits grew from 218 to 5,090.

These circuits formed the base of the southern mutiny in 1779 that divided all the Methodists north of the Hanover circuit from the Methodists south of Hanover.[6] Hanover was the northern vanguard of the Virginia growth center. Sixty miles separated the Virginia growth area from the Maryland growth area at that time. By 1783, the Virginia growth center blanketed most of present-day Virginia and North Carolina with circuits. In that same year, the Holston and Allegheny circuits expanded the Virginia growth center into the western mountains. In 1784, Virginia subdivided four new circuits from existing circuits. Growth by division and by expanding the borders happened simultaneously in the Virginia growth center during this period.

Table 6-1. Numerical analysis of growth centers

	Membership Comparison				Number of Circuits				Number of Itinerants			
Year	M-A	MD	E.S	VA	M-A	MD	E.S.	VA	M-A	MD	E.S.	VA
1776	518	1609	486	2789	4	3	1	5	4	8	3	9
1777	488	1711	720	4049	4	4	1	6	4	10	4	18
1778	150	N.A	N.A	N.A.	1	3	2	9	1	7	6	15
1779	319	1,880	1288	5090	5	4	1	12	5	9	7	12
1780	386	1970	1135	4773	5	4	1	11	5	9	8	20
1781	873	2493	2755	4625	7	5	3	12	8	12	16	19
1782	1174	2485	3952	4164	9	5	4	11	9	12	13	25
1783	1633	2245	4369	5503	12	5	6	20	12	11	17	42
1784	1607	2119	4604	6459	14	5	6	22	14	11	17	38

M-A = Mid-Atlantic, MD = Maryland, E.S. = Eastern Shore (Delmarva), VA = Virginia, N.A. = None Available

Source: Data adapted from MEC *Minutes* (1813).

Table 6-1 documents the growth centers in American Methodism from 1776 to 1784 in terms of membership, circuits, and traveling preachers. Figure 6-1 illustrates the regional pattern of Methodist membership during this period in terms of the growth centers.

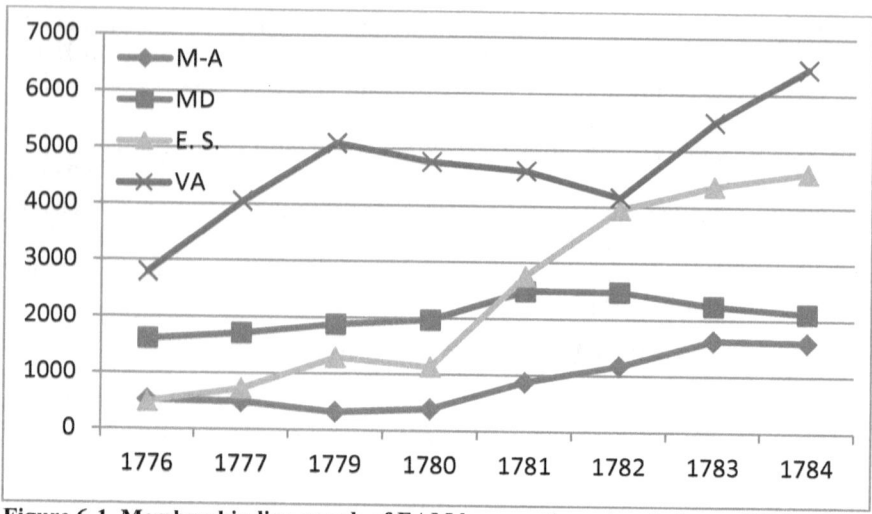

Figure 6-1. Membership line-graph of EAM by growth centers between 1776 and 1784.

The Revolutionary War and Methodist Growth Centers: 1776 through 1784

This section offers a brief history of the war and shows how it intersected with the Methodist growth centers. This is consequential because the war and its associated events are the most significant contextual factors during this time.[7] The Revolutionary War began in April 1775, at Lexington and Concord. It started as a skirmish and ended as a major confrontation that stretched over many miles. In late 1775, Virginian and North Carolinian armies defeated a force of 600 Tories and freed slaves.[8] After a naval bombardment from the British, Loyalists burned portions of Norfolk in January of 1776. American militias recaptured the city but did not extinguish the fires. After the Patriots repelled a British attack against Charleston in 1776, the British abandoned the South for the next three years.

During the spring and early summer of 1776, Washington sought to fortify New York City. As he expected, the British made an all-out attack on New York. The American forces were beaten and had to retreat. Afterward, the British controlled the area between present day Washington and New York. This encompassed most of the Mid-Atlantic growth center.

In December, Washington retreated through New Jersey to Pennsylvania. In the Battle of Trenton, New Jersey, Washington crossed the Delaware River, captured nearly 1,000 Hessian mercenaries, and reoccupied Trenton. The mercenaries were German-speaking. Many requested to remain and settled in the German communities.

From January to June 1777, fighting continued on the frontier and in the Mid-Atlantic region. On the East Coast, the British quickly attacked Washington's new position in Trenton. In January, Washington moved to Princeton, where he inflicted heavy losses on the British. This caused the British to withdraw to New Brunswick, New Jersey. The re-establishing of American control in New Jersey boosted Patriot morale. At the same time, the British attempted to cut off New England from the rest of the colonies along a line that followed the Hudson River.

The summer and fall of 1777 witnessed the most intense fighting of the war. The British landed new armies in Canada and marched them to New York. Other British forces joined them. In July, Patriot troops abandoned Fort Ticonderoga. In September, Washington lost the Battle of Brandywine in Pennsylvania as the British pushed toward Philadelphia. The Continental Congress fled from Philadelphia just before it was occupied in September. In October, the British defeated Washington at Germantown near Philadelphia. Later in October, American forces had great success at Saratoga and Albany in New York. In the Battle of Bemis Heights near Saratoga, the Patriots routed the British. The British retreated to Saratoga. Later that year, Washington withdrew to Valley Forge, Pennsylvania for the winter. In the meantime, the British expanded their occupation around New York City.

In January 1778, American forces launched a mine attack against British shipping in the Delaware River. One ship was destroyed. The incident put British troops and Philadelphians in a panic. Also, fighting occurred with the Indians on the New York border. The Native Americans inflicted substantial losses on American forces and on civilians.

From January to May 1778, all sides attempted to reinforce their positions. At this time, the British had 19,500 troops in Philadelphia, 11,000 in New York and 4,000 in Newport. The Americans had 1,400 regulars at Valley Forge and 1,800 in forts along the Hudson River. They were badly outnumbered. Fortunately, the French sent troops and ships to support the Patriots.

By June 1778, the British had evacuated Philadelphia and headed for New York because of a feared blockade. The French force was turned back by bad weather. At the Battle of Monmouth, New Jersey, Washington defeated the British. In July, Tories and Indians routed Americans and caused great destruction from Niagara to central Pennsylvania. In an attempt to intimidate the Americans and put fear in the hearts of the civilians, they scalped 200 Americans and buried others alive in the Wyoming Valley Massacre. Throughout the fall and early winter Tories and Indians continued attacks on the frontiers. There was little actual combat with British troops during this time. In July 1779, the fort at Stony Point, New York, was captured by the Americans in a brutal battle. By the end of the summer, the Americans had regained all of New Jersey and Rhode Island. The British headed south.

In December 1778, the British captured Savannah, Georgia and moved north to Charleston. Battles and a siege ensued. By May 1780, Charleston and most of the southern army were captured. The British moved out from Charleston to North Carolina. In the following year, they moved directly into the heart of the

Virginia growth center and to Yorktown. Throughout this period, troop movements covered eastern Virginia up to Maryland.

The naval campaigns associated with the Battle of Yorktown came close to the Eastern growth center. However, Delmarva did not see actual combat in the war. In 1781, a large French fleet went to the mouth of the Chesapeake. Britain sent its navy to clear the way for a landing of 16,000 British soldiers from New York. However, after three days of battle, the British ships returned to New York largely because the Crown Prince was with the fleet and they did not want to risk his life. As a result, the British position remained under siege and the escape route was blocked. More than 9,000 American troops and 7,800 French troops held the siege. In October, after days of artillery bombardment and some brilliant tactical moves on the part of the allies, the British force of 8,000 soldiers surrendered at Yorktown. This brought the fighting portion of the Revolutionary War to an end.

During the war, the Americans battled Native Americans on the western front along the Appalachian Mountains and the border with Quebec. The British eagerly supplied these allies with fighting materials, intelligence, and advice. The Indian battles were brutal. Many of the Native Americans fled to the British lines after being defeated. Atrocities were committed by both sides. After the war, American patriots viewed the Native Americans as defeated enemies and wanted to punish them.

The War's Effect on Mid-Atlantic Membership

As a consequence of war, large numbers of people abandoned some of the cities. New York City's population decreased from 22,000 in 1775 to 18,000 in 1780. Many of those people fled to Philadelphia. Its population increased by 3,826 people. Lancaster, Pennsylvania also benefited from people fleeing the war.

Land-based fighting in the Mid-Atlantic began in 1776 and did not flag until July of 1779. From 1775 to 1776, the New York membership declined from 200 to 132. The New Jersey membership declined from 300 to 150. The Pennsylvania membership declined from 264 to 236. New York dropped from the *Minutes* in 1778. Growth did not return to the Mid-Atlantic until 1780, the year after fighting stopped. In that year, New Jersey membership increased from 140 to 196, and Pennsylvania membership increased from 179 to 190. The upward trend was amplified from 1779 to 1783. In those years, the New Jersey membership increased by 888 people and the Pennsylvania membership increased by 426 people. The New York circuit does not reappear in the *Minutes* until 1784. At that time, it reported 84 members. British troops did not leave New York City until November 1783.

Asbury and Methodist histories substantiate that the war was a primary factor that limited growth in the Mid-Atlantic area from 1776 through 1779. However, some *in bello* institutional factors negatively affected the contextual milieu. For example, Wesley's polemic in support of the British monarchy stirred much debate and caused many Patriots to turn from Methodism. In his *Calm*

Address to Our American Colonies, Wesley advocates a royalist position that chides the Americans for their rebellion and espouses a conspiracy theory related to those who want to undermine the Crown. He calls liberty and the establishment of a commonwealth an idol. Point by point, he attempts to counter the philosophical underpinning on which the Americans built their cause for self-rule. Since he demanded that the American Methodists remain loyal to him, his *Calm Address* caused Patriots to doubt the fidelity of American Methodists. In 1776, while passing through Philadelphia, Asbury wrote a journal entry that points to the negative consequences of Wesley's tract in the Mid-Atlantic area. "I also received an affectionate letter from Mr. Wesley, and am truly sorry that the venerable man ever dipped into the politics of America. . . . Some inconsiderate persons have taken occasion to censure the Methodists in America, on account of Mr. Wesley's political sentiments."[9]

In addition to Wesley, many of his missionaries gave conspicuous support to the British cause. Lee opined, "Mr. [Richard] Rodda had taken some imprudent steps in favor of the Tories; a company of them having collected in Delaware state, below Philadelphia. Mr. Rodda's conduct brought many sufferings, and much trouble, on the Methodist preachers and people."[10] Garrettson states, "It was soon circulated through the country that the Methodists were enemies to the American cause: and were embodying themselves to meet the English army. A short time before; and the conduct of Mr. [Rodda] had been very injurious to the persecuted flock."[11] In short, the political posturing of Wesley and his missionaries greatly hurt the cause of Methodism in America at that time.

As a consequence, many of the native preachers experienced a moral dilemma. Should they support Wesley or the cause of their countrymen? Many chose to be conscientious objectors. This also stirred the pot of anti-Methodist sentiment among those who interpreted conscientious objection as a sign of Tory sympathies. According to Nathan Bangs,

> [In 1776,] the state of things rendered the situation of many of the Methodist preachers peculiarly trying, and more especially those of them who were known to be favorable to the British cause. As some of them . . . spoke their sentiments freely against the proceedings of congress and of the American states, they were subject to some persecutions. And although only four out of the twenty-five preachers were from England, yet, as these four were leading men, the others were suspected of favoring the cause of Britain, and therefore were exposed to similar suspicions and treatment.[12]

The war directly caused numerical decline because it hindered the work of ministry and it turned people away from religious duties. In April 1776, Asbury received a letter from a Methodist trustee in Trenton, New Jersey. It said that the preachers neglected their duties in that they did not visit the circuit because of the war.[13] Afterward, he rode to New Jersey and discovered spiritual apathy. He states, "I rode to Burlington, . . . but found, to my grief, that many so imbibed a martial spirit that they had lost the spirit of pure and undefiled religion. . . . I rode to Trenton; and found very little there but spiritual coldness and deadness."[14] Clearly, New Jersey Methodism was not prospering in 1776.

Nathan Bangs was a close friend of the Asbury. He became a presiding elder in Delaware and the head of the Book Concern. His history vividly portrays how the war interfered with itineration.

> It was with no little difficulty that [the preachers] were able to travel some of the circuits, and obliged entirely to abandon others, yet . . . the preachers persevered in their labors wherever they could find access to the people. . . . The war at this time [1776] raged with great violence, so that by the marching and countermarching of armies, enlisting of soldiers, frequent skirmishes between the contending parties, some of the places, even where religion had prevailed to a considerable extent, were not visited at all by the preachers.[15]

In 1776, the war so badly affected New Jersey Methodism that it was reduced to one circuit. In 1777, no itinerants were appointed to New York because of the war. Preachers could not travel in places where hostilities or sieges restricted itineration. Lee adds:

> [In 1777] there was a decrease in the numbers in several circuits to the north, principally owing to the spreading of the war in those parts; where the preachers found great difficulties in keeping their stations, and some were forced to be given up; so that some of the Classes were entirely given up. It might be well said during this year, that without were fighting, and within were fears. War, and the shedding of blood, was heard of in all directions: armies marching back and forth, one after another; and in many places the people were in great confusion, so that religion was almost banished from some neighborhoods where it had been pretty lively. Some of our societies in the north, suffered more from that quarter than we did in the south parts of Virginia.[16]

In 1778, because of the war and the British siege, New York, Philadelphia, Chester, and Frederick were not counted in the *Minutes*. Both New York and Philadelphia were occupied by the British at this time. Lee states,

> In the return of members this year [1778], we found we had lost in numbers 873. This was the first time that we came short of the old number given in the preceding year. This decrease was wholly owing to the breaches made upon many societies and circuits by the distress of war; and some of our preachers had scruples of conscience about taking the oath of allegiance in the different states where we laboured [sic], and of course were forced to leave their station.[17]

The oaths of allegiance required a person to pledge fidelity to the American cause. Many of the state oaths obligated the person to take up arms and fight for that cause if called upon. Fighting gave Methodist preachers great qualms. Some were conscientious objectors. Others did not want to fight because one could not itinerate and be a soldier at the same time. Some of the southern preachers did take up arms. James O'Kelly is an example. Later, he ridiculed the northern preachers for their "pro-British" stance during the war. Most of the preachers were Patriots in heart since they were native born. Previously, Wesley had ordered all the English missionaries to return to England. Asbury was the only one to stay behind. He suffered because he did not take up arms or take the oaths.

Repeatedly, officials asked Garrettson why he would not fight. He contended that he could not kill human flesh with carnal weapons. He fought with spiritual weapons. He always warned the officials about God's judgment on those who do not learn to fight with God's weapons. For this he was subject to mockery and persecution. In 1777, Garrettson wrote an entry in his journal that illustrates the problem with oaths as they related to conscience and ministry.

> About this time the state-oath began to be administered, and was universally complied with, both by preachers and people where I was; but I could by no means be subject to my rulers in this respect, as it touched my conscience towards God: so I was informed that I must leave the state, take the oath, or go to the gaol [jail]. I told those who came to tender the oath to me, that I professed myself a friend to my country: that I would do nothing willingly or knowingly to the prejudice of it: that if they required it, I would give them security of my friendly behavior during my stay in the state. "But why," said they, "will you not take the oath?" "I think" said I, "the oath is too binding on my conscience: moreover, I never swore an oath in my life: and ministers of the gospel have enough to do in their sphere." . . . The rulers said, "You must leave the state." "This I cannot do, for first, the conference appointed me to my labour in this state: and in the second place, I am confident that my appointment is approved of my heavenly Father: and therefore, I dare not leave the state." "Then," said they, "you must away to prison."[18]

After the southern campaign began in late 1778, things began to ease up in the Mid-Atlantic area. In April 1780, Asbury reported, "Received three epistles from the Jerseys, soliciting three or four preachers with good tiding of the work of God reviving in those parts."[19] In 1779, three preachers were assigned jointly to Philadelphia and New Jersey. In 1780, four preachers were assigned to New Jersey by itself. They were appointed to revive the work and recoup previous losses.

The New York society requires special attention. The British occupied New York from September 1776 through November 1783. From the perspective of the *Minutes*, New York Methodism did not exist from 1778 until 1783 because no official preacher was appointed to it and it did not file an annual membership report with the conference. In fact, American preachers could not cross British lines to itinerate in New York. The siege and subsequent occupation isolated New York from EAM.

During the time of its isolation, New York City Methodism prospered under the pastoral leadership of Samuel Spraggs.[20] Spraggs was a Loyalist. In late 1778, he and George Shadford fled to New York. In the safety of that environment, he ministered at Wesley Chapel. As a verification of this, Wesley Chapel lists him as its preacher from 1778 through 1782. He was assisted by a local preacher named John Mann. In 1783, Spraggs reappeared in the *Minutes*. At that time, he and John Dickins were appointed to the New York society.[21]

In *Lost Chapters Recovered from the Early History of American Methodism*, J. B. Wakeley argues that New York Methodism thrived during the war years. To support this thesis, he analyzed recorded expenses paid by Wesley Chapel.

They show that the society prospered financially during its isolation. For example, it paid off its previous debt and purchased 2,000 love feast tickets in 1780.[22] Most of the other churches were closed or used for secular purposes. Thus, people from many denominations attended preaching at Wesley Chapel during the siege.[23]

As the British left New York, most of the Loyalists left with them. A majority relocated to Canada. The immigration helped to jump-start Methodism in Nova Scotia. Among the immigrants were some Methodist leaders to include John Mann, Robert Berry, and Charles White. A few months after being appointed to New York in 1783, Spraggs left the city and withdrew from Methodism. Ultimately, Bishop Samuel Seabury ordained him an Episcopal priest on September 16, 1785 in New Haven, Connecticut. He became a rector in Elizabethtown.[24] The extensive emigration from New York left a vacuum in New York Methodism. According to Coen Pierson,

> Other American sources were contributing to Methodist growth in the northern colonies. The loyalist exodus following the British capitulation at Yorktown brought twenty thousand settlers to Nova Scotia. . . . With them came many Methodists, especially from New York. By 1786, there were 510 Methodists [on the Methodist rolls in Nova Scotia].[25]

Additionally, many New York Patriots felt displeasure with the Methodists for being so amiable and accommodating to the British during the war. Despite sporadic persecution and disruptions, Wakeley argues that the British supported New York Methodism because of Methodism's close relationship with the English church. Otherwise, they would have converted Wesley Chapel into a hospital, armory, or galley. After the war, the systematic persecution of Tories became a matter of policy. Most Tories relocated. Emigration of Loyalists and antipathy toward Methodism explain why the New York society only reported 60 members in 1784 when the British completed their evacuation.

In summary, during the war, New York Methodism flourished because of the occupation and its positive relationship with the British army. However, as the contextual situation changed in 1783, the institutional factors that aided Methodism during the occupation hindered New York Methodism after the occupation. Thus, there is a decrease in members when the 1784 report is compared with the 1777 report.

The Southern Area Membership Summary

The urban population centers in the South decreased from 23,000 to 10,000 from 1775 to 1780. Norfolk, Charleston, and Savannah decreased drastically. The combined population for those cities did not equal the 1775 population until 1790. Each had been occupied and/or destroyed by the British.

The southern membership patterns are different from the Mid-Atlantic ones because the fighting in the South occurred at a different time. Additionally, southern fighting affected the Virginia growth area more than the Maryland or Delmarva growth areas because they escaped the brunt of the fighting.[26]

The membership in the Virginia growth area increased from 1775 through 1776. When Norfolk was razed in January 1776, it ceased to be a circuit. Lee said, "Norfolk was left out of the minutes on account of the war, which had so distressed the town that we could not keep a preacher in that station."[27] Norfolk was the eastern half of the Virginia growth area. It did not participate in the Brunswick revival. The Norfolk circuit does not reappear until the 1790s.[28] Despite the decline in the Norfolk area, the Brunswick area of the Virginia growth area posted very large gains in 1776. Those gains compensated for the Norfolk loss.

From mid-1776 until 1779, the southern arena did not experience combat. This explains why the membership did not decline during these years. In early 1779, the war returned to the South. For the next three years, the membership in the Virginia growth area declined from 5,090 to 4,164. During those same years, Eastern Shore and Mid-Atlantic Methodism tripled their memberships. The Maryland growth area increased by 500 members.

In 1779, Asbury noted a declension among believers and great troubles in the South. The British captured Savannah and occupied Georgia. As they moved north, men were put under arms and others began to flee. The burning of Suffolk and the plundering of Portsmouth, Virginia, caused great anxiety.[29] During this time, intense combat occurred in and around the Virginia growth area. Most of Virginia was controlled by the British in 1781. Of the year 1779, Lee wrote:

> In many places the societies were thrown into great disorder and confusion, by reason of the war which continued to rage through the land. Many of the men were drafted, and taken into the army, and many people left their homes to keep out of the way of the enemy, and to save their property, by carrying it with them.[30]

In reference to 1781, Lee noted that conscription was a problem.

> Many of the male members were drafted, and when the militia were called out, they had to go into the army to fight, in the defense of their country. Some of them lost their lives, and some made shipwreck of the faith, and but few of them returned home with as much religion as they formerly possessed.[31]

Washington's army at this time numbered over 27,000. Other American armies under different generals also numbered in the thousands. Many of those soldiers were drafted by state militias as fighting required. Thus, the total number of American soldiers represented a significant percentage of the adult male population. The draft depleted some societies of most of their men. Asbury complained that there were only two able-bodied men left in a particular society and both were drafted to bear arms.[32]

While itinerating in the war areas of Virginia in 1780, Asbury almost abandoned his travels and returned north to Maryland because the 7th Division of the militia crossed his path. At the same time, an estimated 5,000 British troops tore two counties in pieces within six miles of Williamsburg, Virginia. Asbury was headed in that direction but turned to the north and crossed the river to escape.[33]

A month later, while making his way through Virginia, Asbury complained that the British almost threw themselves in his way. He did not wish to fall into their hands.[34] He lamented that the preachers do not attend to appointments or circuits when the risk is too great. He included himself in that comment.

In reference to 1780, Lee wrote:

> In many places the circuits and societies were so much interrupted by the armies, both of our friends and of our enemy, which were marching through the country, that we had not as many members in society at conference, as we had the year before. Indeed some of the circuits were wholly forsaken, and no return of the members could be made.[35]

Lee remonstrated in similar manner regarding 1781.

> The war was so distressing in [Virginia and some parts of North Carolina], that the preachers could not constantly attend their circuits; and many of the societies were dispersed, and prevented from assembling together.[36]

> During [1781], the societies and circuits in Virginia were more interrupted by the war, than they had ever been before. The British army moved in various directions, and there were many battles fought in the state; which kept the people constantly alarmed, and prevented them from meeting at their usual times and places. And most of the time when they did assemble for divine worship, their conversation was principally turned upon the times, and the distresses of themselves and their friends. Before meeting would begin, and as soon as it was closed, the inquiry was what is the news of the day? One would say my son is killed; another my husband is wounded, or taken prisoner, or sick and likely to die, &c. These things greatly hindered the progress of religion in the south of Virginia.[37]

Of 1782, Lee wrote, "Some of our preachers left their circuits to keep out of the way of the enemy: but others having more courage, continued to travel as usual, and to trust the Lord with their bodies as well as their souls."[38]

The pressing of horses by the militias also hindered the spread of Methodism. When soldiers pressed the circuit riders' horses into government service, the circuit riders could no longer itinerate. On several occasions while itinerating in the Virginia growth area, Asbury reported that the people would not come to preaching because they feared that their horses would be pressed. When word spread that troops were near, many people took their horses and fled from the services. Soldiers went to preaching services for the purpose of taking horses and able-bodied men.[39]

The war in the South ended with Cornwallis' surrender at Yorktown in October 1781. From mid-1782 to mid-1784, the Virginia growth area increased its membership by 2,295, its circuits by 11, and its traveling preachers by 13. That equals a 33 percent increase in members and a 50 percent increase of circuits. As a Virginian who lived through the fighting, Lee's commentary is helpful:

> The revolutionary war being now closed, and a general peace established, we could go into all parts of the country without fear; and to preach in many places where we had not been before. We soon saw the fruit of our labours in the new circuits, and in various parts of the country, even in old places where we had preached in former years with but little success.[40]

> One thing in particular, that opened the way for the spreading of the gospel by our preachers was this: during the war, which had continued seven or eight years, many of the members of our societies had, through fear, necessity, or choice, moved into the back settlements, and into new parts of the country: and as soon as the national peace was settled, and the way was open, they solicited us to come among them; and by their earnest and frequent petitions, both verbal and written, we were prevailed on, and encouraged to go among them.[41]

Lee explained further, "The Lord prospered us much in the thinly settled parts of the country, where, by collecting together the old members of our society, and by joining some new ones with them, the work greatly revived, and the heavenly flame of religion spread far and wide."[42] Of 1784, he said,

> We had a gracious revival of religion this year in many of the frontier circuits, and the way was opening fast for us to enlarge our borders, and to spread the gospel through various places where we had never been before. The call of the people was great, for more labourers to be sent into the harvest.[43]

In summary, warfare negatively impacted the Virginia growth area and caused decline as it displaced people, hindered the itinerating of the preachers, disrupted circuits, depleted male attendance through the draft, and caused people not to attend preaching out of fear of losing their horses. The years of decline and the times and places of fighting correspond with each other. This indicates that the war was the primary contextual factor that caused membership decline in the Virginia growth area from mid-1779 to mid-1782. Following the war, the Virginia growth area experienced tremendous progress.

CHAPTER SEVEN

SPECIAL ISSUES IN EARLY AMERICAN METHODISM FROM 1766 THROUGH 1784

During and following the war years, a cluster of special issues acutely influenced the development and direction of EAM. This chapter examines persecution, rivalry with other denominations, a critical lack of itinerants, and cross-cultural concerns. It also reflects on funeral evangelism.

Problems with Persecution

Persecution hindered the advance of Methodism in the Maryland and Eastern Shore growth centers. The case of the Separatist Baptists in Virginia sheds light on this.[1] In terms of status, preaching, experience, technique, and zeal, Separatist Baptists and Methodist preachers had much in common. The Baptists enjoyed a tremendous revival in Virginia through 1773. However, their revival stopped when the Methodist revival began. Some argue that it stopped because Methodism took it from them.[2] Regardless, the cessation of Baptist persecution in Virginia corresponds with the emergence of the Methodist uprising in Virginia. However, one should not assume that the two are linked.

In the years leading up to the Methodist revival in Virginia, 78 Separatist Baptist preachers endured persecution to include harsh beatings, imprisonment, pelting with stones, dipping their heads in mud, and disruption of services. Baptist persecution was so intense that William Sweet required 18 pages in his history of Virginia Methodism to describe it.[3]

The case of John Ireland illustrates typical persecution. In 1769, the local magistrate sentenced him to prison because he publically proclaimed his religious beliefs while on a preaching tour with the intention of gaining converts. While in prison he continued to agitate by preaching to a large crowd that regularly gathered at his cell. His act of defiance so infuriated the gentry that they often ran their horses at full gallop through the crowd of gathered congregants. In a final act of desperation, they plotted to blow up the imprisoned Baptist preacher.[4]

Gewehr chronicles the Baptist persecution and offers eight reasons for it. One, those who enjoyed a higher social status regarded the Baptist preachers as lawbreakers who deserved to be punished because they arrogated a position in society to which they had no claim. In other words, preaching was a status bearing position that the gentry reserved for educated men with credentials in established church traditions. Two, many feared that Baptist success would lead to the ruin of the Established Church. Three, many felt that the Baptists were a menace to society. They were tried as disturbers of the peace who worked against the common good. Four, the establishment saw the Baptists as false prophets who deceived the poor and less educated by playing on their emotions. Jarratt, the benefactor of southern Methodism and revivalist priest, shared this opinion and did all he could to check their growth. Five, since the Baptists attracted the lower classes, the upper classes complained that they took people from their work. Finally, their social identity as poor, uneducated, enthusiasts who played to the emotions and lacked substance repulsed the gentry and aspiring people.[5]

For their part, the Baptist viciously attacked the Established Church and argued for religious liberty in the same way that patriots argued for political liberty. Their religious protest was encased in political rhetoric. This stirred the invective passions of the Anglican community. Also, Baptist preachers often refused to take state oaths because they did not believe that the state had the authority to regulate religion. Virginian leaders like Thomas Jefferson agreed with this point of their protest. He drafted the Virginia Statue of Religious Freedom in 1777. It gave relief to their grievance.

The reasons that Gewehr listed for persecution could have been leveled against Methodist preachers. Others could have been added to the list. In fact, in Maryland, Methodist preachers suffered in the same way as the Separatist Baptists suffered in Virginia. However, Methodist preachers in Virginia did not suffer from persecution. Many reasons may account for this. First, by the time Methodism began to grow in Virginia, attitudes toward religious liberty and the Anglican Church had changed. As was noted, persecution of Virginian Baptists dissipated at the same time that Methodism began to flower in Virginia. Second, the Methodists in the Virginia growth area were indigenous and patriotic. This becomes very apparent during the 1779 Fluvanna crises that pulled at the institutional fiber of EAM. During a later sectional crisis, James O'Kelly, a war veteran and a presiding elder from Virginia, revived this theme when he contrasted the Patriot Methodists in Virginia to the Tory sympathizing Methodists of northern Methodism. Third, the Tory activism of the English missionaries did not affect Virginia Methodism as much as it affected northern Methodism because geography separated Virginia Methodism from it. Even though the British missionaries had labored in the Virginia revival, they had left Virginia before the start of hostilities. Four, Virginia Methodism found common cause with patriotic Anglican clergy as they worked with them during the great revival. For that reason, Southern Methodism enjoyed a symbiotic relationship with Anglican priests in the revival belt. Consequently, they could not be charged as unlawful dissenters.

On the other hand, persecution of Methodist itinerants in Maryland posed a real challenge. In 1776, Asbury tried to get a Methodist work started in Annapolis, Maryland. He noted that the people raged against Methodism. By April 1777, the opposition to Methodism in Annapolis turned violent. Asbury almost became a victim of it. "Riding after preaching to R.P.'s, my chaise was shot through: but the Lord preserved my person."[6] It is not known whether a bellicose person intentionally shot the bullet at Asbury. On June 27, 1777, Asbury tried to preach in Annapolis but American soldiers purposely made so much noise that they drowned him out. For whatever reason, the Maryland militia did not like Methodism. In March 1778, Annapolis officials cast a Methodist preacher by the name of William Wrenn into prison. Finally, Asbury put the Annapolis work on hold.

On March 18, 1778, Asbury sequestered himself in Delaware on account of the war and his precarious situation. He feared arrest.

> The reason of this retirement was as follows. From March 10, 1778, on conscientious principles I was a non-juror, and could not preach in the state of Maryland; and therefore withdrew to Delaware State, where the clergy were not required to take the State oath; though, with a clear conscience, I could have taken the oath of the Delaware State, had it been required; and would have done it, had I not been prevented by a tender fear of hurting the scrupulous conscience of others.[7]

During his self-imposed confinement, Asbury stayed at Judge White's house. In April 1778, officials took Judge White away under suspicion of being Tory. He was an Episcopalian but was arrested more than once for being a "friend of the Methodists." Because of this, Asbury hid in the swamp.

In April 1778, Asbury reported that a young Methodist circuit rider named Joseph Hartley was arrested in Queen Ann County, Maryland. In September 1778, Asbury lamented that Hartley was still in prison for preaching in Maryland. Antagonists wanted him to quit preaching. Asbury believed his imprisonment illegal because he took the Maryland oath. Officials released him on the condition that he stopped preaching. Afterward, he went to Talbot County to preach and was rearrested. In February of 1780, officials released Hartley from the Talbot jail.[8]

Two months later a former judge accosted Garrettson in Maryland. When Garrettson broke free and fled, he was thrown from his horse, severely beaten, and left to die. Fortunately, a woman came to his rescue. While in Dover, Delaware in September, a large crowd surrounded him and tried to take him. Some wanted to hang him. Town leaders rescued him. The following month a woman came at him with a pistol. The next month, while in Somerset, Maryland, the sheriff served him with an arrest warrant. In June 1779, a company of armed men waylaid him. When they tried to do him harm, women who were accompanying Garrettson to his next preaching location attacked the men. In the same month, a large mob assailed a home thinking that it contained Garrettson. They did great violence to the man who lived there. Afterward, the mob attempted to get Garrettson. Soon after this, while preaching, he was attacked by a man with a gun. Later, the town leaders attempted to drive him away with fire and beating drums. When this did not work, they threatened to drown him. Following this, the sheriff presented him with an arrest warrant. In February 1780, a large group of men captured him and beat his horse. Shortly after this, officials judged and condemned him in Dorchester County for preaching. Two days later, they thrust him into the Cambridge jail. They treated him with severity. Two of his brothers paid a bond for Garrettson's release. Finally, the Delaware governor intervened as a favor to Asbury. In Garrettson's words, "I was carried before the governor of Delaware. This gentleman, was a friend to our society. He met me at the door, and welcomed me in, assuring me he would do anything he could to help me. A recommendatory letter was immediately dispatched to the governor of Maryland; and I was entirely at liberty."[9] This enraged those who wanted him in prison.

In May 1779, Asbury observed that many faithful and zealous men were raised up for the work in the States. They only needed a little instruction in order to be employed. Then he qualified his comment by saying, "We don't have enough proper preachers, some who are gifted can't go into all the states where we need them because of oaths, others are under bail and can't leave the state or local area."[10] This last comment demonstrates the seriousness of Methodist persecution. The bail came as a result of religious prosecution.

In July 1780, while in Delaware, Asbury wrote, "I saw today a political libel; the Methodists are struck at, but every charge is false."[11] The bad press encouraged some people to persecute Methodists. According to Lee, if a person was disposed to persecute a Methodist preacher, it was only necessary to call him a Tory, and the person might treat him as cruelly as he pleased.[12] In this year, Eastern Shore Methodism declined by 153 members.

Asbury complained that Tories and Patriots persecuted the Methodists. He called the Tories "some of our greatest enemies."[13] He noted that the patriot judge at Caroline County court in Maryland was often heard to speak against the Methodists.[14] Later, Asbury said that most people had prejudices against Methodists and opposed them out of nature. However, after they got to know the Methodists better by means of constant preaching and a visible presence, the prejudices began to wear off. When the prejudices wore off, the people would come to hear Methodist preaching. This was Methodism's strategy for dealing with persecution and rejection.[15]

According to Lee, in 1781,"Some of the Methodists were bound in conscience not to fight; and no threatening could compel them to bear arms or hire a man to take their places. In consequence of this, some were whipped, some were fined, and some were imprisoned; others were sent home, and many were much persecuted."[16] According to Jeffrey Williams, the following Methodist preachers refused to take the state oaths or serve in the military: Frances Asbury, Benjamin Abbott, David Abbott, Edward Dromgoole, William Duke, Freeborn Garrettson, Phillip Gatch, William Glendinning, Joseph Hartley, John Littlejohn, Jesse Lee, Nathan Perigrau, Daniel Ruff, Sater Stephenson, William Watters, William Wren, Robert Wooster, and John Young.[17] The above listed itinerants were evenly split between the northern and southern growth centers. The names represent a partial list based on available information. For purposes of perspective, 22 itinerants received an appointment in 1780. EAM did not have an official policy that prevented an itinerant from taking a state oath. However, a group process prevailed so that most circuit riders did not take the state oaths.

Mandatory state oaths, persecution, and the conscription of preachers hindered Methodism in Maryland and the Eastern Shore during this period. Methodists were persecuted for four main reasons. One, Wesley was an outspoken Tory. Two, some of the English missionaries openly supported the British and encouraged others to do the same. Three, American Methodists were suspected of being Tories because of their connections to England. Four, some American preachers became conscientious objectors and most would not take the state oaths. In terms of the last point, American preachers did not become conscientious objectors because Wesley and Methodist doctrine opposed participation in a just war. Rather, they became objectors because their calling to preach was of a higher order than their calling to support a political cause. Also, many sensed affection for the Mother country and felt obligated to obey Wesley's guidance on the issue. Most Methodist persecution came at the hands of Patriots.[18]

Religious Rivalry

Religious rivalry dogged Methodism. However, one cannot measure the extent to which it influenced membership. It is possible that EAM benefitted from its encounter with other traditions. When EAM entered into an area in which well-organized churches existed, the churches opposed Methodist preachers as unwanted competition. The tensions increased as the Methodist movement began to expand because many of the new Methodist affiliates maintained an official membership in a local church. Since EAM engendered a nominal relationship with the English church, Anglican clergy mostly accommodated the Methodists even if they did not approve of them. Asbury detailed the strained relationship that Methodism had with the denominations in a letter he wrote to Wesley in 1783. A redacted summary of the letter will show the extent of the problem as Asbury understood it.

> I have been travelling through various parts of West Jersey. We have within these three years past made large strides in East and West Jersey. In the most public, and some of the extreme parts, a few hundreds have joined us, of different denominations. We are much beset with a mixed people, warm for their own pecu-

liarities in doctrines and forms. I could not have thought that the Reformed churches had so much policy, and stubborn prejudices. No means are left untried to prevent us. . . . The Calvinists on one hand, and the Universalians [sic] on the other, very much retard the work of God, especially in Pennsylvania and the Jerseys, for they both appear to keep people from seeking heart religion. . . . In Virginia, North and South Carolina, and Georgia, the Baptists labour to stand by . . . the good old cause. I think you ought always to keep the front of the Arminian Magazine filled with the best pieces you can get, both ancient and modern, against Calvinism.[19]

At this time, Methodism was not a church. Asbury and Wesley envisioned Methodism as a renewal movement. They welcomed the participation of Christians from all churches who would abide by the Methodist discipline and seek to flee from the wrath to come. This aroused suspicion and generated opposition in the old denominations. Asbury stated,

Is Methodism intended for the benefit of all denominations of reformed Christians? Can a Quaker, as well as a member of any other church, be in Society, and hold his own outward peculiarities, without being forced to receive the ordinances? It is well known that all dissenters, when any of their members join us, turn them out. This is done out of policy, to get them from us altogether; but they will be tired of this when they suffer by it.[20]

The controversies over the sacraments in the South drove many Methodists back to their old churches. Some felt that the Methodist preachers should not serve the sacraments. Others wanted them to serve the sacraments because they no longer belonged to their former churches. Asbury argued that the ordinances are a stumbling block for Methodists for that reason.

I reverence the ordinances of God; . . . but I clearly see they have been made the tools of division and separation. . . . We have joined with us at this time, those who have been Presbyterian, Dutch, and English, Lutherans, Mennonites, low Dutch, and Baptists. If we preach up ordinances to these people, . . . we shall drive them back to their old churches that have disowned them; and who will do all they can to separate them from us.[21]

Problems with Baptists

In the South, continual competition with Baptists caused Asbury great frustration. The Baptist problem was especially severe in the Virginia growth area. In that area, Methodists and Baptists drank from the same revival fountain and appealed to the same populations of people. Asbury referred to the Baptists as "ghosts following us from one place to another." Many times the Baptist preachers would sit in the congregation and heckle. At other times, the Baptists and the Methodists preached to the same people. The people would not know which to choose because they liked the preaching of both. In April 1780, Asbury wrote, "The Baptists show their enmity, and go from house to house persuading weak people to be dipped, and not to hear the Methodists; and they bring their preachers in our absence."[22] While in North Carolina, Asbury complained that the Baptist controversy turned many aside. Later he quipped, "Some of the Baptists rage because we have what they lost."²³ Then he laments, "There is a great falling away; . . . [the Baptists] have preached to them water, more than holiness; and have brought confusion among the Methodists."²⁴ He complained that the Baptists stole Methodists when the preachers were gone to conference. In 1780, he quipped,

> I appointed brother Joseph Wyatt to keep the ground against the Baptists, and to supply our places here instead of the travelling preacher that are going to conference: for John's people [a reference to John the "Baptist"] intent to come a fishing about when we are gone.²⁵

The 1783 *Minutes* told the traveling preachers to engage as many local preachers as can be depended upon to supply the circuits during conference. Since an itinerant had to travel by horse to conference, the absence from his circuit might be prolonged. It was better to fill the vacancies with supply preachers, exhorters, and lay leaders than to leave an opening for the Baptists.

In December 1780, Asbury said a work was breaking out in Delaware but the people were so harassed by the Baptists that it would not last. He wrote, "Called to warn my brethren against the poisonous and false principles of opposing sectarists [*sic*]. I was doing only what it was my bounden duty to do, and, indeed, acting on the defensive."²⁶ In 1784, Asbury complained that a neighborhood in North Carolina had been poisoned by the preaching of Antinomianism (Calvinism) and the "plunging" of Baptists.²⁷ Finally, he determined to avoid Baptist bashing. He was convicted about saying anything evil of any denomination. He vowed that he would not speak about their faults behind their backs and that he would prevent others from doing the same.²⁸

The Baptists pushed the issue of believer's baptism in the South and in other areas to include New England. A woman in Boston recounted a typical encounter with the Baptists. According to Garrettson, "They strove to persuade her to renounce her infant baptism, and enter more deeply into baptismal water. By their continual solicitations and arguments, her mind became confused, so that she was in doubt respecting the matter."²⁹ They were so effective in their preaching on this point that Asbury and other ordained itinerants began to "plunge" Methodists in the South after the Christmas Conference in 1784. Afterward, many Methodist converts who had been sprinkled requested that they be re-baptized by immersion. In an effort to keep Methodists from defecting over this issue, the MEC accommodated them. In the South, the debate over baptism continued to define Baptist and Methodist relations into the late 20th century. David Benedict was an early Baptist apologist of immersion and contemporary of EAM. He traveled extensively in the South. He states,

> On the whole it appears, that baptism is fast returning to its primitive mode. A general conviction seems to be prevailing, that infant sprinkling is an invention of men, and ought to be laid aside; and that believers are the only subjects of the baptismal rite, and that immersion is the only way in which it ought to be administered.³⁰

In sum, during this period most people did not live in a place where they could choose from a variety of churches. Most traditional churches could not operate in sparsely populated areas. Because of the circuit system, Methodism was able to function in these areas. For different reasons, so could the Baptists. The fact that Methodists and Baptists competed for the same people generated conflict that hindered the growth of Methodism. However, the competitive spirit that was inculcated during this period served Methodism well. It fostered an evangelistic zeal that pushed Methodism to work for new converts and it helped to indigenize the movement. Competition with the Baptists was a negative contextual factor to the extent that it caused confusion, took members away from Methodism, and deflected institutional energies. Still, it let to positive institutional adaptations as Methodism recast their polemic in terms of a democratic theology that attacked the elitist encumbrances of election.

Issues Associated with Episcopal Priests

Some Episcopal clergy opposed Methodism out of prejudice or principle. In many places, the clergy attempted to silence the Methodist preachers because they were not ordained or were too evangelical. This was especially true in the Mid-Atlantic area. It was also true in Maryland. For example, in 1780, the Episcopal clergy in Somerset, Maryland, organized a smear campaign based on a book written by Bishop Warburton.[31] In the years following the campaign, the Methodist society in Somerset decreased by 250 members. At the same time, the overall membership of Eastern Shore Methodism skyrocketed as all the other circuits posted annual increases in membership. Even though it is not possible to show that the smear campaign caused the decline in the Somerset circuit, it is likely that the opposition from the local Anglicans contributed to it.

However, many priests were neutral or favorable to Methodism. In August 1783, Asbury reported that four Anglican clergymen worked closely with the Methodists. He listed them as Jarratt in Virginia, Pettigrew in North Carolina, Dr. Magaw in Philadelphia, and Mogden in New Jersey.[32] Asbury promoted a positive relationship with the Episcopal clergy. He worked to avoid a separation from that church. The southern Methodists were not always keen to the idea. In reference to the Virginia preachers, he lamented, "After all my labour to unite the Protestant Episcopal ministry to us, they say, 'We don't want your unconverted ministers; the people will not receive them.'"[33]

A Lack of Traveling Preachers

In 1782, Asbury complained that the people in backwoods areas were greatly wanting in ministers but he was unable to supply their want. The greatest needs were on the fringes of Methodism because those people were ripe for the gospel. For example, in January 1783, Asbury exclaimed that "we have great calls to South Carolina and Georgia."[34] The southern frontier would produce a large harvest in the mid-1780s. However, Methodism's ability to expand and keep up with growth opportunities depended on its ability to recruit, train, maintain, and deploy circuit riders to the new areas.

Marriage took human resources from the ministry. When an itinerant got married, he had to care for his wife and family. That limited his usefulness and his ability to itinerate. Marriage also robbed Methodism of badly needed experience. Anticipating this problem, Asbury pushed the following solution:

> We spoke of a plan for building houses in every circuit for preachers' wives, and the society to supply their families with bread and meat; so the preachers should travel from place to place, as when single: for unless something of the kind be done, we shall have no preachers but young ones, in a few years; they will marry and stop.[35]

The plan was not adopted. In the 1783 conference, Asbury tried to alleviate some of the stress by giving married traveling preachers extra income for the support of their wives. The northern conference raised £200. The southern conference only raised £60. Lee stated, "Some of our leading men in particular circuits did not approve of it; and thought it unreasonable that they should raise money for a woman they never saw; and whose husband never preached among them."[36] The leading men to whom Lee refers were the local preachers in the South. Most were married and enjoyed filling in when there was a lack of traveling preachers. Many had been circuit riders. Others maintained a healthy competition with the traveling preachers. The marrying of circuit riders continued to strain Methodism's ability to expand and fill established circuits as it depleted the itinerancy of needed assets.

Problems with Cultures

EAM struggled with cross-cultural issues. Social and racial barriers hindered ministry with African Americans. Asbury recognized his limitations in preaching to blacks. In 1780, he stated, "If I had two horses, and Harry (a coloured man) to go with, and drive one, and meet the black people, and to spend about six months in Virginia and the Carolinas, it would be attended with a blessing."[37] Blacks were very receptive to Methodism. Black preachers were more effective at evangelizing black people than white preachers. When conditions permitted, EAM reaped a large harvest with black populations. It should be noted that whites also responded well to the preaching of black preachers. The preaching of "Black Harry" Hosier became legend. He may have been the most gifted preacher of his time.

While in western Virginia, Asbury wished he had German-speaking preachers. He believed that Methodism would be successful if it ministered to German-speaking people. He often spoke to the German brethren but could not start a work with them due to a lack of bilingual preachers. Fortunately, the antecedents of the Evangelical Association and the United Brethren were working with the German speaking people.

Early America was a land of immigrants. Many did not speak English as their first language. For example, in Winchester, Virginia, Asbury noted that the polyglot composition of the community made it very difficult for him to minister.[38] Asbury's inability to recruit and deploy preachers who could form culture specific classes greatly hindered Methodism's ability to grow with non-English speaking populations. As immigrants and their children learned English and assimilated into the dominant culture, Methodism was able to reach them more easily. Regardless, it is doubtful if Asbury could have maintained language specific circuits. If he did, they would have overlapped other circuits.

In recent times, attempts have been made to form missionary districts within larger conferences to position United Methodism to evangelize people who speak Korean, Spanish, Haitian Creole, and the like. Because of the racist legacy of the Central Jurisdiction, most refuse to consider the option of a missionary district within a conference that itinerates non-English speaking preachers. Still, it has been shown that non-English speaking people will not cross cultural and linguistic barriers to be assimilated in an English speaking congregation unless the church accommodates the culture gap. From a strategic perspective, missionary districts make a lot of sense in the growing multi-cultural milieu of North America. In fact, the Great Commission obligates United Methodism to take culture seriously as it seeks to make disciples of all the various people groups in American and the world.

Funeral Evangelism

Funeral services continued to be an evangelistic tool during this period. Asbury commented, "About a thousand people attended to hear the funeral sermon of John Laws. . . . His experience and death have wrought powerfully on the hearts of many . . . so even in this unpromising place there is a prospect of religion."[39] Later, Asbury preached a funeral for a young woman. The people were very serious. Joseph Cromwell exhorted. "Strangers attended, that did not, would not before quarterly meeting. These people were drawn. . . . Life begets life."[40] Asbury often spoke of the benefits associated with a funeral sermon and exhortation because unawakened people attended the services. Death was a stark reality and a wonderful object lesson. An opportunity to respond to the message was built into the service.

CHAPTER EIGHT

THE SECTIONAL CRISIS AT FLUVANNA AND ITS CONSEQUENCES

Asbury and the Northern preachers did not attend the regular conference at Fluvanna, Virginia in 1779 because of the war and the problems associated with interstate travel. To accommodate the northern preachers, Asbury held a preparatory conference on April 28 at Judge White's house in Kent County, Delaware. At that conference, the northern preachers designated Asbury as the general assistant for the American work.[1] Previously, Rankin served in that capacity. He and the other missionaries had returned to England. Wesley had not designated Rankin's replacement. Also, they established guidelines to limit the local preachers so that they worked under the supervision of the itinerants.

Since the Delaware conference was a preparatory conference, the preachers at the regular conference in Fluvanna, Virginia did not have to approve its decisions. The preachers at the Virginia conference intended to take American Methodism in a radically different direction. At the regular conference, the southern preachers voted to form a presbytery for the purpose of ordaining preachers who would serve the sacraments. The following southern preachers voted in favor of ordination: Isham Tatum, Charles Hopkins, Nelson Reed, Reuben Ellis, Philip Gatch, Thomas Morris, James Morris, James Foster, John Major, Andrew Yeargin, Henry Willis, Francis Poythress, John Sagman, Leroy Cole, Carter Cole, Carter Cole, James O'Kelly, William Moore, and Samuel Roe. They deemed this necessary because "the Episcopal Establishment is now dissolved and therefore in almost all our circuits the members are without ordinances."[2] The itinerants felt divine approbation for this action because the blessings of God attended to the work when they administered the ordinances. The preachers at the Virginia Conference followed the Presbyterian model of the early church.³ In the absence of a bishop, they ordained three preachers who then formed a presbytery and ordained others to include some local preachers.

A historical marker at the location has this inscription:

> Close by, May 18, 1779, at Roger Thompson's, near the Broken-Back Church, began the "Regular" Methodist Conference composed of some of the most devoted and successful Methodist preachers, a large majority of the whole. Assent was given to the insistent demand for the holy sacraments from those through whom thousands had been converted. A presbytery was appointed, preachers were ordained. After one year, for the sake of peace, they were desisted and appealed to Wesley.⁴

As a Virginian itinerant, Lee was intimate with the preachers and the events that transpired at the Fluvanna Conference. He states:

> In the course of this year there were great troubles and distresses in the Methodist connection, both among preachers and private members; owing to an unhappy division which took place among the travelling preachers. Many of our travelling preachers in Virginia and North Carolina, seeing and feeling the want of the instituted means of grace among our societies; (and there being but few church ministers in that part of the country, and most part of them strangers to heart-felt religion) concluded, that if God had called them to preach, he had called them also to administer the ordinances of baptism and the Lord's Supper. . . . The preachers thus ordained, went forth preaching the gospel in their circuits as formerly, and administered the sacraments wherever they went, provided the people were willing to partake with them. Most part of our preachers in the south, fell in with this new plan; and as the leaders of the party were very zealous, and the greater part of them very pious men, the private members were influenced by them, and pretty generally fell in with their measures. However, some of the old Methodists would not commune with them, but steadily adhered to their former customs.⁵

Asbury did not agree with Lee's assessment. After receiving a letter from Jarratt, an Episcopalian priest and the *de facto* pastor of southern Methodism, on November 13, 1779, Asbury claimed that the "dissenting brethren" planned to purge the southern societies of all who will not accept their ordination. Later entries confirm this. His journal employs negative language when referring to the southern preachers during this time. He bore ill toward them because they thwarted his efforts to connect EAM to the Episcopal Church. From a personal perspective, he felt diminished by their actions. Since he had labored faithfully in their midst and had been the general assistant before Rankin, they should have included him in their deliberations before they began to ordain themselves.

Asbury, Garrettson, and Watters from the northern conference went to the 1780 Virginia conference with an ultimatum. Garrettson and Watters were Strawbridge converts. They had credibility with the southern preachers. Watters served as the spokesman for the northern conference. At first, the Southern preachers stood resolute in their plan. As the northern preachers departed, the southern preachers offered a compromise for the sake of unity. In the compromise, they would cease to administer the sacraments for one year and agreed to unity with the northern preachers under the old Methodist plan until Wesley responded to their petition and acted on their problem.

Asbury estimated that twenty promising preachers and over 3,000 people would have been lost if the Fluvanna separation had not been healed.[6] In actuality, 6,086 people belonged to the southern circuits associated with those who ordained themselves. Even after the southern preachers agreed to Asbury's plan, many southern preachers still believed they were right in what they did. They compromised for the sake of unity.

A curious entry in Asbury Journal may shed additional light upon the southern mutiny. Upon notification of Strawbridge's death in 1781, Asbury wrote, "He is no more; upon the whole I am inclined to think the Lord took him away in judgment because he was in a way to do hurt to his cause."[7] Why did Asbury bear such ill will toward Strawbridge six years after his name dropped from the *Minutes*? It is possible that Rankin pushed Strawbridge out of the itinerancy after Asbury took control of his circuit. It is also possible that Strawbridge withdrew from the itinerancy out of protest. Regardless of the reason, Strawbridge did not leave the ministry. Most likely, he reverted to local status as a located preacher. In that capacity, he continued his work through 1781. As before the arrival of the missionaries, his ministry would have included itineration and the administration of sacraments.

Richard Owings was an early convert of Strawbridge. The 1775 *Minutes* assigned him to the Baltimore Circuit. Like Strawbridge, he dropped from the *Minutes* in that year. In his capacity as a local preacher, he officiated at Strawbridge's funeral service. He returned to the Methodist itinerancy in 1785. Like Strawbridge and Owings, other local preachers also itinerated at will. The 1779 *Minutes* attempted to rein them in by requiring them to get notes from the itinerants. Still, the local preachers in the South remained independent. Following the Fluvanna split, many began to administer the sacraments like Strawbridge and the southern itinerants. After the northern and southern itinerants reached a compromise, some local preachers did not want to give up the sacraments. Asbury did battle with them over this issue.

Even though the primary documents do not mention Strawbridge by name in regards to Fluvanna, his independent ministry and his example may have inspired the actions of the assembled preachers. Additionally, since many of the Southern preachers came into the ministry under Strawbridge's ministry, they may have consulted with him before they took actions that mimicked his precedent. By precept and example, up until the time of his death, Strawbridge remained a threat to Asbury's vision for American Methodism because he had a disproportional influence with the local preachers and the southern itinerants. Plus, he did not submit to the "old Methodist plan." Even worse, he checked Asbury's authority.

In the years following the reunification, Asbury took firm control of Southern Methodism. He itinerated through the area continually as he worked to win the favor of the preachers and the people. He also controlled the southern preachers through his ability to appoint them to different locations. The one year moratorium that the southern preachers agreed to with Asbury at Fluvanna turned into an indefinite suspension as they patiently waited for Wesley's reply to their letter. Since their power base had been weakened and Asbury reined as the general assistant, they did not attempt another separation.

The Significance of the Sectional Crisis

The sectional crisis highlights five factors that influenced the pattern and growth of EAM.[8] First, before the 1780, the conference in Virginia had precedence over the conference in Maryland and Delaware since the northern conference was preparatory to the southern one. Following 1780, Asbury arbitrarily gave the ruling authority to the northern conference. Afterward, it could veto any decisions made by the southern conference. In so doing, he subjugated the decisions of the southern preachers to the will of the northern preachers. The northern conference included the traveling preachers from Maryland, Delmarva, and the Mid-Atlantic region. This was a political move because Asbury enjoyed allegiance in those areas. It also disenfranchised the southern preachers by limiting their ability to influence change. From the perspective of the South, this violated the rules of democracy and equal representation. It gave cause to those who said that Asbury manipulated the rules to his advantage and that he established himself as king. The northern conference had already given Asbury the right of determination in that he had the final say after listening to the debate. This is the same autocratic authority that Wesley enjoyed when he met in conference with the preachers in England.

The emerging slavery debate evinces how the northern conference used its privilege to force an unpopular issue onto the South. Before the reunification of the northern and southern conferences in 1780, the northern conference declared that traveling preachers had to give promise to free their slaves. Furthermore, they stated, "Slavery is contrary to the laws of God, man, and nature, and hurtful to society, contrary to the dictates of conscience and pure religion, and doing that which we would not others should do to us and ours."[9] They voted to disapprove the conduct of all their friends who owned slaves and they pleaded for their freedom. In retrospect, the reprimand seems mild in comparison to the antislavery rhetoric that circulated in some parts of the country at that time. Many of the northern states outlawed slavery during and following the Revolutionary War. Quakers and other religious organizations campaigned for manumission. The slavery issue represented a national debate that divided the country along sectional and ideological lines.

As expected, many southern Methodists felt insulted by the northern conference's resolution and disapprobation. Lee captured the sentiment. "It is evident that the [northern] preachers in this case went too far in their censures; and their language in their resolves was calculated to irritate the minds of our people, and by no means calculated to convince them of their error."[10] The Southern preachers would not have allowed the northern preachers to enact this rule had they had equal vote since they represented the majority of American Methodism at that time. Still, it should be noted that the southern itinerants strongly opposed slavery and did all they could to ameliorate the conditions associated with it. However, the southern local preachers were not as resolute as the circuit riders. For a variety of reasons, the southern itinerants did not push the issue. Regardless, the new rules stirred public opposition to southern Methodism. As a result, many slave owners would not allow their slaves and family members to attend Methodist preaching.

Second, following reunification, many local preachers in the South continued to oppose Asbury and to cause discontent in Methodism over the issue of sacraments and ordination. As was previously noted, some continued to perform sacerdotal duties. Asbury's journal gives insight into the problem.

> A few of the local preachers have made a stir [about the ordinances], and the travelling preachers have withdrawn from them and their adherents.... The local preachers tell of the ordinances, and they catch at them like fish at a bait; but when they are informed that they will have to give up the travelling preachers, I apprehend they will not be so fond of their new plan; and if I judge right, the last struggle of a yielding party will be made at the approaching conference to be held at Manakintown.... There is a considerable distress amongst our societies [in the South], caused by some of the local preachers, who are not satisfied unless they administer the ordinances without ordination, and the whole circuit appears to be more or less tinctured with their spirit.[11]

Seven months later, Asbury added, "I find many of the people and some of the local preachers quite warm about the ordinances on which subject there is much disputation."[12] Even though Asbury quelled the southern revolt, he did not put down the spirit that gave birth to it. Opposition smoldered.

Many local preachers in the South maintained a deep-seated rejection of Asbury's leadership. For that matter, they resented their second class status as local preachers. Local preachers had a long and successful ministry in the Virginia growth area. In their minds, they were combat veterans of the revival. While in the heat of apostolic ministry, they had proven themselves capable spiritual warriors. Their ministry success vouchsafed their calling and their right to preach. In reference to their usefulness during the 1776 revival, Lee asserts, "The work of God thus increased on every side, and more preachers were soon wanting. And the Lord raised up several young men, who were exceeding useful as local preachers."[13] The revival in the South outpaced Methodism's ability to man it with traveling preachers. Southern Methodism grew by more than 3,000 members from 1775 to 1777. The local preachers filled the void and carved out for themselves a respected ministry in that area. They did not want their gifts and abilities to be sidelined by Asbury.

At the same time, Asbury did not want local preachers wandering all over the southern connection because they did not answer to him in the same way as the circuit riders. He could not control them or contain their ministry. Many "pastored" local societies. Others itinerated in the area around their home. Some had been circuit riders. Often, local societies became very attached to them and dependent on them. Asbury tried to contain them through legislation.

Beginning in 1779, a series of rules were put in place to control local preachers. In that year, local preachers were ordered to follow the directions of the traveling preachers and only preach in assigned places. In 1780, they were required to get a note from a traveling preacher on a quarterly basis and give satisfaction in regards to their life, character, and ministry. In 1781, local preachers were forbidden to travel in a circuit even if it was vacant without the consent of Asbury or the nearest traveling preacher. In 1782, the conference asked three questions related to local preachers and the raging controversies surrounding their ministry. The first tried to identify and guard against disorderly local preachers. The second disowned local preachers and their followers who separated from the official Methodist organization. The third tried to guard against impostors.

In 1783, it was clear that many of the local preachers had ignored the 1779 order to manumit their slaves. The 1783 conference decided to try them one more year. After that, they were to be suspended. In 1784, the conference asked, "What shall we do with our local Preachers who will not emancipate their slaves in the states where the laws admit it? Try those in Virginia another year."[14] The local preachers in Delaware, Maryland, New Jersey, and Pennsylvania were to be suspended. Because the local preachers in Virginia were a powerful force, they required special attention.

Third, the southern itinerants had their own leaders. Most came out of the ranks of local preachers. Their ministry reflected Strawbridge's influence and practice. The southern preachers respected Strawbridge and approved of his actions. As American born preachers in the midst of a revolution with England, the southern preachers did not display unmitigated devotion and total submission to Wesley. Since Wesley was an Anglican priest, they may have assumed that they severed their relationship with him when America rejected British rule. Regardless, they did not wait for his directions or seek his input during the Fluvanna Conference. Also, the independent mindset of the conference shows that Asbury did not enjoy the same level of support in the South as he did in the North. Certainly, the southern preachers did not look to him as their general assistant at that time. Furthermore, the events at the northern and southern conferences graphically illustrate the regionalism of EAM. Clearly, an us-versus-them mentality prevailed.

Consequently, Asbury forced the issue of obedience to his rule. At the 1782 southern conference, Asbury asked all the preachers to sign a pledge to "cleave to the old plan" so they could have confidence in each other.[15] The pledge also required them to give up any plan of separation. All but Garrettson signed.[16] He was one of Strawbridge's converts and an itinerant in the Eastern Shore. He suffered great persecution during the war. Out of principle, he also refused to sign the state oaths. Ultimately, Garrettson capitulated on the issue and was warmly greeted by Asbury. The preachers at the northern conference signed the pledge on May 20, 1782.[17]

According to Lee, Philip Gatch, John Dickins, and James O'Kelly gave leadership to the southern mutiny.[18] Asbury included Edward Dromgoole and William Glendinning in that list.[19] Gatch entered the ministry under Strawbridge. Eighteen itinerants approved of the separation.[20] Later, Dickins became the steward of the Book Concern and a dear friend to Asbury.

After unification, some of these leaders continued to oppose Asbury. In 1784, William Glendinning devised a plan to lay Asbury aside and to abridge his powers. Asbury said that Wesley's letter settled the issue.[21] Asbury was not fond of Glendinning. In Asbury's view, he was a charismatic enthusiast who had great dreams and visions. Asbury attributed his clairvoyance to arrogance. Glendinning's visions of Satan garnered him fame and made him a popular preacher after he worked through his falling away. Even after he separated from official Methodism, circuit riders continued to set his appointments and allow him to preach until Asbury stopped it.[22] When he requested to be readmitted, Asbury refused.

James O'Kelly is primarily associated with the 1792 mutiny in which he and other preachers withdrew from Methodism over the issue of Asbury's autocratic authority in the stationing of preachers. The seeds of O'Kelly's future defection began with Strawbridge and continued to germinate during this time. O'Kelly saw how Asbury used his appointment authority as a means to control the southern preachers. For example, in November 1780, the preachers came to consult further about their appointments. All agreed to their appointments except Garrettson. He did not want to return to Baltimore. His case was brought before the assembled preachers. After conferring, their judgment prevailed against Garrettson and he took his appointment. Between this incident and 1792, Asbury assumed the authority to appoint preachers without recourse to the assembled preachers or consultation. He used this power to break-up the southern stronghold.

Fourth, not everyone in the South united behind the southern mutiny. Many opposed it. Some who opposed the mutiny were expelled. Others withdrew voluntarily. During his tour of the South after unification, Asbury noted the deleterious effects of the attempted separation.[23] He emphasized that the separation caused a decline in members, preachers, and the spirit of true religion. In the circuits where the preachers had administered the ordinances, Asbury found coldness and a lack of discipline. He complained that the southern preachers were so concerned with ordinances and their new prestige that they ceased to push the people for holiness. However, he saw a silver lining in the falling away. "I am persuaded this division will cause the sincere, among the preachers and people, to cleave closer to doctrine and discipline, and may be the means of purging our societies of those who are corrupt in their principles."[24]

Fifth, the ordinance issue temporarily separated the southern Methodists from the Episcopal priests. Asbury and Wesley had urged the Methodists to keep to the Episcopal Church and use its priests for their sacramental needs. After reunification, Jarratt resumed his leadership and sacerdotal ministry in

Southern Methodism. If fact, the southern preachers were to consult with him and take his advice when Asbury was not available.[25] Unlike other priests, Jarratt had heart religion and preached like a Methodist.

The following references demonstrate the symbiotic relationship that Asbury wanted Methodism to have with the Episcopal clergy. "Three clergymen attended [our quarterly meeting in Delaware] with great friendship. . . . We had a close conversation with the clergy, who informed themselves of our rules and were willing to give us all the assistance they could by word and deed."[26] After preaching the funeral for a Methodist in a barn filled with 400 people, the Rev. Magaw invited Asbury to help him in the baptizing of the children. The Rev. Neill gave an exhortation.[27] Later, Asbury noted that the preaching of Magaw at a Methodist chapel mitigated the prejudices of the people in that area so that they were more receptive to Methodism.[28] It has already been shown that lawyers, judges, and high officials from Delaware became early innovators of Methodism. It is certain that this influenced Methodism's positive relationship with the official church in Delaware since the lay leadership would have encouraged partnership.

Methodism also benefited the Anglican Church. Good Methodists made good Episcopalians because they attend church and receive the sacrament. After attending communion at an Episcopal church, Asbury mused, "Communicants increase daily, for people get awakened by us; when this is the case, they go to the Lord's supper."[29] In late 1784, Asbury made a keen observation about the relationship between the two organizations. "The Methodists are most likely to have permanent success [in postbellum Virginia], because the inhabitants are generally Episcopalians."[30] For many reasons, Anglicanism declined during and after the war. In the areas where Methodism had a good relationship with the Episcopal Church, Methodist membership benefited from Anglican decline.

In May 1780, Asbury wrote, "Our people's leaving the Episcopal Church has occasioned the people of that church to withdraw from our preaching. . . . I advised our people to attend the Episcopal Church, that prejudice might be removed; then their people will attend us."[31] Methodism used its positive relationship with the Episcopal Church as a means to overcome prejudice against Methodism and to make EAM more appealing to Episcopalians.

In summary, Asbury said that the ordinance issue caused a decline in membership in the Virginia growth area. Undoubtedly, he was correct. However, had he left things alone, the administration of the ordinance may have made southern Methodism more attractive to the disenfranchised masses of Episcopalians. In fact, the conflict that ensued related to the ordinance debate and the manhandling of the southern preachers may have been a greater cause for membership decline. Regardless, the ordinance debate happened during the time when the area was embroiled in combat. It has already been shown that the fighting also caused decline. As such, it is not possible to know how much of the decline was caused by the fighting and how much was caused by the internal strife. The former is a contextual factor; the latter is an institutional factor. Doubtlessly, both contributed.

CHAPTER NINE

THE CHRISTMAS CONFERENCE AND BEYOND, 1785 THROUGH 1800

In December 1784, the MEC came into being. During the next 15 years, the MEC experienced a revival with unprecedented numerical growth, expanded into New England, penetrated the most distant areas of the frontier, endured a series of internal conflicts, weathered a devastating membership meltdown in the South, and positioned itself for massive numerical growth at the turn of the century. By 1800, its national membership totaled 65,098. After a humble start in 1789, New England Methodism burgeoned to 7,236 members and extended into every New England state by 1800. Mid-Atlantic Methodism increased from 3,624 to 15,065 members. Membership on the southern frontier grew from 90 in 1787 to 2,646 in 1794, plateaued and then declined by 349. Following 1800, frontier membership lurched forward on the momentum of camp meetings, immigration, and the impulse of the Second Great Awakening. From 1784 through 1792, southern membership exploded from 12,299 members to 50,192. By 1799, the membership had waned to 38,591. Large gains followed 1800.

The spread of Methodism to New England and the southern decline in the 1790s demonstrate the extensive regionalism of early America and the shaping influence of contextual factors. As the MEC adapted to its regional settings, the church experienced an internal stress that mirrored the stress that conflicted the nation in that Methodism began to embody the national variance. In essence, even though the MEC existed as a national connection that dispatched itinerants between regions, it took on the character of the regions in which it ministered.

The slave debate exemplifies this. The connection lessened its harsh stance against slavery in order to maintain national unity and to stave off radical opposition in the South. Coke and Asbury argued in favor of this compromise based on practical considerations even though they did not like it.[1] Both remained principled abolitionists. However, the slavery controversy flared up on a regular basis and kept the national church in internal turmoil. It pitted itinerants against local preachers, northerners against southerners, and the MEC against state governments.

Additionally, the emerging "republicanism" of the South with its emphasis on egalitarianism and popular vote conflicted with the hierarchical idealism and pro-British bias of Asbury and the institutional church. A series of controversies associated with the Methodist episcopacy, presiding elders, and the ill-fated Council clearly demonstrate the clash between republican values and the Methodist institution. Those conflicts were coupled with the O'Kelly revolt, the continuing discord between the local preachers and the traveling preachers, the rising influence of lay leadership, the de-emphasizing of local discipline, and the changing institutional structure.

At the same time, many national institutional factors aided the growth of Methodism in New England. Examples are the rising of an indigenous ministry, the preaching of Wesleyan-Arminianism, the pushing for the disestablishment of Congregationalism, the building of chapels, the missionary impulse that carried Methodism to every part of New England, the evangelistic zeal of the itinerants, and centralized organization.[2] The enduring spirit of Anti-Federalism, a growing dissatisfaction with the established church order, and the sparse populating of the New England frontier are positive contextual factors that combined with institutional factors to aid Methodist growth in New England.

The Christmas Conference and the Founding of the MEC

The formation of the MEC in 1784 came as the inevitable result of Anglican disestablishment and separation from English control. The long-term significance of the Christmas Conference lay in the patterns that it established. They became a framework around which the church would be built and around which future debates would be argued.

On September 10, 1784, Wesley dispatched a letter and three ordained Methodists to the American connection.[3] By means of the letter and the actions that accompanied it, Wesley formed American Methodism into an independent Methodist church with general superintendents, ordained clergy, articles of religion, a liturgy, and hymns. This represented Wesley's response to the letter sent by the Fluvanna Conference in 1779. The one year moratorium had extended to five years. During those years, Asbury held the American connection together under the old plan. Many southern preachers continued to believe that the actions of the Fluvanna Conference had been correct even if the timing had been poor. Ultimately, they believed that Wesley's actions validated the basic premise and much of the rationale that led to the southern defection in 1779.

Wesley's letter had tremendous implication for Methodists in all parts of the world. It foreshadowed what would happen when Wesley died. Following the ordination of ministers for the American connection, Wesley also ordained Methodists for Scotland, the mission field, and England. Rankin, the former superintendent of American Methodism, received ordination for England. More importantly, Wesley's actions and his justifications for them established a basis from which a Methodist missional ecclesiology can be articulated.

Many factors precipitated the Christmas Conference. Wesley summarized them in the justification letter that he sent to the American conference. First, America was separated from British rule and constituted an independent country. Therefore, the Church of England had no formal jurisdiction in America. Second, Wesley believed that bishops and presbyters were of the same ecclesiastical order.[4] According to him, they are synonymous terms in the New Testament. Wesley believed that he functioned as a missionary bishop in his oversight of American Methodism. In that capacity he had the right to ordain. He did not ordain his preachers before the Christmas Conference because he wanted to avoid open conflict with the Church of England. Third, the situation in America became grave because the Methodists were largely bereft of the sacraments. Consequently, Wesley formed a presbytery of three Anglican priests to ordain Richard Whatcoat and Thomas Vasey as deacons and elders. He also appointed Coke, with the laying on of hands, to be a general superintendent of the Methodists in North America with the authority to ordain. He directed Coke to make Asbury a joint general superintendent upon his arrival in America.

The last paragraph of his letter proved to be prophetic. The American Methodists "are now at full liberty, simply to follow the scriptures and the primitive church. And we judge it best that they should stand fast in that liberty, wherewith God has so strangely made them free."[5] Did full liberty imply separation from Wesley's control? The emphasis on the scriptures and the example of the primitive church are core elements of Methodist evangelicalism and the New Testament Restoration Movement that challenged American Methodism following the O'Kelly schism. Ultimately, the Campbellite Movement of the early 19th century championed Wesley's pronouncement as it used the scriptures and the example of the New Testament church as sources of primary authority. Even though this hermeneutic did not take into consideration the historical context of the scriptures or the social distance of the readers, it appealed to the people with whom the MEC attempted to grow.

The Christmas Conference did not interpret Wesley's letter in the way that he intended. First, Wesley did not ask the American conference its opinion or seek its approval. He simply told the American conference what he wanted it to do and why he wanted it to do it.[6] Upon receiving Wesley's letter, the American conference took an authority upon itself that it did not receive from Wesley. Like good Americans, the delegates contemplated the letter and voted on Wesley's order. In British Methodism, the preachers in conference with Wesley never voted on issues. Wesley consulted with them and they gave him advice, but Wesley had the final word. The conference's actions had long-term implications and far-reaching implications.

Second, under the influence of Coke, the American conference voted to form itself into an "episcopal" church. In common parlance, the term "episcopal" implies "bishop." According to the Minutes,

> Therefore, at this conference we formed ourselves into an Independent Church: and following the counsel of Mr. John Wesley, who recommended the Episcopal mode of government, we thought it best to become an Episcopal church, making the episcopal office elective, and the elected superintendent or bishop, amenable to the body of ministers and preachers.[7]

The above quote came as a result of redaction because the 1785 *Discipline* does not use the term bishop. In the founding documents that Wesley sent to America, he purposely substituted "superintendent" for the office of bishop and elder for the office of priest. The Christmas Conference followed Wesley's guidance at this point. Wesley's letter calls Coke and Asbury joint superintendents over our brethren in North America. Coke arrogated the title bishop and Asbury consented to its use.[8] In fact, a person who directs and ordains clergy is a functional bishop. Also, it is possible that Wesley intended the MEC to become the national church in the same way that Anglicanism had been the established church in many areas before the revolution. However, he did not style Methodism an Episcopal Church.

Third, Asbury refused to be ordained as a superintendent until the conference unanimously voted him into that position. The Conference also elected Coke as one of its superintendents even though Wesley had already consecrated him to that position. If Asbury and Coke had acted without the preachers' approval by taking upon themselves a leadership role and function that the conference did not grant them, their authority and effectiveness would have been challenged. At this point, Asbury understood the American ethos better than Coke.

The issue of the identity and power of the episcopacy was most strongly argued in the South and southern frontier. The conversation paralleled a national debate that argued the role of government and the power of rulers. It was the primary cause for O'Kelly's defection in 1792, and it contributed to the huge decline in southern Methodism in the 1790s. It became a cutting question that caused schisms and determined many future disputes. Was the general superintendent a constitutional monarch or a president who ruled with the consent of the people? Asbury fought for a strong episcopacy. He believed that he walked in the stead of Wesley and needed episcopal authority to carry out the mission of the church. Asbury had a national vision for the MEC. The young church needed a strong leader to guide it and deploy its resources in an effective way so that it could fulfill national goals. In an attempt to do that, he personified the highest ideals of a Methodist circuit rider.

Those who argued against Asbury reflected an emphasis on personal choice and a localized vision for the church in which the authority was vested in the conference with lay representatives. They believed that the conference walked in the stead of Wesley. Issues related to the stationing of the preachers, the ownership of chapels, shared decision-making power in a general conference, and elected presiding elders were heralded by these people. After fighting a revolutionary war with a monarch who abused his powers, many American Methodists were cautious about yielding to an ecclesial autocratic. Their attitudes represented the republican mindset.

In short, institutional conflict and schisms related to the authority of the Methodist episcopacy and the organization of the church distracted the MEC from its primary mission of winning the nation to Christ during this period. Conversely, much of the effectiveness of EAM can be directly attributed to Asbury and his strong leadership.

The MEC Bias for Effective Evangelism

During the week leading up to the Christmas Conference, Coke, Asbury, and others edited Wesley's *Large Minutes* to fit the American situation.[9] The *Discipline* that emerged as a founding document of American Methodism contained some important sections that demonstrate the institutional bias for effective evangelism. The following summarizes relevant points from early *Disciplines*.[10] Section VII detailed the duties of a preacher. It laid a basis for the evangelistic zeal that characterized early Methodism and emphasized the primary task of the ministry.

> You have nothing to do but to save souls. Therefore spend and be spent in this work. And go always not only to those that want, but to those that want you most. Observe. It is not your business to preach so many times, and to take care of this or that society only: but to save as many souls as you can; to bring as many sinners as you possibly can to repentance, and with all your power to build them up in holiness, without which they cannot see the Lord.[11]

Time was a critical commodity for a preacher. He had many obligations related to it. Some preachers wanted to prioritize theological studies and used this as an excuse not to engage in personal evangelism. The *Discipline* affirmed the value of education but not at the expense of saving souls. "Gaining knowledge is a good thing, but saving souls is a better. . . . If you can do but one, let your studies alone. I would throw by all the libraries in the world rather than be guilty of the loss of one soul."[12]

The *Discipline* chided the preachers for a lack of zeal, and it focused them on the primary task. "Our call is to save that which is lost. Now we cannot expect them to seek us. Therefore we should go and seek them. Because we are particularly called, by going into the highways and hedges, to compel them to come in."[13] Some complained that the chapels and meeting places were too small to hold large crowds. This excuse detracted from the primary task of evangelism. The *Discipline* responded, "The house may hold all that come to the house; but not all that would come to the field."[14] Therefore, take the Gospel to the people where they are and preach to them. Afterward, form them into new societies or expand the ones you have. In other words, do not let the size of the meeting place determine the size of the work.

When a person claimed that he was called to preach, he had to show that he had a personal conversion, that he had gifts for preaching, and that his preaching was effective. Effectiveness was measured in terms of people responding to the preaching. "Have they fruit? Are any convinced of sin, and converted to God by their preaching? As long as these three marks concur in any one, we believe he is called of God to preach."[15]

Early Methodism understood that evangelism apart from discipleship was not useful. As such, evangelistic preaching and the forming of the people into societies where they could be nurtured in grace went together. "Is it advisable for us to preach in as many Places as we can, without forming any Societies? By no means: We have made the Trial in various Places; and that for a considerable Time. But all the Seed has fallen by the Way-side."[16]

Methodism anticipated church growth theory related to receptivity and soil testing. "Where should we endeavor to preach most?" Two answers were given. "Where there are the greatest Number [of] quiet and willing Hearers. Where there is the most fruit."[17] When fruit was present, it was a sign that God was moving in that population and that the people were receptive to God. When that happened, the Methodists were to redeploy more preachers to that area so they could more adequately harvest the fruit.

The MEC was hindered in its desire to expand to new areas because it lacked the money to pay preachers to work in new or undeveloped works. To ameliorate this problem, the church decided to raise a special fund. The appeal for the money demonstrates evangelistic zeal.

> Men and Brethren, help! Was there ever a Call like this since you first heard the Gospel-Sound? . . . Help us to send forth able, willing Labourers into your Lord's Harvest: So shall ye be assistant in saving Souls from death. . . . Help to propagate the Gospel of your Salvation to the remotest Corners of the Earth.[18]

Implications Following the Formation of the MEC

Because EAM did not constitute a church before the Christmas Conference, its members received the sacraments from an institutional church. Most attended the Anglican Church. When American Methodism organized itself into a church, church membership became problematic for those who had to choose between churches. Many devout members left Methodism. Asbury wrote, "Nothing could have better pleased our old church folks [Anglicans] than the late step we have taken in administering the ordinances; to the *catholic* Presbyterians it also gives satisfaction; but the Baptists are discontented."[19]

Before the Christmas Conference, great numbers of Anglicans began to attend Methodist programming. In the absence of a functioning Anglican Church, Methodism had become their church of choice. The formation of the MEC in 1784 gave these people a place to receive the sacraments and legitimized their church experience. In many areas like Delmarva, Methodist gains were proportional to Anglican losses. Disestablishment and the decline of Anglicanism were major growth factors that favored Methodism following the Revolutionary War in areas where Anglicanism had been established.[20] The following quotation from Barclay confirms the contextual situation and its consequences.

Religious conditions throughout the South—more particularly in Virginia—greatly favored the growth of a vigorous, warm evangelical movement such as was represented by the Methodist. . . . The majority of the clergy of the Established Church had deserted their congregation during the Revolution and returned to England. Many parishes continued for years without incumbents. . . . Many [Anglicans] welcomed the coming of the Methodist itinerants to their communities, attended their preaching services, and eventually united with the Methodist Church.[21]

Before the Christmas Conference Asbury worked with Anglican priests in an effort to win them and their parishioners over. As has been shown, many priests aligned themselves with American Methodism because Asbury represented Methodism as a "church within the Church." Like Pietism, Methodism did not see itself as a separate church. Rather, it worked as a nondenominational renewal movement that sought to grow spiritual vitality through its various classes and societies. It de-emphasized dogma so it could build common ground with a variety of traditions around a shared experience of God that manifested itself in external holiness and the use of spiritual disciplines. The Christmas Conference shattered the arrangement because EAM became a church with dogma and liturgy. Afterward, the Anglican priests stopped cooperating with Methodism because participation conflicted with their primary allegiance to the Anglican Church. They also urged their parishioners to avoid Methodism because the MEC had become competition.

Before the Christmas Conference, strong similarities existed between Baptists and Methodists. According to Coleman, they shared the same evangelistic fervor, missionary emphasis, sociological appeal, political association, democratic aspirations, ministerial training, and preaching emphasis. One was Arminian; the other Calvinistic.[22] For its part, Methodism attracted many Baptists. To counter this, following the Christmas Conference, the Baptists began to emphasize believer's baptism by immersion and church government as points of controversy and distinction. This proved to be an effective strategy that targeted a weak spot in Methodism. As was shown in a previous chapter, the Baptist preachers argued that believer's baptism was the only biblical alternative and that congregations should hire and support a pastor. A centralized government with a strong bishop who arbitrarily appointed preachers did not resonate with the democratic ideals of the South or their exegesis of the New Testament. Many Methodists shared their critique.

The issue of sacraments caused a big debate with the Baptists who attended Methodist services. As long as the Methodists did not administer the ordinances, neither the mode nor the subject of baptism mattered. Afterward, the issue became a major point of conflict. Many Baptists left, and others would not participate. Interestingly, in areas where the Baptists had strong influence, Asbury and other Methodist preachers immersed adults due to the debates that surrounded infant baptism. Baptists had gained much ground on that point in terms of public opinion. Even as late as 1795, former Baptists within the MEC complained at a conference about baptism. Asbury lamented that the old people were stirred up by the Baptists over the issue.[23]

Because so many people of that time believed that believer's baptism by immersion was the scriptural way to be baptized,[24] the 1785 *Discipline* asked an important question. "What shall be done with those who were baptized in their infancy, but have now scruples concerning the validity of Infant-Baptism? Remove their scruples by argument, if you can; if not, the office may be performed by immersion, pouring, or sprinkling, as the person desires."[25] Shortly following the Christmas Conference, Asbury wrote, "Here I plunged four adults, at their own request, they being persuaded that it was the most proper mode of baptizing."[26] A few months later, Asbury contended that plunging people increased the size of his congregations.[27]

In summary, the Christmas Conference inaugurated the MEC and began a new era within global Methodism. Becoming a denomination was a necessary development. American Methodism was fortunate that Wesley acted in regard to this before he died. Otherwise, it is doubtful that the MEC would have maintained the connection. A period of tremendous membership growth followed the Christmas Conference. Still, unsettled issues related to the form and order of the new church would foment conflict in the near future. Without a doubt, the seeds of institutionalism were planted in the years following 1784. Institutionalism would work against the dynamic of movementalism.

CHAPTER TEN

DEMOGRAPHICS, ECONOMY, AND POLITICS: HOW THESE CONTEXTUAL FACTORS SHAPED EAM FROM 1785 THROUGH 1800

The following sections highlight relevant national contextual and national institutional factors that had a direct influence on Methodist growth and decline from 1785 through 1800. Because of the 1790 Census, much can be known about the demographics of early America. For that reason, a statistical analysis of 1790 will reveal much about the contextual milieu in which EAM labored.

Statistical Analysis of 1790

According to the 1790 Census, 3,929,214 people lived in the United States. Seventy-nine percent claimed European heritage. Twenty percent were of African origins. Germans composed the largest non-English speaking white population.[1] They accounted for one third of the population of Pennsylvania and more than seven percent of the total population. Almost seven percent were unassigned because of blending. Most of these assimilated into English speaking populations.[2] Sixty-two percent were from English-speaking ancestry. Ninety-five percent lived in a rural environment.[3] Of the 201,655 persons who lived in an urban environment, 32,305 lived in New York and 42,520 lived in Philadelphia.[4] Native American tribal populations were not included in the 1790 Census.

The black population numbered 757,208. Over 697,000 were slaves. Of the 67,424 blacks in the Northeast, 40,354 were slaves. Of the 635 blacks in the North-central areas, 135 were slaves. Of the 689,784 blacks in the South, 657,372 were slaves. The four states with the greatest population of slaves were Virginia, 292,627; South Carolina, 107,094; Maryland, 103,036; and North Carolina, 100,783. By comparison, New York had 21,193 slaves and Kentucky had 12,430 slaves. Slaves composed the following percentages of respective state populations: 42 Virginia, 42 South Carolina, 32 Maryland, 26 North Carolina, 17 Kentucky, and six New York. More blacks lived along the coasts of Georgia, South Carolina, and Virginia than white people. Along the South Carolina coast, the black population equaled 70 to 95 percent of the population.[5] A dense population of blacks also existed in east-central Virginia. On the frontier, blacks clustered around Nashville and the area from Cincinnati to Lexington.

Regionally, the Southeast was the most populated area with 1,851,806 people. The southern population was greatest along the eastern seacoast. It gradually diffused as it moved west. The Georgia population clustered along the South Carolina border. A large community grew around Athens, Georgia. Unlike other rural areas, that population included more women than men. The coastal area of southern North Carolina and northern South Carolina was sparsely populated. The Norfolk and Savannah areas were still recovering from the war. The southern frontier of Kentucky and Tennessee contained 109,368 people. An area south of Cincinnati in Kentucky had a population greater than 45,000. Present day Fayette County (Lexington) had a population of 18,440 in 1790. The area stands out as a population island in a sea of sparsely settled frontier towns. It decreased to 14,028 in 1800 and grew to 21,370 by 1810. The frontier population was distinctively male.

The areas around Utica, New York and Pittsburgh had growing populations. The New England states totaled 1,009,408 persons. The areas along Lake Champlain and the Vermont/New Hampshire border had growing populations. Much of the New England population clustered around cities. The Mid-Atlantic had a population of 958,632. Long Island, southern New Jersey, and Delaware were less densely populated than the areas immediately to their west. The densest population in America ran from Boston to northeastern Virginia.[6]

There were 557,889 households in 1790 with a median size of 5.48. The average life expectancy in Massachusetts was 35 for children at birth. Only 15 percent lived to 60.[7] The average life expectancy decreased on the frontier and in rural areas. This statistic played large in Methodism's ability to sustain its ministry. Most itinerants died young. Amazingly, Asbury itinerated for 50 years. When the Christmas Conference reviewed the proposed *Discipline*, provisions were made for Asbury's death because many assumed that he would die shortly.

In terms of percent population increase, from 1775 to 1790, growth was greatest on the frontier. By 1790, the pattern of western migration was heterogeneous rather than homogeneous. That is, people moved out as families and as individuals rather than as ethnic communities. This accelerated the "melting pot" effect or blending. Westward migration was greatest from the middle states and the South.

In New England, Maine, New Hampshire, and Vermont showed population increases. The southern New England states showed the slowest rate of growth for the entire country. They only grew by 74 percent. After 1790, southern New England had the slowest rate of growth in the country largely because it was the most densely populated. The southern and middle states grew fastest. Georgia increased by 762 percent. Georgia was a part of the southern frontier in the same way that Maine was a part of the northern frontier. Virginia and the Carolinas doubled their populations. In 1790, Virginia had the largest population and the fasted growth rate. At that time, Methodism was growing at a very fast rate in Virginia. Respectively, New York and Pennsylvania increased their populations by 190 and 136 percent. Conversely, Delaware, New Jersey, and Maryland showed less than 100 percent growth. Delaware had a very slow growth rate.[8]

According to Table 10-1, New England had the most cities but the Mid-Atlantic had the largest cities with the fasted growth in 1790. Much of the urban population in New England scattered during the Revolution due to combat. Many relocated to the New England frontier. Others headed to the West. By 1800, the urban population of the Mid-Atlantic doubled that of New England. By contrast, in 1790, the combined urban population of the South barely equaled its 1775 level. Emigration and conflict from the war accounted for this. Before the formation of the Federal District, Methodism already had a strong work in the Arlington area. The Federal Circuit was carved out in 1795. Its creation was a testimony to the growth that surrounded the formation of Washington, DC.

Table 10-1. Growth of selected cities by region from 1775 to 1810

	1775*	1780	1790	1800	1810
Boston, MA	16,000	10,000	18,038	24,973	33,786
Gloucester, MA	0	0	3,000	5,313	5,943
Hartford, CT	3,000	3,000	3,000	3,523	3,955
Marblehead, MA	4,812	4,142	5,661	5,211	5,900
New Haven, CT	0	3,356	4,487	3,704	5,772
Newburyport, MA	3,000	3,080	4,817	5,946	7,634
Newport, RI	9,209	5,330	6,744	6,739	7,907
Portsmouth, NH	4,590	4,222	4,720	5,339	6,934
Providence, RI	4,321	4,310	6,371	7,614	10,071
Salem, MA	5,000	4,008	7,917	9,457	12,613
N.E. Totals	**49,932**	**41,448**	**64,755**	**77,819**	**100,515**
Albany, NY	3,700	3,050	3,494	5,289	10,762
Baltimore, MD	6,734	8,000	13,503	26,514	33,787
Lancaster, PA	0	3,919	3,762	4,292	5,405
New York, NY	22,000	18,000	32,305	60,515	96,373
Philadelphia, PA	23,739	27,565	42,520	61,559	87,303
Mid-Atl Totals	**56,173**	**60,534**	**95,584**	**158,169**	**233,630**

Table 10-1. Growth of selected cities by region from 1775 to 1810, continued

	1775	1780	1790	1800	1810
Charleston, SC	14,000	10,000	16,359	18,824	24,711
Norfolk, VA	6,000	0	3,000	6,926	9,163
Richmond, VA	0	0	3,761	5,737	9,735
Savannah, GA	3,000	0	0	5,146	5,215
Washington, DC†	NA	NA	0	10,467	20,383
South Totals	**23,000**	**10,000**	**23,120**	**47,100**	**69,207**
New Orleans, LA	0	4,980	5,338	N.R.	17,242

Sources: Cappon, *Atlas,* 97; and Bureau of Census Reports for 1790, 1800, and 1810.[9]
* A zero indicates a population of less than 3,000
† Washington, DC includes Alexandria, Washington City, and Georgetown

The Mid-Atlantic region had the greatest population increase from 1790 to 1810. However, the frontier grew at a faster rate. From 1790 to 1800, the mean center of the population for the United States moved 41 miles west and was located 18 miles west of Baltimore. In 1810, the population center moved another 46 miles west-southwest. By 1810, many western cities had populations of 3,000. They are not shown on Table 10-1. New Orleans stood out with a population of 17,242. It was the seventh largest city in America. Pittsburgh, Pennsylvania; Lexington, Kentucky; and Cincinnati, Ohio all had populations greater than 3,000. Kentucky's population illustrates the growth of the frontier. In 1790, it was 73,677. In 1800, it grew to 220,955. By 1810, it expanded to 406,511.[10]

Migration and the MEC[11]

Table 10-2 shows that population growth did not cause membership growth. Doubtlessly, population growth influenced membership growth because it increased the size of the harvest. When population growth came as a result of migration, it detached people from a previous tradition and gave Methodism an advantage because the MEC had the mechanism and infrastructure to win them. However, if population growth was an independent factor that caused membership growth, Southern Methodism would have grown in the 1790s. Methodist membership grew with the expanding population in the Mid-Atlantic and it greatly outpaced population growth in New England. Emigration from southern New England to northern New England aided membership growth in the last years of the decade. From 1800 to 1810, Methodism grew at a faster rate than the population in all the regions. Methodism in the South and Frontier accentuate accelerated growth.

Table 10-2. Methodist membership as a percent of regional populations between 1790 and 1810

Regional Population				Methodism as Percent of Population			
	1790	1800	1810		1790	1800	1810
N. Eng	1,009,408	1,233,011	1,471,973	N. Eng	0.002	0.47	1.2
Mid-Atl	958,632	1,402,565	2,014,702	Mid-Atl	1	1	2.1
South	1,851,806	2,286,494	2,674,891	South	2.4	1.7	3.1
Frontier	109,368	335,407	768,208	Frontier	3.3	1.2	3.5

Source: Data from U.S. Bureau of the Census. Available at www.census.gov/prod/cen1990/cph2/cph-2-1-1.pdf (accessed August 1, 2011).

Migration was a positive and negative contextual factor in EAM. Migrating local preachers and members helped to plant Methodism in new places. Migration also helped Methodism because other churches were not active in the places where most of the people migrated. For example, because of migration, many New Englanders converted to Methodism long before Lee planted Methodism in Massachusetts. According to Samuel Hill,

> A sizable proportion of New Englanders decided to leave the more settled society of the seaboard for a venture into the West. . . . Once removed from the more delineated civilization these thousands found a need to adjust their religious forms. One expression was to neglect or forsake religion. . . . Another was to transplant their old faith, with some called-for modifications. Some became Methodists, or Methodist-like, as the enthusiasm of vital piety redirected their spiritual practices.[12]

Migrants were receptive to Methodism because they did not have a social attachment to an existing church in their new location. Since the Methodists, Baptists, and Presbyterians actively evangelized in the frontier, they benefited the most from migration. However, emigration was a negative contextual factor when it took members from a local society. This caused Methodist circuits in the eastern sections of the Mid-Atlantic states and upper South to decline. According to Coleman, westward emigration from Maryland and Virginia was a primary cause for the southern decline in the 1790s.

> The membership of the church, however, experienced a notable readjustment in the areas of former concentration of strength [during the years of decline]. The states of Maryland and Virginia, whose populations had been depleted by the extensive westward immigrations, actually showed a decrease in membership between the years of 1790 and 1800. . . . Nowhere were there gains except in the rapidly developing virgin areas of the west and south and newly discovered fields to Methodism in New England.[13]

Coleman offers a tempting thesis. Unfortunately, the data show that frontier Methodism followed a similar pattern of decline in the 1790s. Nonetheless, he captures the reality of emigration. It took from existing societies.

In 1786, people from Maryland were moving to the western Pennsylvania frontier. While on the Redstone circuit, Asbury commented, "I am now among some old friends that moved from Maryland to this country."[14] One of Strawbridge's preachers from Maryland lived in this area and helped to start a society there. Later, Asbury was in the company of Brother Smith and other old friends from Maryland.[15]

A similar occurrence happened in South Carolina. According to Lee, a located preacher moved to South Carolina in 1785. He found many Methodist families who had moved there from Virginia. They formed the basis for the Broad River circuit.[16] Asbury stated, "Many who had no religion in Virginia, have found it after their removal into Georgia and South Carolina."[17] In 1789, Asbury stayed at the home of Thomas Hayes. Hayes left Virginia to escape the Methodist preachers who converted his wife. He got converted in Georgia.[18] The next week Asbury conducted a district conference at the Grant house in Georgia. The Grants had been Presbyterians before relocating from Virginia.

While in the North Carolina mountains, Asbury met with some Methodists from Maryland, Delaware, and Virginia who he had known for 22 years. Delmarva is called the "Garden of Methodism" because its members started Methodist works in many different places as they emigrated.[19] While in Carroll's Meeting House in Georgia, Asbury said, "Some of the people of the congregation are from the east and west parts of Maryland."[20] East refers to the Delmarva area or Eastern Shore.

While at the Deer Creek chapel in Maryland, Asbury noted that death, emigration, and backsliding hindered the society. "But, O, how many are dead! And some have fled to the woods, and some gone back to the world. The society is all gone that we had formed here more than twenty years back. . . . Poor Deer Creek! The preachers have left the place for want of hearers."[21] A similar reality occurred with the circuit in the Brownsville and Marion area of South Carolina. According to Asbury, "This is an unhappy country: it is thinly settled and many are moving away to Georgia and the Natchez; our societies are small, and the prospect low."[22] The area that Asbury mentioned had a diminished population at the turn of the century. In 1780, the area had been well populated.[23]

In sum, migration dominated the period of 1785 through 1800. Before 1785, throngs of people had relocated in order to escape the war. Many had clustered on the western border regions with the intention of moving further west as soon as conditions permitted. Some of the migrants took Methodism with them. Others found Methodism after they disassociated from a church tradition that did not exist in the new location. Wherever the people migrated, Methodist circuit riders followed close behind.

The Economic Situation

The economic situation directly affected the MEC and its ability to grow. From 1700 through 1770, per capita income rose at a steady one percent. In 1770, the average American made the equivalency of $200 per year. A severe economic depression gripped America following the Revolutionary War. The depression bottomed out in 1788. However, the economy did not improve until 1791. From 1791 through 1800, the per capita income recouped. It remained steady through 1810.[24]

Excessive importation of British goods and an unstable currency caused the economic downturn following the war. The British banking crisis compounded the problem. A deflation in commodity prices in England lowered the value of American goods. Accordingly, Americans made less profit for the same products because they had to compete with cheaper British imports. In 1789, the commodity rate was the same as it was before the war in 1775. Farm wages and other salaries were down 20 percent from their 1780 levels. Insistent creditors caused havoc and panic for many. The people demanded relief through the issuance of more paper money and stay laws to protect them from their creditors.

The situation was particularly bad in New England.[25] It produced local meetings of protest and agrarian demonstrations in Massachusetts, New Hampshire, and Vermont. Farmers from Connecticut and Rhode Island were some of the most distressed demonstrators.[26] Many were veterans from the Revolutionary War who had not been paid for their service. Upon discharge, they faced debtor's prison and the confiscation of their property. Ironically, those who most benefited from the service of the soldiers were the ones who sought to take advantage of their situation.

Massachusetts was a bulwark of Federalist idealism. Its laws favored the standing order and the ruling classes. The plutocrats would not heed the cries for the issuance of paper money from debt-ridden farmers or for laws to protect them from foreclosures. A convention of 50 towns at Hatfield condemned the Massachusetts Senate, lawyers, the high cost of justice, and the tax system. They complained that it was a self-serving system that benefited the wealthy and those in power at the expense of the people. Mob action shut down courts to prevent them from issuing orders to foreclose on properties. More than 600 soldiers and 500 insurgents met at the state supreme court. The magistrates averted violence by the adjournment of the court.

The insurgencies in the eastern part of the state collapsed quickly. However, a threat still existed in the western part of the state. Daniel Shays, a Captain in the Revolutionary Army and a destitute farmer with nothing to lose, organized an army of 1,200 men. His force planned to scatter General Shepherd's militia of 900 troops and take the arsenal in Springfield. As the ragtag soldiers marched to Springfield to join forces with another army under Luke Day, miscommunication and bad luck overwhelmed them. The operation fell apart. Four insurgents died. The rest received pardons. The insurrection resulted in new laws for the good of the common people. Massachusetts canceled the direct tax. Fees for court were lowered. Clothing, household goods, and tools for one's trade were exempt from debt collection.[27]

In the South, plantation owners also suffered from high debt, damage to their material infrastructure, poor harvests, export restrictions, and the loss of labor. During the havoc of the Revolutionary War, many slaves escaped. Retreating British troops acquired others.[28] Like the small businessmen and the tradesmen in the North, the plantation owners needed special protection from lenders.

Before the 1790s, the agricultural base in the South required a lot of capital and cheap labor. Most whites worked for the rich or eked out a meeker living on a subsistence farm because they could not enter the market. The invention of the cotton gin changed the social structure of the South. With its aid, the working poor could buy land and sell cotton. Many used their profits to enlarge their farms. The majority did not need and could not afford large numbers of slaves. In time, they moved up the social latter and severed their dependence on the rich land owners. By the end of the century, a strong middle class of entrepreneurs began to emerge in the South.[29]

As was previously noted, following 1791, agriculture boomed and the exports of the states tripled. Shipping and real estate also advanced. The 1790s were a time of economic prosperity. Except for a minor setback from 1796 through 1798, the period between 1791 and 1800 was one of exceptional prosperity.[30]

Economic Implications Related to the MEC

The bear market before 1791 adversely affected Methodism's institutional infrastructure. The following from Asbury in November 1789 summarized this reality:

> The school for the charity boys much occupies my mind [Cokesbury College]. The poverty of the people, and the general scarcity of money, is the great source of our difficulties. The support of our preachers, who have families, absorbs our collections, so that neither do our elders nor the charity school get much. We have the poor, but they have no money; and the worldly, wicked rich we do not choose to ask.[31]

His commentary highlights five important realities related to money and the MEC. First, the typical Methodist suffered from the economic depression. As Asbury itinerated during this period, he often reflected on the general scarcity of food and the lack of disposable money.[32] Often, he would stay in homes that suffered from acute material want. Second, Methodism maintained an oppositional attitude toward the rich and a positive bias toward the poor. In the above quote Asbury called the former "the worldly, wicked rich." The wicked rich owned slaves, pursued vanities, and cared not for the things of God. The institutional church needed money from the rich but did not want to be compromised by them. Like the itinerating Jesus, early American Methodism received some support from rich benefactors without allowing that support to change the character of the ministry. Third, married itinerants placed an enormous stress on the limited resources of the MEC. They received extra income for the support of their family. Already, Methodism did not have enough money to pay the itinerants and expand the work by hiring more circuit riders. Fourth, Cokesbury College ate up economic resources. Asbury had to divert scarce assets from the support of preachers, the establishing of new works, and the building of chapels to maintain that institution. Finally, Asbury believed that the poverty of the people and the corresponding lack of money was the "great source of our difficulties."

Cokesbury College constantly irritated Asbury. In 1788, Asbury complained, "Knowing the obligations I am under to pay money to several persons to whom the college is indebted, my mind is much exercised, I feel very heavily the weight of such responsibility."[33] In 1789, Asbury complained that he had to spend time visiting from house to house to beg money for the college.[34] In fact, almost every reference he makes about the school is negative. When fire consumed the school on December 7, 1795, Asbury made some very telling remarks. "We have now a second and confirmed account that Cokesbury College is consumed to ashes, a sacrifice of 10,000 £ in about ten years! . . . Would any man give me 10,000 £ per year to do and suffer again what I have done for that house, I would not do it."[35] Wesley scolded Asbury for establishing the college and for naming it after himself. In truth, Coke was the one who wanted it. He pushed Asbury for it. Asbury had to manage it in his absence.

The Poverty of the Itinerants and Issues Associated with It

The paucity of money hindered Methodism in its ability to recruit and retain traveling preachers.[36] This had the additional consequence of limiting the numerical and geographic growth of the church. At first, the MEC made token responses to the problem. When the implications became overwhelming, the MEC attempted to fix the problem. The chronology that follows documents the institution's response.

During this entire period, the MEC struggled to pay its traveling preachers their wages. For example, in 1788, many of the preachers did not receive more than £18 or £20 per annum, and several not more than £15 per annum.[37] As was previously stated, married itinerants and those on the frontier or in new works posed a special problem. Married preachers required more income than single preachers, and those appointed to the frontier or new works did not have large enough constituencies to pay their salaries.[38] The 1785 *Discipline* addressed this issue. It required a yearly collection and, if needed, a quarterly one for the purpose of supporting preachers in new works and for supporting preachers and their families who had special needs. The church feared that a lack of money to support distressed preachers would hurt their morale and cause them to leave the itinerancy.[39] The yearly collections did not solve the problem.

Rarely was there enough money to pay the full wage. Because married preachers received an additional year's wage for their wives and additional money for each child, single itinerants felt short-changed when the money was distributed because the money given to married preachers reduced their earnings. This caused tension. That tension was reflected in the 1787 *Minutes*.[40] "Are not many of our Preachers and people dissatisfied with the salaries allowed our married Preachers, who have children? Ans. They are. Therefore, for the future, no married preacher shall demand more than £48." Evidently, this rule caused many married itinerants to cease from traveling. This was indicated by a new question that was asked in 1788. "What Preachers have a partial location on account of their families, and are subject to the order of the conference?" Six were listed.[41]

In 1790, the *Minutes* indicated that the church responded to the special financial needs of the itinerants working on the frontier.

> At the Baltimore conference there was a collection of 721£ 9s 6d. And as the brethren in the Kentucky and Ohio districts appear to be in the greatest need, the conference generously voted two thirds of the said sum, as a partial supply for the preachers in the Ohio district, and one third for the brethren in Kentucky. The whole to be sent in books. There was also a collection of 48£. 18s. 11d. at the Duck-Creek conference, which was sent as a partial supply for those in the extremities of the states of New York and Connecticut.[42]

When Asbury entered into Tennessee in 1790, he described the overwhelming poverty of the itinerants. "I found the poor preachers indifferently clad, with emaciated bodies, and subject to hard fare; yet I hope they are rich in faith."[43] This comment takes on deeper meaning when one realizes that Asbury shared in their poverty, constant toils, and physical ailments.

The MEC expanded the use of collections and regulated them. The question was, "How many collections are to be made in a year?" The answer came in five parts.

> 1. A quarterly collection from the members of the society, to supply the Preachers; and when that is deficient, a public quarterly collection: If there be any overplus, let one third of it be reserved for future deficiencies; one third be given to the poor in general; and one third for the building or improving of our churches.

> 2. A yearly collection from all our members that are of ability, for the building of convenient churches. [This was expanded in 1792 to include the paying off of debt for the churches already built.]

> 3. A collection, at love-feasts and on sacramental occasions, for the poor of our society.

> 4. An annual collection or subscription for the college.

> 5. An annual public collection for the contingencies of the Conference; which shall be applied,

>> 1. To discharge the deficiencies of those Preachers who shall not have received their full salary in their circuits; and,

>> 2. To defray the expense of our missions to distant parts of the continent.[44]

In 1792, the General Conference disassociated the word "regular" from salary in the discipline to indicate that the preachers did not receive a regular salary or even the small amount specified. As an expression of frustration, this General Conference broke a long standing policy and allowed itinerants to collect a "marriage fee" for the first time. However, it was to be given to the Stewards who would combine it with the other available funds to pay off the salary deficiencies of all the preachers. The General Conference specified,

> No Minister or Preacher whatsoever shall receive any money for deficiencies, or any other account, out of any of our funds or collections, without first giving an exact account of all the money, clothes, and other presents of any kind, which he has received the preceding year.[45]

Local preachers were allowed to keep money that they received for marriage ceremonies and funerals. This was a constant point of irritation for the itinerants. This fact points to the "pastoral" nature of their ministry. They had a deeper relationship with the people because they did not itinerate and were never transferred. Plus, they were present when rites of passage happened.

In 1794, Asbury commented, "The poverty of the church is exceedingly great for preachers, yet not so great as the demands to different and distant parts. [As such,] I have declined taking a person that is fit for the circuits with me, the call is great."[46] Poverty notwithstanding, Asbury demonstrated his commitment to evangelism. Even though he was authorized a paid traveling assistant, he chose to ride alone so that the money and person could be used in the service of the cause. Usually, the presiding elder of the district in which he traveled accompanied him.

In 1796, Asbury made an entry that illustrates the integrated relationship between money and evangelism.

> I came to Nixon's, on the road to Wilmington; here I found a kind people, but the preachers had left them because they did not immediately join in fellowship. Perhaps I was called this way to feel for souls in and round about Wilmington: if we had men and money, it would be well to station a preacher in such places as Wilmington.[47]

At this point, money determined how long an itinerant could work an unproductive area. Because of the lack of financial backing, the itinerants abandoned some areas before the growth potential of the area was realized.

In 1796, the General Conference approved a charter fund for itinerants, worn-out preachers, their widows, and orphans. The money in the preacher's fund that had been collected prior to this time was deposited in the charter fund. Additionally, future profits from the Book Concern would also go into the fund.[48] Before the General Conference, Asbury foreshadowed the creation of this fund when he wrote,

> I drew the outlines of a subscription, that may form a part of a constitution of a general fund, for the sole purpose of supporting the travelling ministry; to have respect, First, To the single men that suffer and are in want. Secondly, To the

married travelling preachers. Thirdly, To the worn-out preachers. Fourthly, The widows and orphans of those who have lived and died in the work. And Fifthly, To enable the yearly conference to employ more married men; and finally, to supply the wants of all the travelling preachers, under certain regulations and restrictions, as the state of the fund will admit.[49]

The quote clearly demonstrates the need and the priority in distributing available funds. Asbury wanted to keep the itinerants traveling, to support those who were worn-out, and to employ new itinerants. The support of worn-out preachers and their families was more than a moral obligation. It was a necessity. Preachers who gave themselves to the work had to be reassured that the church would care for them once they were used-up. Without this safety net, itinerants would have left the traveling ministry before wearing themselves out in the work.

The following justification for the Charter Fund appeared in the 1796 General Conference report. It shows the relationship between a lack of adequate salaries and the numerical strength of itinerants.

> Our brethren who have laboured on the mountains, on the western waters, and in the poorer circuits in general, have suffered unspeakable hardships, merely for the want of some established fund. . . . On the same account, many of our worn-out preachers, some of whom quickly consumed their strength by their great exertions for the salvation of souls, have been brought into deep distress. . . . And it is to be lamented, if possible, with tears of blood, that we have lost scores of our most able married ministers—men who, like good householders, could, upon all occasions, bring things new and old out of their treasury, but were obliged to retire from the general work, because they saw nothing before them for their wives and children, if they continued itinerants, but misery and ruin. But the present institution will, we trust, under the blessing of God, greatly relieve us in, if not entirely deliver us from, these mighty evils.[50]

The charter fund did not solve the whole problem. Of 1797, Lee wrote, "So many preachers located this year, that we could not well supply the circuits, or enlarge our borders in new places, as we wished to have done."[51]

According to Table 10-3, between 1796 and 1799, the MEC had a net loss of 19 traveling preachers. In 1800, the MEC posted an increase of 15 preachers. Lee made an insightful remark about this "gain."

> Notwithstanding we took more preachers into the travelling connection this year, than we lost out of it, I consider ourselves not as well supplied as we were before: for we had only taken in young preachers; and many of them that had located were old and successful labourers in the ministry, and were well qualified to guide the Lord's flock.[52]

More adjustments were necessary.

Table 10-3. Numerical Analysis of Traveling Preachers in the MEC between 1785 and 1800

Year	Total # of Itinerants*	Desist/ Withdrew	Located/ Supernumerated	Expelled	Died	Total Lost	Admitted on Trial	Difference
1785	104	3	0	1	2	6	14	8
1786	117	4	0	0	2	6	24	18
1787	133	2	0	0	1	3	18	15
1788	166	3	6	0	4	13	48	35
1789	196	1	1	0	5	7	43	36
1790	227	0	8	0	3	11	47	36
1791	250	2	9	0	4	15	50	35
1792	266	0	14	2	3	19	39	20
1793	269	4	18	1	2	25	44	19
1794	301	2	28	4	4	38	40	2
1795	313	3	32	0	5	40	45	5
1796	293	2	28	1	9	40	32	-8
1797	262	0	43	2	2	47	39	-8
1798†	267	1	16	0	3	20	24‡	4
1799	272	0	38	0	3	41	36	-5
1800	287	3	21§	0	4	29	41	12

Source: MEC, Minutes (1813).[53]

* Each year the *Minutes* list those who had located, desisted, withdrew, been expelled, and died. They also list the names of those admitted and the total number of traveling preachers. Due to other circumstances, the difference column and the total number of itinerants column cannot be reconciled.

† In October 1798, Asbury listed from memory the names of ten preachers that died. Of those, six died from the "malignant fever."[54] All of these names cannot be reconciled with the *Minutes*. It must be assumed that some are located preachers or itinerants who died in previous years.

‡ In this year and in some others, Lee has different numbers. His source is undetermined.

§ From 1798 through 1800, a person could switch from the supernumerated category to the location category or he could remain in the supernumerated status for successive years. Because of this, the numbers in the located/supernumerated column have been altered so no person is counted more than once. For the purposes of this table, a person should only be counted as a loss once unless he moves from location/supernumerary to full itinerancy and back to location/supernumerary. Thomas Morrell is an example of this. He was located in 1796, returned to the itinerancy in 1797, supernumerated in 1798, and then returned to itinerating.

The 1800 General Conference determined to make big changes. First, the General Conference removed the rule respecting presents to preachers. Preachers no longer had to account for gifts before receiving their pay. However, the marriage fee rule still applied. A motion to eliminate it failed. Next, it was argued that the salary of $64 was inadequate because of the inflation in the 1790s. Supporters contended that the rate of inflation had doubled since the time that the $64 salary rate was set. The ballot by the traveling elders to raise their salary to $80 only passed by five votes. For the itinerants, austerity became a badge of honor. Following this, the General Conference required each circuit to build a parsonage and to furnish it with heavy furniture. If a country circuit could not afford to buy land and build a parsonage, it had to rent a house when a married preacher was assigned to it.[55] Finally, the itinerants were authorized a 15 to 25 percent commission for all the books they sold on behalf of the Book Concern. All traveling preachers were required to carry and sell books. In actuality, they served as agents for the Book Concern. The cut represented their share of the profits, and it served as an incentive for them to sell more books.[56] Methodist literature helped to promote Methodism. For this reason, it was a win/win situation for the MEC.

The MEC wanted to win the nation. Organizationally, it was structured to do that. During this period, it attempted to have a substantial presence in every section of the country. However, to maintain the threefold evangelistic thrust of expanding the borders, sending missionaries to unreached areas, and dividing existing circuits, the MEC needed an abundance of traveling preachers. The MEC's system of growth was held hostage to the availability of deployable preachers. In 1796, Asbury wrote, "At present we have more work, than faithful workmen. We have a state or two out of 17 states and territories, that call for help, and we are not able to supply them and support it."[57]

Marriage was an enemy to the itinerancy because it located good preachers. However, the root problem was a lack of money. A preacher could not support a family on his salary. In 1805, upon receiving news of Coke's marriage, Asbury made his most famous comments about the effect of marriage on the itinerancy. "Marriage is honourable in all—but to me it is a ceremony awful as death. Well may it be so, when I calculate we have lost the travelling labours of two hundred of the best men in America, or the world, by marriage and consequent location."[58]

Asbury fought a desperate battle to keep the itinerants in effective ministry and to recruit new ones. That is why money was a critical issue to Asbury and to the MEC. They understood the critical relationship between wages, numbers of preachers, and numerical growth.

The Building of Chapels and Preaching Houses

Poverty also hurt the MEC because the church could not build or buy enough preaching houses and/or chapels to keep up with growth needs. In places where public opposition to Methodism existed, the lack of a preaching house or chapel hampered growth. In such a case, Methodists had to use a privately owned building like a barn, rent from another congregation, or use public accommodations like school houses or courtrooms. As Methodism struggled to get a foothold in New England, this issue became very ominous. In populated areas, a positive relationship existed between the building of preaching houses and the numerical growth of the MEC. Asbury knew this. For that reason, he made the building of preaching houses a main priority in the 1790s. This rationale is demonstrated by a quote from 1797. "The more [preaching] houses the more people; and the more preaching, and the more converted."[59] In the explanatory notes in the 1798 *Discipline*, the MEC moved away from an earlier emphasis on field preaching. It realized the necessity of chapels. "The preachers who are sent of God, must have a place to assemble their hearers, otherwise they can but seldom deliver their message. Little good will be done, if they have only the open air to preach in."[60]

The Political Scene

The Continental Congress adopted the Articles of Confederation in 1777. The states ratified them in 1781. The Articles united sovereign states in a common war effort and created a weak central government to accomplish essential tasks. During the revolution, 11 of the 13 colonies adopted state constitutions. All of them had strong legislatures and weak executive branches. Bills of rights and enlightenment ideals were written into many of the constitutions.[61]

Proposals to revise the Articles of Confederation began in 1786. In part, Shays' Rebellion caused some to believe that America needed a strong standing army. Delegates to a constitutional convention approved a basic draft in September 1787. Anti-Federalists demanded a national bill of rights. In 1789, James Madison produced one for consideration. Many proposed articles were rejected and others were redacted. Eventually, ten of them won approval and were added to the Constitution.

Proponents of ratification (Federalists) had their political base in big cities, seaports, New England, and the Tidewater plantations in the South. They included most of the rich and gentry classes, along with educated ministers, lawyers, editors, and craftsmen. Most favored England and a stratified society that gave the primary responsibility for ruling to the aristocrats and landed gentry. The Federalists also enjoyed popular support in the Ohio River area and along the southern frontier because the inhabitants wanted a strong army to protect them from Indian raids.

Opposition to ratification (Anti-Federalists) came from people in the South and rural areas where a large percent of Americans lived. According to Kagan, "The postwar hard times and depreciated currency hit small farmers and veterans the hardest: they were in no mood to approve a new central government with swarms of paid officials and tax collectors."[62]

Alexander Hamilton was the lead author of the Federalists Papers. John Jay and James Madison made substantial contributions. Madison made common cause with Hamilton because he wanted the Constitution to be ratified. However, they were not political allies.[63] The essays reached a large readership. They argued for a strong central government. In 1790, President Washington nominated Hamilton to become the Secretary of Treasury. For the next 10 years, the Federalists maintained control over the central government. However, Jefferson and other Anti-Federalists maintained a strong opposition during these years.

In 1791, Jefferson and Madison took to the streets to build support for Anti-Federalism. In a tour of New York and New England, they sounded out Anti-Federalist sentiments for the purpose of forming a national coalition. Aaron Burr's Anti-Federalist faction gained strength in New York and the surrounding region. They published the *National Gazette*. It featured the Hamilton and Jefferson's feud. Others entered into the fray. National sentiment sided with the Anti-Federalists. They formed themselves into the Democratic-Republican Party (Republican Party) as a response to Hamilton forming his movement into the Federalist Party. In the 1792 congressional elections, the Anti-Federalists gained 24 seats in the House of Representatives and became the majority party (cf. Table 10-4). However, they lost control of the house in the 1796 elections and did not regain control again until 1800.[64]

Table 10-4. Balance of Power in U.S. Congress from 1788 through 1806

House of Representatives										
	1788	1790	1792	1794	1796	1798	1800	1802	1804	1806
Federalist	37	39	51	47	57	60	38	39	25	24
Republican	28	30	54	59	49	46	65	103	116	118
Senate										
Federalist	18	16	16	21	22	22	15	9	7	6
Republican	8	13	14	11	10	10	17	25	17	28

Source: Kenneth C. Martisk, *The Historical Atlas of Political Parties in the United States Congress: 1789-1989* (New York: Macmillan, 1989).
Note: the numbers are estimates before 1796 because many members had not declared a political affiliation. The House membership is a better bellwether of the American sentiment than the senate because members have to be re-elected every two years.

The French Revolution widened the gap between the Federalists and their antagonists. Hamilton's sympathies rested with Great Britain. Jefferson favored the democratic and religious idealism of France. By the end of the year, Washington sided with Hamilton and favored the British in the war and in trade. As such, he sought more advice from Hamilton than Jefferson, his Secretary of State. Consequently, Jefferson resigned from the cabinet. In 1795, Washington reorganized his Cabinet to include only Federalists.[65] In that year, Hamilton resigned from the cabinet so he could make more money by practicing law.

The election of 1796 was the first contested election for president. It showed that the country was split along regional lines. The traditional South, the frontier, and Pennsylvania voted for Jefferson and Republican candidates. New England, the Mid-Atlantic States, and Maryland voted for John Adams and the Federalists. The vice president, Adams, won that election. He received 71 electoral votes. Jefferson received 68 votes.

In order to protect America from French influence or subversion, the Federalists passed two controversial laws in 1798. The Sedition Act made it illegal to criticize a government official. The Alien Act authorized the deportation of "dangerous" people.[66] A dangerous person could be someone who espoused politically incorrect views. Twenty-five Republicans were tried and ten were convicted for political rhetoric. The Republicans blasted this legislation as unconstitutional, despotic, and un-American. In fact, Jefferson and Madison secretly advocated a theory called nullification. By means of it, states could nullify unconstitutional laws. The proposal never gained traction with the states. Still, the American public sided with the Republicans. In the 1800 election, New York voted with the South, and Maryland split its vote. The Republicans won a landslide victory and received a national mandate.[67]

The Hamilton and Jefferson Debate

Hamilton and the federalism espoused the following six principles that favored the industrial cause of the North: (1) a balanced and diversified economic order; (2) active governmental encouragement of finances, industry, commerce and shipping; (3) sympathy for creditor interests; (4) advocacy of a strong national government under executive leadership; (5) distrust of the people's capacity to govern; and (6) a belief that the best government was that of an elite.[68]

The undergirding ideology of the Federalists shows that they favored a plutocracy. In some sense, they held the common person in contempt. They advocated a modified social stratification in which wealth and property determined status and worth. Barclay sums it up well.

> Hamilton believed in an intimate and necessary connection between property and liberty. He frankly declared the rule of property to be not only inevitable but desirable. By nature and choice an aristocrat, he deliberately sought to ally government with wealth. Give, he contended, to the rich and the wellborn the ruling hand and all will be well with the nation. "The people are turbulent and changing; they seldom judge or determine right. . . . The people!—the people is a great beast!" The principle of exploitation is not to be condemned, but defended. The increase of national wealth accrued by levying toll upon the weak and the helpless is to be accepted and contemplated with satisfaction.[69]

Jefferson and Anti-Federalism reflected the philosophy of the Enlightenment. They were heavily influenced by French ideals. They embraced the following seven following principles: (1) a democratic agrarian order based on the individual freeholder; (2) a broad diffusion of wealth; (3) relative freedom from industrialism, urbanism, and organized finance; (4) sympathy for debtor interests; (5) distrust of centralized government; (6) belief in the perfectibility of humankind; and (7) confidence in the view that the people, acting through representative institutions, could be left to govern themselves.[70]

Anti-Federalists sympathized with the common people. Barclay sates, "It was for these people that Jefferson wrote the Declaration of Independence and introduced his great reforms abolishing entail and primogeniture, establishing freedom of religion, and inaugurating his comprehensive plans for [general education].”[71] Anti-Federalists fought for a limited federal government. At the same time, Federalists wanted to expand the role and power of the federal government. This led to sectional disputes.

In 1790, Hamilton proposed that the federal government should assume the debts incurred by the states during the Revolutionary War. New England states favored this proposal because they had large debts. Southern states strongly resisted the plan because they had paid their debts or had made arrangements to pay them. They also feared that Hamilton's proposal was another attempt to take power away from the states. According to Morris, "The Virginians protested that the assumption schemes established and perpetuated a moneyed interest, subordinated agriculture to commercial interests, and was inimical to republican institutions and the federal form of government and that they could 'find no clause in the constitution authorizing Congress to assume the debts of the states!'"[72]

As a compromise, the South agreed to the "assumption of debts" and the North agreed to establish the national Capital along the Potomac River in the heart of the South as it existed at that time.

In 1791, Hamilton's report on the proposed national bank offers another example of the disparity between the Federalists and Anti-Federalists. Jefferson reported to Washington that the concept was not constitutional. As a strict constructionist, he championed states' rights. He argued that the Constitution did not give the federal government the power to incorporate a central bank. Hamilton's response elaborated the doctrine of "implied powers." He became the father of "loose constructionists." He contended that, "The proposed bank was related to the Congressional power to collect taxes and regulate trade: a delegated power implied the employment of such means as were proper for its execution."[73] Washington favored Hamilton in the debate.

Following this, Hamilton recommended a stiff tax on the manufacture of distilled liquors. This imposed a heavy burden on frontier farmers. For them, distilling provided a profitable way to dispose of excess grain because difficulties hindered the shipment of grain from the frontier to the East Coast. The tax caused much debate in the South and on the frontier. Western Pennsylvanian counties and North Carolina united to produce a series of resolutions denouncing the tax. Citizens promised to oppose its enforcement. Washington declared that he would enforce it. From July 1794 to May 1795, the "Whisky Insurrection" ensued in the Pennsylvania back country. Washington ordered the people to return to their homes. Finally, he sent 15,000 troops to negotiate. When negotiations failed, he ordered the military to force the issue. The federal troops put down the insurrection. Hamilton was present for the fight. This disagreement is one of the reasons that Pennsylvania voted with the South in the 1796 elections. In 1799, there was another uprising in western Pennsylvania over a personal property tax issue.

Because of its emphasis on holiness, the Methodist leadership did not favor cheap liquor. Still, it appreciated the plight of the poor farmers. Methodism did not push prohibition until the 1840s when it joined with others in the temperance movement. Asbury's attitude toward alcohol presaged later conflicts. In 1795, Asbury and his traveling companions lectured a member about his distillery and the consequences of his actions. He opined that alcohol corrupts the family, the neighborhood, and the society.[74] While traveling through the North Carolina backcountry, he lamented, "This country improves in . . . stills, a prophet of strong drink would be acceptable to many of these people. I believe that the Methodist preachers keep clear, both by precept and example; would to God the members did so too."[75]

In sum, national political debates were played out in EAM. Methodism was a national church that existed in each of the regions. Largely, it pulled members from the Anti-Federalist class. Still, many of its prominent preachers, to include Asbury, espoused Federalist sympathies. The slavery debate clearly indicates that the membership from the various regions did not agree with each other. The next chapter will show how the institutional disputes reflected the national debate and affected membership in the regions.

CHAPTER ELEVEN

REVIVALS AND DECLINE IN SOUTHERN METHODISM FROM 1786 THROUGH 1800

The southern states show nearly identical membership patterns for 1786 through 1800. As an aggregate, the membership grew from 1785 to 1791, plateaued from 1791 through 1793, declined from 1794 through 1796, and stabilized from 1797 through 1799. From 1800 forward, membership grew rapidly. Due to the severity of the membership declines in the 1790s, the combined southern membership did not surpass the 1792 membership high until 1803.

Southern Methodism from 1786 through 1792

According to Table 11-1, southern Methodism experienced a numerical increase of 31,019 from 1786 to 1790. Membership grew in Maryland by 9,367, in Virginia by 12,088, in North Carolina by 4,528, in South Carolina by 2,820, and in Georgia by 2,266.

Table 11-1. Membership of Southern States between 1786 and 1793

	1786	1787	1788	1789	1790	1791	1792	1793
Maryland	6040	7735	9951	11127	15407	15281	15552	15193
Virginia	4434	6431	11642	15609	16522	17289	17709	17541
North Carolina	4275	5061	5615	7662	8803	9737	10458	10063
South Carolina	638	1766	2470	2784	3458	4650	4397	4457
Georgia	78	450	1227	2011	2294	2250	2086	2151
Totals	15465	21443	30905	39193	46484	49207	50202	49405

Source: MEC, Minutes (1813).

According to Table 11-2, the number of southern circuits increased by 29 from 1786 to 1790. That equals one new circuit for every 1,070 new members. The number of southern itinerants increased from 90 to 166. That equals one new itinerant for every 408 new members. The optimal growth ratio for EAM was one circuit to two preachers to 500 members. The southern ratio during this period was one circuit to 2.5 itinerants to 1000 members. In order to match the optimal growth ratio from the perspective of membership, southern Methodism needed to add 60 new circuits and 120 itinerants from 1786 to 1790. Whenever EAM could not expand the number of circuits and preachers to assimilate, supervise, and disciple large numbers of new members, a numerical loss ensued or the quality of the program diminished.

Table 11-2. Number of Circuits in Southern States between 1786 and 1793

	1786	1787	1788	1789	1790	1791	1792	1793
Maryland	10	10	11	14	16	17	20	20
Virginia	10	12	16	19	22	28	28	31
North Carolina	11	12	12	13	13	17	18	18
South Carolina	4	5	8	9	10	13	12	11
Georgia	1	1	3	4	4	4	6	5
Totals	36	40	50	59	65	79	84	85

Source: MEC, Minutes (1813).

Figure 11-1 shows that the national ratio between circuits, itinerants, and members remained within the ration of 1 circuit to 2 itinerants to 500 members. This happened because the MEC expanded into New England and the Frontier with circuits and itinerants. Those areas had more circuits and preachers than the membership required. From a strategic perspective, the MEC extended its infrastructure in order to grow membership in new areas. Ultimately, this paid big dividends. However, the missionary outreach of the MEC inadvertently compromised southern Methodism's ability to assimilate its numerical growth because it redirected vital institutional resources needed to sustain and increase the southern harvest. Large circuits required the focused attention of one to two itinerants. As such, the missionary thrust that propelled the MEC into new areas may have contributed to the Southern decline following 1792. However, for reasons that will be discussed, that point cannot be argued with certitude.

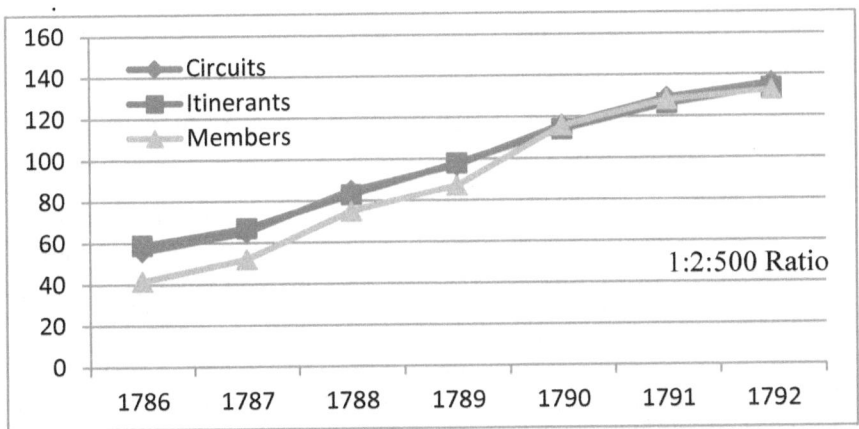

Figure 11-1. Number of Circuits, Circuit Riders, and Members for the MEC between 1786 and 1792.

Figure 11-2 graphically depicts the growth rate of southern Methodism from 1786 through 1790. It shows that Virginia Methodism grew at the fastest rate. Virginia Methodism slowed in 1789. In that year, Maryland Methodism surged.

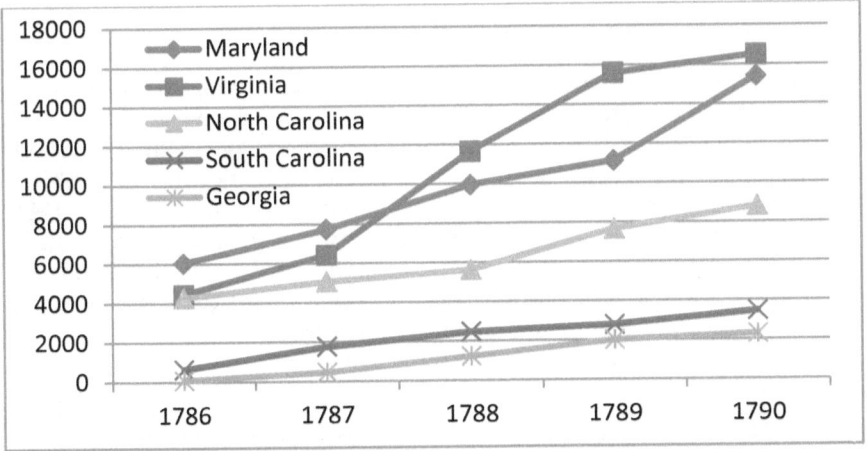

Figure 11-2. Line-graphs of Methodist Membership in Southern States between 1786 and 1790.

Southern Revivals

As was previously noted, the Methodist work in southern Virginia and North Carolina grew out of the 1775 revival. That revival raged until the war displaced it. In 1787, a second revival submerged the area under the rising tide of God's numinous presence. People remembered the first revival and made comparisons to it. Also, many of the itinerants who worked the South in 1787 came out of the first revival and were transformed by their participation in it. Additionally, migrating local preachers, class leaders, and run-of-the-mill laity who had participated in the 1775 revival carried the experience and revival expectation to other areas of the South and Frontier. Those who had been touched by the revival hungered for a new outpouring. The hunger became contagious as they told stories and shared testimonies.

The 1775 and 1787 revivals taught the MEC to expect revivals. In turn, expectation turned to "do those things that make for revivals." During the period of southern decline in the 1790s, leaders tried to manufacture revivals by encouraging prayer meetings and other activities associated with them. After revival rain returned to the parched soil of southern Methodism in 1800, the southern church regularized revivals and purposely promoted them. Lee's firsthand description of the various revivals shows how the MEC used the phenomenon of revival to increase its membership. Lee argues for a direct correlation between revival and church growth.

One could argue that the 1775 revival was the spiritual mother that gave birth to other revivals that dominated EAM. In time, revivals reshaped the character of American Methodism, popularized evangelism, gave birth to new movements, and helped to form American Evangelicalism.

The Virginia Revival of 1787

When the old revival area in southern Virginia received another blessing in 1787, membership skyrocketed. Asbury claimed that the revival added 1,400 members to the Sussex circuits and more in the Brunswick circuit. The revival included whites and blacks.[1] In 1787, Brunswick and Sussex had a combined membership of 1,055. The next year the membership jumped to 3,215. In 1789, the Sussex circuit divided and formed the Surry circuit. Before dividing, it had a membership of 1,806. More than 500 of the members were black.[2] During the revival years, Virginia Methodism added 19 circuits. Some came from dividing old circuits. Others came from expanding into new areas.

The following excerpts from Lee describe the revival:

> The greatest revival was in the south parts of Virginia, which began in July [1787], and continued to prosper throughout the year. . . . Prayer meetings were frequently held both in the town and the country, souls were frequently converted at those meetings, even when there was no preacher present; for the prayers and exhortations of the members were greatly owned.[3]

> The most remarkable work was in Sussex, and Brunswick circuits, where the meetings would frequently continue for five or six hours together, and some all night. . . . At one quarterly meeting . . . in Brunswick circuit . . . some hundreds were awakened; and it was supposed that above one hundred souls were converted at that meeting. . . . The next quarterly meeting . . . in Sussex . . . was favored with more divine presence than any other that had been known before. . . . Before the preachers came together, many of the young converts, had come together, and uniting with christians [sic] in singing and praying, the heavenly fire had began

[*sic*] to kindle.... By the time the preachers came within half a mile of the chapel, they heard the people shouting and praising God.[4]

While the society was collected in the house, some of the preachers went into the woods to preach, and while they were preaching the power of the Lord was felt among the people in such a manner, that they roared and screamed so loud that the preacher could not be heard, and was compelled to stop. Many scores of both white and black people fell to the earth.... Many of the wealthy people fell to the earth; and some lay in the deepest distress until evening. Many of these people who were happily converted, left their houses and came to the meeting with great opposition to the work of God; but were struck down in an unexpected manner, and converted in a few hours.[5]

It was thought, that in the course of that summer, there were as many as sixteen hundred souls converted in Sussex circuit; in Brunswick circuit eighteen hundred; and in Amelia circuit about eight hundred. In these three circuits we had the greatest revival of religion; but in many other circuits there was a gracious work and hundreds were brought to God in the course of the year.[6]

Sussex, Brunswick, and Amelia were ground zero for the previous revival. One wonders why this area was so receptive to the outpourings of God. History shows that certain locations tend to attract revival. For example, Asbury University in Wilmore, Kentucky has experienced eight revivals dating back to 1905. Perhaps it relates to expectations. When people live in an area in which there has been revival saturation, they learn about it and are taught to desire it. This makes them open to it. As was noted before, revival veterans sow the seeds for revival. Revivals are contagious events.

The Maryland Revival

From 1786 to 1790, the MEC did not organize any new circuits in the Eastern Shore. Even still, its membership increased from 3,266 to 4,622. In 1789 and 1790, tremendous growth also happened in the Baltimore area. The exceptional growth gave birth to seven new circuits. Membership in the Baltimore area grew from 766 to 5,578 in a five-year period.

The membership growth in the Eastern Shore and Baltimore areas came as a result of revival. At first, over 300 came to Christ. As the excitement grew, the preachers desired to expand the blessing to the community. Since they did not have access to the majority of the population on Sunday mornings, they held open services on Sunday afternoon. This innovation met with great success. According to Lee,

The work of God greatly increased in Baltimore town in the course of the summer 1788, owing to a plan that was adopted, of preaching on the common, or in the Market-house on Howard's-hill, every Sunday in the afternoon, after the public service was ended in all the churches. By this means we had thousands to hear us, who did not usually attend our meetings. Many persons had been converted in town before the conference came on in September.[7]

The evangelistic pleading of the preachers and the testimonies of the redeemed also raised the level of expectation in the town. In this way, the open air preaching prepared the people for revival. The revival took off at the Baltimore conference meeting in September. It produced external manifestations of God's presence. Many fell to the ground, loss use of their limbs, shouted for mercy, and cried for joy. Such external manifestations were commonly associated with the southern revivals. All night prayer meetings continued. People spread the word, and invited friends and relatives. Throngs received grace and professed faith. After the conference, the Methodists returned to the open air preaching with more success. As a result, the 1788 outpouring continued for a long time.

Asbury described his experience while at the revival the following September in 1789:

> Preached in the town and at the [Fell's] Point. The last quarterly meeting was a wonder-working time: fifty or sixty souls . . . appeared to be brought to God; people were daily praying from house to house; some crying for mercy, others rejoicing in God, and not a few, day after day, joining in society for the benefit of religious fellowship. . . . Many of the children of the Methodists are the happy subjects of this glorious revival. We have more members in Baltimore (town and Point) than in any city or town on the continent.[8]

The 1787 through 1789 revival did not exist as a continuous activity. Rather, it had highs and lows. It would begin in one spot and soar for a few weeks. When the flame burned low, it would pick-up in another location. At times, the 1789 revival in Maryland took on the character of a generalized revival. A generalized revival burns in all the areas at the same time. Asbury claimed that the 1800 revival was generalized.[9] According to Lee,

> About ten in the morning, a company of mourners assembled at a private house, where the work of conversion began. First one, and then another, entered into the liberty of the children of God. The news spread; the people collected till the house and street were filled with a crown of believers, and a wondering multitude: and this continued without intermission till night. They them repaired to the church which was presently filled, they continued there until two o'clock the next morning. . . . At the same time the country circuits throughout Maryland, seemed to flame with holy love. On the Eastern Shore there was a powerful work; hundreds in different parts were turning to God.[10]

From 1787 through 1790, revivals added large numbers of people to the church. Whether the revivals came as an act of God, were psycho-social phenomena, or were manufactured by the church, matters not. They were used by the MEC in the South to bring sinners to faith and to increase its membership. In fact, they became a defining characteristic of the southern church.

Revival Returns

During a long hiatus in the 1790s, southern Methodism did not experience any revivals. Asbury bemoaned the spiritual dryness of the people. Even when he earnestly entreated the circuits to establish prayer meetings as a means to sow seeds for revival, he lamented that the spirit of prayer was not among the people.[11] In 1800, the revival rains returned to the South. The showers started as a sprinkle and turned into a torrent. The storm began at the 1800 General Conference in Baltimore. Lee describes it.

> The revival of religion which took place in Baltimore during conference, began particularly in Old Town, where the people held meeting in a private house. . . . The work then began to spread, and souls were converted in the different meeting-houses, and in different private houses, both by day and by night. The old christians [sic] were wonderfully stirred up to cry to God more earnestly, and the preachers that tarried in town for a few days were all on fire of love. Such a time of refreshing from the presence of the Lord had not been felt in that town for some years.[12]

Two weeks later, the revival intensified at the Duck Creek Conference:

> [It] had such an effect on the inhabitants, that 117 persons, in and about that little village, joined our society in the course of a few days. . . . In all our societies in that neighborhood, there was a considerable ingathering of precious souls. . . . From that time and place, the heavenly flame spread through the Eastern Shore of Maryland, and the lower counties of the Delaware state, in an uncommon manner. The preachers and people carried the fire of love with them to their different circuits, and places of abode. Thousands of people will have cause to bless God for that conference.[13]

Lee filled up three pages describing all the different places that experienced revival in 1800. Asbury shared Lee's exuberance regarding the Maryland portion of the outpouring.

> Brother George Roberts wrote that they are a thousand strong in Baltimore. That there hath been a work in Annapolis is certain: indeed it begins to be more and more general in the towns, and in the country. . . . God hath begun to pour out his Spirit; and almost generally through Montgomery and Frederick circuits. . . . Some hundreds in three months have been under awakenings and conversions, upon the western shore, District of Maryland. . . . Perhaps six hundred souls, in this district and in Baltimore, have been converted since General Conference. Hartford, Baltimore, Calvert, Federal, Montgomery, and Frederick feel the flame. . . . My soul hath been agonizing for a revival upon the western shore of Maryland for many years, and now the Lord hath sent it.[14]

Asbury referred to the southern revivals as "our Pentecost." The term harkens back to Acts 2 and associates the revival with the outpouring of the Holy Spirit. According to Asbury, revival hotspots existed all over the South in 1800.

> Surely we may say our Pentecost is fully come this year, when we recollect what God hath wrought in Edisto in South, and Guilford in North Carolina; Franklin, Amelia, and Glouster, in Virginia; in Baltimore, and Cecil, in Maryland; in Dover, Duck Creek, and Milford, in Delaware![15]

When Asbury traveled to Virginia to conduct the conference, people expected great things. They were so excited that they gathered around Asbury's carriage as if he "had a cake and cider cart."[16] God did not disappoint the hungry souls. At the same time, revival surfaced on the Frontier in the form of the camp meeting. Of a particular meeting at Drake's Creek meeting house, Asbury says,

> Methodists and Presbyterians united their labours and mingled with the childlike simplicity of primitive times. Fires blazing here and there dispelled the darkness and the shouts of the redeemed captives, and the cries of precious souls struggling into life, broke the silence of midnight. . . . Mercy flowed in abundant streams of salvation to the perishing sinners.[17]

The membership summaries confirm the positive relationship between revival and church growth. From 1799 to 1804, the combined membership of Maryland and Virginia increase from 24,479 to 41,763. On the Frontier, the combined membership of Kentucky and Tennessee increased from 2,269 to 6,554. The 1775 and 1788 revivals produced a similar growth spurt. Even though all the growth cannot be attributed to revival and the things associated with revival, much of it can be.

Southern decline from 1792 through 1799

Before the advent of camp meetings and the 1800 revival, Methodism had found a meager harvest from 1793 through 1799. The period was associated with numerical decline, institutional turmoil, French idealism, economic growth, migration, a general unconcern for the things of God, and a striking lack of revivals. According to Table 11-3, the total number of circuits did not decline until 1794. As such, the membership decline preceded the decline in the number of circuits.[18] Consequently, the membership decline did not happen because the MEC stopped starting new works in the South or because it closed existing works. On the contrary, despite membership decreases and a shortage of preachers, the MEC continued to assign preachers to new circuits in the South. For example, between 1793 and 1798, Virginia Methodism started seven new circuits that posted returns for at least two consecutive years. Many others were attempted. In the same period, Virginia membership decreased by 4,778. Additionally, during the South Carolina conference in 1796, the preachers agreed to send two of their itinerants as missionaries to Savannah and the "ancient parts of Georgia." Georgia circuits decline because of a defection and the establishment of alternative Methodist churches that sucked people away from the MEC.

Table 11-3. Number of Circuits in Southern States between 1792 and 1799

	1792	1793	1794	1795	1796	1797	1798	1799
Maryland	20	20	19	18	16	18	18	17
Virginia	28	31	32	25	25	21	20	20
North Carolina	18	18	17	18	18	19	16	16
South Carolina	12	11	13	11	10	11	10	10
Georgia	6	5	3	3	3	2	2	4
Totals	84	85	84	75	72	71	66	67

Source: MEC, *Minutes* (1813).

Asbury appointed 168 preachers to the South in 1792, 198 in 1795, and 132 in 1799. Even though the membership decreased between 1792 and 1795, the number of appointed preachers increased. Finally, the reality of decline required Asbury to cut back on the number of appointed itinerants. As a consequence, after 1795, many of the circuits that had multiple preachers assigned to them in previous years only received one itinerant.[19] Most established circuits had two preachers before the decline. Larger ones had three.

Starting in 1793, some circuits received a "to be supplied" designation. Typically, local preachers worked those circuits. Fortunately, southern Methodism had an abundance of local preachers who tended to circuits, societies, and chapels in the absence of the itinerants.[20] Also, in 1794, four presiding elders received appointments to circuits. The 1798 *Discipline* acknowledges that many argued against the office of presiding elder because it kept an experienced itinerant from serving in a local circuit.[21] Of course, presiding elders traveled their districts and preached constantly. They also mentored junior preachers and solved problems.

Even though an acute shortage of traveling preachers in the 1790s prevented the MEC from filling some circuits, nationally, the number of traveling preacher grew by 147 from 1788-1795. It was not until 1796 that the total number of itinerants declined. Since Asbury sent itinerants from the center to the circumference and in any other direction he deemed necessary, a decline in the number of traveling preachers in one region affected every region because the regions shared preachers.[22] As such, the southern malaise adversely affected all the regions.

In sum, this chapter shows that revival spurred numerical growth. It also shows that revival growth cannot be sustained when the number of itinerants and circuits do not increase in a proportional manner. Methodist converts had to be discipled or they fell away. The Methodist system of classes, bands, and societies was perfectly structured to turn awakened people into discipled Methodists. When the itinerants could not build the infrastructure, decline ensued. However, the southern decline in the 1790s cannot be solely attributed to the lack of revivals or the failure to build the infrastructure. Others contextual and institutional factors contributed to it.

CHAPTER TWELVE

REPUBLICANISM AND THE REJECTION OF WESLEY

The French Revolution began in 1789. From its inception, it pitted the people against the nobility and the church. Anticlericalism went to its core. During the "de-Christianization" campaign from 1793-1794, churches were closed and clergy were forced to abdicate. The animosity against the church was intensified because most clergy sided with the king. More than 2,000 priests died by violent means.

The escalation of French radicalism coincided with the emergence of the Jacobins in 1792. In America, Jacobins were people who supported the French Revolution. The Federalists labeled Jefferson and those who collaborated with him as the Jacobin Party. The Jacobin rhetoric became most intense in the election of 1798. Jefferson was not a friend of the church. He pushed for disestablishment, was a rational deist, and did not favor experiential religion.

The popularization of republicanism with its admiration of French ideology adversely influenced Methodist membership in the South for several reasons. First, it made parts of the South unreceptive to the preaching of an evangelical Christianity that focused on personal sin and the need for personal salvation. Anti-Federalism believed in the perfectibility of humankind and it was very optimistic about human nature. Its deistic leaders were humanistic. Second, in the guise of rational humanism, Anti-Federalist leaders believed that religion should serve a functional purpose defined in terms of personal morality and the improvement of society. Dogmatic debates and church allegiance were of little concern to them. People who espoused humanistic ideology were unlikely to embrace Methodism or any evangelical faith. Third, French republicanism and Anti-Federalism eschewed old world monarchies and the institutions that supported them. They believed in the equality of all people and sought to destroy institutional structures that valued or elevated one class of people above another. State religion was of particular concern.

Generally, the masses favored the democratic gospel of the MEC preachers (free grace and free will) and the Methodist worship experience that allowed for individual expression. However, many of the same people disliked Methodism's ecclesiastical structure because it reflected Federalists ideals. The MEC's organization minimized the democratic participation of the people and reinforced an exclusive and arbitrary institutional organization. The episcopacy and rigid itinerancy exemplify this. Hierarchy was written all over the MEC. This made EAM vulnerable to critics who espoused republicanism. The detractors of Methodism were very good at casting their criticisms in organizational and structural terms. The internal debates and large scale defections within the MEC reflect this reality. Additionally, the bad publicity associated with these debates pushed many would-be converts away from Methodism.

The following section provides background material that describes the origins and influence of Anti-Federalism and French republicanism in the South during the 1790s. These fall under the category of regional contextual factors.

French Republicanism and Anti-Federalism in the South

The fathers of "Republicanism" in Virginia (Thomas Jefferson, James Madison, Patrick Henry, and George Mason) were also strong proponents of deism and admirers of the French Revolution.[1] These statesmen were affected by the French Revolution in 1789, and adopted its value system.[2] They supported Thomas Paine and the new French Republic. According to J. Edwin Orr, "Thomas Jefferson, father of the American republic, lent much aid to the rapid spread of rationalistic deism in the newly independent United States."[3] He opposed organized religion and remained bitterly anticlerical. His personal correspondence shows him to be a strong Deist. Jefferson demonstrated his commitment to deistic values when he wrote Article 16 of the Virginia constitution. It reads, "Religion, or the duty which we owe our creator [sic], and the manner of discharging it, can be directed only by reason, and conviction, not by force or violence; and therefore, all men are equally entitled to the free exercise of religion according to the dictates of conscience."[4] True to his values, Jefferson pushed for disestablishment of the Anglican Church, championed individual rights with equal protection, encourage universal suffrage for men (slaves excluded), and advocated for republicanism. As evidenced by voting patterns, much of his sentiment was shared by the common people in the South, the very people with whom the MEC attempted to align itself.

However, many of the wealthy people in the South, especially those on large slave plantations and those along the coast, were sympathetic to federalism and Great Britain. They enjoyed the benefits of a ranked society that gave them special privilege. The implications of Anti-Federalism and the French Revolution frightened them.[5] Also, they feared that France would seed a slave revolt in the South.

According to Barclay, at times, republican idealism and Anti-Federalism were merged so that they were indistinguishable to the average person.

> [The French Revolution] popularized the ideal of democratic government and provided a body of philosophy for those who had been instinctively sympathetic with the largely unformulated democratic ideals of the new nation. It supplied the masses with effective slogans in support of democracy. But unfortunately the association of atheism with the French Revolution gave the enemies of political democracy and social equality in America a powerful weapon. Federalists charged that the word "Republican" was synonymous with atheism. . . . As a result a strong *odium theologicum* became attached to the advocacy of democratic principles—an explanation, at least in part, of the estimates of wide prevalence of atheism preceding the close of the eighteenth century.[6]

The connection between the rise of republican values and the decline of Christianity was not unfounded. J. Edwin Orr analyzed the history of this period. According to him, it was a dark season for Christianity. French influence, deism, practical atheism, and the Enlightenment were the main culprits.[7] He wrote,

> But there was also the blistering Tom Paine, champion of American independence and French revolution, proposing rationalistic deism as the proper doctrine of emerging democracies. Paine's writings were immensely popular and masses of restless people took hold of his ideas and abandoned orthodox Christianity.[8]

Before the XYZ Affair in 1797-1798, Jefferson and his colleagues favored a close diplomatic relationship with France and the cancellation of the favorable trade treaty with England. They believed that English monarchialism would be the downfall of America. Also, as has been shown, they distrusted organized religion and were inimical to evangelical Christianity. Their sentiment was a very powerful force in the South and on the frontier in the 1790s. The ubiquitous common press trumpeted it. As such, the ideals of "republicanism" were widespread and widely accepted in those parts before 1798.[9]

During the period following the Revolutionary War to 1798, people in the South and on the frontier felt great appreciation for the French because of their support in the war against Great Britain. The latter years of the war were fought in the South. America would not have defeated the British without the heroic efforts for the French Navy and General Lafayette. As evidence of their admiration, many newly incorporated municipalities were given French names. For example, 33 cities in South Carolina end in "ville." Without counting cities with a French suffix, sixty southern municipalities in Georgia, South Carolina, North Carolina, and Virginia bear French names. Most were named during this period. Lafayette, Fayette, or Fayetteville are the most common French names.

Since large portions of the southern frontier were being settled at this time, many municipalities were given French names. For example, Nashborough, Tennessee became Nashville in 1784 and Hopewell, Kentucky was renamed Paris in 1790.[10] Versailles, Kentucky was named in honor of the French in 1792. On a 1783-1803 map of Kentucky and Tennessee, 13 localities have the French suffix "ville." By contrast, only eight localities end with "town," "boro," "burg," or "borough."[11] Most were named during the period of French romance. A 1794 county map of Kentucky lists Bourbon, Fayette, and Mercer (from *mercier*) counties. Bourbon and Mercer were named in 1792. Fayette was named after Lafayette. By contrast, an 1818 county map of Kentucky shows 47 new counties that were established since 1803. None were given French names or French suffixes.[12] This can be explained. After the XYZ Affair went public, people in the South and the frontier stopped giving their cities and their children French names. This fact shows the drastic change in sentiment toward the French.

Contextual Factors at Work in South Carolina

The history of South Carolina during this period illustrates the influence of French ideology and Anti-Federalism in the public arena. Even though the following historical sketch is specific to South Carolina, the storyline is very similar to the rest of the South; that is, the specifics are different but the themes are the same. For that reason, it serves as a good case study.

When the state convention met in 1790, the state capital had been moved to Columbia from Charleston. This was done to give the common people more ownership of the government. The wealthy, landed gentry, and slaves were concentrated along the coastal regions. The masses of white people populated the central and western regions of the state. They argued that the state capital should be central to the people and not in the pocket of the aristocrats. Government was for the people, of the people, and by the people.

The 1790 convention was called, "in order to strengthen the principles of republicanism enjoined on the Legislature as soon as might be convenient, 'to pass laws for the abolition of the rights of primogeniture, and for giving and equitable distribution of the real estate of intestates.'"[13] According to *Ramsay's History of South Carolina*,

> In old countries where the feudal system had long prevailed, the entailing of real estate on the eldest males in succession, was a common practice; this was transferred from Europe to America while the colonies were British provinces, and was by many thought an useful appendage to royal government, as favoring the distinction of ranks in society. To republicanize the rising generation, the convention of the people of South Carolina made it the duty of the constituted authorities to do away this accompaniment of royalty as far as was compatible with liberty. . . . The aristocracy which had attached itself to some of the old families in Carolina, received a check.[14]

At the same convention, the state also disestablished the Episcopal Church. Both were key provisions in the Anti-Federalist platform and stated goals of Jefferson.

In 1793, Charleston celebrated Bastille Day with a great parade and pageantry. In France, the celebration commemorated the storming of the Bastille on July 14, 1789. It was a symbol of the French Revolution. During the original celebration in 1790, people went naked through Paris as a way to demonstrate their complete freedom. In South Carolina, the people enthusiastically welcomed Citizen Genet, the first minister from Republican France. Because of its great admiration of all things French, South Carolina opened its ports to French privateers and allowed them to arm and equip within its borders. This was in violation America's policy of neutrality.[15]

Additionally, Jacobinism influenced many of the young men in Charleston. As the Pitt Statue was being moved in 1794, its head fell off. This received publicity and was said to be an ominous sign for the aristocrats. This was taken as a veiled threat and deepened the animosity and distrust between the rich and the other classes.[16] According to Robert Molloy's history of Charleston:

> And even while the enthusiasts had been crying up the French Revolution and denouncing the upper classes, they had welcomed the [French] refugees from Santo Domingo [Haiti], some five hundred of whom, in 1792 arrived in [Charleston] after fleeing the [slave revolt] in the island. The Santo Dominicans, added to the Huguenots, could not but have deepened the French tinge of the town's culture.[17]

Thus, the contextual context of South Carolina reflected the spirit of humanism, French Republicanism, and Anti-Federalism. These philosophical underpinnings diminished the MEC because of its hierarchical structures, its association with Wesley, and its advocacy for the emancipation of slaves.

The Rejection of the MEC in Charleston

As one who spent much time in Charleston during this period, Asbury's observations are invaluable. His remarks and the membership statistics indicate that the white male population of Charleston rejected Methodism. Some tried to intimidate the Methodist preachers and those who aligned with them. The mockery and animosity of the detractors reflected the attitude of the Jacobins in France. Furthermore, their acrimonious actions mirrored the attitudes that were associated with Thomas Paine and French idealists throughout the South. Asbury's commentary elaborates the situation and shows the connection between it and membership.

> While another was speaking in the morning to a very crowded house, and many outside, a man made a riot at the door; an alarm at once took place; the ladies leaped out at the windows of the church, and a dreadful confusion ensued. Again whilst I was speaking at night, a stone was thrown against the north side of the church; then another on the south; a third came through the pulpit window, and struck near me inside the pulpit.[18]

The year 1795 was particularly bad for Methodists in Charleston. Asbury wrote, "One young man behaved amiss, for which I removed him: perhaps he might be among those in the evening who made a riot, broke the windows, and beat open the doors."[19] Did this man come to the service to disrupt it? Most likely he did. Afterward, the bishop was verbally abused. "I was insulted on the pavement with some as horrible sayings as could come out of a creature's month on this side of hell. When I pray in my room, . . . those who walk the street will shout at me."[20] Two years later Asbury still felt the sting of Charleston's irreverent ire: "No justice for Cumberland Street Methodists. A young Scot shouted in the church, and after he was taken out of the house struck three or four men: no bill was found against him; and we are insulted every night by candlelight."[21] Persecution and intimidation were a part of life for Methodist preachers in Charleston. Asbury states, "I lament the wickedness of this city, and their great hatred against us."[22] Also, "In Charleston, I doubt that I had seventy white hearers because the vast number in the city do not attend to the worship of God anywhere."[23] From this one could intuit that the people did not abandon the MEC and go to other churches. Rather, they became unchurched in keeping with the sentiments of the time.

Asbury confirms that the white male population in Charleston disassociated itself from the MEC.

> The white and worldly people are intolerably ignorant of God; playing, dancing, swearing, racing; these are their common practices and pursuits. Our few male members do not attend preaching; and I fear there is hardly one who walks with God: the woman and Africans attend our meetings, and some few strangers also.[24]

The white population's rejection of all things spiritual greatly grieved Asbury. "The city now appears to be running mad for races, plays, and balls. . . . I have thought if we had entered here to preach only to the Africans, we should probably have done better."[25] Because of the opposition to the MEC, in 1797, Asbury determined that the MEC was not sent to the white people in Charleston.[26] During these years, the white membership in Charleston never reached 75. The slave membership reached 420.

The Changing Tide

In 1792, the French and the British were at war. The British had attempted to enact a naval blockade. The British did not want the French Revolution to spread. At the same time, the British were seizing neutral American ships and impressing their crews. This act of aggression stirred the patriotic passions of the Anti-Federalists and was used to their political advantage. It is one of the reasons that they won the congressional elections of 1792. Jay's Treaty in 1794 ended the controversy.[27] Hamilton was the force behind the successful treaty. Afterward, America enjoyed a prosperous trade that helped to fuel an economic boom. However, Jefferson and his allies hotly contested the treaty. They feared that it would lead to closer ties with England and aid the newly formed Federalist Party. Washington strongly supported the treaty.

The treaty provoked France. In retaliation, France renounced the commercial treaty of 1778 and issued a decree that allowed it to seize neutral American ships. Afterward, France refused to receive Charles Pinckney who was sent to France as an American minister. In an attempt to avoid war, John Adams dispatched a delegation to work out a new treaty and resolve the tensions. Three anonymous Frenchmen named X, Y, and Z approached the delegation and demanded a bribe of $250,000 for the French foreign minister, and a loan of ten million dollars to France as a cost of doing business. Also they required a formal apology from the American president. The American delegation refused to comply. Afterward, Adams sent an account of the affair to congress. The American people became enraged. French enthusiasm quickly waned in South Carolina.[28]

In 1798, South Carolinians expected war with France. Ironically, the same city that welcomed Genet now built and fortified Castle Pinckney to defend the city of Charleston. They named the fort after the hometown hero who defied the French Directory.[29] Pinckney was a mayor of Charleston, two-time governor of South Carolina, Senator, Congressman, signer of the U.S. Constitution, and ran for President on the Federalist ticket in 1800 and 1804. Despite his popularity, his state voted for the Anti-Federalist Burr in the 1800 election.[30] As such, even though public sentiment turned away from France, it remained firmly attached to American republicanism.

It has been shown that the popular rise of Anti-Federalism in 1791 coincided with the beginning of the Methodist numerical slowdown and eventual decline in the South. Jefferson and allies were a force behind Anti-Federalism as they swayed the people to their point of view. Their political rhetoric was so effective that they won the House of Representative with a large majority of southern votes in the 1792 elections. On the other hand, the publication of the XYZ Affair and the waning of French idealism in 1798 marked the beginning of southern Methodism's recovery in the South. Even though this does not prove a direct correlation between the rise of republicanism and the decline of southern Methodism in the 1790s, a correlation can be inferred since the renewal of southern Methodism occurred when French idealism diminished.

As it turned out, republican ideals and French romanticism were two different realities. America's republican ideals rose out of the Revolution and were codified in national benchmarks like the Bill of Rights and the Declaration of Independence. They were influenced by French thought. Also, French support in the southern campaign of the war greatly aided the American cause and was a major reason for victory. The South was drawn to France and appreciated its help. For a time, republican ideals and French romanticism were intertwined. When they were disentangled by the XYZ Affair, republicanism remained and French idealism evaporated.

The Clash of English and Republican Ideals within the MEC

The former section examined the conflict between Southern Methodism and the contextual factors related to the rise of republicanism. This section examines internal conflicts within the MEC. As Southern Methodism adapted to its context, it accepted much of the criticism that was levied against it. In a short period, it attempted to lessen conflict with the external environment by making internal adjustments. Initial adjustments came in the form of "Americanizing" the MEC. The on-going process of contextualization engendered internal conflict and open schisms.

Methodism was founded in England and established within an English milieu. It appealed to the working people and to those who were the dispossessed of society. Wesley had a passion for the people. However, British Methodism assumed an English identity and worked out its issues in that context. Wesley was an Anglican priest who enjoyed the benefits of establishment. Additionally, he was a monarchist who lived in a stratified world. That is, in his Methodist kingdom, he assumed the role of an absolute monarch. Most of all, he remained patriotic and loyal to England and its colonial cause. These values were antithetical to republicanism and caused tension whenever their implications were played out in America.

To a great extent, Coke shared Wesley's prejudices. To a lesser extent, Asbury also shared Wesley's views. However, Asbury attempted to conceal and modify his bias as he endeavored to adapt American Methodism to its various contexts. For his efforts, he had conflict with Wesley and those who supported Wesley, e.g., Coke, Vasey, and Hammett. Also, he had conflict with those who pushed for the complete "Americanization" of Methodism, e.g., O'Kelly and allies. The latter group threatened to destroy Methodism's essence. Asbury stood between these opposing forces as he tried to mold American Methodism into a national church that was true to its Wesleyan core and true to the American experience.

Institutional conflict exposed the fault lines in EAM. As they relate to numerical growth and decline, the fault lines are points of debarkation. The following discussions give brief sketches of several contextual issues and institutional conflicts in order to show the relationship between them and numerical decline.

Wesley's Authority Rejected by the American Conference

The preachers at the Christmas Conference promised that they would submit to Wesley in matters of government. Soon, that promise was broken. In a letter to Coke on September 6, 1786, Wesley wrote, "I desire that you would appoint a General Conference of all our preachers in the United States, to meet at Baltimore on May 1st, 1787, and that Mr. Whatcoat may be appointed a superintendent with Mr. Francis Asbury."[31] The 1786 *Minutes* scheduled the conference for June 19, 1787 at Petersburg. Many preachers did not receive notice of the change or were inconvenience by it so that they did not attend the called General Conference.

Coke opened the conference and presided. He read Wesley's letter. Not only was Whatcoat to be appointed a general superintendent with Asbury, Garrettson was to be appointed a superintendent to Nova Scotia.[32] A heated debate ensued. Coke pushed the point and reminded the preachers that they were bound to obey

Wesley. However, the conference determined not to abide by Wesley's order. Furthermore, the preachers repudiated their earlier promise to submit to Wesley. According to Lee, "Many of the members of that conference argued that they were not at the conference when that engagement [to obey Wesley] was entered into, and they did not consider themselves bound by it. Other preachers who said they were 'Ready to obey his commands,' said they did not feel ready *now* to obey his commands."[33]

Lee offered two reasons why the preachers disobeyed Wesley. First, Whatcoat was not qualified to take charge of the American connection. Unlike Asbury, he was relatively new to America. Second, they did not want Wesley to recall Asbury to England. They assumed that to be his plan.[34] To make the point more clear, they struck Wesley's name from the *Minutes*. In effect, they expelled Wesley from the American connection.[35] Asbury did not participate in the debate or encourage the outcome.

Before the conference, Coke wrote letters to the preachers while he was out of the States. He functioned as Wesley's intermediary, and in that capacity he acted like the bishop-in-charge of American Methodism. When this information came to light, the conference was very displeased with Coke. According to Lee,

> The preachers complained of Dr. Coke, because he had taken upon himself a right which they never gave him, of altering the time and place of holding our conference, after it had been settled and fixed on at the previous conference. Another complaint was brought against him for writing improper letters to some of our preachers, such as were calculated to stir up strife and contention among them.[36]

Consequently, Coke was forced to sign a pledge not to exercise any government whatever in the MEC during his absences from the United States. Furthermore, he agreed to limit his episcopal authority while in the United States.[37] This action humbled and minimized Coke.

O'Kelly was the primary antagonist who spoke for the preachers against Wesley and Coke. However, since Asbury arrogated the negative, he could have annulled the actions and kept the MEC aligned with Wesley. Wesley understood this. That is why Wesley blamed Asbury for the outcome and held him responsible for it.[38]

After the vote, Asbury wrote a letter that expressed his feelings on the issue. His letter placed the debate in a political context. According to his reasoning, Wesley could not be a monarch in America because that role did not exist in the States. America was free from English control. As such, the MEC must be free from Wesley's autocratic control. Practically speaking, Wesley could not know what was best for the American connection because he was not intimately familiar with that connection or the preachers in it. His opinions were determined by the biased words of others. Asbury believed that he was qualified and called to be the leader of American Methodism by virtue of his long service and intimate knowledge of every part of it.[39]

> For myself, this I had submitted to;[40] but the American's were too jealous to bind themselves to yield to him in all things relative to Church government. Mr. Wesley was a man they had never seen—was three thousand miles off—how might submission, in such a case, be expected? Brother Coke and myself gave offense to the connexion by enforcing Mr. Wesley's will in some matters.[41]

O'Kelly also argued against Wesley's order based on American independence and expediency. Wesley and the MEC bishops should not determine things without the consent of the preachers. America fought a war to win its freedom from England and the preachers have worked hard in difficult times to build up the flock. They are competent to govern themselves by means of the conference. O'Kelly did not oppose the idea of another bishop. Rather, he demanded that the preachers in connection have the right to make their own decisions related to their leaders and their governance.

> [I] am perfectly willing if Brother Asbury thinks well to chuse [sic] one or two superintendents as the work is too great for Brother Asbury to act in conjunction with him as the younger; and all in subordination to the Conference, but let our dear preachers have this liberty, to choose their master.[35]

Underlying the entire debate was the issue of authority. America was an independent nation, governed under republican principles. Emerging republican ideals infiltrated the people and the MEC. The new church had to conform to those expectations in order to be acceptable to the Methodist people in the South. Based on that, the bishops derived their power to govern and ordain from the conference, and they were amenable to the conference for its use. They were to act like a constitutional president, not a king. In this scenario, there was no room for a meddling ecclesiastical monarch from England to interfere with the conference or interject his control via letter or emissary. Ultimately, Wesley's expulsion and Coke's *mea culpa* left Asbury in full control of the connection. However, O'Kelly, by virtue of his war service, long tenure in the connection, eloquent articulation on behalf of the preachers, and leadership office as a presiding elder, was in a position to check Asbury if he used his power in a monocratic way.

CHAPTER THIRTEEN

THE RISE OF O'KELLY AND HIS DEFECTION

After taking the lead in the dethroning of Wesley and the humbling of Coke, O'Kelly next turned his eyes to Asbury. Asbury stood to receive his ire because he had become the Wesley of American Methodism. Like Wesley and Coke, Asbury was British, affirmed church hierarchy, and assumed the authority of an ecclesial dictator. The battle began when O'Kelly observed Asbury's autocratic tendencies. As a member of the ill-fated Council, O'Kelly complained that Asbury manipulated the proceedings in order to control the outcome in that he presided like a monarch and changed the end results when it suited him. He did not encourage discussion. Rather, he told the members what he wanted. All was done to secure his power.

The free use of his "negative" was a particular point of concern to O'Kelly. During the Fluvanna crisis in 1777, the northern conference had given Asbury the same authority that Wesley had in regard to negating. That is, after the assembled preachers decided on something, Asbury could disaffirm it. That authority was never confirmed by the wider connection. His use of the negative repulsed O'Kelly. He believed that Asbury needed to be checked so that American Methodists could enjoy ecclesial freedom in accordance with the ideals of southern republicanism and gospel liberty.

The Council Controversy

Like the wandering charismatic apostles of early Christianity, Asbury was a peripatetic preacher. Annually, he journeyed throughout America conducting conferences. Often, his travels were accompanied by severe hardship and bad health. Still, he stayed on his horse until old age made him use a carriage. Literally, he died on the job. In his ministration of the episcopacy, he personified the highest ideals of the itinerancy. Because of his constant itineration, he knew the totality of the American connection to include the abilities and personalities of the circuit riders. No one understood the character of the various regions in which American Methodism existed better than he. Asbury was so ubiquitous in his travels that he was one of the most recognized people in early America. Most of the participants in EAM had personal contact with Asbury. Even though he was not a fiery preacher, the rank and file preachers held him in awe. Normally, his presence generated a consensus even when the preachers might be predisposed to argue a point with a lesser figure. More than anyone else, Asbury determined the form and character of EAM.

Before the formation of the Council, American Methodism functioned like a confederacy of conferences without a regularly scheduled general conference. During the various conferences, the preachers voted on local and national business. Before the Fluvanna controversy, the Baltimore conference served as a preparatory conference to the one in Virginia. Afterward, Asbury conducted the preparatory conference in Virginia and the regular conference in Baltimore. In the aftermath, the northern conference seasoned the deliberations of the southern conference and made the final determination. As was mentioned in the section on the sectional crisis, this was advantageous to Asbury because he carried more influence with the northern preachers.

After the Christmas Conference in 1784, the MEC increased the number of conferences to three. They met in North Carolina, Virginia, and Maryland. The 1787 *Minutes* increased the number of conferences to six. They extended from Charleston to Baltimore. The 1788 *Minutes* increased the number to 11. The new list included New York and the frontier districts. The 1789 *Minutes* scheduled 14 conferences. In 1789, the conference cycle no longer ended in Maryland and Baltimore no longer enjoyed its privileged status. In 1790, Asbury's itineration began in Georgia, continued to the west through the frontier regions, and concluded in New York. It took Asbury eight months to complete his "circuit." When Lee opened up New England, Asbury's annual trek expanded to include that region. The 1792 *Minutes* scheduled an incredible 20 district conferences that ran from November 1792 through October 1793. In eight years, the MEC grew from two to 20 yearly conferences. The increasing number of district conferences points to the rapid numerical and geographic expansion of EAM.

Under the new plan, Asbury replaced the regional conferences with a series of district conferences. In the new plan, Asbury increased the number of conference to accommodate the preachers. Also, he did not want them to abandon their circuits in order to travel to a distant conference. Plus, smaller conferences were easier for him to manage. However, O'Kelly averred that Asbury increased the number of conferences to keep the preachers from having a critical mass in one place. He opined that Asbury attempted to control the preachers and minimize their criticism by means of many smaller conferences. Lee shared this sentiment. In a small conference, the presence of Asbury loomed very large and the preachers were less likely to vote against him. Plus, the assistants had enjoyed the camaraderie of the protracted regional conferences and wanted to assemble together in larger groups.

The regional conferences of previous years had gathered a large number of circuit riders from many different districts. The conferences were a protracted event in which the preachers encouraged one another, built community, and did a fair amount of politicking. When Asbury travel through a district, the presiding elder of the district accompanied him. This increased the prestige of the presiding elders and gave the districts a legislative function.

In 1789, Asbury and Coke traveled together as they conducted all the conferences. In that year the conferences began on March 9th and ended on May 28th. During the various conferences, the bishops told the preachers that the MEC needed an instrument to bring administrative unity to the connection. An annual general conference would be the preferred means to maintain administrative unity, but the growth of the MEC made it impractical. In the ensuing debates Asbury and Coke strongly advocated for the formation of the Council. Some dissenting preachers were not dissuaded by the dominating presence of the two bishops. They believed that the proposed plan would strengthen Asbury's hand and allow him more executive privileges. The heated discussions presaged things to come.

On paper, the Council seemed like the perfect tool. It allowed the church to receive input from the preachers and it allowed the MEC to respond quickly to emerging issues. Additionally, it was a representative form of government in that it would be formed of "chosen men out of the several districts as representatives of the whole connection, to meet at stated times."[1] The "chosen men" refer to the presiding elders. Lee's *History* includes the charter of the Council and gives commentary on it.

> These shall have authority to mature every thing [sic] they shall judge expedient. 1. To preserve the general union: 2. to render and preserve the external form of worship similar in all our societies through the continent: 3. To preserve the essentials of the Methodist doctrines and disciplines pure and uncorrupted: And, lastly, they are authorized to mature every thing [sic] they may see necessary for the good of the church, and for the promoting and improving our colleges and plan of education. Provided nevertheless, that nothing shall be received as the resolution of the council, unless it be assented to unanimously by the council; and nothing so assented to by the council, shall be binding in any district, till it has been agreed upon by a majority of the conference which is held for that district.[2]

The assembled preachers of the first Council changed the last part of its charter. They determined that a majority of the district conferences could ratify the resolutions of the Council and make them binding on all the districts. Before this, it was stated that the rulings of the Council would only be binding on the districts that ratified them. Such a rule would have divided American Methodism so that one area would have been governed by one set of rules and another part by a different set of rules. In his *Apology*, O'Kelly takes credit for this idea.[3] Also, majority rule through representative government was in line with the emerging values of the American people.

However, the new rule met with strong opposition in the South. Lee wrote that the plan for the Council was "exceedingly dangerous." According to him, the preachers who voted for it soon realized their error. The Council was composed of the bishops and the presiding elders. However, the elders were not free to represent the people because they were not elected by the preachers or amenable to them. In fact, Asbury selected them and could remove them at will. The preachers assumed that the presiding elders were pawns in the hands of Asbury and that they would do what Asbury directed. As such, the ability of the preachers to maintain representative government through the various district conferences was thwarted by the Council when it changed its charter. In the eyes of many, the Council had become an instrument of oligarchy over which Asbury ruled like a despot.

The debate surrounding the Council gave impetus to a movement to elect presiding elders. Proponents argued that elected presiding elders would represent the people and be free to disagree with the bishops. In effect, they would function like an elected congress. Many continued to question the motives and probity of the bishops following the Council debacle. Consequently, even after the problem with the Council was settled, preachers still wanted to elect the presiding elders as a means to check the bishops. Asbury argued that presiding elders derived their authority from him and that they exercised it on his behalf. They were like the president's cabinet, not like the congress. As such, presiding elders needed to be amenable to him. The explanatory notes in the 1798 Discipline clearly show the bishops' perspective.

> The only branch of the presiding elder's office, the importance and usefulness of which is not so obvious to some persons, but which is, at the same time, perhaps the most expedient of all, is *the suspending power,* for the preservation of *the purity* of our ministry, and that our people may never be burdened with preachers of *insufficient* gifts. Here we must not forget, that the presiding elder acts as agent to the bishops; and that the bishops are, the greatest part of their time, at a vast distance from him, he must, therefore, exercise episcopal authority (ordination excepted) or he cannot act as their agent.[4]

O'Kelly emerged as the strongest voice in opposition to the Council. He was a presiding elder and a member of the first Council. After he returned to his district in south Virginia, he spoke bitterly against it. Asbury reported,

> I received a letter from the presiding elder of this district, James O'Kelly; he makes heavy complaints of my power, and bids me stop for one year, or he must use his influence against me. Power! power! there is not a vote given in a conference in which the presiding elder had not greatly the advantage of me; all the influence I am to gain over a company of young men in a district must be done in three weeks; the greater part of them, perhaps, are seen by me only at conference,

whilst the presiding elder has had them with him all the year, and has the greatest opportunity of gaining influence; this advantage may be abused; let the bishops look to it; but who has the power to lay an embargo on me, and to make of none effect the decisions of the conferences of the union?[5]

O'Kelly's request for a one year suspension was not coincidental. He was a member of the Fluvanna Conference. Asbury appealed to the southern preachers at that conference to put away the sacraments for one year in order to maintain connectional unity and allow Wesley time to respond to the presenting problem. They complied. However, the wounds from that conference still lingered with many southern preachers. The one year suspension became an indefinite period. During the hiatus, Asbury used his positional authority to establish himself as the prelate of American Methodism. Through the appointment setting process, he broke up the southern stronghold. In his *Apology*, O'Kelly made reference to the Fluvanna Conference. His choice of words in the letter that he sent to Asbury imply that Asbury's action through the Council threaten the connection and could be a reason for a sectional split.

After the Council met, its resolutions had to be affirmed by the various district conferences. When Asbury came to O'Kelly's district in 1790, all but two of the 21 itinerants voted against the bishop. Afterward, Asbury complained that the young men were totally under the influences of their elders.[6] According to O'Kelly, when Asbury brought the resolutions of the council to Petersburg, Virginia, the preachers had a private meeting to discuss them. Under his leadership, the group opposed Asbury. In the heat of the moment, Asbury responded by expelling the preachers to include O'Kelly.[7]

O'Kelly was shocked that he and his fellow conspirators could be expelled from the connection because they dared to challenge Asbury in conference. According to him, their crime was voting their consciences. Afterward, the young preachers repented of their wrong, agreed to submit to Asbury, and received their appointments and O'Kelly remained the presiding elder. In the immediate aftermath, O'Kelly sought to organize a grassroots resistance to the Council and Asbury. He proposed that two preachers from each district should meet to debate the issue. Asbury refused. He then requested to speak to the northern conference about the form of church government since preachers from the northern conferences had spoken to the southern conferences on behalf of Asbury's plan. Again, Asbury refused.[8]

Before the 1790 meeting of the Council, Asbury confessed, "I have felt grieved in mind that there is a link broken out of the twelve that should form a chain of union. I hope God will sanctify some providence to the explanation of this matter, and heal the whole."[9] O'Kelly was the broken link. In an effort to mend the breach, Asbury sent a letter to O'Kelly in which he promised "to take his seat in the council as another member; and in that point, at least, wave the claims of the episcopacy; yea, I would lie down and be trodden upon, rather than knowingly injure one soul."[10] This implies that he would not use his negative. In a previous letter, O'Kelly requested that Asbury suspend the council for one year or lay down his negative. For the sake of unity, the 1790 Council did not send out any resolutions to the district conferences. However, Asbury's overture did not assuage O'Kelly. After the 1790 meeting, O'Kelly continued his campaign to check Asbury by writing letters to influential preacher in America and England. In his letters, he accused Asbury of "dreadful things."[11]

The Conspiracy of Coke and O'Kelly

Ironically, despite his opposition to the episcopacy, Wesley's authority in America, and Coke's previous actions on behalf of Wesley, O'Kelly sought a political alliance with Coke to check Asbury and disestablish the council. Previously, Coke had worked with Asbury to convince the preachers to establish the institution. In a letter to O'Kelly, after the death of Wesley on March 2, 1791, Coke showed his hand:

> Methodism is gone. But remember when we meet together and overthrow the new institution [the Council] as I believe we shall, if Mr. Asbury is not satisfied with the government as it stood before, we will contend for a Republican government. Give me thy hand—fear not; I am a friend of America.[12]

Coke showed further animosity toward Asbury in the funeral sermon he preached for Wesley. "Two of those actors in Mr. Wesley's expulsion are dead and damned, and the others, with their patron, will go to hell except they repent."[13] O'Kelly was one of the main actors in Wesley's expulsion. Coke seems to be ignorant of this fact. Coke blamed Asbury for his previous censor and for the actions of the preachers when they insulted Wesley by removing his name from the *Minutes* because Asbury did not use his negative and did not speak against it. Also, Coke intimated in a letter to O'Kelly that Asbury's actions hastened the death of Wesley. In actuality, Coke wanted to be the lead bishop in America and thought that he would be the leader of world Methodism when Wesley died. He cared nothing for republicanism or for the deeper principles for which O'Kelly fought. Unbeknownst to O'Kelly, Asbury, and the American preachers, Coke was seeking to unite American Methodism with the newly formed Protestant Episcopal Church in America at this time. He sought an audience with Bishop White for this purpose. O'Kelly would have been mortified had he known this.

The following exert from a letter to Bishop White shows Coke's designs and his malice toward Asbury. It also shows that he does not understand the character of American Methodism.

> But what can be done for a reunion, which I wish for, and to accomplish which, Mr. Wesley, I have no doubt, would use his influence to the utmost? The affection of a very considerable number of the preachers and most of the people, is very strong toward him, notwithstanding the excessive ill-usage he received from a few. . . . Yet Mr. Asbury whose influence is very capital, will not easily comply; nay, I know he will be exceedingly averse to it.[14]

Asbury sensed the urgency and the growing level of discontent in the MEC. He stated, "Long-looked-for Doctor Coke came to town. . . . I found the Doctor's sentiments, with regard to the council, quite changed. James O'Kelly's letters had reached London. I felt perfectly calm, and accented to a general conference, for the sake of peace."[15]

After receiving O'Kelly's letter, Coke returned to America determined to intervene on his behalf. Some have suggested that Wesley had charged him to check Asbury and disestablish the Council.[16] Regardless, Coke pushed for the general conference when he returned. Lee reflected on the situation:

> We have sufficient reason to believe that the establishment of the council was very injurious to the Methodist connection. The plan produced such difficulties in the minds of the preachers and the people, and brought on such opposition, that it was hard to reconcile them one to another. Nothing would give satisfaction to the preachers but the calling together all the travelling preachers in a general conference; to which after some time the bishop consented.[17]

Lee agreed with the other preachers. In 1791, he attempted to change Asbury's mind related to the Council when the bishop was in his district. He devised a plan for a delegated general conference of two to four itinerants from each district to meet annually in Baltimore. Such a plan would have solved the problem and assuaged most of Asbury's stated objections.[18]

During the year and a half leading up to the general conference, O'Kelly worked to marshal his troops against Asbury. In the general conference, O'Kelly would have an equal standing with the bishop. In that democratic setting, he could change the MEC and minimize Asbury in the same way that he had minimized Coke and Wesley at an earlier general conference. To do that, he had to have the popular support of the preachers.

May's assessment of the O'Kelly conflict accurately reflects the situation:

> The crux of the difference between Asbury and O'Kelly lay in their contrasting views of the ministry. O'Kelly's passionate devotion to the principles of the Revolution, to the sovereignty of the people and the right of representation, stood in diametric opposition to the hierarchical concept of the ministry, with its rigid discrimination between clergy and laity, and its clerical domination of church government and discipline.[19]

In order to understand Asbury's recalcitrance in regards to O'Kelly and his criticism, one must understand how Richard Baxter's writings influenced Asbury's thinking. Asbury was so impressed with Baxter that he mentions him by name and includes portions of his work in the 1787 *Discipline*.[20] The material was printed by the Book Concern in 1792 under the title, *The Causes, Evils, and Cures, of Heart and Church Divisions, Extracted from the Works of Mr. Richard Baxter, and Mr. Jeremiah Burroughs*.[21]

Based on his study of Baxter, Asbury determined two things. First, unity is primary for discipline and order. Scripture can be misused by unscrupulous people to promote disunity. Scriptural arguments that promote disunity in the church must be rejected. Well-meaning people can be sincerely wrong. Problems in the church cannot be solved by schism or division. When pursued, external unity will yield internal unity. When unity is the goal, controversy is minimized.

Second, those who separate from the church, reject those with whom they disagree and arrogate to themselves a power not given to them. The minister's power of the keys is to be exercised under the direction of the chief pastor. As the chief pastor of EAM, Asbury carried the keys. From this, Asbury rejected democratic interpretations of church. "Read these with judgment, and then believe if you can that the power of the keys or government is in the people. Show us what text doth give them that power. And where the scripture calleth them to exercise it by votes. . . . Tell us where the people are authorized to baptize: or to rule the church."[22]

The Hammett Defection and Related Membership Declines in South Carolina and Georgia

As if the problems with O'Kelly were not enough, Asbury and southern Methodism were rocked by William Hammett's defection before the 1792 General Conference. In 1786, Hammett was ordained by Wesley and dispatched with Coke and others to serve as a missionary in Newfoundland. Due to bad weather, he ended up in Antigua. Undeterred, Hammett began to preach and formed a society of 700 members. On January 4, 1791, Coke returned to the West Indies. During an extensive itineration over many islands, he discovered that Hammett had done a wonderful job. He also noted that Hammett suffered from severe persecution and grave illness. He states,

> Mr. Hammett lay dangerously ill of a fever and ague, and a violent inflammation in one of his eyes, and was worn almost to the skeleton with opposition and fatigue. He had not been able to preach for near a month. . . . Dr. Harris, a man of great honour as well as great skill who assured me that there was not the least hope of his recovery, but by his removal for some time to a colder climate.[23]

Coke intended to return him to settle a mission at Montego Bay, Jamaica when his health permitted. While *en route* to America, they were shipwrecked at Edisto, 28 miles south of Charleston on February 21, 1791. When they arrived in Charleston, Asbury was concluding a conference that began on February 14th. The preachers agreed to remain an additional day in order to spend time with Coke. Hammett preached before the conference and was received enthusiastically. The members of the circuit requested that Hammett be made their pastor. Asbury ignored the request and left town with no explanation to the society or Hammett.[24] While leaving the town, Asbury wrote, "I am somewhat distressed at the uneasiness of our people [in Charleston], who claim a right to choose their own preachers; a thing quite new amongst Methodists. None but Mr. Hammett will do for them."[25] Hammett took the approbation of the society to heart and followed after Asbury in an effort to persuade the bishop. He found Asbury in Philadelphia and conversed with him. Asbury states, "Mr. Hammett came from Charleston with a wonderful list of petitioners desiring his return: to this, as far as I had to say, I submitted, but I see and hear many things that might wound my spirit."²⁶ Interestingly, even though Coke brought Hammett to the Charleston and witnessed the proceedings, his journal does not mention the controversy.

After his encounter with Hammett in Philadelphia, Asbury wrote to Nelson Reed, the presiding elder of the Maryland area with the following guidance: "Mr. Hammett will stay sometime as a stranger, but let the discipline and government be with Brother Pryor [spelled Prior in the *Minutes*]. . . . Be prudent how you speak and act when spies are around."²⁷ Pryor was in charge of the Baltimore-town circuit. Following this, there were many problems in the Baltimore circuit. Asbury was accused of irregularities. Certain preachers said he was partial to Dickins, Willis, and Haskins.²⁸ It is not certain if Hammett played any part in this, but it seems possible. Hammett did not like Asbury's episcopal power or the fact that Asbury consented to the striking out of Wesley's name. He was a close companion of Coke and owed his allegiance to Wesley. Asbury realized the problem and demanded action.

> I am grieved . . . that simple and happy society in Baltimore, famed and respected for many years for hospitality, simplicity and union, should be distressed and disturbed with restless spirits. . . . Call a solemn meeting of the society the first opportunity and read the minutes pointing at those members who shall rise up against the government of the church, that such persons being found guilty shall be expelled. You may plead my authority over it if you please. It was early sent to this town that some person has written . . . that the minority²⁹ had departed from us, and gave advise to Mr. Hammett to come forth to meet these disaffected men. . . . Opposition to the laws, union, and government is treason against the Church: to defame the Conference. . . . Put the law in force against such.³⁰

By this time, the southern preachers were aware of O'Kelly's complaints and were discussing the points among themselves. Northern preachers also discussed the issues even though they were not as passionate about the debate as their southern brethren. Undoubtedly, some of the Maryland preachers favored O'Kelly's arguments. As such, the preaching and presence of Hammett in Baltimore may have given focus to their displeasure. However, the same cannot be said of the rank and file northern preachers. When preaching at the New York conference, Hammett was not well received by the preachers there.³¹ Hammett does not appear in the 1791 *Minutes*. Regardless, before the coming of Hammett, Baltimore was not in turmoil. When he left, a spirit of contention remained.

After this, Hammett led a major schism in the Charleston circuit. He formed his followers into the Primitive Methodist Church. The name reflected his protest. The primitive church was governed by presbyters and elders, not by bishops who abused their authority. Hammett then published a series of pamphlets in which he assailed Asbury and the office of the presiding elder. He called Asbury and Coke "tyrants." Hammett argued for religious liberty and against a "rigid, unscriptural episcopacy."³²

Hammett was very successful in pulling away preachers and other Methodists, and in starting new churches. According to Lee, "In the course of the next year, 1792, he drew off a great part of the society in [Charleston]. . . . He got Mr. P. Matthews, a Methodist preacher to unite to him. Some time after that a few more preachers joined him. But none of our travelling preachers joined him."[33] Hammett's followers erected two churches in Charleston; one in Georgetown, Georgia; another in Savannah; and one in Wilmington, North Carolina.[34] There was a large decline in MEC membership in and around the Charleston area following Hammett's schism. More importantly, Hammett influenced membership decline in Georgia. Asbury's *Journal* shows the connection between Hammett and Georgia membership decline. "Some of them may think with Hammett, in Georgia, that I am the greatest villain on the continent. . . . If we lose some children, God will give us more. Ah! this is the mercy, the justice of some who, under God owe their all to me, and my *tyrants*, so called."[35]

Immediately following the Hammett problem, Methodism in Georgia registered membership declines in 1791 and 1792. The Savannah area was especially hard hit by Hammett's faction. The area had three circuits in 1792. The work withered to two circuits in 1793, to one in 1794, and to none in 1795. During the same period, the population of Savannah grew rapidly. In 1796, the South Carolina conference sent missionaries to restart the work in Savannah. However, the MEC was not able to start another circuit in the Savannah area until 1808. Hammett's influence also touched the North. In 1791, after its brief encounter with Hammett, Maryland Methodism posted a one-year loss.

From the beginning, Hammett sided with the local society against Asbury. In so doing, he divided the ministry and lessened the authority of Asbury. Asbury guarded his power to appoint and believed that it was essential to the welfare of the MEC. Hammett's desire to please the people by letting them pick their preachers threatened that power and would have established a very bad precedent. Hammett was not a republican in the same manner as O'Kelly was. In fact, he was a high churchman who identified with Wesley. Preaching gowns and powder were important to him.[36] However, when it suited him; he wrapped his protest in a republican garb. To this extent, he was an opportunist who understood how to use the spirit of the time to suit his cause.

According to Coke, Hammett's popularity did not last. While in Charleston in 1797, he made the following observation:

> Poor William Hammett is now come to nothing. When he began his schism, his popularity was such, that he soon erected a Church, nearby, if not quite as large as our New-Chapel in London; which was crowded on the Lord's-day. But, alas! He has now upon Sunday evening, only about thirty white people with their dependent blacks. He has indeed gained a sufficiency of money to procure a plantation, and to stock it with slaves; though no one was more strenuous against slavery than he, while destitute of the power of enslaving. During his popularity we lost almost all our congregation and Society: but, blessed be God, we have now a crowded church; and a Society, inclusive of the blacks, amounting to treble the number which we had, when the division took place: and our people intend immediately to erect a second Church.[37]

Hammett was not the only reason for membership declines in Georgia and South Carolina. Barclay attributed the long decline to four factors. First, prosperous trade with the Indians and slave labor "engrossed the minds of the people." Second, there was a shortage of preachers. Third, theological controversies raged with Calvinists. Methodists did not fare well in these debates, and they distracted the preachers from their main work. Fourth, in 1792, many preachers left the field and others were leaving.[38] Some left out of sympathy with Hammett. One was expelled. Two got married.[39] Also, there was controversy between the local preachers and the itinerants. The people were not kind to their preachers. In 1793, Asbury wrote that the Georgia brethren were much humbled. They feared that Asbury would not send them any more traveling preachers.[40]

In 1792, Georgia and South Carolina Methodism was also hurt when Beverly Allen was expelled for a flagrant crime. Previously, he was a presiding elder. He served in the Charleston area at Edisto. He was an extremely popular preacher. Before Coke shipwrecked in Edisto, the MEC did not have a work there. Allen volunteered to start the work. After his expulsion, Allen spoke against Asbury to the preachers and the laity in South Carolina and Georgia from 1792 through 1794. He also wrote letters to Coke. Asbury claimed that he was "the source of most of the mischief that has followed."[41] In 1795, a warrant was issued for his arrest. Allen killed the U.S. Marshall who issued the warrant. After being imprisoned, he escaped by bribing the jailer. While being recaptured, the posse burned his home. Because the people in Georgia were opposed to anything "federal," they helped Allen escape from jail a second time. Anti-Federalism was very strong in Georgia at that time.[42] Allen fled to Logan County, Kentucky as a fugitive. Asbury cringed under the bad publicity. "The poor Methodists must unjustly be put to the rack on his account, even though he has been expelled from us for two years."[43] Allen caused much reproach to Methodism and gave Hammett more ammunition.

The O'Kelly Revolt and Its Consequence

When the General Conference convened in November 1792, almost every preacher in full connection was present. Most came with big expectations. Others assumed that it would be the last general conference. For practical reasons, they thought that future general conferences would be delegated conferences.[44]

Coke nearly missed the general conference because of traveling problems while *en route* from England. He arrived at the last moment. Asbury expected trouble. He knew that O'Kelly planned to make a motion for the "right of appeal." He also knew the real issue. In the absence of Coke, Asbury had planned to delay the controversial debate for ten days. During those days, he wanted the preachers to share their testimonies, pray, and celebrate the great revival over which they presided. This would change the focus from the Council and the fiasco that attended to it. Because most of the controversy was aimed at him, Asbury asked Coke to preside. Additionally, Asbury relinquished his episcopal prerogative to include his negative and refrained from debating (see below). It should also be noted that Coke moderated the debate with great care and did not attempt to use his position to sway the vote toward O'Kelly. It appears that Coke and Asbury reconciled before the general conference and that Coke realized that O'Kelly was the greater danger to the connection. In hindsight, O'Kelly would contend that Coke betrayed him and his word:

> MY DEAR BRETHREN:—Let my absence give you no pain—Dr. Coke presides. I am happily excused from assisting to make laws by which myself am to be governed: I have only to obey and execute. I am happy in the consideration that I never stationed a preacher through enmity, or as a punishment. I have acted for the glory of God, the good of the people, and to promote the usefulness of the preachers. . . . I am one—ye are many. I am as willing to serve you as ever. I want not to sit in any man's way. I scorn to solicit votes.[45]

This left the door open for O'Kelly and his followers. They wanted to discuss the Council and Asbury's conduct in relation to it. However, Coke did not permit that. At length, O'Kelly pushed his motion for appeal:

> After the bishop appoints the preachers at conference to their several circuits, if anyone think himself injured by the appointment, he shall have liberty to appeal to the conference and state his objections; and if the conference approve his objections, the bishop shall appoint him to another circuit.[46]

During the early stages of the debate, a large majority seemed to favor O'Kelly's motion. Things began to change when Dickins had the question divided. During the Fluvanna crisis, Dickins argued against the episcopacy and argued in favor of a Presbyterian form of church government. He had made his case from the scriptures. Later, he became good friends with Asbury. When the divided motion was debated, everyone agreed that the bishop should appoint the preachers to their circuits. However, the right to appeal produced three days of intense debate. Because it was determined that the second question was an amendment of an existing rule and not a new rule, O'Kelly only needed a majority vote to carry his motion.

During the debate, some of the supporters of the motion spoke harshly. This caused them to lose ground with the other preachers. For example, when an elder who was against the motion asked if anyone had been injured by an appointment, Rice Haggard told the conference of two who had been injured. For this, other preachers accused Haggard of improperly impeaching the conduct of the bishop. Finally, the motioned was rejected by a large majority. The next morning, O'Kelly and two fellow preachers withdrew from the MEC.[47] Afterward, the conference voted that no presiding elder could be stationed in the same district for more than four consecutive years. O'Kelly had been stationed in his for ten years and had used that tenure to build up his own kingdom from which he challenged the MEC.

O'Kelly offers a blow-by-blow account of the conference proceedings. According to him, the leading elders attempted to make him bind himself to the outcome of the debate before the conference began. He refused. One must assume that the threat of schism was a weapon in his arsenal. After his motion was defeated and he adjourned to a home, a committee came to him in an effort to reconcile. Coke also met with him. When he sent his letter of resignation, Coke read it to the conference. Afterward, he was allowed to preach in MEC chapels and was offered a $40 a year stipend for his long work in the ministry.[48]

On the surface, the preachers agreed with the sentiment of O'Kelly's motion. However, most backed off when the ensuing debate exposed the intent. The northern preachers were especially cold to the motion and the impassioned pleading of O'Kelly and those who spoke in favor of it. Also, leading up to the general conference, O'Kelly repeatedly stated that the northern preachers were not like the southern ones. After the debate, O'Kelly complained that the "Elders to the North... make me their table laugh."[49] These comments point to regionalism and show how the MEC took on the character of the regions in which it labored. In actuality, O'Kelly was just as suspicious of northerners as he was of Asbury. He stated,

> The kind of government which Asbury and Coke preferred may answer better to the north of this [Virginia], where the British armies were long suffered to plunder the honest patriots. But when they came to exercise their felonious practices in Virginia, they were sent back in the degraded situation of prisoners.[50]

Republican idealism was not a main concern of the northern preachers. For that reason, the seeming monarchial nature of the MEC did not offend them. Because of this, Asbury's leadership style and the Council were not negative institutional factors that caused numerical decline in their area of ministry. This may be one reason why the northern circuits did not plateau and decline like the ones in the South following 1792.[51]

Immediately after withdrawing from the MEC, O'Kelly stated that he would send his converts to the Methodist societies. However, a fellow defector showed him the folly of the plan. If the MEC was unscriptural, why would one send people to it? They will become corrupted by it and their blood will be required on the preacher's head. Indeed, people did respond to O'Kelly's ministry. He organized these followers into the Republican Methodist Church. According to Lee,

> At that time there were great struggles and contentions about politics. In Virginia republican principles prevailed, and it was considered advantageous to a man to be a republican. The divisive party, with O'Kelly at the head, therefore called themselves Republican Methodists.[52]

In 1793, the new group began to form societies. Many Methodists joined with the new church. In fact, whole societies went with them. In other places, the societies split between those who favored O'Kelly and those who wanted to remain in the MEC. The infighting between the groups became personal and bitter. Lee observed, "In some places they scattered the flock and separated the people one from the other, without securing them to their own party."[53] In other words, because of the acrimonious discourse, many members left the MEC and did not join the Republican Methodists. Of those who withdrew because of the controversy, a large percentage did not align with another church. "Many religious people . . . began to contend about church government, and neglect the duties of religion, till they were turned back to the world, and gave up religion altogether."[54] The MEC also lost many chapels and portions of its infrastructure to the schism.[55]

Lee avers that all were to be on equal footing within the Republican Methodist Church. "One preacher was not to be above another; nor higher in office or in power, than the other preacher. No superiority, or subordination, was to be known among them. They promised to the lay members of the church greater liberties."[56] O'Kelly states, "We formed our ministers on an equality; gave the lay-members a balance of power in the legislature; and left the executive business in the church collectively."[57] This message especially appealed to local preachers who had felt like second-class preachers in the MEC. In fact, O'Kelly's protest foreshadowed future protests with the MEC.

After O'Kelly split, the issue of baptism worked its way into the debate. According to David Benedict, Methodists were split on the issue and many divided over it. Later, O'Kelly merged with the New Testament Restoration Movement that began to take shape at this time. They called themselves Christians. Benedict gives a first-hand description of the debate and its aftermath in a section for 1790-1813. Much of his insights were collaborated by John Asplund. Starting in 1790, he traveled 7,000 by foot over an 18 month period to collect data and report on issues. According to his report,

> Believers baptism by immersion has prevailed much in the United States, within ten or twenty years past. Multitudes of the Methodists have adopted it. . . . In Virginia and the southern States, there has been a great schism in the Methodist church. A large party has come off, which denominate themselves Christians. A similar party has separated from the Presbyterians and Methodists in Kentucky, and the western States, and a great number of these Christian people have lately been buried in baptism.[58]

Additionally, the rise of Republican Methodism caused negative publicity for the MEC. According to Lee,

> The disaffected party then began to pour out a flood of abuse against us, to ridicule us, and to say all manner of evil against us; and with all, they took unjustifiable steps in order to set our members against the preachers. The bishop was more despised by them, than any other man. The name bishop they abhorred.[59]

At first, the defection was contained to southern Virginia and North Carolina. This was the area of O'Kelly's base and greatest influence. However, because of the negative publicity and rapid immigration, his ideas quickly spread to other sections of the connection in the South and on the frontier. The controversy haunted Asbury and the MEC throughout the decade of the 1790s. As late as 1800, Asbury still struggled with O'Kelly as he continued to cause numerical decline and institutional tension. While at Craney Island Chapel in Virginia, Asbury wrote,

> Here a dreadful havoc hath been made by James O'Kelly; a peaceable society of nearly fifty souls are divided, and I fear in the end some may be destroyed: how he hath done this work we may know by reading his Apology. . . . It is astonishing to hear the falsehoods published against me.[60]

The primary sources from this period contain frequent references to the defection of local preachers in the South and to their support of O'Kelly and his ideals. The local preachers were swayed by his republican vision of the church. As they left the MEC and sided with O'Kelly, they attempted to take the laity with them. As has already been shown, the lay people felt a close bond to the local preachers because they ministered to them when the itinerants were traveling. Also, they were never reappointed. Because of the defection and great influence of the local preachers in the South, the MEC made special rules to govern local preachers more carefully in 1796.

The following quotations from selected primary sources are provided to demonstrate the relationship between O'Kelly, local preachers, institutional stress, and numerical decline:

> If we (the itinerant connexion) would give the government into the hands of a local ministry, as some would have it, and tax the people to pay preachers for Sabbath work—this would please such men: but this we dare not do.[61]

> Rice Haggard was the only travelling preacher that went off with O'Kelly, and continued to travel. Some of the local preachers became warmly attached to the old man, and fell in with him, and with his plan. . . . Several of our local preachers, and many of our private members were drawn away from us. . . . These preachers who turned aside from the truth, did abundance of mischief among the people that were not religious: many of whom became so deeply prejudiced against religion that they would hardly attend on preaching at all.[62]

> I learn that mischief is begun in the lower parts of Virginia; J. O'Kelly, and some of the local preachers, are the promoters and encouragers of divisions among the brethren. . . . I wrote many letters to the south district of Virginia, to confirm the souls of the people, and guard them against the division that is attempted there.[63]

> I was concerned to bring in better order among the local line of the ministry [in Virginia], by classing them together, and then, being thus classed, by making them take regular stations on Sabbath days. I also appointed them a leader, to meet once in three or six months. . . . Some of our local preachers complain that they have not a seat in the General Annual Conference. We answer, if they will do the duty of a member of the yearly conference, they may have the seat and privilege of the travelling line. The travelling ministry may complain, We must go at a minute's warning to our circuits, far and near; and attend with the greatest strictness to our appointments and societies. The local preachers go where and when they please; can preach anywhere and nowhere; they can keep plantations and slaves, and have them bought or given by their parents. The local preachers can receive fifty or a hundred dollars per year, for marriages; but we travellers, if we receive a few dollars for marriages, must return them at the conference, or be called refractory or disobedient. Let us not have the grace of our Lord Jesus Christ with respect of persons in ministries, any more than in members—in local preachers, any more than travelling ones.[64]

In 1798, Lee took the first survey of the local preachers. He discovered that there were 850 local preachers in the connection and only 269 travelling preachers. Local preachers were distributed as follows: Georgia 33, South Carolina 55,

North Carolina 148, Virginia 251, Maryland 103, Delaware 21, Pennsylvania 50, New Jersey 53, New York 51, Connecticut 13, Rhode Island 3, Massachusetts 3, Maine 6, and Kentucky/Tennessee 60.[65]

Summary of the O'Kelly and Hammett Decline

Both Hammett and O'Kelly caused numerical declines in the South when they deserted the MEC. Hammett's defection caused an immediate decline in the Charleston circuit. He pulled away members, local preachers, and a chapel. He also set up rival churches in Charleston, Wilmington, Savannah, and Georgetown. Following this, the Savannah circuits were devastated. Likewise, O'Kelly led a populist revolt as he siphoned away local preachers, members, and chapels from the MEC. Hammett and O'Kelly appealed to republican ideals and attacked the hierarchical government of the MEC. The bishop's power to appoint was central to their complaints. They both turned to the scriptures for biblical models of church government. At the 1792 General Conference, O'Kelly proposed a motion that the scriptures be the final authority and ultimate guide in the ensuing debates. The appeal to scripture carried much weight in the eyes of the laity. Because of attacks on the unscriptural basis of the MEC, the bishops added 70 pages of biblical references and notes to the 1796 *Discipline*. Also, the Book Concern published *The Causes, Evil, and Cures, of Heart and Church Division*. It included a point counter point defense of the MEC and its form of government by appeal to scripture.

When the criticisms of O'Kelly and Hammett are examined in light of the political climate that existed in the South at that time, the relationship between the two becomes clear. The Methodist structure reflected many federalist ideals that conflicted with republican thinking. The concept of a strong national government under executive leadership was reflected by the bishops and their strong leadership. The distrust of the people's ability to govern themselves is reflected by the MEC's executive control. The people and local preachers did not vote in conference, there was no lay representation at General Conference, and Asbury demanded that he make all the appointments for the preachers. No one could challenge his decisions because he arrogated that power to himself.

The belief that the best government was that of the elite is reflected by Asbury's arguments as to why he and the itinerants were the only people qualified to make rules for the church, that is, they had a national vision for the church, they were impartial in what they did, and the Bible gave the elders and bishops that authority. Asbury contended that local preachers and lay people could not lead the church because they lacked a national vision. Lay delegates would "endeavour [*sic*] to obtain the most able and lively preachers for their respective circuits, without entering, perhaps at all, into the enlarged, apostolic spirit which would endeavor, whatever might be the sacrifice, to make all things tally."[66] Yearly conferences could not appoint for the same reason.

> [If yearly conferences made the appointments] the connection would no longer be able to send missionaries to the western states and territories, in proportion to their rapid population. The grand circulation of ministers would be at an end, and

a moral stab given to the itinerant plan. . . . There is nothing like [the itinerant plan] for keeping the whole body alive from the centre to the circumference, and from the continual extension of the circumference on every hand.[67]

In short, local circuits and preachers were focused on their local needs and could not be trusted to make decisions for the national good of the church. Asbury treated the entire connection as if it were one big circuit. In that regard, he subordinated the individual needs of the itinerants and the local circuits to the overall best interest of the church in mission.

O'Kelly and Hammett argued against Asbury on the basis of republican principles. The distrust of centralized government is reflected in their attempt to minimize the control of Asbury and the Council. They wanted a limited national church that gave maximum control to the local churches and preachers. They challenged the fundamental underpinning of episcopal control over central government, the bishop's right to set the appointments. They strongly affirmed that the people, acting through representative institutions, could be left to govern themselves. Hence, they favored an open General Conference, the election of presiding elders, and voice for local preachers and laity in the decision making process of the MEC at every level.

In light of the political and philosophical environment that prevailed in the South and the controversies and defections during this time period, one can conclude that the MEC's strong episcopacy and church government were negative institutional factors in the South because they conflicted with southern values, incited schisms, and dissuaded others from affiliating with the church. The defensive posture of the MEC and the workings of the damage control machinery that ensued deflected the southern church from its evangelistic effort. At the same time, the MEC's strong episcopacy and government were positive institutional factors that caused growth in New England and other areas where the MEC was expanding its borders. An expanding church needed the national vision and the strong leadership that Asbury gave to it. Additionally, Asbury argued that the church's strong government managed the conflict well and prevented the agitators from doing more damage.

CHAPTER FOURTEEN

SLAVERY AND OTHER CONTRIBUTING FACTORS TO THE SOUTHERN DECLINE

The previous chapter demonstrated that schisms associated with O'Kelly and Hammett contributed to the southern membership down-turn in the 1790s. Also, local histories show that O'Kelly sympathizers caused membership decline and confusion in Kentucky because migrating Methodists and local preachers carried the controversy to the frontier.[1] Robert Coleman argues that 25 percent of the MEC's total membership was lost to O'Kelly by 1794.[2] He does not factor in regional variations, measure the losses to 1799, or isolate O'Kelly's district from the rest of the MEC. If he did, he would have noted that the South declined by 12,747 or 22.5 percent from 1793 through 1799. However, the circuits in O'Kelly's district declined by 4,165 members or 43 percent from 1793 through 1799. His district included three circuits in North Carolina. They declined by 674. In total, O'Kelly's district accounted for 25 percent of the southern decline. Interestingly, the Virginia circuits not in O'Kelly's district only declined by 1,872 or 18 percent. This indicates that O'Kelly's influence had a limited sway outside his area of influence. Certainly, he was not the force behind the decline in Maryland. As such, O'Kelly cannot be the primary reason for the southern decline.

Table 14-1 shows the numerical declines of the circuits in O'Kelly's district during and before his defection. The main decline happened between 1793 and 1796.

Table 14-1. Membership Summary of O'Kelly's Circuits in Virginia between 1788 and 1799

	1788	1789	1790	1791	1792	1793	1794	1795	1796	1797	1798	1799
Franklin				314	635	658	600	562	457	411	411	398
Cumberland		404	385	422	422	459	437	417	485	426	426	347
Mecklenburg	1,109	790	510	503	511	511						
Amelia	807	908	898	783	784	784	647	496	437	407	414	392
Brunswick	1604	1500	942	827	910	814	802	701	687	529	555	650
Greenville			1,076	1,103	954	1,012	1,238	1,277	912	1,224	1,224	1,006
Sussex	1,611	1,808	835	814	753	654	2,354*	1,090	824	823	823	584
Surry			921	1,475	1,631	1,769†						
Bertie	690	530	731	770	761	792	792	670	579	577	577	530
Portsmouth	649	953	1,642	1,393	1,344	1,168	1,018	1,202	990	887	877	778
Camden‡	452	509	803	814	817	902	784	518	618	502	596	662
Banks				438	178	178	219	198	170	112		
Totals	6,922	7,402	8,743	9,656	9,680	9,701	8,891	7,131	6,159	5,898	5,903	5,539

Source: MEC, *Minutes* (1813).

*Combined with Surry.

†O'Kelly began his new church in Surry County in 1793[3]

‡ Camden, Banks and Bertie circuits are in north-central North Carolina.

This regional decline is significant because every southern state sustained a significant decline during the 1790s. Since the protracted period of decline followed a period of tremendous growth and since it was a regional phenomenon, it begs to be studied. As was indicated in Chapter Three, Southern Methodism lost 4,945 members in Virginia, 4,217 members in Maryland, 2,907 members in North Carolina, and 1,152 in South Carolina during the decline. That equals 28, 27, 28, and 25 percent of the total membership in the respective states.

As a point of reference, it should be noted that the Baptists in Virginia had a substantial membership loss during a period that paralleled Methodism's loss in Virginia. *A History of Kentucky Baptists from 1769 to 1885* alludes to membership declines for many churches in the 1790s.[4] Robert Semple offers a documentary analysis of the decline in the Virginia associations. It may be surmised that the Baptists in other southern states also declined during the 1790s. According to Semple, the Virginia Baptists blamed their losses on the cessation of revivals and westward migration.[5] The following quotation is dated October 13, 1792. It was from the Dover Association meeting of the Baptist Church and it precedes the MEC's decline in Virginia:

> By then it appeared that in the Dover District the harvest was past and the summer ended. Coldness and languor were generally complained of. The great revival had now subsided and the ax of discipline was laid at the root of the tree. Many barren and fruitless trees were already cut down. In many of the churches the number excluded surpassed the number received.[6]

Reports from the Goshen Association in present day West Virginia describe a time of coldness and languor from 1792 to 1802. The Culpepper Association said that its membership declined. They attributed the decline to the "the great numbers of removals to the Western Country."[7] The Middle District reported that from 1792 to 1797, there were reports of the cold state of religion.[8] The following is a fascinating quote:

> Since the great revival the Baptist cause has considerably declined in most parts of the Ketocton Association. The decrease is certainly not universal; there are some flourishing churches within the district. As the Baptists have decreased, the Methodists in many places have increased. It is not easy to account for the change. Does it arise from the Arminian doctrine being more palatable to the self-righteous heart of man? Or, have they succeeded in driving the Baptist preachers to dwell too much on high Calvinistic points, to the neglect of more simple but more important principles of Christianity?[9]

Unlike the Methodists, the Baptists were not burdened by bishops or a central government that minimized lay participation and aroused political sentiments in the people. In fact, they personified a democratic church. They fought for disestablishment in Virginia and had popular appeal. In terms of preaching style and evangelistic zeal, however, they were very similar to the Methodists. They differed in terms of Calvinism, congregational government, and believer's baptism by immersion. Coleman argues that the Baptists and Methodists targeted the same people and that they were very similar:

> In evangelistic fervor, missionary emphasis, sociological appeal, political association, democratic aspirations, ministerial training, and even in their preaching emphasis, there was a great similarity between the two most rapidly growing denominations in America in the late eighteenth and early nineteenth centuries. . . . The two bodies were very similar, particularly in the Gospel that was presented, the way it was proclaimed, and the class of people attracted to it. For this very reason there was an intense rivalry between the Baptists and the Methodists.[10]

The situation in Maryland also mitigates the "republican" theory for decline. Unlike the rest of the South, it remained a stronghold of Federalism. In fact, it voted for Federalist candidates in every national election through 1816. It never gave its vote to Jefferson. Nor is there any evidence that O'Kelly or his followers influenced that state. Yet, Maryland Methodism has the same overall membership pattern of decline as Virginia. In fact, the white membership in Maryland declined at a much faster rate than the white membership in Virginia.

In an effort to hold onto the republican theory as the main cause of southern decline, one might suggest that the MEC in Maryland declined like the MEC in Virginia because its members were republicans and that they shared the egalitarian values of the members from the other declining areas. Strawbridge, the founder of Maryland Methodism fits that pattern. Also, Maryland, like Virginia, had many local preachers. However, Asbury was the father of Eastern Shore Methodism. He birthed that work in his own image.[11] As Strawbridge and his preachers faded away, Maryland Methodism fell under Asbury's sway. During the early 1780s, Maryland was called the northern conference. Its preachers did not participate in the mutiny at the Virginia Conference in Fluvanna. In fact, the Maryland Conference sent delegates to Virginia in an attempt to correct the Virginia brethren and bring them back into the fold under the control of Asbury.

The Virginia growth area grew to include most of the South and southern frontier. However, it never assimilated the growth areas in Maryland or Delmarva. As such, one cannot assume that the Methodists in Maryland were enamored with republican ideals or imbibed the theological poison of French atheism.

In sum, without a doubt, the membership decline in O'Kelly's district was larger than the decline in the rest of the South. However, it cannot be argued that O'Kelly caused the southern decline in the 1790s because the Baptist Associations in Virginia had a parallel membership decline with the MEC in Virginia. The Methodists and Baptists were very similar except that the Baptists were not hindered by the O'Kelly schism, an episcopacy, or a church government that reflected federalist ideals. It must be assumed that other factors besides the ones related to political concerns and church government also influenced decline in the South during the 1790s. In other words, if southern Methodism and the Baptist churches both declined at a similar rate during the 1790s, the primary cause should be a contextual factor that equally affected both traditions. The entire South shared one contextual factor. That is the institution of slavery. The MEC's response to it and the reality of it influenced the southern membership of whites and blacks.

The Slavery Issue

Leading up to the Christmas Conference in 1784, EAM passed a series of slavery rules. At the northern Conference held in Baltimore in 1780, the preachers declared their "Disapprobation on all our friends who keep slaves, and advise their freedom."[12] Additionally, they determined that traveling preachers who owned slaves had to give promise to set them free. At the time of this conference, the preachers in the northern conference were separated from the southern preachers. Consequently, the southern preachers did not participate in the debate or vote for the rule. After the breach was healed, Asbury required the entire connection to abide by the decisions of the small conference in Maryland. It seems that Asbury took advantage of the temporary separation to push through rules that would not have been passed had all the preachers been consulted. As expected, when the slave rule was applied to local preachers, a lack of consensus emerged. In 1783, the conference agreed to try slave-holding local preachers for one more year.[13] In 1784, the traveling preachers determined to suspend the local preachers in Maryland, Delaware, Pennsylvania, and New Jersey who did not emancipate their slaves and to try those in Virginia for one more year.[14] The local preachers in Virginia formed a powerful lobby that challenged the authority of the conference. As the conferences became more aggressive with the slavery rules, the local preachers in Virginia became more vocal in their opposition.

In the first MEC *Discipline* in 1785, the church, under the leadership of Coke, showed a strong resolve to deal decisively with the slavery issue. In order to "extirpate the abomination of slavery from among us," the MEC added new rules. First, every member who held slaves had to make provision for their gradual manumission. Second, the traveling preachers had to keep a journal to record the ages and names of every slave and the date when they were to be set free.

They also had to list where the signed documents from the slave-holding Methodists were recorded. Third, every member not wishing to abide by the rule could withdraw from society within the next 12 months. After that period, non-compliant members would be expelled. Fourth, after withdrawing or being expelled, the former members could not participate in the sacrament with the Methodists. Fifth, no new people would be admitted to the society or the Lord's Supper until they signed documents to emancipate their slaves.[15] According to Richard Cameron,

> These rules [in the 1785 *Discipline*], however, were to be applied only as far as they were consistent with the laws of the states in which the members resided. This fateful exception referred to the laws forbidding emancipation which had been enacted in some southern states. The conference felt that it was not the province of the church to contravene established legal provisions of the civil authority.[16]

As was previously noted, Asbury and Coke conducted three conferences in 1785. The first was held in North Carolina on 20 April; the second in Virginia on 1 May; and the last in Baltimore on 1 June. During these meetings, Coke used aggressive rhetoric and ecclesial threats to push his antislavery views. While at the North Carolina Conference, Coke spoke in a very harsh tone. Lee responded to Coke so that Coke thought Lee was "unfriendly to the cause." Afterward, during the examination of character, Coke objected to Lee's. When Lee defended his position, he was interrupted by Coke. This led to a heated exchange. Later, Coke apologized. After the debate, the North Carolina Conference agreed to send the state legislature a petition asking that residents be allowed to emancipate slaves. North Carolina did not allow for the emancipation of slaves. Barclay notes that the MEC appealed directly to the states in order to change laws that prohibited emancipation.

> Methodists at that time were active in circulating petitions to be presented to state legislatures in behalf of emancipation. A petition had been circulated by Methodists in North Carolina praying for the repeal of the law against emancipation of slaves and Coke states that Asbury visited the governor and "gained him over." The legislature, however, failed to act. In November [1785] at least nine petitions were presented to the Virginia Legislature—four of which were from Halifax, Amelia, Mecklenburg, and Pittsylvania—in the heart of Methodist country. No legislative action resulted.[17]

Because the rule in the 1785 Discipline made an exception for Methodists who lived in states that forbid the emancipation of slaves, Coke was more restrained in North Carolina. However, while in Virginia, he was pointed in his outspoken opposition to slavery because Virginia law allowed for emancipation. Evidently, this caused a great deal of internal and external opposition. In reference to this period, Lee said,

> [Coke] was much respected in the United States; but he met with some opposition in the south parts of Virginia, owing to his imprudent manner of preaching

against slavery.... When he printed his journal in England, he acknowledged that he was wrong in preaching publicly against slavery in Virginia, where the practice was tolerated by law.[18]

The phrase "south parts of Virginia" refers to O'Kelly's citadel. In this case, the opposition was not from him. He was a very strong abolitionist who took an active stand against slavery. Evidently, the local preachers and other slaveholding members opposed Coke.

If one follows Lee's logic, there was no "proper" time to preach against slavery. The *Discipline* protected slave owners in states where it was not legal to emancipate slaves. One should not force the issue there. Additionally, one should not preach against slave-holding in states where it was legal because it was legal. At this point, Lee displayed the characteristics of a true Virginian. His logic betrayed the deep regional divide related to this issue. According to Samuel Hill,

> [White Methodists in the South] were not averse to benevolent reform if that meant encouraging personal temperance and helping the orphan or widow, the deaf, the dumb, the blind, the insane. But, if it meant rearranging the social order, tampering with slavery, interfering with state sovereignty, defending the Indians' right to remain on good farm and cotton land, then benevolent reform was totally misguided. It was in fact, un-Christian, since it created political tests for spiritual organizations. Whether a man held slaves or not was irrelevant to his right to join a church.[19]

As a consequence of his preaching against slavery, Coke had several narrow escapes from violent handling. Bucke provides numerous examples.[20] Asbury offered the following one:

> I found the minds of the people greatly agitated with our rules against slavery, and a proposed petition to the general assembly for the emancipation of Blacks. Colonel Bedford and Doctor Coke disputed on the subject, and the Colonel used some threats: next day, brother O'Kelly let fly at them and they were made angry enough; we, however, came on with whole bones.[21]

At the Virginia Conference, many petitions were presented asking that the minutes on slavery be suspended. Coke replied that they must be retained and threatened that preaching would be withdrawn from circuits where they could not be enforced. The Virginia legislature did not act on the petitions that it received.[22] After the Virginia Conference, Coke and Asbury visited George Washington and handed him a petition against slavery. They were received politely and were able to discuss the issue with him. However, he refused to sign it.[23] While in Virginia, Asbury dined with General Roberdeau. They conversed on slavery, the difficulties attending emancipation, and the resentment some of the members of the Virginia legislature express against those who favor a general abolition.[24]

While in Virginia, Coke met with Devereux Jarratt who was an Anglican priest and a great friend of southern Methodism. They disagreed about the minute on slavery. Coke wrote that Jarratt was "a violent assertor of the justice and propriety of Negro slavery."[25] Jarratt responded by saying:

The truth is, the little man read the minutes to me, and asked my opinion of them. I told him I was no friend of slavery; but however I did not think the minutes proper, for two reasons. First, The disturbance it would make and the opposition it would meet with in the societies. Second, He ought not to make a disputable matter a positive term of communion. And as he was a stranger in the land, I told him the spirit of Virginia would not brook force.[26]

In less than one month, the Baltimore conference did what the Virginia conference would not. They suspended the rule on slavery. Little is reported on the debate or the change. Coke stated, "We thought it prudent to suspend the minute concerning slavery, on account of the great opposition that had been given it, especially in the new circuits, our work being too infantile a state to push things to extremity."[27] "Indeed, I now acknowledge that, however just my sentiments may be concerning slavery, it was ill-judged of me to deliver them from the pulpit."[28] Coke, Asbury, Lee, and others contended that the suspension of the minute was the only option open to them. All of them justify this concession because of the damage the antislavery rhetoric had on membership and continuity in the MEC. This concern is partially substantiated by the Virginia membership figures. In 1783 and 1784, while the slavery rules were being applied to local preachers and the people as a whole, Virginia Methodism suffered large declines. Numbers for 1785 are not available. By 1786, a year after the rule was suspended, Virginia Methodism showed a large increase in members.

The slavery issue inflamed passions in the South and caused division in a small denomination that could not withstand the struggle. When the traveling preachers who were more intimately connected to the people saw the negative affect that the issue was having on membership and the viability of the MEC, they begged for relief from the rules. Coke and Asbury were still against slavery after the suspension of the rule. However, for the sake of numerical growth and lack of controversy, they minimized the slavery issue.

The issue of slavery did not emerge again until the 1789 *Discipline*. It stated that the buying or selling the bodies and souls of men, women, or children, with an intention to enslave them, was forbidden. However, this rule did not forbid the holding of slaves.[29]

The 1796 General Conference reached a more decisive conclusion. Question 12 asked, "What regulations shall be made for the extirpation of the crying evil of African Slavery?"[30] First, anyone admitted to an "official satiation" in the church who owned slaves had to emancipate them immediately or gradually, depending on the laws of the state where the person lived. Every level of church organization was required to supervise this issue. The annual conferences were permitted to make their own rules respecting the admission of persons to official stations in the MEC. This allowed for a local response to the problem. It also permitted the MEC to have a divided stand on the issue. Second, no slave-holder could be admitted into the local society until the appointed preacher talked to the person about the evil of slave-holding. Third, any member who sold a slave would be expelled from society. Any member who bought a slave or came into the possession of a slave had to make provisions for gradual emancipation. Fourth, each itinerant was to give the issue of slavery great attention and send his thoughts to the next General Conference so that the MEC could "eradicate this enormous evil" from the church.[31]

The 1800 General Conference entertained six motions related to slavery. It was a hot topic of debate that lasted for many days. One motion sought to expel any traveling preacher who became the owner of slaves by virtue of marriage unless he emancipated them immediately. Another sought to require every person uniting with a society in the MEC to emancipate his or her slaves within one year. These were defeated. Finally, the conference agreed to appoint a committee to study the issue and to issue a report on the evils of slavery to the Methodist societies. William McKendree moved that each annual conference draw up an address to the various state legislatures, from year to year, for the gradual abolition of slavery. The motion passed.[32] Thus, the 1800 General Conference did not follow through with the determination of the 1796 General Conference. It allowed the issue to smolder.

A survey of Asbury's and Lee's writings shows that the slavery issue was very complicated. In 1788, Asbury wrote, "Their minister boldly preaches against the freedom of slaves. Our Joseph Everett with no less zeal and boldness, cries aloud for their liberty—emancipation."[33] Everett was in Maryland. Then Asbury bragged, "most of our members in these parts [Delmarva] have freed their slaves."[34] While in Virginia in 1789, Asbury was rejected by a former friend over the slave issue. He stated, "We found ourselves not at home. . . . My spirit has been wounded not a little. I know not which to pity most—the slaves or their masters."[35] While in Virginia in 1790, Asbury wrote that the disputes about slavery have been harmful to growth.[36] While in conference in South Carolina in 1794, many of the preachers voiced concern about the rule that forbade members from selling slaves. They feared that there would be no one left to pay their salaries if they did not retain slave traders in the societies. Asbury was more concerned with his ability to supply the state with preachers.[37]

In 1795, while in Charleston, Asbury observed that their meetings were filled with woman and slaves. He urged the preachers to meet with the slaves by themselves and to teach them how to read. The slaves would not come to mixed meetings. Forcing the issue caused the MEC to lose African members.[38] Later, he met with the African Americans in Maryland and talked about forming a distinct African, yet Methodist Church.[39] He complained that the African Americans in Baltimore desired a church, which, in temporal, would be altogether under their own direction, and asked greater privileges than the white stewards and trustees ever had right to claim.[40] The blacks responded positively to the MEC in Maryland. Between 1786 and 1800, black membership increased by 3,418 persons and white membership only increased by 2,189.

In 1795, Asbury complained that the southern preachers were being battered on the subject of slaves. Public opinion was not in their favor. Yet, the preachers in the north were at peace. He resolved that there was a regional split on this issue. Then he concluded, "It will not do; we must be Methodists in one place as well as another."[41]

While in North Carolina, Asbury wrote, "My spirit was grieved at the conduct of some Methodists, that hire out slaves at public places to the highest bidder, to cut, skin, and starve them; I think such members ought to be dealt with: on the side of the oppressors there are law and power, but where are justice and mercy to the poor slaves?"[42]

Because of his strong feelings about slavery, Asbury moderated his language so he would not offend people. While in Virginia he stated, "I rose in the morning, in some fear lest I had or should say too much on slavery."[43] In another place, Asbury chastened himself for his strong feelings on the subject:

> What blanks are in this country—and how much worse are rice plantations! If a man-of-war is a "floating hell," these are standing ones: wicked masters, overseers, and Negroes—cursing, drinking—no Sabbaths, no sermons. But hush! Perhaps my journal will never see the light; and if it does, matters may mend before that time. . . . O wretched priests, thus to lead the people on in blindness![44]

At times, Asbury appeared resigned to the evil of slavery:

> O! to be dependent on slaveholders [for money and support] is in part to be a slave, and I was free born. I am brought to conclude that slavery will exist in Virginia perhaps for ages; there is not a sufficient sense of religion nor liberty to destroy it; Methodists, Baptists, Presbyterians, in the highest flights or rapturous piety, still maintain and defend it.[45]

In 1797, Asbury wrote a startling justification for the MEC's mollified stance on slavery. He said,

> I am perfectly satisfied with the part I took in the [1796] General Conference relative to the slaves. It is of great consequence to us to have proper access to the masters and the slaves. I had a case, a family I visited more than a year ago, a tyrannical old Welshmen. I saw there he was cruel, his people were wicked, and treated like dogs. "Well," say you, "I would not go near such a man's house." That would be just as the devil would have it. In one year I saw that man much softened, his people admitted into the house of prayer, the whole plantation, 40 or 50 singing and praising God. What now can sweeten the bitter cup like religion? The slaves soon see the preachers are their friends, and soften their owners towards them. There are thousands here of slaves who if we could come to them would embrace religion.[46]

Later, in the same year he declared, "If any had asked the Lord on the subject of slavery, as on polygamy, he must have said, Moses, as a man, suffered this, a less evil, to prevent greater evil; but it was not so from the beginning of the creation: it is the fall which hath done this, not a holy God."[47]

In sum, in order to have access to slaves, Asbury advocated a non-confrontational approach. He wanted to reach people with the Gospel and was willing to ignore a social injustice if he could achieve a spiritual victory by it. He may have been justified in this from his perspective at that time. In his mind, the institutions of society were less important than a person's salvation. However, this attitude gave rise to a pacifistic church in the South that lost its prophetic voice. In time, it also lost most of its black members.

As previously noted, Asbury and the MEC struggled with the local preachers in Virginia. Many of them acted with an independent spirit. In an effort to bring them in line with the other preachers, Asbury organized them in groups so they could be better supervised. He met with many of the groups. After one meeting he noted that seven out of ten were not slave-holders.[48] Then he instructed Philip Sands to draw up an agreement for the local preachers to sign stating that they were opposed to slavery. In 1798, he wrote,

> Thus we may know the real sentiments of our local preachers. It appears to me, that we can never fully reform the people, until we reform the preachers; and that hitherto, expect purging the travelling connexion, we have been working at the wrong end. But if it is lawful for local preachers to hold slaves, then it is lawful for travelling preachers also; and they may keep plantations and overseers upon their quarters: but this reproach of inconsistency must be rolled away.[49]

While in Charleston, Asbury noted that Methodism grew most with the slaves. He had a preferential option for them and desired them more than he did the slave owners. Because of this, many of the white people in Charleston had negative feelings toward Methodism. Some were aggressive in their opposition. The General Conference in 1800 sent an address to the state legislatures about slavery. The South Carolina legislature was very angry about it. Asbury comments,

> I saw one of the members of the General Assembly of South Carolina, who informed me that our address from the General Conference had been read and reprobated; and furthermore, that it had been the occasion of producing a law which prohibited a minister's attempting to instruct any number of blacks with the doors shut; and authorizing a peace officer to break open the door in such cases, and disperse or whip the offenders.[50]

The dangers of discussing slavery were increased enormously after 1793 when 500,000 slaves revolted and won their freedom in Haiti. Refugees from Haiti recounted ghastly stories. The insurrection inspired slaves in America and caused slave owners to fear slave revolts. Along the coastal regions in South Carolina, slaves outnumbered whites. According to Ferguson,

> Guards in the South were stepped up, patrols increased, church services among slaves forbidden unless they were held in open and unless whites could be present, it having been long suspected that it was in religious meetings that plots of insurrection were hatched. . . . [After many unsuccessful slave uprisings in the South] it came to light that Methodists, Quakers, and Frenchmen were to be spared if the armed slaves carried out their designs.[51]

The long-term consequences of the antislavery rhetoric of the MEC, mild as it was in 1800, was far reaching in terms of the church's ability to do ministry in South Carolina. Asbury wrote,

> Sure nothing could so effectually alarm and arm the citizens of South Carolina against the Methodists as the *Address of the General Conference*. The rich among the people never thought us worth to preach to them: they did indeed give their

slaves liberty to hear and join our Church; but now it appears the poor Africans will no longer have this indulgence. Perhaps we shall soon be thought unfit for the company of their dogs.[52]

Not only was it difficult to do ministry in South Carolina because of the negative sentiments from the white people toward the MEC, it was also dangerous.

> I had thought our address would move their majesties and the peers of Charleston. Report says they have pumped poor George Dougherty until they had almost deprived him of breath; and John Harper committed the apology to the flames before the intendant of the city: I have seen his apology for receiving them.[53]

Northern abolitionists had sent some printed antislavery addresses to John Harper, the itinerate at Charleston. He stored them away, but a copy got into circulation. It enraged the people. Harper was brought before the authorities. After he explained the situation he burned the remaining papers. No charge was laid against him. Unfortunately, George Dougherty was seized at the prayer meeting the following night and held under the spout of a pump until he was nearly drowned. Finally, he was saved by an intrepid woman who pushed through the mob and used her shawl to stop up the pipe.

Methodism struggled with the issue of ordaining African preachers. This hindered the MEC from having an indigenous ministry with that population. According to Lee, in May 1800:

> There was a new rule formed respecting the ordination of coloured, or black people, to the office of [local] deacon, among us. . . . "The bishops have obtained leave by the suffrages of the general conference, to ordain local deacons of our African brethren in places where they have built a house or houses for the worship of God; provided they have a person among them qualified for that office, and he can obtain an election of two-thirds of the male members of the society to which he belongs, and a recommendation from the minister who has the charge, and from his fellow-labourers in the city or circuit.[54]

This rule was never printed during the life of Lee. He was the first to make it public. He said,

> When the rule was formed, there were many of the preachers, especially from the southern states, that were much opposed to it. . . . Some who were opposed to it moved that it not be printed in our Form of Discipline, and a vote of the conference was obtained to enter it on the journals only, and most of the preachers were opposed to it's [sic] being made public.[55]

Richard Allen of Philadelphia was ordained a deacon on June 11, 1799. He was the first African American to be ordained. According to Lee, others were ordained in New York, Philadelphia, and Lynchburg, Virginia.[56]

Based on the information in this section, the institution of slavery was a negative contextual factor that hindered the growth of the MEC in the South. As the Methodism responded to the slavery issue, it encountered an opposition that militated against growth. The opposition took the form of negative media attention; withdrawing members; and internal conflict that pitted members against members, local preachers against traveling preachers, the bishops against traveling preachers, and the North against the South. The MEC's response to slavery issue contributed to the southern decline during the 1790s.

The slavery issue also revealed a strong regional difference of opinion. Lee represented the opinion of the South. Even though he opposed slavery, he resented the church's meddling in that issue by means of its many rules. Slavery was ingrained into the life and fabric of his society and was a culturally accepted institution. Even devout people learned to tolerate it. For that matter, many of the South's prominent Methodists and local preachers were slave owners. The local preachers were affectionately tied to the people and were very influential. Attempts to expel these preachers because they owned slaves only made matters worse. Furthermore, the Methodist preachers in the South did not want to enforce all the rules because they would lose slave-owning members who paid their wages. They also believed that the people would become disaffected by the rhetoric. Ultimately, they feared that the church's strong antislavery stance would hinder its ability to maintain its membership with the white population. Additionally, it would compromise it efforts to evangelize the slaves because hostile slave owners would not give the preachers access to their slaves.

On the other hand, Coke and many of the preachers who challenged slavery at the various conferences believed that the moral and social implications of being Methodist required the MEC to speak out against slavery in every way possible. At first, the pragmatic issues related to church growth and the continued viability of American Methodism were of secondary importance.

In short, people's opinions on the issue were largely colored by the context in which they lived. Most northern preachers believed that slavery was a social justice issue that demanded a prophetic voice in opposition to it. For a time, they were willing to prioritize evangelism and internal cohesion for the sake of growth, but they never shared the opinion of the southern Methodists who tolerated slavery under the guise of the evangelistic priority, i.e., a mollified stance that permitted the evangelization of slaves and lessened the acrimony of southerners who were sympathetic to slavery. This set the stage for continuous conflict and a future confrontation.

The slavery issue and the general prejudice against all blacks kept Methodism from having an indigenous ministry with this population. Blacks resisted mixed societies because they wanted to be segregated from the whites in order to enjoy culture specific worship with their own leaders. Asbury instructed southern preachers to do this. However, in some places, laws prevented this. For a short period, Asbury took a black traveling companion with him so he could preach more effectively to the blacks.

Asbury tried to establish an African Methodist Church because he recognized the problem. If an African church had been established, the black Methodists would have been free to build their own chapels and ordain their own preachers where laws permitted. Also, they would have been free from white control and able to become fully indigenous. As late as 1797, Asbury commented that he was still trying to organize an independent African church in Maryland.[57] That dream was not realized in this time period. Still, Asbury encouraged the societies and preachers to build chapels dedicated to ministry with black people. In those chapels, black men could be ordained to preach. This laid the foundation for the black Methodist churches.

The following provides a point of reference. In 1790, blacks equaled 19.2 percent of the U.S. population[58] and 20.3 percent of the MEC's membership. In the South, blacks equaled 23 percent of the MEC membership. However, an obvious disparity occurs when black membership in the MEC is compared with the percent of black population in the various southern states. Blacks equaled 42 percent of the general population in Virginia and South Carolina in 1790. However, they only equaled 20.6 and 14.3 percent of the respective MEC membership in those states. In North Carolina, blacks accounted for 26 percent of the state population and 17 percent of the MEC membership. Of the 29,264 slaves in Georgia, only 184 (0.68 percent) were members of the MEC. On the other hand, in 1790, blacks equaled 32 percent of the Maryland population and 32 percent of the MEC membership in that state. In 1800, blacks accounted for 47 percent of the MEC membership in Maryland. In that year, there were 11,672 black MEC members in the southern states to include 5,497 black members in Maryland. The black membership in Maryland equaled 47 percent of the total black membership in the South in 1800. By comparison, the white membership in Maryland only equaled 23.2 percent of the total white membership for the South in 1800. Excluding Maryland, in 1790, blacks equaled 16.9 percent of southern membership. By 1800, they equaled 21.9 percent. In short, even though the MEC grew with the black population in all the southern states, it experienced rapid growth with the black population in Maryland.

The data show that Maryland Methodism more effectively reached and integrated the black population within the structure of the MEC in the 1790s than the other southern states. Asbury attempted to accommodate the blacks in Maryland. He tried to build them separate buildings and to give them more control over their internal operations. At the same time, the cultural climate in Maryland was less oppressive to blacks, and the preachers in that state spoke out more intentionally against slavery. However, its white membership declined at a faster rate than the white membership in the other southern states from 1793 through 1799. In that period, the white membership in Maryland declined by 31 percent. The rest of the southern states to include O'Kelly's district only declined by 21.5 percent. From 1793 through 1799, the black membership in Maryland declined by 10 percent. For the rest of the southern states, it declined by 27.5 percent. From 1790 to 1800, the white membership dropped from 10,425 to 6,363 or by 41 percent. By contrast, the black membership shows an increase from 4,982 to 5,497. Things turned around in 1801. In that year, the white membership increased by 2,230 and the black membership by 1,052.

Table 14-2 shows that the black membership of Maryland remained fairly constant during the 1790s. It only fluctuated by 799 people.

Table 14-2. Membership Totals for Maryland Methodism between 1790 and 1799

	1790		1791		1792		1793		1794	
	Black	White	Black	White	Black	White	Black	White	Black	White
Total by Race	4982	10425	5522	9759	5593	9959	5683	9510	5749	8952
Combined Total	15407		15281		15552		15193		14701	
	1795		1796		1797		1798		1799	
	Black	White	Black	White	Black	White	Black	White	Black	White
Total by Race	5523	8641	4910	7496	5096	6982	4950	6885	5079	6568
Combined Total	14164		12406		12078		11835		11647	

Source: MEC, *Minutes* (1813).

In summary, Maryland Methodism attempted to appeal to the blacks and to evangelize them. Plus, it was not as hindered by restrictive laws. As a consequence, it reaped a fast growing ministry with blacks. In Charleston, Asbury believed that the Methodists were sent primarily to the blacks. Because he wintered in Charleston, he focused the circuit on that priority. Consequently, the black membership in Charleston grew from 77 to 440 from 1790 to 1800. The white membership only grew by nine persons.

It appears that southern whites did not want to participate in a church that valued blacks as their equals. Advocacy on behalf of blacks and aggressively seeking to evangelize them sounded a counter-cultural signal that humanized the slaves and made the whites conscience of their misanthropy. As the black membership increased, Maryland Methodism may have been stigmatized as a black person's church. If this is the case, it would explain why the white membership declined so fast. In the other southern states, the black membership was dependent on the goodwill of the slave owners. As the MEC ratcheted up its rhetoric and its efforts to evangelize blacks, a growing number of slave owners may have prevented their slaves from participating since most slaves attended services at their plantation.

This study has not accumulated enough facts to be incontrovertible, but, from the data gathered, it appears that the white membership in the South declined proportionally to the MEC's efforts to evangelize and advocate for blacks. Based on this, one can postulate that aggressive ministry to blacks in the South during the 1790s was a negative institutional factor in terms of white membership growth. It was a positive institutional factor for black membership growth in areas where the slave owners were not disaffected by the antislavery rhetoric. In those areas, both the white and black membership declined at a similar rate. The reality of the latter caused principled preachers to abandoned the MEC's historic antislavery stance in order to remain a viable church in the South.

In retrospect, the church must keep the moral mandate and the evangelistic mandate in balance. Asbury and others argued that evangelism should be prioritized. According to the argument, when evil people fall under the influence of the church, God changes them and the society they sway. The church is salt and light. Like yeast, it leavens society. Direct confrontation pushes potential converts away from God and makes them more resolved in their evil. Ultimately, the church is called to preach the gospel and disciple those who come to it. In time, God will change the world as the church changes people via its witness of radical faith. Unfortunately, this facile postulation only postponed the inevitable, brought evil people into the church without changing them, and helped to perpetuate the unjust treatment of African Americans. The mass exodus of blacks from the MEC into the black Methodist churches (AME 1816, AME Zion 1821, and CME 1870) is a sad consequence of this. Additionally, the slavery controversy hastened the split between the MEC and the MEC South in 1844. The split presaged things to come.

Methodism's Bias toward the Poor

An earlier section discussed the economic condition of early America. A depression lasted until 1788. The economy gradually improved through 1791 and then surged forward. In the South, slaves contributed to the prosperity and were considered necessary for its continuance.[59] Before the economic upswing, the South did not have a large middle class. It lacked the industrial base of the North. Ninety percent of the people lived in a rural environment. This hindered the growth of a middle class. Most white people worked for the rich or lived on a subsistence farm. Southern inhabitants were largely polarized between the rich, the masses, and the slaves. However, the invention of the cotton gin helped to change that. It enabled poor white farmers to enjoy the benefits of the bull economy. Land suitable for raising cotton was cheap and could be purchased or rented. As a consequence, a new class of white farmer emerged in the South. He worked small farms and expanded as opportunity allowed. As these farmers began to fill-in the gap between the poor and the rich, some became slave owners. The new ordering changed life in the South and inspired the masses to improve their situation. The resignation of the depression years was replaced with an optimism that was embodied by Jefferson and republicanism.[60]

The years of the economic boom and the changing social structure in the South corresponded with the years of numerical decline and low receptivity for the MEC in the South. It is possible that Methodism's bias against slave owning, the acquisition of wealth, and the wealthy classes made the church unattractive to people who aspired to improve their material condition. This would include most of the white people in the South. The MEC failed to inspire the white masses to the extent that it was out of step with the spirit of the age in regard to upward mobility.

The following paragraphs attempt to demonstrate Methodism's bias to the poor and its negative attitude toward wealth. It quotes from official documents and Asbury. The quotations show that the bias was a national institutional factor. However, the bias did not mean that Methodists of this time were primarily poor or that the MEC opposed the ruling class. In fact, during the 1790s, Methodists were rising in social rank and in wealth. It was a natural consequence of redemption and lift, and the economic upswing. The MEC struggled in its efforts to reconcile this new reality with its self-perception.

In earlier years, Southern Methodism grew by means of great revivals. The revivals particularly appealed to the poor. By focusing on the poor, both in England and in America, Methodism found a receptive niche in the social landscape. During the time of economic prosperity, the traditional niche became increasingly smaller. Additionally, many who became Methodists when they were poor were now experiencing a more comfortable lifestyle. For example, in the 1790s, Methodism in the Mid-Atlantic cities was "still an artisan's church, but its artisan members were moving from a disproportionate number of lower-class artisans to a disproportionate number of large-workshop artisans."[61] Doris Andrews captured the irony of the situation. She argues that the trustees and the well-off members of the church were more influential than Asbury or his preachers in determining the local ethos of individual churches.

> In some respects James O'Kelly's attacks on Asbury's authority may have been misdirected . . . because the preachers in the long run continued to depend on the largess of their followers, many of them with an increasing investment in the materialistic world that the Methodists in general condemned.[62]

If this analysis is true, it highlights the conflict between a national institutional expectation and a local institutional preference. The contextual reality of an economic upswing was not a positive or a negative factor. The church's response to it determined its character. In fact, the MEC's bias for the poor placed it in conflict with the contextual reality of the South and the expectation of the local societies. Because of this, some members left the church as they progressed up the economic latter. It kept other advancing people from affiliating with the MEC.

While in Maryland in late 1785, Asbury claimed that the principle members were not successful in business. They were poor. According to Asbury, if they were well-off they would not be Methodists. However, he stated, once a person became a Methodist, the person was better able to handle prosperity without losing his soul. He encouraged the people to relocate to the western frontier "where the means of rearing a family, and the advancing in the world, were more within the reach of the inhabitants."[63] In 1790, Asbury wrote, "Our society in the city of Philadelphia are [sic] generally poor: perhaps it is well; when men become rich, they sometimes forget that they are Methodists."[64] This was a statement based on personal observation. The statement was validated by his experiences in Charleston.

While in Charleston in 1793, Wesley's maxim, "It is a mere miracle for a Methodist to increase in wealth and not decrease in grace," burned on his mind.[65] To Asbury, a negative relationship existed between acquiring wealth and staying a Methodist. During the time of economic prosperity in 1797, Asbury lamented the state of some Charleston Methodists who gained wealth and prestige. "Too often, when any rise in their circumstances, they seek for offices, or become slave traders, and much too great to be Methodists."[66] As people climbed the economic and social ladder in Charleston most did not continue to identify with the MEC. He continued, "I am ready to conclude we are not sent to the whites of this place, except a very few; but to the poor Africans."[67] Slaves accounted for over 50 percent of Charleston's population. While traveling in the countryside 12 miles north of Sumpter, South Carolina, Asbury said, "Religion is reviving here among the Africans; several are joined in society: they are the poor; these are the people we are more immediately called to preach to."[68]

Asbury and the MEC had a special passion for the poor and dispossessed. While in New York, Asbury observed, "The people on this island, who hear the Gospel, are generally poor, and these are the kind I want, and expect to get."[69] Throughout his ministry, Asbury targeted poor people. Additionally, by word and example, he directed the itinerants to do the same.

A Connecticut resident lamented to Asbury, "It was the misfortune of the Methodists to fall in with some of the most ignorant, poor, and disreputable people in the State."[70] The person viewed this as a negative factor because rich people would not socialize in a church that sided with and was composed of the poor. Asbury took it as a compliment and bragged that the poor had the gospel preached to them. Then he quipped, "Have any of the rulers believed on him?"[71]

Asbury detested the indulgent pursuits that characterized wealthy people. While in western Virginia he stated, "When I behold the conduct of the people who attend the Springs, particularly the gentry, I am led to thank God that I was not born to riches; I rather bless God, that I am not in hell."[72] In reference to the white people of Charleston, in 1795 Asbury wrote,

> The white and worldly people are intolerably ignorant of God; playing, dancing, swearing, racing; these are their common practices and pursuits. Our few male members do not attend preaching; and I fear there is hardly one who walks with God: the women and Africans attend our meetings and some few strangers.[73]

While preaching in Connecticut in 1800, Asbury commented,

> We had a finely-dressed congregation—a good name is a great matter with these people. O Baxter! are these thy apostate children? Will Methodism ever live in such whited walls and painted sepulchers as these people, who delight to dwell insensible to the life of religion, and closed up in their own formality and imaginary security?[74]

Asbury's bias for the poor became a hallmark of the institution. In 1789 he wrote, "To begin at the right end of the work is to go first to the poor; these *will*, the rich *may possibly*, hear the truth: there are those among us who have blundered here."[75] In other words, go to the poor first and build the work around them. Then the rich may be converted to God. Do not build the church around the rich because they will corrupt it, and the poor will be beholden to the means of the rich. This sentiment is contained in the General Minutes and all the MEC Disciplines during this period:

> Let all our churches be built plain and decent; but not more expensively than is absolutely unavoidable; otherwise the necessity of raising money will make rich

men necessary to us. But if so, we must be dependent on them, yea, and governed by them. And then farewell to Methodist discipline, if not doctrine too.[76]

As demonstrated earlier, most itinerants were poor. This caused them to be in conflict with some of the local preachers and members who took advantage of the good economy. Many itinerants located so they could improve their lot. Prosperous local preachers served as a temptation for this. Some local preachers became slave holders. Itinerants were required to counsel against this. Ultimately, the local preachers were more indigenous to the local populations than the traveling preachers because they identified with the aspiring people in a way that the itinerants could not. Andrews sums up the situation.

> Preachers might do what they could to mitigate the effects on the followers of this new attachment to commerce and its consequences; but the old paternal model did not fit well with the new republican society.... Many preachers concerned with respectability themselves tended to ally with the elite in the local societies.... As it turned out, the Jeffersonian republic argued in a kind of cultural renaissance for religion.[77]

In sum, Methodism's institutional bias for the poor made the MEC a church of the masses. The church attracted common people because the MEC spoke their language. This positive institutional factor fostered numerical growth because it allowed the MEC to target the masses with an indigenous ministry. However, the focus on the poor alienated the wealthy and those that aspired to wealth. A bias for the poor can become a bias against the wealthy. During the economic boom in the 1790s, the number of white poor shrunk as the masses improved their economic situation. When this occurred, the MEC's institutional bias for the poor conflicted with a dominant contextual factor and caused upwardly mobile white members to leave the church to the extent that the MEC would not flex with their changing social status. As has already been stated, when the poor became Methodist, they acquired a disciplined lifestyle that promoted redemption and lift. That is, Methodist discipline coupled with economic boom generated upward mobility. In fact, many Methodists became successful businesspeople. A disproportionate number of local preachers fall into this category. Some owned slaves. The lifestyle of the prosperous local preachers beckoned to itinerants who wanted to settle down and marry.

Second, the pursuit of "worldly riches" may have distracted the unchurched because they did not have time for Methodism or feel a need for experiential religion. Studies have shown that receptivity levels diminish as a poor population gains access to the benefits of material society. Asbury sensed this when he traveled through New England and when he wintered in Charleston.

Third, Asbury hints that upward mobility and the propensity to acquire land also predisposed people to get slaves. During the 1790s, the MEC restated its strong stance against buying or selling slaves. One who did such things could not be a Methodist. Methodists who had slaves in states where slaves could not be manumitted were allowed to keep them provided they treated them humanely. Because of Methodism's antislavery stance and its diatribe against the wealthy lifestyle, many slave owners felt negatively disposed toward Methodism. In turn, growing numbers would not give the Methodist preachers access to their slaves. One can assume that much of the decrease in the black southern membership in the 1790s relates to this. Slaves represented one of the most receptive populations in early America. Their receptivity was not lessened by French republicanism or economic prosperity. EAM grew or declined with this population in relationship to its ability to gain access to it.

Fourth, even though Asbury said that Methodism targeted the poor and despised the gentry's lifestyle, he does not speak for the entire connection. The itinerants, local preachers, and lay leadership were the public face of Methodism. The journals of prominent circuit riders seem to support Asbury's claims. However, it cannot be asserted that the institutional bias was shared by a majority of those who aligned with EAM.

A Shortage of Preachers Caused a Numerical Decline in Southern Methodism

As has been shown in Chapter 10, Methodism lost members because it suffered from a shortage of itinerants.[78] According to Table 10-3, from 1788 through 1791 the MEC had a net gain of 35 to 36 traveling preachers each year. Consequently, the MEC could expand its borders, split circuits, and send missionaries to nonadjacent locations. In fact, from 1788 to 1792 the MEC added 31 new circuits in the South and 29 in other locations.

From 1792 through 1799, the number of itinerants who located increased dramatically. A majority of the locations occurred in the South. Most of the locations happened because of financial stress. Only a few traveling preachers left with the O'Kelly and Hammett schisms. Asbury claimed that 200 of the best preachers located because of marriage. The Methodist system could not support married preachers.[79] Other preachers wore themselves out. By 1794, the shortage of itinerants became critical and remained that way until the 1800 General Conference made some colossal changes so that the MEC could attract and retain more traveling preachers.[80] In some cases, local preachers could serve a vacant circuit. However, the apostolic calling of the MEC depended on circuit riders to expand the boundaries and increase its membership by itinerating.

Asbury continued to increase the number of circuits and itinerants in the South until 1794; two years after the southern decline began. As such, the southern membership plateau and subsequent decline did not happen because of a lack of traveling preachers. However, the lack of preachers did hinder the MEC from expanding into new areas. In 1796, Asbury lamented that he did not have enough itinerants to meet the missionary obligation on the frontier.[81] At that time, the missionary effort in New England borrowed 26 preachers from the other regions.[82] The New England expansion put a huge strain on internal resources and reduced the MEC's ability to man the South at the optimal level to sustain growth. Even though this did not cause the southern decline, it contributed to the MEC's inability to disciple the masses who had flooded into the church during the revival period.

A Law of Revival

As was detailed in Chapter 11, the lack of revivals contributed to numerical decline in southern Methodism during the 1790s. A clear relationship exists between revivals and church growth. Many historians of Methodism have credited "revivals" or the "revival spirit" with numerical success. Likewise, from the *prima facie* evidence, there is a clear relationship between a lack of revivals and numerical decline.

There were no significant revivals in the South during the years of decline. The 1789 revivals were the last recorded ones. In the late 1790s, Asbury tried to revitalize the church by encouraging prayer meetings and spiritual disciplines, hoping to produce revivals. However, he was not successful. The membership decline was not halted until 1800. In that year, revivals returned to the South. Like rain on dessert soil, they produced instant growth.

Based on the data, one can deduce a pattern. Before the 1790s, southern Methodism experienced periodic revivals. During each revival, the membership of the effected circuits increased dramatically. After the revivals, the membership plateaued and slowly dipped as the implications of discipleship became clear. Many people who joined the society in the excitement of revival soon lost interest or were distracted. Jesus' parable of the soils seems to speak to this phenomenon. However, before the revival energy dissipated, the societies experienced another revival. The energy from the new revival pushed the societies to new membership highs. After the new zenith was reach, the cycle of decline and progress continued.

From 1785 through 1788, it appears that southern Methodist membership did not follow the revival cycle because it did not plateau or decline. However, a close look at the data shows that individual circuits within that region did follow the pattern. When the memberships of the various circuits are studied, the pattern appears. As an aggregate, Southern Methodism grew during these years because it added circuits and preachers. The unabated growth of the mid-1780s following the earlier revivals was aided by aggressive church planting.

Beginning in 1788, revivals returned to four areas that had previously plateaued. They are the Brunswick (south), Berkley (north-central), and Fairfax (east-central) areas in Virginia, and the Baltimore area in Maryland. As these circuits grew during times of revival, state memberships lurched forward for two years, plateaued for three, and then declined. The revival model anticipated a state membership plateau in the early 1790s and a gradual decline. Based on the revival model, after the plateau and gradual decline, a new revival was necessary to continue the pattern of growth. That did not happen. Consequently, the lack of any subsequent revivals predisposed the membership declines in those states to continue until the chaff had been blown away. Once revivals returned to the southern MEC in 1800, the revival pattern and membership growth continued as before.

Why there were no revivals in the 1790s becomes the next question. If revivals are sovereign acts that God sends in accordance with God's timing, the question is mute. However, if revivals happen as a consequence of receptivity factors, environmental forces, and spiritual preparation, then the answer to the question becomes very important.

Summary of Southern Membership Decline

While there is no single explanation for the southern decline of the MEC from 1793 to 1800, contributing factors to the decline have been identified. Although, it is not possible to weigh or quantify the contributing factors.

A primary cause of decline was the clash between Republican values that prevailed in the South and institutional Federalism. The conflict between O'Kelly and Asbury exemplified this. Hammett's and O'Kelly's defections stole away members, preachers, and property. More importantly, they engaged the MEC in a public controversy that caused bad public relations and deflected the church from evangelism. To some extent, it pitted local preachers against itinerants. However, the fact that the Baptist Associations of Virginia and Federalist Maryland had identical membership declines raises important questions about the overall significance of this factor. Certainly, it cannot be offered as a single cause explanation.

Slavery and Methodism's response to it caused membership decline. As the MEC challenged slavery in the state legislatures and made rules to eradicate slavery from the church, it alienated southern members and potential members who did not share that view. Many southern members with an opposing view on the subject stayed in the church and caused internal conflict. Some of those who stayed were local preachers with influence. Because of Methodism's anti-slavery stance and the fear of slave revolts, many slave owners did not let the church have access to their slaves. Furthermore, wherever the MEC made strong efforts to evangelize blacks or prioritize ministry to them, it suffered a corresponding decline in white membership. This fact represents an observation. Its cause is not specified. However, one can guess at the relationship between the two. The South was a very segregated society in which many whites detested any personal association with blacks. In the hierarchy of the South, poor whites prided themselves on not being slaves. They were turned-off by a church that valued blacks and prioritized ministry to them.

The MEC's bias for the poor was a contributing factor to southern decline to the extent that it conflicted with the spirit of the age. Republicanism and the good economy encouraged people to be optimistic about life and to strive to improve their condition. Methodists experienced redemption and lift. As they moved up the social ladder and acquired more material means, they received a contradictory message from their church. It valued simplicity and feared economic improvement. At this point, there was a disconnect between the national church and the regional character of the South. This caused some members to leave the church and it kept others from joining it.

The poverty of the itinerants and its related issues were major causes for decline in the South. Limited financial resources kept the MEC from paying its preachers a living wage, which, in turn, caused many to locate before they were worn-out. When a preacher married, usually he had to locate to support his family. A lack of a living salary also kept others from becoming itinerants. A deficit of preachers kept the MEC from expanding its borders or from adequately supplying its circuits. There is a close correlation between the number of itinerants, the number of circuits, and the number of members. Whenever one portion of the equation is reduced, it lowers the other two parts of it.

Emigration had a tremendous influence on the decline of membership in the eastern areas of the South. Additionally, the lack of revivals contributed to numerical decline in southern Methodism during the 1790s. Southern Methodism depended on revivals for growth. No significant revivals occurred in the South during the years of decline. In fact, the membership decline did not abate until revivals returned to the South in 1800. Also, theological controversies, persecution, a lack of preaching houses, Indian hostilities, and epidemics also hindered numerical growth and contributed to decline.

Kentucky Methodism

This chapter has alluded to the frontier but has not attempted to analyze it. In fact, Kentucky and Tennessee shared many contextual factors with the South. Redford's *History of Methodism in Kentucky*[83] offers important insights into the southern decline in the 1790s by means of its analysis of the decline in Kentucky. In fact, Kentucky remained attached to Virginia until it gained statehood in 1792.

Redford argues that many contextual and institutional factors combined to cause numerical decline. First, between 1795 and 1800, emigration to other parts of the expanding frontier took large numbers of people from Kentucky. The people who were drawn to Kentucky were also drawn to new lands to the West as they became available. In some places large circuits were broken up so that few remained. These were the seeds of the MEC. They took Methodism to the new frontier. Second, O'Kelly's influence was strong and his followers wreaked havoc in many parts of Kentucky and Tennessee. He states, "Kentucky had chiefly been settled by emigrants from Virginia and the infant Church in the West became involved in the controversy. Some prominent preachers were beguiled by [O'Kelly's] teachings."[84] He mentions some local preachers by name and says that whole societies were destroyed by them. Third, religious controversy distracted preachers and members from the primary task of the church. Religious controversy may be necessary to promote orthodoxy or to free people from ecclesial bondage. However, it is harmful to spiritual growth and happiness. Methodism had a running battle with Baptists and Calvinists from New England to Georgia. The arguments loom large in the writings of early circuit riders. Fourth, the church's stance on slavery alienated many members and turned away potential members. It also engendered negative publicity. Because of its assumed political position, many detractors argued that the MEC meddled in the affairs of the civil government. The people did not like this and instinctively favored a separation of church and state. Furthermore, many families of high social status who were drawn to Methodism because of the zeal of its preachers, the simplicity of its worship, and the truth of its doctrines; joined other denominations because of the MEC's renewed effort to combat slavery in the 1790s. These were the ones who gave the most financial support to the frontier circuits. Fifth, America's romance with French philosophy and deism were most hurtful. France's infidelity bled over to America and caused a corresponding spiritual and moral decline in the South and on the frontier. Sixth, conflicts with Native Americans to include raids on frontier outposts posed a problem and kept the people anxious. This may have drawn people to the MEC. Asbury and Garrettson advocated for the fair treatment of the Native Americans and applauded efforts to honor land rights. However, frontier people did not share that sentiment. Finally, the declines in members were checked and reversed by the great western revivals that started in 1799.

CHAPTER FIFTEEN

METHODISM IN NEW ENGLAND: 1789 THROUGH 1800

American Methodism made its first permanent inroad into the forbidding land of New England in 1789 when Jesse Lee was appointed there as a missionary. However, he was not the first Methodist to preach in New England. George Whitefield began to preach in New England in 1740. Whitefield was a sensational success. Large crowds eagerly waited on his words. During his many preaching tours in New England through 1770, Whitefield procured a large following. Next to Jonathan Edwards, Whitefield was the most influential preacher in New England during the time of the Great Awakening. However, when he died in Newburyport, Massachusetts in 1770, New England Methodism died with him. He did not organize his converts or rise up native preachers to continue his work in the United States. Additionally, Whitefield separated from the Wesley brothers before beginning his preaching tours in New England. He became a Calvinist. Unlike Whitefield, Lee "planted" Methodism in New England. For that reason, Lee is considered to be the father of New England Methodism. His story is legend.[1]

Lee had wanted to go to New England for a long time. In 1788, he left the South and received an appointment in New Jersey. In 1789 Asbury appointed him to Boston. Previously, Asbury had consented to dispatch Garrettson to Boston. However, Garrettson was delayed in Albany, New York. Afterward, he became the presiding elder of the Northern District of Northeast New York. Starting in August 1789, he and his preachers made constant preaching forays into neighboring New England. His journal details the early development of Methodism in New England. In his New England travels, he preached to large congregations, formed societies, and baptized converts. At times, he met Lee on the road and preached with him.

Garrettson relates a story that validated Methodism's divine calling to New England and strengthened the fortitude of the MEC preachers. While making a preaching tour through Hartford, Farmington, Litchfield, Cornwall, and Canaan, Connecticut in 1790, he met a woman who related a dream she had in 1783. In the dream a man came to her. He was of low stature and dressed in black like a Methodist preacher. A bright light shone around him. He took out a book and wrote her name in it. Afterward, he told her that she would have a crown of life if she lived as a faithful servant of Christ. The woman related the dream to her husband and began to search everywhere for the man. Upon seeing Garrettson, she immediately recognized him as the man from her dream. She was filled with great relief and much joy. She believed that the Methodists came to New England with the divinely appointed word of truth.[2]

Before 1789, Asbury did not feel that Methodism was called to New England. He did not want to commit the church's scarce resources to that unpromising place for three reasons. First, the people on the frontier and in other areas were destitute of all religion. Some of these people begged for Methodist preaching. Asbury was unable to accommodate their requests because of a lack of itinerants. Second, New England was covered with churches and ministers. Furthermore, Congregationalism was established by law and supported by tax in most of the inhabited parts. Third, Arminian dissenters would not be welcomed in that bastion of Calvinism. Persecution would be likely.[3]

Growth of MEC in New England from 1789 through 1800

Methodism was not native to New England, and it did not take root easily. However, when it began to grow, its organization spread out like a wild vine under a warm sun as its crawling branches penetrated into every area of the region. In 1790, New England Methodism consisted of three circuits in Connecticut. By 1795, New England Methodism consisted of 17 circuits in four states. By 1800, it consisted of 33 circuits in all six New England states and it boasted a membership of 5,812.

Table 15-1. Number of Itinerants, Circuits, and Members in New England between 1789 and 1800

Year	Itinerants	Circuits	Members		Year	Itinerants	Circuits	Members
1789	2	0	0		1795	28	17	2,525
1790	5	3	181		1796	32	20	2,519
1791	13	7	608		1797	38	22	2,999
1792	17	8	1,377		1798	39	26	4,155
1793	21	12	1,739		1799	42	30	4,954
1794	30	12	2,358		1800	48	33	5,812

Source: MEC, Minutes (1813).

In 1789, Lee was appointed to Stamford, Connecticut.[4] The bounds of his circuit included Norwalk, Fairfield, Stradford, Milford, New Haven, Derby, Newtown, Reading, Danbury, and Canaan. Those cities are located in southeast Connecticut. In 1790, circuits enclosed the entire western portion of the state to Hartford. By 1793, Connecticut was covered by circuits. In that same year, the MEC pushed east and claimed Rhode Island. Two circuits were mapped out around the major cities of Greenwich and Warren. In 1795, eight circuits covered those states. No more circuits were added in Connecticut and Rhode Island until 1807. In 1796, the MEC had a membership of 1,470 in those states. By 1800, the combined membership had inched its way to 1,798. From 1795 to 1800, Rhode Island Methodism did not have any numerical growth.

In 1790, Methodism had a false start in Boston. On one Sunday in that year, Lee preached in the Commons to a large crowd. He estimated that the crowd numbered two to three thousand. The following Sunday afternoon, he preached to a larger crowd. This was the method that worked in Baltimore. However, it did not work in Boston because Lee was unable to form a class or society.[5] The MEC had to wait until 1792 to form a small society in Boston. In the meantime, the traveling preachers discovered that Lynn, Massachusetts was ripe unto harvest. When they preached there, they had immediate success. Lynn became Methodist-central for that part of New England. From there, the MEC covered Massachusetts with ten circuits by 1800. In that year, the membership in the state was 1,577 and climbing.

The MEC had good success in the unsettled regions of Maine, New Hampshire, and Vermont. In 1793, Lee was sent as a missionary to Maine. He traveled that area for a year before he determined the most receptive place to form a circuit. The new circuit was 200 miles from the nearest circuit. After the MEC got a foothold in Maine, it moved from several directions to enclose the rest of the northern New England states. Lee stated, "Our greatest success at first was in places where the people were but thinly settled, the people could but seldom hear a sermon of any kind. Where there were ministers regularly settled, the people were not so fond of hearing us as they were in other places."[6] The Congregational church did not have a thick presence in these states, and it was not established in all of them. The MEC proceeded in these states like it did in other sparsely settled areas. Itinerants traveled the land, made preaching appointments, formed small groups, organized societies, and built chapels. At first, the circuits were large in area and small in membership. As the area was worked more closely, the large circuits were divided. By 1800, Methodism in Maine, New Hampshire, and Vermont contained 13 circuits and 2,437 members. In 1803, there were more Methodists in Vermont than in any other New England state. Vermont and Maine proved to be very receptive to Methodism.

From 1800 to 1812, Methodism grew in all the New England states. In Massachusetts, it doubled its membership to 3,643. In Connecticut, it doubled its membership to 2,884. Rhode Island Methodism gained 554 members. New Hampshire Methodism grew from 224 to 1,750. Maine Methodism tripled its membership to 3,450. Vermont membership increased five-fold from 1,016 to 5,535.

Figure 15-1 shows the rate of growth and the correlation between circuits, itinerants and membership. The national ratio was one circuit to two preachers to 500 members. However, the ratio in New England was one circuit to two preachers to 175 members. That ratio remained fairly constant until 1794. From 1794 to 1796, the number of preachers remained constant. However, the number of circuits was increased from 12 to 20. With that type of expansion of the system, numerical growth was inevitable. From 1797 to 1800, the MEC averaged 938 new members each year. Sixty-three percent of those members came from Maine, New Hampshire, and Vermont. Adding preachers and increasing the number of circuits by expansion or by division was a formula that the MEC used to increase membership.

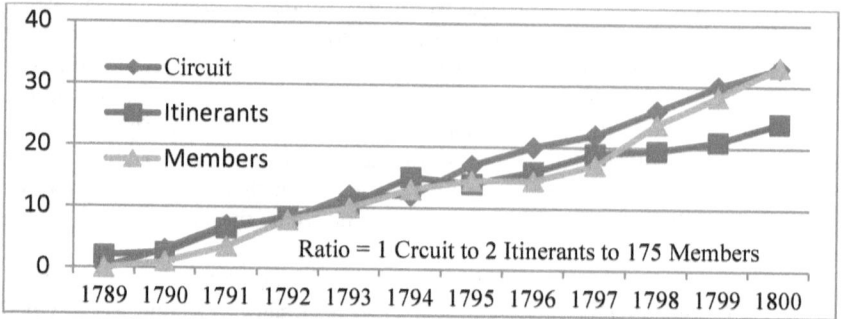

Figure 15-1. Number of Itinerants, Circuits, and Members in New England between 1789 and 1800.

Missionary Character

During the 1790s, the MEC had a critical shortage of itinerants and money to pay them. At the same time, Asbury committed a disproportionate number of preachers to New England. His decision demonstrated the missionary character of the MEC. Asbury was a strategist with a vision. Methodism's commitment to "spreading scriptural holiness throughout the nation" compelled him to take a chance in New England. But it was not a blind gamble. He believed that religion was on the decline in New England and that God might use the MEC to ignite a renewal in that land.[7]

Before sending the first preacher to New England in the early part of 1789, Asbury wrote an article in *The Arminian Magazine* that showed why he was concerned for the people in New England.

> We are not ignorant that the Gospel has been preached in the eastern and northern parts of these United States, from the earliest settlement of the country; but this has been done chiefly . . . through the Calvinistic medium: the consequence of which has been, that the religious books in general which have been circulated in those parts, and in some measure through the southern states, have more or less maintained the doctrines of unconditional election and reprobation—that "GOD is" not "loving to every man," and that "his mercy is" not "over all his works";

and consequently, that "Christ did" not "die for all," but only for a small select number of mankind; by means of which opinions, Antinomianism has increasingly gained ground, and the great duties of self-denial, mortification, crucifixion to the world, and all the other severe but essential necessary duties of religion, have been too much neglected and despised.[8]

In 1791, during his first visit to New England, he stated,

> We are now in Connecticut; and never out of sight of a house; and sometimes we have a view of many churches and steeples. . . . I do feel as if there had been religion in this country once; and I apprehend there is a little in form and theory left. There may have been a praying ministry and people here; but I fear they are now spiritually dead; and am persuaded that family and private prayer is very little practiced: could these people be brought to constant, fervent prayer, the Lord would come down and work wonderfully among them.[9]

According to W. A. Chandler, the Second Great Awakening in New England (*c.*1798) "was preceded by a period of great religious declension. . . . Churches were gloomy by reason of faith decay and hearts grown cold. Iniquity abounded and skepticism prevailed on all sides."[10] According to Barclay, establishment compromised the spiritual life of the New England churches. Under the influence of establishment, the religious culture assumed that people who belonged to the church were right with God. This blurred the line between personal faith and institutionalism. Ultimately, this caused an attitude of apathy and a decline in personal religion. In short, establishment sucked the spiritual ardor out of New England and Calvinism lessened the motive for evangelism.

The spirit of the times caused people in New England to be restless. The theological construct that laid a foundation for New England in previous generations was crumbling. The emergence of "liberal" theology hammered at Calvinism from without and from within. Unitarianism is an example of a religious organization that grew out of the unrest. It filled an intellectual niche that Calvinism could not satisfy. According to Barclay,

> As a doctrinal system the New England theology had gone to seed. Its spiritual barrenness had become generally evident. . . . Universalism and Unitarianism were making constant inroads within them and . . . were being openly advocated in most of the prominent pulpits. The spirit of the age rebelled [against Calvinism].[11]

> The supremacy of orthodox Calvinism—the "New England theology"—was sharply challenged during this period in two separate quarters. In reaction against Puritan legalism and literalism in Biblical interpretation and theological doctrines of original sin, predestination, and the Trinity, Unitarianism [developed] at the very centers of Calvinism, Boston and Cambridge.[12]

Unitarians and Universalists represented an intellectual revolt against traditional orthodoxy. They fought from the outside. Christian Deists offered a greater challenge because they fought against the theological assumptions of the established church from within the church itself. Deism contended that the tenants of Calvinism and the systems that were derived from it were in error to the extent that they were not scientific. Furthermore, the teaching of scripture contained moral examples, not ultimate truth. Barclay argues that the rationalistic philosophy of deism "aimed to infuse religion into all culture by bringing theological formulas into harmony with scientific knowledge and developing systems of ethics and politics on a rational basis."[13] Deism emphasized the person over the system, was very compatible with democratic thought, encouraged philanthropy, and hailed the rediscovery of reason as a gift from God to be used for the purposes of good. However, it distorted the truth of biblical Christianity since it denied miracles, the resurrection, the incarnation, the authority of scripture, and historical orthodoxy. Early detractors argued that deism lacked a spiritual foundation for moral behavior and minimized personal religious. Faith was rationalistic; not dogmatic or experiential. Church attendance and heart religion declined wherever Universalism and deism gained a stronghold.[14]

As New Englanders began to question the rightness of Calvinism and the systems founded on it, many attempted to disestablish the Congregational Church. Unitarians, Baptists, and others tore away at the fabric of the Puritan hegemony. During this time, the winds of religious and political change blew hard in New England. Change brings opportunity. Opportunity beckoned to the Methodists.[15] From Asbury's perspective in 1789, it appeared that the iron wall of Congregationalism was cracking and that a new niche was opening on the religious landscape. Coupled with the absence of vital religion, this was the perfect time to launch a Methodist invasion. Ultimately, Asbury sent preachers to New England because he knew that Methodism could prosper there and that the people were becoming persuadable. Additionally, he wanted to test receptivity. When he discovered a high level of receptivity, he was willing to commit a proportionally larger number of itinerants to that work.

Asbury's experience at Lynn in 1793 demonstrates the last point. He said, "We have only three hundred members in this district [Massachusetts and Rhode Island], yet we have a call for seven or eight preachers; although our members are few, our hearers are many."[16] The extra preachers were necessary because the potential harvest was great. In established circuits in the South and Mid-Atlantic regions, local preachers could take up the slack when the itinerants were reassigned to a mission field. In the early 1790s, New England Methodism lacked an indigenous ministry and local preachers. It could not evangelize itself. As such, the priorities of evangelism and organizing the participants into societies required that Asbury send extra itinerants to New England. The itinerants were the infantry of the MEC army, and they functioned like an expeditionary force.

Also, Asbury knew that parts of the New England frontier were just being settled. In those areas, the religious marketplace invited competition. The organization and missionary character of Methodism were perfectly suited for that environment. Plus, the MEC had experience and success in other frontier settings. In reference to being sent to Maine as a missionary, Lee affirmed this point. "It was commonly understood that they were in want of preaching, and that our manner of travelling and preaching would be very suitable for that part of the country."[17]

Finally, as New England Methodism took root, Asbury knew that it would recruit its own preachers and pay its own way. From this perspective, Asbury was making an investment when he sent itinerants to New England. A large number of itinerants were needed to get the work started, but once the work was established it would grow local leaders and produce other itinerants. Starting as early as 1793, Asbury ordained new preachers in Connecticut.

In sum, it required more resources to begin a new work than it did to maintain one. However, the missionary character of the MEC required risk. Asbury wanted growth and he was willing to take the risk. That is why he committed his resources to New England.

William Umbel succinctly sums up why the MEC had success in New England.

> New England Methodist leaders came directly out of a society in which plain people were predominant. They were products of one transformation - the decline of Calvinism and the disestablishment of Congregationalism - and participants in another - the emergence of a new religious culture. Methodism succeeded in the region by capitalizing on its minority status and its theological and churchy uniqueness; by capturing the hearts and minds of a younger generation who had, like some of their parents, grown discontent with the established religion; and by promoting its ideas to virtually all groups and locations of New England. They successfully maintained a balance between authority and egalitarian appeal. Methodism's theology invited all to come; its organization bound converts to Wesley's ideas and developed religious communities who adapted as their own its task of spreading "scriptural holiness" and reforming the nation.[18]

Methodism capitalized on a convergence of favorable contextual and institutional factors. In a fascinating way, the MEC turned negative contextual factors into positive factors. Methodism's controversy and interaction with the "establish order" illustrates this point.

Establishment's Prejudice and Its Historical Basis

According to Methodist apologists, the established church and those who benefited from it resisted Methodism. Theological controversy; negative propaganda; denying the legitimacy of its ordination; and persecution to include forced taxation, destroying property, and threatened violence were a part of the Methodist experience in New England. Those who advocated a tight link between church and state had a long history of challenging heterodoxy. Sweet made the following statement about the source of establishment prejudice.

> Massachusetts intolerance was one of the principal reasons for the formation of other New England colonies. With the exception of New Haven [Connecticut] all other New England colonies established after Massachusetts Bay owe their origin in a greater or less degree to the clash of religion and politics in the Bay colony.[19]

New Haven, Connecticut, was organized in 1637. It was founded by Thomas Hooker and 250 new immigrants who were disgusted by the situation in Newton, Massachusetts. He and his followers left the Bay Colony and walked to present day Connecticut. He pushed against the aristocratic autocracy in Boston. He believed that all the people should have a voice in matters that affected the common good. Still, New Haven was strictly Puritanical and did not allow dissenters.

Rhode Island was created by a group of exiles from Boston between 1636 and 1656. They were banished for protesting the religious intolerance of the Puritans. Roger Williams was the leader of this Separatist defection. Anne Hutchinson found refuge in Rhode Island for some years. She had become a very popular bible teacher and religious commentator in Boston. Men and women crowded her weekly meetings. She accused the Puritan ministers of preaching a covenant of works. She and her followers were banished. Ultimately, she relocated to the Dutch Colonies because she thought the Congregationalists were going to annex Rhode Island. While in the Dutch Colonies, she and her children were gruesomely killed by a Native raiding party. Rhode Island welcomed both Jews and Quakers. However, it became predominantly Baptist.

New Hampshire was established in 1638 under the leadership of John Wheelwright. He advocated freedom of speech and opinion. He was the brother-in-law to Anne Hutchinson. He and his followers were expelled from Massachusetts because their theology was incorrect. They signed the Exeter Compact, which was patterned after the Mayflower Compact.

Maine and its inhabitants also sought independence from the Bay Colony on many occasions. Under the original charter, Maine was a part of Massachusetts and remained that way until 1820, when it was separated to become the twenty-third state.

Not only did settlers want to escape from Massachusetts, Massachusetts wanted to rid itself of all those who were of a different mind. The Puritans sought to force their religion on every aspect of life. Those who held contrary views were a danger to their hegemony. Hence, they sought to limit the influence of dissenters and to further their own cause by means of laws. Those who contested were marginalized in society or forced to leave.

Citizenship, suffrage and church membership went hand-in-hand in the Bay Colony. In 1643, of the 15,000 residents, only 1,708 were citizens. Such a small minority guaranteed that the will of the religious leaders would be followed. In the event of dissent, the religious leaders expelled the disagreeing members. This kept them from voicing their displeasure in a public forum. However, such un-American principles could not last forever. Cracks began to appear in the structure. The Half-Way Covenant of 1657 was one of the first internal challenges. What do you do when the second and third generations do not evidence conversion and the same vision/lifestyle as the founders? Answer, you let them be baptized, but you deny them the benefits of Church membership. The Half-Way Covenant became a way of life for the masses. Efforts to maintain orthodoxy and strict control continued, but the hearts of the people grew cold and indifferent. The Puritan dream of pure religion and theocracy was at odds with the popular sentiments of the times.

Methodism and Establishment

Virginians like O'Kelly criticized the MEC for not being republican enough because it was tinged with federalistic appendages. Ironically, in New England, the MEC became the voice for republican ideals. In other words, in much the same way that O'Kelly criticized the MEC, the MEC criticized the standing order in New England. To the extent that Lee and other southern preachers brought their political prejudices with them, one would expect this. However, in the New England context, advocacy for republicanism benefited the MEC. As one would expect, the open promotion of republican ideals caused conflict with the standing order. The following quotation from Barclay beautifully captures the essence of the New England hierarchy's mindset:

> The clergy—constituting, along with merchants and lawyers, the hierarchy of officialdom—believing that they governed by divine right, were alarmed by the rising democratic spirit in both politics and religion. Anything that pointed in the direction of a free Church was regarded by them as a menace, in self-defense to be resisted by every possible means.[20]

Methodism's grandiloquence against the church tax issue is a perfect example of its republican orientation and its willingness to wrap an issue in political language when it suited its cause. While touring New England in 1794, Asbury made stirring comments that reflected the hot rhetoric of the Methodist preachers.

> Here [is] the iron wall of prejudice. . . . Out of fifteen United States, thirteen are free; but two are fettered with ecclesiastical chains–taxed to support ministers, who are chosen by a small committee, and settled for life. . . . Who began the war? Was it not Connecticut and Massachusetts? and priests are now saddled upon them. O what a happy people would these be if they were not thus priest-ridden![21]

A true patriot could not have penned a more poignant critique of the standing order. On the surface, this reversal of opinion seems hypocritical or self-serving since Asbury did not style himself a republican. Asbury came from England and was accustomed to establishment. He never spoke against the establishment of the Anglican Church before 1785. In fact, before the Christmas Conference, Asbury sought to work with Anglican priests in a mutually beneficial way. On the one hand, Methodists needed sacerdotal support from the Anglican priests. On the other hand, by cooperating with Methodist preachers the Anglicans increased their attendance. It was a symbiotic relationship. Plus, Methodism's partnership with the Anglican Church deflected criticism from those who opposed dissenters.[22] However, the New England situation in the 1790s was very different for many reasons.

First, the MEC had become its own church with a national vision. That vision propelled it into New England. Second, the establishment of the Congregational Church represented a vexing contextual obstacle that needed to be hurdled. America fought a war over the principles of freedom. Third, Anglicanism had been disestablished in the states where it had enjoyed that privilege. An antiestablishment clause existed in the national constitution. Establishment was antithetical to the democratic ethos in the new republic. Fourth, in most places, the longstanding churches of other denominations also received support from church taxes. This practice worked against the principle of tithing to a voluntary organization. Fifth, Methodists refused to buy into that system. For example, in 1793, Asbury commented that the majority of people in Needham, Massachusetts preferred the preaching of the Methodists and wanted to pay them by a tax on the people. However, the appointed preachers absolutely refused this plan.[23] Even if the MEC would have bought into the church tax plan, its membership was small and the amount raised by taxes would not have supported it. It needed sacrificial giving, not the pittance that came from tax support. Congregational Churches could survive on tax support because they were the default recipient of the taxes that came from the masses who did not participate in church. Every adult male had to pay a church tax. Sixth, Methodism was in direct competition with the other churches. Its membership in New England came as the result of defections from the other churches. This produced antagonism. The fact that many of the defecting members were unchurched or disenchanted before joining the MEC did not matter. Finally, the Methodist message resonated with large numbers of disaffected people who desperately wanted an alternative church. The MEC successfully attracted these people largely because it defined itself in contradistinction to Congregationalism. Campaigning against state sponsored religion helped to position the MEC in the religious marketplace and made the church an option for those who wanted change.

Disagreement related to the church tax debate became intense at times. For example, in 1794, the Lynn society was incorporated so its members would not have to pay the church tax to the Congregational Church. Before this, its members took certificates to show that they were Methodists and financially supported that church. That angered the standing order who argued that they were still responsible for the church tax. While at the new chapel at Wilbraham, Massachusetts, Asbury commented on this point. Asbury adamantly believed that they were very mistaken. The following week, while in Windsor, Connecticut, Asbury complained, "Not withstanding [Brother Stoughton's] certificate from the Methodists he has been taxed to pay a minister he heareth not. O liberty! O priestcraft! So all that withdraw must pay the ministry."[24]

Methodism struggled with this issue more than other dissenting churches because, at times and in places, it was not a recognized church. When a convert joined a Methodist society, it did not mean that he or she ceased to be a Congregationalist in the eyes of the state. For this reason, the standing order argued that Methodist converts had to pay the church tax. In their eyes it was a matter of "tax evasion." Also, it was an attempt to intimidate an aspiring and unwelcomed sect who sought to grow by taking members from the recognized churches. The issues of recognition, proselytism, and the church tax caused tension and rancor between the MEC and the standing order.

This was important because Methodism attracted the poorer people. Consequently, the church tax that was paid to the established church reduced the amount of money that the Methodist converts could contribute to their new church. The maintenance and growth of the MEC in New England depended on its ability to pay its own way and raise funds. For example, building meeting places and chapels was a big priority. Where the MEC did not have one, its growth was severely hampered. As such, the church tax was a negative contextual factor that hurt the MEC to the extent that it reduced the potential contributions of its members and hindered the growth of the organization's infrastructure. However, Methodism's campaign against the church tax and establishment was a positive regional institutional factor that facilitated membership growth with the populations who favored the message.

A Democratic Gospel with an Emphasis on Salvation

The MEC preached against the elitism of the established church in that the message of free will and free grace ran contrary to the prevailing ideas of Calvinism and New England politics. Methodists proclaimed a "democratic" gospel that emphasized salvation and sanctification. The perfectibility of human nature through the grace of God reflected a human optimism that was popularized by Jefferson and republicanism.[25] Salvation was not for an elect group of chosen people. Rather, the gift was for all who would respond to it and conform to God's demands as they grew in grace. These emphases prioritized personal decision and evangelistic preaching. God was a loving God who offered his grace to all people. The preacher worked in tandem with God in accordance with Wesley's order of salvation. Being a baptized member of an established church would not save one who did not have personal faith. Salvation required an individual response. The damned were those who would not respond to God's love and the message of salvation. However, no one was predetermined to be damned and no one was predetermined to be saved. Also, one could have an assurance of salvation and rejoice in God's love, but no one was beyond the possibility of backsliding. Always, the Methodist preachers lambasted antinomianism. This spoke against the doctrine of the perseverance of the saints and placed an emphasis on faithfulness. Growth in grace was a primary purpose of the local MEC organization. The experience of salvation, the assurance of salvation, the need for sanctification, and the preaching for response were central to the Methodist message.[26]

Methodism cared about learning and wanted its preachers to study, but the priority on effective evangelism superseded everything else. According to Umbel,

> Early New England Methodists valued schooling, but they valued saving souls more. They did not wish to confine notions of education to the classroom or to

the reading of classical texts. They also gathered their knowledge from "everyday's experience" and believed that people generally followed those who taught from experience rather than those who taught "from books only." They especially abhorred "godless" learning. . . . Settled clergymen who had acquired a classical education but did not know how to win souls repelled them.[27]

In the 1790s, Methodist preachers in New England were not educated in the same way as other pastors. They understood Arminian principles and were able to articulate the gospel message from that perspective. They also knew how to pick at Calvinism. One did not have to be a scholar to exploit the weaknesses of the theological system. Additionally, Wesley and Fletcher wrote extensive responses to Calvinism. This provided the itinerants with good ammunition as it shot holes in the dominant theology. Plus, the course of study for itinerants and learning from exposure to other preachers prepared the Methodist itinerants in New England to preach effectively against the undemocratic ramifications of Calvinism. Methodism was aggressive in challenging the standing order and in appealing to a segment of the population that was receptive to its arguments.[28]

Not only did Methodism learn to exploit the undemocratic nature of Calvinistic thought, at times preachers mocked it. Lee stated,

> I did not spare Calvinism but bore solemn testimony against the doctrine which prevails in this part of the world, which in substance is this: "The sinner must repent, and can't repent; and he will go to hell if he don't repent," or, as a lawyer expressed in my hearing, "You must believe, or be damned: and you can't believe, if you are to be damned." But some of these people begin to see that something must be done before justification; though some of the preachers teach that a sinner cannot repent until he is born again. From this doctrine, good Lord, deliver us.[29]

Lee's argument was very facile and could be challenged by a trained theologian. I am sure the standing ordered mocked him. However, Lee did not address his critique to the educated scholars or attempt to persuade them. Rather, he preached to the common people. His folk theology and simplistic characterization of the chauvinistic tenants of Calvinism appealed to them. More importantly, the people responded to it. Traditional Calvinism had given a theological foundation for the ranked society that existed in parts of New England. It ossified a social stratification that benefitted a privileged class of lawyers, clergy, business barons, and government officials. To the disenfranchised, the message of Methodism offered an appealing alternative that resonated with emerging political ideas. It told them that they had value before God and that no person was more valuable than another.

To be sure, Universalists made many of the same claims as the Methodists. They also rode a wave of popular appeal. However, they did not appeal to the same segment of the population. Plus, the Universalists were liberal in theology and quiet on the need for personal salvation and sanctification. Also, Methodism never preached that all would be saved. Rather, it preached that all could be saved. The Universalists were very similar to the Unitarians in appearance, and appealed to the ideals of deism.[30]

Social Status and Political Orientation of New England Methodists

In an earlier section, this book showed that the MEC targeted the poor and that it had a bias for them. The same was true in New England. According to George Baker,

> The Methodist preachers were not preaching to the best educated and most cultured people of New England. The leaders went among and appealed to those whom the standing-order clergy were not effectively reaching with their more erudite and carefully worked-out sermons. In a pamphlet, printed in Norwich in 1800, the Methodists were described as follows: ". . . their church is made up of the most weak, unlearned, ignorant and base part of mankind."[31]

Circuit riders came to seek and to save those who were lost; the very same people that Jesus targeted. Some of the criticisms that the standing order levied against the Methodist preachers sounds very similar to the criticisms that the standing order levied against Jesus because he was a friend of sinners and tax collectors. According to Matthew's gospel,

> As Jesus was walking along, he saw a man called Matthew sitting at the Tax booth; and he said to him, "Follow me." And he got up and followed him. And as he sat at the table in the house, many tax collectors and sinners came and were sitting with him and his disciples. When the Pharisees saw this, they said to his disciples, "Why does your teacher eat with tax collectors and sinners?" But when he heard this, he said, "Those who are well have no need of a physician, but those who are sick. Go and learn what this means," "I desire mercy, not sacrifice." For I have come to call not the righteous but the sinners. (Matt. 9:9-13 NRSV)

Methodism took great pride in the divine comparison. It was most apostolic when it sought after the poorer people to include the middling folk and intentionally built their societies around them. Farmers, seamen, petty merchants, apprentices, and tradesmen were especially attracted to Methodism. These people were the working core of society. Women associated with these categories were even more receptive to Methodism.[32] However, like Jesus, Methodism preached to all classes of people and it won converts from every class.[33] Methodism did not segregate the wealthy from the poor in the society or the class. Furthermore, Methodism's requirement for intimate association deterred the upper echelons because it was difficult for prominent and/or people of means to associate in an intimate way with the lower classes. In time, Methodism did reach the wealthy and educated people in New England as the church indigenized to its context and became more respectable.[34] An emphasis on an "educated" clergy and married preachers who lived as if they were settled pastors are two examples.

Besides being poor, Methodists of this period were mostly republican in their leanings. From a demographic and social perspective, this should be expected. This fact had special significance for New England Methodism because Federalism reigned there. Baker showed that the Federalists in New England found their strength in the standing order. He identified them with the Calvinists and "nearly every lawyer of repute, most physicians, every member of the Yale faculty, and the leaders in business. . . . The dissenters 'were generally found on the side of Jefferson.'"[35] Barclay shared a similar view:

> In New England the clergy of the Established Church were predominantly on the side of the conservative, property-holding class. The dissenters, for the greater part, advocated the doctrines of Jefferson. In fact, the overthrow of the Federalist dynasty of New England was chiefly attributed . . . to the Methodists, [and other dissenting denominations] cooperating with the new democratic political forces in undermining "the old and established order of things."[36]

It has already been shown that Methodism grew in New England during a time of political, religious, and social upheaval. This was a time of "mounting theological debate, growing denominational pluralism, a weakening of Congregationalism's legal and social authority, and increased public involvement in partisan politics."[37] In this social milieu, New England Methodism aligned itself with a growing opposition party that included political outsiders and dissenters of every sort. With these groups, the MEC waged a fierce war against establishment and it rode the rising tide of Anti-Federalism. In so doing, it appealed to and gave voice to a growing segment of the dissenting population.[38] Umbel rightly points this out.

> [The] religious transformation [in New England] mirrored those taking place in politics, the economy, and the family. Numerous social analogies worked to Methodist's advantage. . . . A loss of social power, the decline of Calvinism, and the overwhelming repudiation of religious establishment occurred simultaneously with a bulging pluralism of groups and the ascendency of [Methodism] which was committed to revivalism, missions, and social reform.[39]

In summary, Methodism took advantage of the changing tide and the new receptivity that it brought. In fact, the MEC identified with the changing order and gave voice to a segment of the population that wanted change. A New England Methodist was a Republican in a bastion of Federalism. Becoming a Methodist at this time was a conscious protest against the standing order. This fact was chronicled by Asbury, Lee, and a host of New England itinerants. It was one of the primary reasons why the MEC was successful in New England at this time. A missionary character and an effective organization were key to Methodism's success, but, by themselves, they would not have produced a large harvest if the contextual factors were not working in Methodism's favor. The people wanted social, political, and religious change, and Methodism gave voice to what they wanted. The changing environment of New England was a regional contextual factor. Methodism's response to the changing social milieu took the form of institutional factors.

Issues of Special Consideration

This section addresses the lack of chapels, the society at Lynn, the failure of Methodism in Rhode Island, a spontaneous revival, and a legend about Lee.

Each sheds light on New England Methodism and helps to explain reasons for growth and lack of growth.

Chapels and Growth

Asbury prioritized the building of chapels in the 1790s. The lack of chapels was a national and local institutional factor. Wherever the local societies lacked a place to meet and preach they were limited in their ability to attract and hold a congregation. When they built a chapel, attendance typically increased. The chapel problem was particularly critical in New England because the social environment was hostile to the MEC and the attendees were so poor that they struggled to build their own chapels. While in Stratford, Connecticut in 1791, Asbury wrote,

> They have voted that the town house shall be shut: well–where shall we meet? Some of the selectmen–one at least, granted access. I felt unwilling to go. . . . I refuse to preach there any more; and it was well I did–two of the esquires were quite displeased at our admittance. . . . The Methodists have a society consisting of twenty members. . . . but they have no house of worship–they may now make a benefit of a calamity–being denied the use of other houses, they will the more earnestly labour to get one of their own.[40]

In 1791, while in Boston, Massachusetts, small crowds attended Asbury's preaching. He blamed the problem on two things. First, the people who attended Methodist preaching appeared to be ashamed or embarrassed of Asbury and the MEC. As such, they did not take an active role in promoting the church to the larger community. Second, Asbury did not have adequate places in which to preach. Without their own chapels, Methodists had to use other church buildings or local accommodations. This did not work out well. Asbury concluded, "I have done with Boston until we can obtain a lodging house to preach in, and some to join us [as members]."[41]

Lee had a similar experience in Boston. Of his ministry there in 1790, he stated, "In Boston it was hard to procure a place to preach in, and the word took but little hold on the minds of the hearers."[42] Notice the connection between effective preaching and a chapel. At another point, Lee demonstrated the connection between the lack of an adequate meeting place and the ability to grow a society:

> We preached a long time in Boston, before we formed a society, but on the 13th day of July, 1792, we joined a few in society, and after a short time they began to increase in number. We met with uncommon difficulties here from the beginning, for the want of a convenient house to preach in. We began in private houses, and could seldom keep possession of them long. At last we obtained liberty to hold meetings in a school house; but that too was soon denied us. We then rented a chamber in the north end of the town, where we continued to meet a considerable time regularly. The society then undertook to get them a meeting house, but being poor, and but few in number, they could do but little. We begged money for them in Baltimore, on the Eastern Shore of Maryland, and in Delaware state, in Phila-

delphia, and in New York, and by these exertions we were able to proceed, and began the building. On the 28th day of August, 1795, the *Corner Stone* was laid of the first Methodist meeting house in Boston. . . . After we began to preach in the new meeting house, we had large congregations to hear us.[43]

While in Boston in 1795, Asbury wrote, "I have no doubt but that if we had a house, we should command a large congregation; but we labour under great inconveniences where we preach at present."[44] It took three years of preaching in Boston before the MEC formed a society and another three years of preaching before they could build a chapel and attract a crowd. In New London, Connecticut, it took the MEC three years to form an adequate circuit and another five years to build a meeting house.[45] Its problem was similar to the one in Boston. In both cases, as soon as the society built a meeting house, it experienced sustained growth.

In New England, there was a positive relationship between a building and growth. To become a Methodist in Boston required a tremendous sacrifice in social status. Most likely, a new convert would be disowned to some extent by family members and former friends. Understandably, the perspective convert wanted to be sure that the MEC was going to stay around and provide community before the person committed to it. A building represented permanence. In other words, after a building was erected, it was safer to become a Methodist. People did not want to make a personal sacrifice to a transitory church.

The Lynn Society

The society at Lynn started from nothing and became a strong society in a very short time. After recounting how disappointed he was with Boston, Lee stated, "But as soon as we began to preach in Lynn, the word had a powerful effect on the hearers who flocked to hear by the hundreds. It soon appeared that Lynn was the place that should be attended to, in preference to others."[46] Lynn was close to Boston. Immediately, the Lynn society determined to build a meeting house. It was dedicated in June 1791. Afterward, Methodism continued to prosper in Lynn for many months without any declension. While in Lynn in 1791, Asbury wrote, "I was greatly surprised to find a house raised for the Methodists. . . . Here we shall make a firm stand, and from this central point, from Lynn, shall the light of Methodism and truth radiate through the State."[47] Asbury was right. Because of the strong foothold in Lynn, the MEC began to have great success in the areas around Lynn.[48]

The success in Lynn was caused by a combination of contextual and institutional factors. First, the Methodists were invited to come to Lynn by a prominent shoe manufacturer.[49] Second, the people of Lynn were dissatisfied with the Congregational Church. According to Lee,

> There were abundance of people in this town who were fond of hearing the Methodists, and wished to attend their meetings constantly; and on the 9th day of May [1791], upwards of seventy men who paid the tax, came together and took certificates showing that they attended public worship with the Methodists, and

paid to keep them, as far as possible from being compelled by law to pay the support of their settled congregational minister, whom they did not like.[50]

Before the preaching of the MEC in Lynn, the people protested against the oligarchy of the Congregational Church. In particular, they were in conflict with the pastor. The pastor was said to be "more devoted to his own pleasures than to the work of the ministry."[51] In another place Barclay said that the growth of the Lynn society came as a result of a mass defection from the First Congregational Church. "A list of one hundred and eight names was handed in, indicating that so many had become members of a Methodist society, and ceased to be taxable to the first parish. This occurred in May, 1791. . . . [It included] some of the . . . leading men of the parish."[52] This fact explains why the people in Lynn were so eager to embrace the Methodists and why they were able to build a meeting house so quickly. This defection also served to give the Methodists credibility in the eyes of the neighbors who witnessed the situation. Many of them were also frustrated with their churches and gladly followed the example of the people in Lynn. By 1793, the membership in Lynn grew to 166 and the attendance was much greater.

Unfortunately, internal conflict in the Lynn society nearly destroyed the congregation. Apparently, Lee was the main point of contention. From 1793 to 1803, the Lynn society decreased until it reached a low of 83 members. In 1793, Asbury wrote that the Lynn conference was more painful than any other single conference. In that conference, Lee was appointed to Maine and did not take his appointment because he did not want to leave Lynn. The *Minutes* list him as Lynn and Maine. However, the people in Lynn did not want him and they threatened to return to the Congregational Church if he stayed. He angered them by introducing fugue tunes in the music.[53] In New England, fugue tunes emphasized hymns with one part of the melody dominating as it was repeated. It was sung with the accompaniment of an organ. People of higher status tended to look down on fugue tunes. In 1794, Asbury lamented, "I now go to Lynn; once the joy, now the grief of our hearts."[54] The problem in Lynn also caused Lee and Asbury to argue. In 1795, Asbury wrote, "I received an original letter from Mr. Lee, not like what I wrote; so I bid him farewell: I will not give him another opportunity to abuse me; neither shall I lay to heart what he saith to afflict me."[55]

Lee was from Virginia and he was opinionated and dominating. Past conflict with Coke, Asbury, and O'Kelly point to this. This may have been the real source of conflict in the Lynn society. The Lynn members were not typical Methodists in that they represented a true cross-section of the town. Because the society came into existence through a schism in the Congregational Church, "leading men" were members of the Lynn society. It must be assumed that these men did not become Methodists because they were converted to it. Rather, they became Methodists because they rejected the Congregational Church in town. The Lynn society was born out of conflict and schism. The people joined the Methodists with their social structure intact. Because of this, it is possible that they resisted being "Methodized." Methodist preachers, especially Lee, may have seemed autocratic to people who were accustomed to the Congregational Church. Their former preacher ignored them and the Methodist preacher controlled them. That may have been the primary cause of the internal tension. The issue with fugue tunes may have been the presenting problem but, most likely, it was not the real issue. Most Methodist societies began as small groups and grew to become large societies. As they grew, they formed their Methodist identity and established their own social structure. The Lynn society was an aberration from this perspective.

Rhode Island Methodism

Rhode Island presents a special problem because it successfully repulsed the Methodist invasion of New England. From the time that the MEC began to work in the state its membership grew to 220 in 1796, declined to 162 in 1798, and then grew to 227 in 1800. Lee was unable to explain why the MEC was not effective there.

> It is almost twenty years since we first began to preach in Rhode Island, and at present we have only four or five hundred members in that state. We have had as little success in that place, as in any of the states where we have been; yet we have not as much opposition there, as we have commonly had in most places; neither are the people as much prejudiced against us and our plan, as they are in the rest of the New-England States. In this state they have no ministers settled by law: they neither have any law to tax the people for the support of ministers. The people hear such preachers as they like, and pay toward their support just as much as they please. In a word, they enjoy religious liberty: and are the happiest people in this respect of any that dwell in New England. Yet, they are not more religious than the people of the neighboring states.[56]

In 1793, Asbury resonated with Lee's sentiment:

> I came upon the State of Rhode Island; stopped in Coventry, and found that the two preachers stationed here have been running over almost the whole State, and formed but few societies. When I came to Providence, I. Martin told me, that under the present difficulties they had agreed not to forward the preachers of the Methodists among them, nor to befriend them.[57]

Rhode Island was founded as a safe-haven for religious dissidents. Baptists were in the majority. Quakers and Jews also enjoyed the religious climate of tolerance. Congregationalists equaled less than 17 percent of the population.[58] Additionally, the state was covered with churches. Since there was religious freedom, and since evangelical churches already staked out claims in the state, there was little openness for the Methodists in that they did not fill any void in the religious marketplace or appeal to any disaffected population. The MEC entered the state with the same missionary character and organization that helped to make it effective in other locations, but those qualities did not make the church successful in Rhode Island. If this assessment is correct, the negative contextual factors in Rhode Island negated the positive institutional factors of the MEC to the extent that the MEC did not grow rapidly. In short, there were unchurched people in Rhode Island. Those people and their associated characteristics have not been identified. However, the MEC did not position itself to harvest them. Often, an abundance of religious liberty leads to spiritual apathy. Most likely, the people did not sense a felt need or feel drawn to the brand of religion that ardent Methodists peddled.

Additionally, receptivity to the MEC in the Providence area was lessened in 1793 just as the MEC was getting started in the state. Asbury blamed the opposition and lack of members in Providence on a Mr. Wilson. Wilson was a member of the Irish Conference until he was returned to the local ranks for getting married. He then immigrated to America. Later he worked with William Hammett in Baltimore during its time of numerical decline and internal conflict. Afterward, he became a colleague of the Rev. Snow of Broad Street Congregational Church in Providence. While there, he wrote an extremely critical book called *Apostolic Church Government, and Massachusetts the Government and System of the M. E. Church Investigated*.[59] He led a local opposition to Methodism and disdained Asbury for many of the same reasons as Hammett.[60]

A Spontaneous Revival in Province-Town, Massachusetts

At times, God providentially prepared the way for the MEC. The revival of religion in Province-Town is an example. The community was located on the extreme northern tip of the Massachusetts peninsula by Cape Cod. When religious excitement began to move the people in Province-Town, they had neither organized religion nor any person to guide them in it. A few were converted and began to employ spiritual disciplines. They met together, sang, read the Bible, and talked about their religious experiences. Soon after this, a Methodist preacher was blown ashore and stumbled upon them. He met with them, organized them, and ministered to them. When he left, he directed them to Boston so they could get an itinerant assigned to them. When the MEC established an official presence in the town, it was overwhelmed by the positive response. The society was formed in 1795 and soon registered 166 members. Since this was a small town in a very isolated place, it must be assumed that 166 people represented a large percentage of the population. Interestingly, those who did not embrace the MEC were very violent in their opposition to it. For example, when the new converts cut and prepared lumber in preparation to build a chapel, a mob went to the site of the proposed chapel, cut the lumber up, threw it into the sea, and tarred and feathered an effigy. Lee stated that it was the "most violent opposition that we had met with in that part of New-England."[61] Later in the year, they did build a chapel.

A Legend

As itinerant evangelists without a permanent dwelling, Methodist circuit riders resembled mendicant preachers. Since most were from other regions and none acted like the ordained clergy in New England, they must have seemed quite strange to the inhabitants. Lee epitomized the caricature. He weighed 300 pounds and was very extroverted. One might call him peculiar. New England United Methodists tell the following story:

> Jesse Lee was travelling through New England with hopes of establishing new [classes and societies]. Unfortunately the further north he went, the less receptive the people were. After repeatedly failing to gain the interest of locals, he decided to take a different route. Throwing caution to the wind, Jesse hitched his horse to a tree right outside of a school house, climbed on up, and started to sing from his hymnal. As you can imagine, this caused quite a stir among the children. Soon a crowd of kids joined him around the tree and joined in the impromptu sing along. After doing this for an hour or two, he looked down at the kids, and said; "Maybe I can do this at one of your houses. I could give a service, and we could sing. Would any of you like me to come to your house?" With that all hands shot up. Jesse Lee would follow them home, introduce himself to their parents and tell them what he wanted to do. At first the parents would oppose the idea . . . until they looked at the pleading eyes of their children. Looking down at them their minds were quickly changed. He would hold the service and capture the spirit of those gathered, and a new Methodist Society was born. This soon became his standard operating procedure upon entering any new town.[62]

Even though no other sources corroborate this story, the legend is in-line with Lee's character and ministry. He did not mind being a spectacle for the sake of attracting a crowd. Lee tells the following story about himself:

> I went to the Common, and standing on a table began to sing with only a few persons present. But having prayed and begun to preach, the number encreased [sic] so that there were two or three thousand attentive hearers. The number greatly encreased the next Sabbath day, at the same place, at six o'clock in the afternoon.[63]

Lee had learned this method from the Baltimore revivals. During that time, Methodist preachers began to preach outside in the afternoon after all the other churches had let out for the day. The innovation proved to be very effective. Unfortunately, the method failed in Boston in that none of the assembled people joined to a society. Actually, the large crowd came together because it wanted to see Lee; not because the people were interested in becoming Methodists. He was a curiosity like John the Baptist who dressed in camel skins as he cried out in the wilderness for people to repent. His method was as strange as his message. In many ways, Lee was like a clown at the circus. People enjoyed his performance and talked about it among themselves, but no one took the content seriously. When Paul went to the Areopagus in Athens, he experienced a similar fate. They took him before the council because of his preaching. The leaders called him a babbler (cf, Acts 17:19-20). The people patiently listened to him. Still, no church was started as a consequence of his preaching in that place. In the early 1790s, everything about the Methodist preachers sounded bizarre to the people in New England. Many listened but few united in fellowship. In later years, Methodism would discover positive receptivity and strong growth when it contextualized its methods and its organization to the region and employed local people as its itinerants.

It is no accident that New England Methodism led the MEC into higher education and respectable religion. At the same time, those innovations and adaptations that made Methodism grow in New England worked against growth in other regions. New England Methodism, Southern Methodism, and frontier Methodism all took on the form and character of the regions in which they ministered. In essence, there was no standard Methodism at this time. Rather, Methodism prospered when it adapted to its various contexts.

CHAPTER SIXTEEN

UNDERSTANDING THE DATA IN TERMS OF SOCIOLOGICAL THEORY

This chapter examines two sociological theories in light of EAM. The material is exploratory and not intended to be exhaustive. First, it reviews Dean Kelley's theory on strict and socially strong churches. Afterward, it examines the sect-to-church typology as it is described by Reinhold Niebuhr. Sociology of religion uses terms and categories in specific ways. "Church" refers to an organization like colonial Anglicanism or New England Congregationalism in the late eighteen century. Sect refers to a religious movement that breaks away from a dominant church. Usually, it is a renewal movement. Specific characteristics are associated with sects and churches. A cult is similar to a sect. However, it does not have to break away from a parent church. Typically, it claims new revelation. Sects and cults are protest movements. Mostly, they are inspired by a charismatic leader. In general parlance, the terms are not use with sociological specification. The sect-church typology goes back to Max Weber. However, Niebuhr popularized the concept to the American audience. In his usage of the theory, he polarized the extremes and put them on a continuum. This enabled the theory to be applied to an evolutionary process by which a sect becomes a church.

According to Finke and Stark, the continuum between sect and church represents the degree of tension that exists between religious organizations and their socio-cultural environments. For example, sects live in tension with the prevailing culture because they have beliefs and practices that set them apart. On the other hand, churches live in a smooth homeostasis with the prevailing culture. Of course, having achieved equilibrium does not guarantee that a church will remain in equilibrium. The social landscape can change. Typically, a church will change with the culture because it is embedded in the society. On the other hand, sects tend to be counter-cultural. In fact, a sect may split off from a church over the issue of cultural accommodation, religious lethargy, and institutionalism. American history is full of "new light" movements that emerged from revivals.

Kelley's Theory

Dean Kelley participated in the Hartford Project that articulated the national/local, contextual/institutional factor typology. Additionally, he was an active member of the National Council of Churches and the American Civil Liberties Union. He graduated from Iliff School of Theology and was a clergy member of the UMC. He successfully led a national lobbying effort to defeat the school prayer amendment to the constitution that was championed by Evangelicals. As was stated in Chapter One, he is best known for his seminal book entitled *Why Conservative Churches Are Growing*.[1] In his book, he does not reject the typology that the Hartford Project articulated; rather, he challenges the group's overemphasis on the "determinative" nature of contextual factors. In the preface of his book, he says that it should have been titled "Why Strict Churches Are Strong." In fact, that is his theory. Kelley does not deny that contextual factors influence growth and decline. Rather, he thinks that a focus on the determinative nature of contextual factors does not accomplish anything because the institutional qualities of a church determine whether it will grow or decline in a given contextual milieu. Furthermore, according to Kelley, if a religious organization has the right institutional qualities; it will grow even in an era of negative contextual factors. His theory was rejected by most mainline academics but embraced by conservative church growth experts.

During the mainline malaise in the 1970s, Kelley made a stunning claim that sounded a warning to the declining churches who embraced liberalism.

> The sectarian and theologically conservative religious groups have made amazing gains in recent years. Amid the current neglect and hostility toward organized religion in general [a national contextual factor], the conservative churches, holding to seemingly outmoded theology and making strict demands on their members, have equaled or surpassed in growth the yearly percentage increases of the nation's population. And while the mainline churches have tried to support the political and economic claims of our society's minorities and outcasts, it is the sectarian groups that have had most success in attracting new members from these very sectors of society.[2]

By way of critique, Kelley noted that sectarian churches prospered in the same "negative" environment in which mainline churches declined. As such, he argued that institutional factors internal to mainline churches caused them to decline. The sectarian churches grew because institutional factors internal to their organizations allowed them to adapt to the changing context so that they were favorably situated for growth.[3] In fact, the fields were ripe unto harvest and people were coming to Christ. However, they were not coming to churches that did not emphasize evangelism, vibrant worship, heart religion, and strong community. Droves responded to the gospel so that evangelical, Pentecostal, Non-denominational, and fundamentalist churches realized excellent growth. Others turned to Mormonism, Eastern religions, New Age religions, and an assortment of cults. The hippie culture, drug usage, and peace protests factored large in this equation. In general, the cultural turmoil of the 1960s fostered disillusionment with traditional Protestantism and a yearning for culturally relevant, experiential religion in a community that transcended the traditional church. The Jesus Movement, parachurch organizations, and the rise of the Charismatic renewal movement are examples of evangelical trends that successfully engaged the culture shift and the spirit of the age. Still, one cannot show that the evangelical surge penetrated to the heart of the counter-cultural rebellion or countered the secularizing forces that were unleashed by those who rebelled. Also, one cannot show that the evangelical surge successfully appealed to the entire unchurched population. Its harvest may have come from a segment of the unchurched population that was most predisposed to its cultural forms and its ideology.

In the subsequent decades, America polarized between two competing visions for the country. One group pushed for the disestablishment of the dominant religious traditions, the separation of church and state, social justice, civil rights, sexual liberty, environmentalism, and political liberalism. This group continued the protest of the 1960s. The other gave birth to organizations like the Moral Majority, the Christian Coalition, and Focus on the Family. They advocated the resurgence of biblical Christianity, experiential faith, capitalism, a strong America, and political conservatism. Some refer to this as the Reagan Revolution.

The mainline churches self-identified with the first group. Unfortunately, the first group did not identify with the mainline churches or align with organized religion. That is, even though the mainline churches shared many of the same values and attitudes as the liberals of the first group, they were not able to attract large numbers of unchurched liberals or sustain their membership base. For the liberals, the church no longer served a vital function. In fact, one committed to the liberal vision did not need the church to achieve one's goals. Actually, a plethora of liberal organizations competed for the time, talents, and resources of the liberal base. In the wake of this sea change, mainliners embraced the spirit of secularism and found common cause with political liberalism in an effort to remain a central force in the changing culture.

On the other hand, traditional America and disaffected people from the mainline churches flowed into conservative churches. The new evangelicals sensed a cultural shift that threatened them and their way of life. For them, the church became an ark of safety, a vehicle of protest, and a means to sustain their identity. In short, the conservative groundswell turned to the evangelical churches for direction and meaning. As a result, conservative churches registered large membership increases during the same period in which liberal churches declined. Conservative leaders like James Dobson and Jerry Falwell coalesced large associations of likeminded conservatives to give them a collective voice. This type of conservatism gave birth to a new form of a socially strong, strict church that distinguished itself and its members from the growing secularism and moral relativism of the dominant culture that had emerged during the cultural upheavals of the 1960s. In addition to providing their members with meaning and being a source of vital spirituality, the emerging evangelical churches evangelized with zeal, fought against moral decay, demanded allegiance, promoted traditional values, and mobilized their members to battle against secularism and the expanding agenda of liberalism.[4]

According to Kelley, strict churches communicate ultimate meaning to their followers, make substantial demands on them, and require commitment. One of the primary functions of religion is to infuse life with purpose and meaning. Motivation and commitment flow from this. When people believe in something with great passion, they will be passionate in their commitment to the faith system that embodies the passion. The failure to communicate meaning is one of the primary reasons why people abandoned the mainline churches.

It should be noted that liberalism could organize itself so that it acted like a strict religion. In fact, some have argued that the "radical left" functions like a strict religion with its own dogma, rituals, priests, denominations, and messiah figures. According to Kelley, conservative churches do not grow because they are conservative. They grow because they are socially strong and strict. In cities and other sectors of America, liberalism is winning the day. If the mainline churches could become a central organizing force for liberalism, they would realize substantial growth in members and cultural influence. To do this, they would have to jettison portions of their religious heritage, identify new sources of authority, make common cause with non-Christian traditions, and redefine what it means to be a disciple in a multi-faith setting. In part, they have already accomplished this; that is, in order to become culturally relevant the mainline churches have compromised with a liberalism that rejects the moral, historical and biblical essence of orthodox Christianity. This has produced a relativistic pluralism that has sucked the heart and soul out of mainline Christianity. Not surprisingly, the ecclesial shift has made the mainline tradition sterile in that it has no means by which it can reproduce itself since it has rejected the classical case for missions and evangelism. For this reason, one can assume that the liberal churches will continue to decline. In the cycle of sect to church, once a church matures it must recreate itself by virtue of renewal or it will die of old age. The mainline churches are dying from old age.

A Cautionary Digression

A warning should be sounded for evangelical churches that have aligned with the conservative resurgence. Modern American evangelicalism was birthed as a social movement in the aftermath of the 1960s. In the process, it made common cause with the Republican Party in order to gain access to political power and to use the political apparatus of the GOP to spread its message. When the evangelicals won people to Christ, it was assumed that the converts would be won to the GOP. Previously, the black church did the same thing with the Democratic Party in order to concretize the gains of the Civil Rights Movement. The Democratic Party advocated for African Americans and championed their cause.

In the aftermath, the black church gave its unwavering support to the Democratic Party even when the Democratic Party required the black church to affirm portions of its platform that went contrary to the traditional position of the black church. Such is the reality of forming an allegiance with a national party.

In the new era, traditional Christianity is not the primary force in society or at the center of the culture. Even though it has partnered with the GOP in order to gain and maintain its influence, it does not own or direct the conservative movement any more than the mainline churches own or direct modern liberalism. Bluntly stated, political conservatism is not a synonym with Christian. Aspects of its agenda run contrary to biblical faith and historical Christianity. When Evangelical became a synonym for politically conservative, the evangelical movement was co-opted and compromised. Worse, it had to depend on the political party for its legitimacy. To the extent that evangelicalism is yoked to the GOP, it will share its fate. Additionally, a large percentage of unchurched Americans will not become evangelical because of the political stigma attached to the term. Since the mainline churches do not push apostolic evangelism, for all practical purposes, this growing segment of society is cutoff from a witnessing church by which it can be discipled because the population thinks one has to become a Republican in order to become a Christian. At its core, the church is not called to be a political movement or to join itself to Caesar.

To the extent that American Christianity has been identified with the political parties, it has been divided against itself. Furthermore, it shares in the polarization of America and in the toxic environment that has been generated by the present political climate. Frankly, the allegiance to the prevailing political parties has caused evangelicals and liberals to compromise the gospel they preach. The hostile divide has become caustic. In the meantime, a growing groundswell is calling for change. The American people do not like the present situation or trust the political parties to lead America. Because the political process has bred dislike, distrust, disunity, and distain, people are desperate for a different direction. They are looking for vision. In short, this is a very bad time for the church to be aligned with political parties or to be identified with them! As the groundswell of discontent grows, evangelical churches may take a big hit and begin to lose members as quickly as the mainline churches lost members following the cultural revolution in the 1960s if they remained culturally and ideologically yoked to the GOP.

The present situation beckons to the churches and offers them an opportunity to become cultural change agents. God is not calling the church to lead a political revolution. Rather, God is calling the church to model the ideals of biblical Christianity as it embodies the kingdom of God in word, deed, and sign in the midst of the American people. When the church learns to give public witness to the incarnated Christ who dwells among us, it will become a source for hope and healing. Before that can happen, the church needs to break its bondage to the political parties and re-establish the unity of the Body of Christ. When this happens, evangelicals and liberals will discover that they have more in common with each other than they do with the political parties. If all the Christians in America joined together and began to work toward common solutions based on their shared values as people of faith, the American people would follow them to Christ. In the aftermath, a united Christianity would be a strong force for cultural renewal and the resurgence of biblical faith.

Evidence of Social Strength

According to Kelley, commitment, discipline, and missionary zeal indicate social strength in a strict church.[5] He does not define the sociological distinction between sect and cult. Because of commitment, believers in a strict church will demonstrate such a strong adherence to the group's beliefs that they will suffer persecution for them. Additionally, they will sacrifice status, possessions, safety, and life itself for the organization's convictions and goals. Individual believers subsume their personal agendas to that of the group. Additionally, believers willingly submit themselves to the discipline of the group. They obey the decisions of the leadership. Being punished for an offense is better than being expelled. The group and its members are consumed with a missionary zeal. They are eager to tell the "Good News" and will not be silenced by opposition or contrary views. Evangelism invites others to join their family. They talk more than they listen.[6]

EAM Examined for Evidences of Social Strength

EAM possessed the characteristics of social strength. Generally, early American Methodists had great commitment to the church. Many suffered repeated persecution for it. Ridicule and social ostracism were common at different times and places, especially when Methodism was new to an area and/or had the status of a minority religion. Other churches and many non-Christians were threatened by Methodism. They were very critical of the church and the zeal of its converts. Violence was not uncommon. Opposition also took the form of coercion. A husband trying to keep his wife from converting is a classic example. Persecution evaporated when Methodism became the dominant religion in an area. For example, in the 1790s, Asbury and Lee did not write about organized persecution in Virginia or Maryland, but they did write about persecution in New England and Charleston. Additionally, Coke wrote about virulent persecution in the Caribbean. Persecution happened in areas where the church did not have a strong presence, or in areas where it challenged the dominant culture or some power structure.

Discipline was central to the experience of EAM because it was a means of grace and essential for growth in grace. New members remained on probation as they moved forward in the order of salvation. In the class meetings, discipline was very strong. People confessed their sins and faults to each other and were corrected by their leaders and fellow classmates. People who did not attend class meetings, violated the rules, or caused division were expelled from the society. General love feasts were banned. Admittance to the society required a ticket that evidenced the bearer's commitment to the "discipline" and willingness to submit to the church. Coleman wrote,

> Those who violated these rules were admonished of the error of their ways, but if they persisted in their disobedience, their names were to be dropped from the church rolls. The unusual thing about these rules was not their severity, but that they were actually enforced. The records of early American Methodism abound with testimony to the frequency of expulsions from the membership because of persons' negligence in following the *General Rules*. . . . Even for a member to murmur persistently against the Methodist discipline or doctrine was sufficient grounds for him to be expelled from the society. Failure to attend regularly the class meeting meant lost membership. A formal charge of delinquency in this case was not required. The mere record of non-attendance was enough to exclude him from the rolls. . . . Even after becoming a member of the society he had to have his character reviewed and passed upon annually. In every way, the emphasis was upon a strict enforcement of the Methodist discipline. To be a member of the church was serious business. . . . The local church organization was designed to assure the maximum efficiency of spiritual guidance to the individual members while at the same time permitting and stimulating the primary purpose of the denomination which was to evangelize the continent.[7]

In the early years, Asbury and other circuit riders gloried in trying the classes and purging the societies. In fact, Asbury boasted about it. However, the people gradually rebelled against this. They saw it as an arbitrary abuse of power. It was un-American. As such, the MEC made new rules that regulated the application of discipline and limited the discretion of the circuit rider in expelling members without due process. Rules that governed the disciplining and expelling of local preachers and itinerants also were developed. Eventually, the right of appeal was instituted as a safeguard for members. A person could appeal all the way to the quarterly conference. Preachers also had the right of appeal.

The following statement from Asbury in 1796 demonstrates the evolution of local discipline and the struggle that local societies had with it. Notice that it became a "democratic" process in which local leaders voted on a person's disposition.

> I had a meeting with the leaders in close conference and found it necessary to explain some parts of our discipline to them particularly that of the right of preachers to expel members, when tried before the society or a "select number," and found guilty of a breach of the law of God and our rules; and that if an appeal were made, it should be brought before the quarterly meeting conference, composed of travelling and local preachers, leaders, and stewards, and finally be determined by a majority of votes. I found it also needful to observe there was such a thing as heresy in the church. . . . Schism is . . . dividing real Christians from each other, and breaking the unity of the Spirit.[8]

From its beginnings, American Methodism struggled with the issue of discipline because strict discipline was not a part of its founding. Asbury and other British missionaries tried to infuse discipline into the organization when they arrived. They met with resistance from native-born preachers in the South and from members who wanted to have a congregational model of church government in the Mid-Atlantic area. Southern schisms reflected the same ethos. Even though early American Methodists were committed to the organization, they struggled with an institutional discipline that expelled members. In many societies, there was a level of distrust between the people and the circuit riders who represented the "central government." Oftentimes, that distrust was fomented by disgruntled local preachers.

Previous chapters have demonstrated the missionary character of the Methodist institution. The itinerants were wandering evangelists who sought to spread Methodism everywhere they went. The organization developed an aggressive strategy for bringing Methodism to every part of America. The circuit system was unparalleled in its missionary effectiveness and in its ability to foster numerical growth. The circuit riders and the institution were consumed by a missionary zeal. The traveling preachers were so committed to the vision that they suffered for it. Poverty, chastity, and obedience were hallmarks of their calling.

Also, within the societies the local preachers, exhorters, and other leaders were very committed and evangelistic. Lay people were expected to have a personal experience of God. From that encounter, they formed their testimonies. The literature from EAM demonstrates that testimonies re-enforced the evangelistic ethos of the movement. After a revival season in Virginia, Asbury reports that the people shared the faith with their friends and neighbors. "The multitudes . . . returning home all alive to God, spread the flame through their respective neighborhoods, which ran from family to family: so that within four weeks, several hundreds found the peace of God."[9] Methodist laity would witness to others so that co-workers and friends would be converted. Lee states, "It was often the case that people in the cornfields, white people, or black, and sometimes both together would begin to sing, and being affected would begin to pray . . . . And by that means [Methodism] spread all through the United States."[10] At other places it is very obvious that Methodism spread like a web movement. Friends invited friends and family members brought other family members. Web dynamics are typical of growing churches that are strict. When a itinerant passed through an area and was scheduled to preach, he expected that the people would invite their friends and have a crowd ready for him. EAM could not have grown as quickly as it did if the itinerants were the only ones with a missionary zeal.

In sum, by Kelley's category, EAM was a socially strong religious organization. The level of strength varied between regions and time periods depending on external conditions. On the whole, Methodists were committed to the church, were disciplined in their lives, and were evangelistic in their behavior.

Evidence of Strictness

Kelley identified three traits of strictness, absolutism, group conformity, and fanaticism.

> If the members of a religious group show high commitment to its goals or beliefs, and a willingness to suffer and sacrifice for them, etc., they also tend to show a

kind of absolutism about those aims, beliefs, [and] explanations of life. One would think that knowledge began with them, that all other attempts to explain life are sadly in error and hardly worthy of notice, let alone respect or credence.[11]

Those who hold to absolutistic tendencies live in a closed system. Their inspiration comes from a special truth. They have a sense of superiority that borders on arrogance. Kelley states, "If the members of a religious group willingly accept a rigorous discipline, obey their leaders unquestioningly, and suffer punishment without abandoning the group, they also require of one another a fairly strict conformity."[12] Conformity applies to matters of faith and lifestyle issues. Lifestyle issues include how one dresses, what leisure activities one enjoys, who one marries, how one raise one's children, and other issues of personal choice. Conformity identifies the individual with the group and serves the social function of binding the members together. It is a shared stigma and a badge of honor. Kelley says, "The ridicule and persecution it draws down . . . is an important element in reinforcing the mutual support within the group and in increasing their separation from the hostile outside world."[13] Persecution reinforces the social strength of the church by raising the cost of belonging and re-enforcing the idea of separation from a hostile world.

Fanaticism relates to the missionary zeal of the individuals in the church. They talk more than they listen and do not listen when the others talk because they already know the truth and are on a crusade to convert the other person.

Methodism Examined for Evidences of Strictness

Without a doubt, circuit riders and preachers showed absolutistic tendencies. They came up through the system as class leaders, exhorters, and preachers. They learned the essence of Methodism through experience, on-the-job training, and personal study. Early American Methodist preachers were converted to the faith. They believed in it and they preached it with passion. They earnestly contended with people who did not share their views. For them the truths of Methodism were self-evident. People who are absolutistic are the opposite of those who are ecumenical or relativistic. Early American Methodist preachers were in competition with other preachers. They emphasized their differences, not what they shared in common. For example, before the Christmas Conference they had to go to the Anglican Church for sacraments and were encouraged to go to the Sunday morning service. The people and the preachers complained that the priests were unconverted and their services were not edifying.[14] In time they developed an us-against-the-world mentality that reinforced an exclusive institutional identity. Events in the world were interpreted in terms of their existing worldview. The Methodists found ample causation to believe that they were Mount Zion in the midst of a pagan Canaan land.

The appeal of Methodism extended beyond its doctrines, organizational prowess, or great missionary zeal. People believed in Methodism because it was experiential. For common people, the experience of God in the inner soul was more important than the erudite words of an educated minister who did not feel what he preached. The experience of God validated the message and the messenger. That is why giving testimonies (exhorting) were a part of every Methodist service. It is also why Methodist preachers used personal illustrations to make their points. A preacher had to believe it and live it. He had to be a living spring that gushed forth with life-giving spiritual water.

Kelley says that in an absolutistic church, there is willful submission to a charismatic leader who interprets truth. His authoritative teaching is an unchanging standard that is binding on all members. Of British Methodism, Kelley stated that Wesley fulfilled this function. British Methodism fit all of his categories very nicely and is used as an example in every section. Early American Methodist preachers rejected the authority of Wesley without rejecting the authority of his teachings. In terms of personal charisma, Asbury was the Wesley of American Methodism. To an extent, he was minimized in the aftermath of the Council debacle. As a consequence, the preachers transferred their allegiance to the conference. The conference was more than an institution. It was an idea to which the preachers aspired, i.e., a tightly knit fellowship of traveling preachers who were united together by experience, calling, belief, deprivation, and commitment. Being a member of the conference gave the preacher status and meaning. It took on the function of the charismatic leader and provided a source of authority to which all were obligated to submit. For this reason, when the popular O'Kelly challenged the conference and withdrew from it, only one itinerant went with him even though many were sympathetic to his cause. On the other hand, the laity and local preachers were not as attached to it or the MEC because they did not belong to the "conference." As such, a large number of them willingly parted from the MEC and followed O'Kelly and other schismatic preachers of that period.

It is difficult to determine to what extent the laity held absolutistic tendencies. When people left a dominant church to become Methodist or chose to be a Methodist while living in an environment in which several organizations vied for their allegiance, it can be assumed that they were serious about Methodism. On the other hand, in places where Methodism was the only show in town or where it was the dominant religion, it can be assumed that Methodists in those areas were less absolutistic about their faith. Regardless of the laity's level of absolutism, the Methodist system promoted an absolutistic agenda in all the places where it existed.

There is evidence of widespread and general conformity in EAM. This is most readily seen in terms of lifestyle issues. Methodists preached against the carefree life and were very critical of those who indulged in it. In a letter to a Quaker friend, Asbury summarized all the things that Methodists should not do.

> I wish Methodists . . . would bear a stronger testimony against races, fairs, plays, and balls; I wish they would reprove swearing, lying, and foolish talking; watch their young people in their companies; instruct them in the doctrines of Christ; call upon them to feel after the spirit of prayer, morning and evening, and strive to bring them to God.[15]

Also, Methodists were supposed to marry other awakened people. When a Methodist married an unbeliever or a person from another church whose religious experience was questioned, that person was expelled. In the course of time, the preachers modified the rule so that the person who married an unbeliever was placed on probation for six months. Methodists were to wear plain clothes and were not to adorn their bodies with jewelry. In worship, the men and the women sat apart. The distilling and use of spirituous liquors was strongly frowned upon. In time, rules forbade it. Conformity was so generalized that it is possible to describe a Methodist in terms of what he or she did not do.

EAM did have a strong missionary zeal, and some called it fanatical. A quotation from Nathan Bangs helps to demonstrate this last point. He was a New Englander who converted to Methodism at the age of 22 in 1800 while the MEC was still young in that region.

> There was no regular religious worship yet in the settlement, but a Methodist itinerant occasionally reached us and gave us a sermon, and a small Methodist class met in the neighborhood. These people were considered, by those with whom I associated, as fanatics, and were treated with contempt.[16]

In sum, EAM demonstrated strictness tendencies. However, it is difficult to determine to what extent EAM was strict. Certainly, the circuit riders and local leaders evidenced strictness in every category. Also, as a whole, the laity was strict in the area of conformity. Most were strict in the other categories of absolutism and fanaticism. When a person became a Methodist in early America, a wall that separated the person from the world was built around the person's life. That wall re-enforced the ideals of Methodism and the community that made it possible.

Implications of Kelley's Theory When Applied to EAM

Kelley opined that membership gain over a long period indicates social strength. He states,

> To recapitulate: membership gain or loss is significant over time; what that significance may be is subject to interpretation. The explanation offered here is that . . . strong organizations tend to increase in membership and weak ones to diminish. Thus membership gain or loss is used as a useful, though not sole or infallible, indicator of social strength.[17]

Loosening membership rules or lowering the standards may yield numerical growth for those who want to join but do not want to pay the cost to join. However, this weakens the church and sets in motion a process that will lead to future membership decline. Strong organizations tend to be strict organizations. When social strength and strictness are combined they reinforce each other. Ultimately, when a strong organization loses its strictness it will also lose its strength. Therefore, growing churches that do not maintain strictness will degenerate over time. Social weakness replaces social strength as a church declines in numbers and influence. Redemption and lift and the inability to pass on the dynamic charisma of the faith to the next generation are primary reasons for decay. Once a denomination begins to decay, short of divine intervention or a revival, human interventions will not stop the process. Usually the process corrects itself because new churches that are socially strong and strict split off from the one that has become weak. This is the genesis of sects and the lifecycle of vital religion.

If Kelley is correct, his theory offers a compelling explanation as to why EAM grew. However, Kelley's theory is problematic when applied to EAM for several reasons. First, Kelley's theory will be flawed if applied to the MEC as a whole because the various regions responded to different sets of contextual factors. Plus, EAM contextualized itself in the various regions so that the institution adapted to the contexts. To use his theory properly, each region of EAM would have to be examined separately. Second, EAM did not grow well in some places like Rhode Island or Savannah, Georgia. According to Kelley, strong organizations can grow in any context. He states, "A really vigorous religious movement is not hindered by an inhospitable cultural climate–it makes its own plausibility-structure."[18] Granted, EAM could have grown in places where it did not grow if it made its own plausibility-structure. If making a plausibility-structure is a quality of a strong organization, then at times and in places, EAM was not strong. Third, how would Kelley's theory explain the fluctuating periods of membership growth and decline in various regions of EAM? For example, after eight years of decline, southern Methodism had an explosion of growth starting in 1800. Can the decline and the revival both be explained by means of Kelley's theory? Do strong organizations cease to be strong for a period and then become strong again? It seems that Kelley surrenders to a type of determinism with an all-or-nothing mentality.

One could use Kelley's theory to argue that the southern decline happened because southern Methodism ceased to be socially strong and strict. In fact, this is true to an extent. Widespread conflict, schism, and general membership loss in the 1790s give evidence to this. However, one could just as easily argue that the organization became weak because it could not surmount negative contextual factors that drained the vitality out of the institutional church. That is, negative contextual and institutional factors combined to check the church's growth and contributed to the internal stress that weakened the organization. It becomes a question of primary causation. Since Kelley's theory makes no provision for negative contextual factors, he cannot address this important issue.

From the perspective of this church growth study, Kelley's theory is useful when applied in a narrow way, but it does not explain the reality of regional growth and decline in EAM as well as the Hartford typology.

The Sect-to-Church Theory

Many have used the sect-to-church typology in part or in whole to describe the life cycle dynamics of American Methodism.[19] When used as an interpretive model, it explains why American Methodism grew rapidly in its youth and stumbled in later years. The theory assumes that "sect" qualities made EAM grow. The loss of those qualities signaled accommodation to the culture and eventual numerical decline.

The Sect-to-Church Theory According to Niebuhr

In the book *The Social Sources of Denominations*, Niebuhr shows that there is an intricate connection between sects and churches. Sects become churches and churches give birth to sects. This accounts for the sociological distinction between the two. It also explains why the religious landscape is dotted with so many different religious organizations. In the following paragraph, Niebuhr describes the sociological difference between a sect and a church from his perspective in the early nineteenth century.

> The difference has been well described as lying primarily in the fact that members are born into the church while they must join the sect. Churches are inclusive institutions, frequently are national in scope, and emphasize the universalism of the gospel; while sects are exclusive in character, appeal to the individualistic element in Christianity, and emphasize its ethical demands. Membership in a church is socially obligatory, the necessary consequence of birth into a family or nation, and no special requirements condition its privileges; the sect, on the other hand, is likely to demand some definite type of religious experience as a prerequisite of membership.[20]

Churches attach high importance to official status. They rightly administer the sacraments, have a professional clergy who are set apart for "sacerdotal" ministry, and interpret the scriptures for their members. Emphasis is on participation and training. The church is closely allied with national, economic, and cultural interests. By its nature, it accommodates its ethics to the ethics of civilization. "It represents the morality of the respectable majority, not of the heroic minority."[21] Leadership is institutional, not charismatic.

On the other hand, sects attach primary importance to the religious experience of their members as prerequisites to membership, the priesthood of all believers, and to the sacraments as symbols of fellowship and pledges of allegiance. Typically, they reject the official clergy and rely upon lay preachers who are indigenous to the people. The lay preachers share the same experience in faith and in life. A personal religious experience that is attached to a true interpretation of scripture is more important than the educated teaching of an elite clergy. Leadership is charismatic. The members are a minority group in society and are counter-cultural. Usually, they are from the disaffected, poorer classes.

Often sects function as a protest movement against the established order and the established churches.²²

> The sociological character of sectarianism, however, is almost always modified in the course of time by the natural processes of birth and death, and on this change in structure, changes in doctrine and ethics inevitably follow. By its very nature the sectarian type of organization is valid only for one generation. . . . Rarely does a second generation hold the convictions it has inherited with a fervor equal to that of its fathers, who fashioned these convictions in the heat of conflict and at the risk of martyrdom. As generation succeeds generation, the isolation of the community from the world becomes more difficult. Furthermore, wealth frequently increases when the sect subjects itself to the discipline of asceticism in work and expenditure; with the increase of wealth the possibilities for culture also become more numerous and involvement in the economic life of the nation as a whole can less easily be limited.²³

The training of the children in the faith requires an emphasis on a dogmatic and less charismatic presentation of the truth. Creeds are substituted for personal experience. A class of educated, professional clergy separate themselves from the membership. The emergence of the denomination is not bad. It is a necessary phase. However, the failure of the institution to maintain the vision and the loyalty of the entire membership becomes apparent when new sects rise up in its midst. New church bodies almost always begin as sects. If they attract members and survive, they will be transformed into churches over time.

Niebuhr appealed to EAM to illustrate his theory. He was especially attracted to the frontier manifestation of it.²⁴ Ironically, Niebuhr credited EAM's success to its ability to adapt itself to its cultural and geographic environments. Adaptation to cultural norms is not a typical quality associated with emerging sects. He says that EAM almost died during the Revolutionary War because of its association with Anglicanism. After the war, Asbury was able to redefine the MEC and configure its organization to the missionary task at hand and to the context of the American scene. The "Americanizing" of Methodism was necessary for its survival. He states,

> With its fervent piety, its lay preaching, its early sectarian polity, it accorded well with the spirit of the West, while the itinerancy and the circuit system were admirable devices for the evangelization of the frontier. While it is true that the centralization of control in the Wesleyan church ran counter to the provincial and individualistic temper of isolated pioneer communities, yet this form of organization gave Methodism direction and concentration of energy which the loose polity of the Baptist movement lacked. This centralization of control was a corollary of the itinerancy; in combination they constituted a missionary strategy which conquered the West.²⁵

According to Niebuhr, in an attempt to lessen the tension between the organization and the culture, Methodism sought to cloak its organization in republican forms or to describe it in Anti-Federalist terms. In both cases, the MEC appealed to government as an example. For sociological reasons, Federalists were not very attracted to Methodism or its message. However, Anti-Federalists were. For that reason, it was in the best interest of the MEC to identify with that group.[26] For example, Asbury was not a monarch like Wesley. The assembled preachers voted him into office. In turn, he was amenable to the preachers via the conference. The MEC behaved like a constitutional organization. For the sake of organizational effectiveness, Asbury appointed the preachers. They did not have a right to appeal. Also, the MEC did not allow the election of presiding elders or lay representation in conference. However, the negative effect of these organizational necessities was mitigated because the preachers were not as distinguished from the people as to become a separate class. Consequently, they were not in violation of the democratic spirit.

Schisms and internal conflict furthered the process of cultural adaptation and accommodation. Niebuhr states, "Despite the fact that Asbury often expressed an autocratic spirit, he nevertheless accommodated the character of the church to the new environment and so enabled it to become the representative frontier denomination."[27] Accommodated means that he adapted the organization to its context. By definition, that is a quality of an effective organization. According to Niebuhr, Methodism was bred to win the West. He says, "With these modifications of its character as a sect of the poor and a child of an aristocratic church, Methodism was able to enter upon an unprecedented career of frontier conquest."[28] In other words, it had the character of a sect and the organization of an effective denomination. As a result of its accommodations to the spirit of the West, its missionary zeal, and its effective organization, EAM championed over the older established churches. It became America's church to the extent that it embodied its values and gave meaning to them. In the early 1800s, while Methodism was growing at a meteoric rate, Federalism was a spent force. To the extent that the mainline churches of that time were associated with Federalism, they shared its fate.

According to Niebuhr's description, EAM had a missionary character in that it was contextualized to the spirit of the West and was driven by an evangelistic zeal. Its effective organization was suited to the demography of the West and its missionary task. Additionally, it evidenced sect-like qualities. By means of its sect-like qualities it appealed to the people of the West, notwithstanding the fact that tension existed between the organizational structure and the people to whom it appealed. The church's missionary character and its effective organization united with the church's sect-like qualities to make it numerically successful in the West. The sect-like qualities of the MEC attracted the people of the West because the inhabitants were poor, socially isolated, largely uneducated, and republican in their orientation. EAM was at home in that context.

By contrast, Methodism entered New England as a sect. In time, it carved out a small niche with some disaffected people who were attracted to its sect-like qualities and its counter-cultural message. Slow but steady growth ensued. The greatest growth happened in the New England frontier where the population density was low. In the 1790s, the MEC appealed to the people who moved to that region more than it did to the people in southern New England.

It must be assumed that some of the immigrants to the New England frontier were counter-cultural people in their orientation. They left Massachusetts and Connecticut to escape from establishment and to find opportunity. In many ways, they were like the people who ventured into the western frontier. It has already been demonstrated that western immigrants were receptive to Methodism. The sect-like attributes of Methodism appealed to frontier people. In general, the sect-like qualities of a religious organization will attract counter-cultural people with whom those qualities resonate. However, the MEC did not grow rapidly in southern New England in terms of percent population until the 1800s when it modified some of its sect-like qualities so that it appealed to more people. In other words, the MEC had to adapt to the normative culture of southern New England before it experience significant growth. To do this, it modified many of its sect-like qualities. An emphasis on an educated clergy with the appearance of a parish pastor is an example. In so doing, it accelerated the process by which it became a church. This was a positive adaptation for southern New England but did not bode well for the other regions in which the MEC labored.

By means of its sect-like qualities and missionary zeal, EAM was able to get a foothold in every region of the country because there were people in every region who were attracted by them. The social upheaval and national transition that was taking place during this time made the sect-like qualities of EAM very appealing to a large portion of the population. As long as there was a growing population of people that was attracted to the sect-like qualities of the MEC in a given area, the sect-like qualities of the church helped it to grow. However, after the MEC established a strong presence in an area, the process of indigenization pushed it into the cultural mainstream. In time, the sect-like qualities were sacrificed at the altar of respectability.

Summary

Sect-like qualities are institutional factors that cause growth to the extent that they mesh with positive contextual factors. The missionary zeal and strong organizational dynamics that are embedded in a church with sect-like qualities are positive institutional factors that favor growth in every context. However, without the benefit of an effective organization, a church with sect-like qualities will limit its growth potential. Additionally, if a church with sect-like qualities has an effective organization so that it grows large, at some point, it will cease to be a sect.

It has been argued that EAM and other sect-like churches of the late eighteenth and early nineteenth centuries were so successful in reaching the people that they actually were a primary force in changing the value system that undergirded America at that time. This is the argument of Nathan Hatch and his students. It parallels Frederick Turner's Frontier Thesis. During the period of Methodism's fastest growth, America went through a profound "Christianization." Hatch called this the "democratization of American Christianity."[29] Democracy does not refer to Republican ideology. Rather, it is the incarnation of the church into popular culture. When evangelical Christianity was diffused through the general population, it ceased to be the exclusive concern of a clerical elite or an elect oligarchy. At that point, it became a subject of vital interest to the masses.[30] A religious organization that is diffused through the general population and incarnated into the culture is not a sect. As such, during the time of its greatest growth, the MEC had a missionary character and an effective organization, and it was socially strong; but, it was not a sect.

When American Methodism began its gradual decline after 1850, the MEC and MEC South stopped being socially strong churches and they diminished their missionary character. When Methodism lessened its missionary character, it also confused the reasons for its existence. An effective organization serves the self-defined purposes of the organization. When the MECs compromised the priorities of evangelism, conversion, and discipleship, their organizations changed so that they no longer promoted those causes to the same extent as they did before. This led to numerical decline and was the process by which the MECs became socially weak and ineffective organizations.

According to Finke and Stark, the MECs stopped growing after the 1850s because they stopped acting like "upstart sects."[31] The authors blame this on the growing professionalization of the clergy. They argue that clericalism signaled the change from sect to church. Their documentation shows that a strong correlation existed between the institutionalization of the MECs and their numerical declines. They conclude that Methodist membership began to slump when it began to act like a church. The theory as they use it unnecessarily blurs their point because their discussion focuses on the extremes of the sect-to-church continuum. By their definition of sect, the MEC stopped being one as soon as it became socially acceptable and the dominant church in America. This happened before 1820 because the MEC was the largest church in America by that time. Indeed, for many decades, Methodism had rapid growth with the general population because it was not a sect. This rapid growth occurred after the 1820 and continued to the 1860s.

Umbel acknowledges the sect-to-church theory but is not tied to it. In no other region did EAM transition from sect to church as quickly as it did in New England. Since New England is Umbel's point of reference, one would expect that he would reference the theory. His words validate the observations that Niebuhr made about EAM on the frontier.

> American Methodism travelled from sect to church. And yet these categories do not adequately describe Methodism's uniqueness. Historians look at movements and structures. We must also look at the process from one to the other. I argue here that Methodism initially possessed both the spirit of a popular religious movement [a sect] and the structure of a fully organized religious institution [a church]. Indeed, its early success lay in its rapid organization of new converts into societies, its stream of leadership to target locations, and it system of denominational order.[32]

Sociologically, EAM displayed the genuine qualities of a sect. Institutionally, it functioned like a well-oiled church growth machine complete with all the marks of a fully formed denomination. From this perspective, Kelley's theory and the sect-to-church theory both provide important insights. However, by themselves, they do not give a full explanation for the regional growth and decline of EAM.

Instead of focusing on the sect-to-church process, it may be more productive to focus on the in-between state when a church is not a sect and before it becomes socially weak. During the in-between phase, a church has maximum potential for numerical growth because it can appeal to the larger population and it has the internal resources to grow large. While in this phase, the MEC retained some sect-like qualities, evidenced social strength, and squarely focused on its missionary task. In fact, EAM remained in this phase for an extended period of time. While in this phase, it dominated the religious landscape of most of the regions in a relatively short period.

In conclusion, it has been demonstrated that EAM possessed a missionary character, an effective organization, and sect-like qualities that made it socially strong. In the regions where Methodism grew, these interdependent qualities meshed with each other so that Methodism was able to maximize growth opportunities. Also, it has been shown that a church does not have to become a sect in order to display these qualities. The MEC had its strongest growth when it adapted to the cultural context in the various regions without compromising its social strength, missionary character, or effective organization. A countercultural sect will never win a region. By definition, it will remain a minority faith. In order to dominate the religious landscape and shape the culture, the sect has to take on church-like qualities without losing its social strength or appeal to the masses. A religious organization that successfully makes this transition may become a force to change the culture. However, if the culture changes it, it will lose its dynamism and begin the process of social decay.

CHAPTER SEVENTEEN

LOOKING BACK TO LOOK FORWARD

By way of review, this book has shown that the missionary character, effective organization, and social strength of EAM caused it to grow when it was contextualized into the various regions in which it existed. Contextualization and the process by which the church becomes indigenous relate to missionary character. An evangelistic zeal that pushes the church into the world to make disciples is another aspect of missionary character. Both hark back to the Great Commission. EAM's effective organization gave vision to its primary task and mobilized the church to fulfill its mission. Every member was a preacher by word or deed.

Additionally, the book has concluded that missionary character, effective organization, and social strength are interdependent variables that will foster numerical growth in any context. These institutional factors are hampered by negative contextual factors but are not neutralized by them because they require the church to adapt to its context. Some negative contextual factors may counteract positive institutional factors for a period. However, when the opportunity for growth exists, the above listed interdependent variables will maximize the growth potential in a given area. Specifically, adaptation is a key component of an effective organization. An effective organization adjusts itself and its processes so it interacts with the external environment in ways that facilitate its purpose and progress. This does not mean that a church with an effective organization cannot be prophetic. Even though EAM capitulated on the issue of slavery; it successfully challenged the gentry's lifestyle, the manufacturing of hard liquor, and many activities that worked against holiness.

Likewise, a socially strong church is purpose-driven and motivated by a shared vision that grips the membership and focuses it on a common task. A religious organization cannot have a missionary character, as defined by this church growth study, without being socially strong. Also, a church does not need to be a sect in order to be socially strong. However, a socially strong church needs to be united by a strong vision that compels it to fulfill its purposes. An apostolic church is a type of socially strong church that has a missionary character and an effective organization. An apostolic church exists to make disciples out of all who repent, assimilate in the local church, grow into the image of Christ, and work to further the cause of God in the world. Apostolic churches invade their communities with a persistent presence and a continuous invitation to come to God. EAM behaved like an apostolic church. Without compromising the end goal, EAM had an effective organization that maximized membership growth as it permeated early America with the gospel and its expanding infrastructure of circuits, societies, chapels, and classes.

The above listed discussion on missionary character, effective organization, and social strength represents the central insight of this book. I offer it as a general church growth theorem. I hope that others will evaluate it and test it. Church growth is an applied science. Insights are gained so they can be used in the task of making disciples of all nations. The end goal of church growth research is to equip the church to fulfill the task of world evangelization.

Second, this book has demonstrated the usefulness of the Hartford typology (contextual-institutional factors, national-local factors). Previous chapters establish the following principle related to the typology: positive contextual factors combined with positive institutional factors will produce numerical growth. Positive contextual factors combined with negative institutional factors or negative contextual factors combined with positive institutional factors may produce anemic growth or decline. Negative contextual factors combined with negative institutional factors will produce numerical decline. This principle is related to the mechanical analogy. That is, several gears must engage before a shaft can turn. When the gears mesh, applied force will move the gears and turn the shaft so that work is accomplished. If the gears do not mesh, force will still be applied but it will meet with resistance. When this occurs, the gears will not turn the shaft efficiently and little work will be accomplished. When a socially strong church with a missionary character and effective organization meshes with its external context, the force of evangelism will awaken people. In turn, the awakened people will assimilate into churches and be discipled. When this happens, the work of church growth is accomplished.

The principle relates to the proposed theorem. A church may not be able to change its context. By definition, the church has little control over contextual factors. However, a church can circumvent most negative contextual factors by adjusting its internal mechanisms. The ability to turn negative contextual factors into growth opportunities is a hallmark of churches with a missionary character and an effective organization that are socially strong. As such, churches should seek to identify negative contextual factors so they can develop strategies to circumvent them. Churches should never surrender to the context. In America, the worst context exists when the general population is rapidly declining and no new people are moving into the community or region. Even then, unchurched people with varying degrees of receptivity will be present in the community. To attract this population, the church must be externally focused, culturally relevant, ministry oriented, and willing to give itself away.

Third, professional social scientists believed that contextual factors were more determinative to growth than institutional factors. Conservative Protestant church professionals prioritized institutional factors. Ultimately, contextual factors will cause numerical decline to the extent that a religious organization cannot adapt to the context and develop effective strategies to capitalize on opportunities for growth. Even though context is critical, the church's response to context is more critical. As such, this research sides with the conservative Protestant church professionals. The Church Growth discipline is very pragmatic. It prioritizes institutional factors so it can achieve its goal of disciple-making. However, this research does not suggest that contextual factors are less determinative to church growth or decline than institutional factors.

Fourth, this research has demonstrated the importance of regional factors. It recommends that the category of "regional factors" be added to the Hartford typology that includes national and local factors. One could also make the case for global factors since the world has become more interrelated. For example, global weather patterns, the global economy, global transportation systems, the development of a global lingua franca, global diasporas, and the work of global jihadists are global contextual factors that influence evangelism and church growth. Also, since denominations, parachurch organizations, and non-governmental organizations work all over the world, global institutional factors exists. For example, a decision to give UM annual conferences in Africa equal representation at General Conference would radically change the internal dynamics of United Methodism.

Fifth, according to Roozen and Hadaway, in early America, large numbers of unchurched people held traditional religious beliefs. However, because of massive migration, large percentages lived in places where there were no churches. In that environment, it was relatively easy for an aggressive church with a missionary character and an effective organization to grow quickly. Accordingly, the MEC capitalized on the opportunities that migration brought, and grew rapidly because of it. Through the 1850s, the MECs planted churches in every new community and aggressively sought to make converts of the unchurched. However, after the country was covered in a network of circuits and local churches, Methodist circuit riders settled down and acted like the established clergy. When they did this, they supplanted the local leadership and stopped planting new churches. According to Finke and Stark, before this happened,

> The actual pastoral functions were performed in most Methodist churches by unpaid, local "amateurs" just like those serving in the Baptist congregations up the road. A professional clergy had not yet centralized control of the Methodist organization. True, the circuit riders were full-time professionals vested with sub-

stantial authority. But they only visited a congregation from time to time and played a minor role of visiting bishop and evangelist more than the role of pastor. It is only when the circuit riders dismounted and accepted "settled" pastorates that the "episcopal" structure of Methodism came to the fore. Indeed, it may well be that to the extent that the Methodists were able to create a national organization based on circuit riders, they had the best of both worlds—centralized direction and local control.[1]

After America was settled, there was a period in which families remained fairly stable. It was not uncommon for three and four generations to be born and raised in the same community. This maintained strong filial bonds within communities and permitted local churches to become community institutions. Local churches that served stable communities enjoyed continuity. Churches could focus on ministering to the flock and not be consumed with the task of evangelistic outreach. Churches maintained their membership by biological growth. In time, evangelism directed at outsiders diminished. Many small churches became extended families in which one was born or joined through marriage. In time, the appointed preachers became chaplains who ministered to an insulated flock. Education, pastoral skills, and administrative abilities made pastors successful. Successful pastors who were well connected worked their way up the system. A pastor who did well would get a larger charge with more prestige. However, mediocre pastors also received an appointment.

In the previous period, the Methodist circuit rider was an itinerant evangelist who evangelized the masses, took the church into new areas, planted churches, and held the connection together. After the itinerant preachers displaced the local preachers and took control of the local churches, no one assumed the evangelistic task of the circuit rider. At this point, Methodism stopped expanding and began to occupy the land. This explains why Methodist membership declined in terms of percent population during the late nineteenth century. As an occupation force, Methodism did not seek to expand its presence. It only sought to hold onto what it had.

George Hunter, in his book *To Spread the Power: Church Growth in the Wesleyan Spirit*, captures the essence of this phenomenon. He stated,

> There is, however, something tragically seductive about a denomination reaching a stage . . . where the pins on a map show an established church in virtually every town in a state or society; the denomination begins to think of outreach as "finished" and settles in for the nurture and care of Christians. These churches then experience net membership decline until they rediscover their perennial apostolic mission.[2]

Today, an aging membership fills the pews in a growing number of UM churches. The children and grandchildren have moved away and only come back for visits. Biological growth will not propel the aging churches into the future. Without a strong emphasis on evangelism, the churches will eventually die. The members remember the old days and lament that their churches are dying, but they are unwilling to pay the price necessary to revive their churches. For many, it is better to die than to change.

When Methodism was young, immigration was a contextual factor that combined with the church's missionary character and effective organization to make the church grow rapidly. Today, emigration from small town America and the rapidly changing demographics of urban centers do not have to be the doom of United Methodism in those areas. A UM congregation can grow in a changing community. Furthermore, if it focused on the external context, it could become a source for revitalization. Regardless, conferences and districts need to prioritize church extension. They should do this in partnership with local churches. The strategic planting of new churches in areas of population change is crucial. In growing communities, new residents are attracted to new churches. Additionally, newly planted congregations want to grow. Plus, they do not have to overcome the inertia of transition in order to grow. Second, old churches can attract new crowds by starting specialized services that target specific populations. For example, static churches can revitalize their aging congregations by starting a new service that targets the new families who have moved into their aging communities. Or, a local church can sponsor a special-needs ministry to a targeted group.

In the past, the connection extended Methodism into new areas and started new churches. In the future, local churches will become the lead agents in church extension and evangelism. They can do this by starting new services within the present church building, or by starting satellite ministries that grow into new congregations, or by a missionary method of seeding a new church in a new area. Some local churches should partner with ethnic people to plant culture-specific congregations both near and far. In the growing polyglot context of America, this is an important strategy. America is a missionary field and requires a missionary strategy.

Most importantly, the UMC needs to design and deploy a functional equivalent for the circuit rider. Modern pastors are not circuit-riding evangelists or church planters. Missional mergers may help the UMC to conceptualize an updated model for an American itinerant. Missional mergers have become a popular way for some churches to extend themselves and grow. In a missional merger, two or more strong congregations combine resources for the sake of better reaching the larger community. Some want to evangelize an entire city and realize that they need to cooperate with likeminded churches to make that happen. The end result includes additional ministry sites, increased participation, shared leadership, gifted ministry, more compassionate outreach, expanded influence in the community, and pure excitement for those who are involved. Preachers appointed to missional mergers do not belong to a local congregation. Rather, they work on a team of ministers who function like circuit riders as they keep the merged congregations focused on an expanding ministry to the larger geographic area. Some members of the appointed team may have specialized ministry skills that they exercise on behalf of the merged congregations. The various congregations may not be united in one location for Sunday morning services. That would work against the end goal of planting the church in every part of the expanded area. Ultimately, the merged congregations may become the equivalency of a large circuit with many preaching points. When the ordained clergy focus on the expanded ministry front, lay ministers are freed to take their rightful places in the local assemblies. When this happens, the exaggerated dichotomy between clergy and laity becomes less noticeable. Both are called and dispatched to gifted ministry. Unfortunately, most churches merge as a way to postpone death. The end result is a loss of identity, disgruntled members who fight with each other, a power struggle, and decreased attendance.

Whatever the UMC does, it must reconsider the pastoral model that has emerged since the itinerants took over the local churches. Does United Methodism want its clergy to be highly educated priests who manage a local congregation as they dispense professional services to a dependent people? I think not. Early Methodism released the lay people and formed a ministry partnership with them. It also released the clergy to go forth as they reformed the nation and spread scriptural holiness throughout the land by making disciples and planting churches in every settlement. The time to challenge the professional clergy model is now!

Since I work in a seminary that prepares called people to become professional clergy, I should be intimidated by my cajoling. In fact, my seminary faithfully and proficiently equips its students to do effective minister in the congregation and the world in accordance with the expectations that the denominations, trustees, and accrediting agency give us. After all, seminaries work in partnership with the denominations to train people for effective ministry. UM clergy need to be tooled. Even Wesley required his preachers to go through the course of study. Additionally, junior preachers were mentored by senior preachers. Before a person accepted the call to the itinerancy, the person was trained in the local church as a class leader and an exhorter. If the denominations changed their expectations, seminaries would change their curriculum. The denominations pull the cart of seminary education. A curriculum review that focuses on the apostolic calling of the church is in order.

Sixth, considerable immigration occurred in America before 1800. Afterward, immigration rapidly increased. EAM's failure to evangelize and disciple non-English speaking immigrants was a major factor in its inability to grow its membership with those populations after the 1850s. The Roman Catholic Church in America grew and continues to grow because it actively assimilates Roman Catholic immigrants. Because of Roman Catholic immigration, the Roman Catholic Church passed the Methodist churches as the largest denomination in America before the end of the nineteenth century.[3] The lesson is obvious. A denomination that wants to grow in terms of percent population must prioritize ministry to immigrants and other categories of unchurched people. Additionally, a church with a missionary character will welcome the opportunities and blessings that ministry with immigrants brings.

In America today, Hispanics are the fastest growing immigrant population. According to the Census Bureau, from 2001 to 2006 the Hispanic population increased in the Deep South by 58 percent. The national Hispanic population increased by an incredible nine million in that time period. The Census Bureau projects that Hispanics will equal 24.4 percent of the total American population within forty years. Already, Hispanics equal 25 percent of the population in south Florida and much of the Southwest. Hispanics became the largest American ethnic minority in 2003.[4]

Most Hispanics are disconnected from church structures. Nominally, they are Roman Catholics, but in practice the overwhelming majority remains functionally unchurched. New immigrants are very receptive to the gospel and the ministry efforts of the church. This receptivity does not last long. As the foreign born Hispanic population grows and becomes more stable, it will develop patterns that limit the effectiveness of Methodist evangelism. Specifically, new arrivals will be assimilated into a broad based Hispanic social network that will isolate them from the UMC. To have a meaningful ministry with immigrant Hispanics and to grow with this burgeoning population in the future, UM churches need to establish that ministry now! If United Methodism learned the lessons from the past, Hispanic church planting will become the top ministry priority of the UMC today. Otherwise, the UMC will be cut-off from this population in the future.

Seventh, the contextual reality of modern America is very similar to the contextual reality of early America preceding the Second Great Awakening. The 1790s were a time of tremendous social upheaval and decline for American Christianity. A host of contextual factors combined to decimate the established churches. The rise of republicanism, the decline of federalism, the ascent of rationalistic denominations in New England, the emergence of an aspiring middle class in the South, the romance with French agnosticism, the prevalence of deism, spirited national debates, disestablishment laws, rapid emigration from established areas, new technologies, and rumors of war all give evidence to this truth. In the wake of the groundswell of negative contextual factors, the Episcopalians, Congregationalists, and Baptists all floundered. The decline of religion did not bypass the MEC. Methodism struggled to grow in the Mid-Atlantic and suffered enormous declines in the South. By 1800, a very small percentage of Americans regularly participated in church.

After 1800, America went through a period of profound "Christianization." Like a snake that sheds its old skin so it can grow new skin, America embraced evangelical Christianity under the influence of the Second Great Awakening. From 1800 through 1812, American Methodism experienced sustained numerical growth in every region. In the years leading up to 1800, few would have predicted the strong resurgence of biblical faith and popular religion. Certainly, Thomas Paine and the Virginia Fathers who gave primary political leadership to America did not anticipate a revival of biblical proportions. Many hoped that religion in America would fall to the same fate as religion in France. They were not friends of evangelicalism. In fact, secularism has continued to erode the core of Christianity in Western Europe. The fire of vital Christian has almost burned out in secular Europe. Some predict that the inevitable march of secularism in America will destroy evangelicalism as it douses the fires of Christian vitality.

They envision a post-Christian America. Hadaway and Roozen offer an important analysis of the religious situation in modern America:

> The erosion of the cultural center and the disestablishment of mainstream Protestantism provide the keys to understand "where we are" from a religious perspective. The decreasing power of the mainstream is only a reflection of a general breakdown of the "dominant culture" that was supported and defined by white Protestant Americans. The primary losers in this process were the mainstream denominations which collectively constitute "established" religion for American society. These institutions have much less influence, and the culture has become much more fragmented and secular, no longer serving as a general plausibility structure for a religious people.[5]

Finke and Stark have documented the disestablishment of early America and the rise of the upstart sects to include the Methodists. Hatch and others have shown how the new evangelical churches radically reoriented the American religious landscape. In the late eighteenth and early nineteenth centuries, the dominant churches of America passed into the shadows as the Methodists and Baptists made their move to center-stage. As the contextual reality of early America changed, the established churches were not able to adapt to the new reality or to compete in the open economy of the emerging religious marketplace. The new context favored evangelical theology and the aggressive evangelization of the new churches. In particular, Methodism had an organization that allowed it to go to the people. Dominant churches made the people come to them. Now, the UMC is numbered with the declining mainline churches. It has become the very thing it repudiated.

Today, Pentecostal, non-denominational, and evangelical churches of every sort are attempting to do the same thing that Methodism did 200 years ago. In so doing, they are redrawing the map of religious America. However, there is a new challenge and a host of new players. World religions, cults, new religious movements, and sects of every sort are also competing for American adherents. At this point, no single religious organization dominates the American scene to the extent that Methodism did in the first-half of the nineteenth century. The Roman Catholic Church boasts of growth. However, much of its growth comes from Latino immigration. It is not making inroads with the growing population of church dropouts, agnostics, functional atheists, and practitioners of other faiths. It should be noted that Islam and Mormonism are two of the fasted growing religious organizations in America.

The aftermath of 9/11 and two wars have drained the American economy. Additionally, America is mired in a season of political turmoil. The nation is deeply divided along sectional and social lines. "Culture wars" are raging. The forces of secularism have aligned to make a frontal attack on the values of evangelical Christianity. Massive immigration from Latin America and Asia has reshaped the American mosaic and caused the cultural center to shift. Migration is constant. Large sections of the population are relocating from the rust-belt to the sun-belt. Other groups move on a regular basis as they transfer between jobs or look for new opportunities. New technologies in farming, medicine, communications, computers, and the space industry have had a fundamental impact on

America. Globalization and terrorism have drastically changed the world. The economic boom of the 1990s, with its low unemployment has been replaced with an unyielding economic downturn. No one knows the real unemployment rate. Some suggest that it is at 23 percent. Many Americans who want to relocate to find a new job can't sell their existing homes. Individual bankruptcy rates are at all-time highs. At the same time, the rich have gotten richer.

As I write this, Occupy Wall Street protesters have set up in the major cities and are demanding economic change and the redistribution of wealth. Some are anarchists. Few base their discontent and protest on biblical or Christian principles. Evangelicals are striking by their absence. How should the evangelical church engage this population of restless and angry people? Could Evangelicals restate their core convictions in biblical terms? The protesters will not be evangelized and discipled by a church that ignores them and remains deaf to their concerns.

In the midst of the current upheaval, the UMC is holding its own in the Southeast to Texas largely due to emigration from other regions. However, the UMC is posting large losses in the other regions of America. At the same time, the African conferences have posted extraordinary gains. Their increases have padded the large membership decreases in the American connection. Africa is in revival.

Methodists in the 1790s prayed for revival. Not only did they pray for it, they worked for it. Perhaps, the conditions of today have made America ripe for another general revival. If that be the case, American Methodism could be on the verge of revitalization and membership growth.

Eighth, the Hartford typology has an inherently naturalistic bias that discounts spiritual factors. As was stated in Chapter One, this book assumes spiritual factors but has not tendered spiritual explanations. However, the primary data and church growth theory do not delimit spiritual factors. C. Peter Wagner's *Strategies for Churches: Tools for Effective Evangelism and Missions* advocates for the inclusion of spiritual factors.[6] Also, Wagner includes a section on spiritual factors in a revised edition of Donald McGavran's groundbreaking book on church growth.[7] According to social scientists, spiritual factors relate to theology and perceived experience. They cannot be quantified or tested by means of the scientific method. In the mind of the social scientist, a person of faith reads spiritual factors back onto natural causations.

Besides Wagner, many others argue for the inclusion of spiritual factors. Recent research on spiritual mapping, revival, spiritual warfare, signs and wonders, prayer evangelism, and the like identify spiritual factors that influence church growth and decline. The Bible also affirms the relationship between spiritual factors and church growth. Some spiritual factors relate to the institution, others to the context. For example, the work of God in the church to bring about anointed worship, clear preaching, holiness, church unity, and obedience are spiritual factors that relate to the institution. On the other hand, a plighted community that is plagued by persistent cycles of crime, disease, violence, sexual perversion, blasphemy, sorcery, disrupted families, addictions, and natural calamities may be under the influence of demonic forces. These are examples of negative spiritual factors that relate to the context in which the church operates.

The Sentinel Group has documented a plethora of cases in which the presence of God has swept into a plighted area so that the people, churches, governments, communities, and the land were transformed when the people turned to God and rebelled against the reign of Satan.[8] In their extensive research, they have documented spiritual factors and developed templates by which transformation events can be analyzed and compared. According to the Sentinel Group, transformation always includes a deep repentance and a renunciation of dark allegiances. Even though this book does not attempt to quantify spiritual factors related to the growth and decline of EAM, modern practitioners who have a biblical worldview should be trained to discern them and respond to them.[9] It should be noted that the journals of early American circuit riders are full of references to perceived spiritual factors.

Additional Theories for Further Study

Many theories of conversion and church growth have been offered as explanations for the substantial Christian penetration of a group or culture. Each theory examines the phenomenon of mass conversion and the spread of Christianity from a unique perspective. Each was developed and articulated within a specific context. Each has its own assumptions. Each answered the questions for which it was developed. When these theories are applied to EAM, all fit to some extent and contribute to the knowledge base. However, the growth dynamics of EAM are too complicated to be explained by any single theory to include the one offered at the beginning of this chapter. For this reason, it is helpful to examine Methodist growth data from the perspective of a cluster of theories.

Revival theory explains, describes, and quantifies a spiritual factor. It assumes that God works through the agency of his Holy Spirit to awaken people and cause church growth. Furthermore, it believes that the church and its leaders are tools through which God accomplishes the work of evangelism and cultural transformation. However, God is the primary force.

During the many revivals that descended on the southern revival belt from 1771 through 1789, the Methodist preachers learned to cooperate with God. They expected revival and worked with revival to harvest large numbers of converts as they grew the church and matured the saints. In time, Methodism institutionalized revivalism. Previous chapters show the relationship between the incidence of revivals and the growth and decline of southern Methodism. That is, one can discern a predictable pattern of growth and decline in Southern Methodism based on the sequence of revivals.

Revivals are not restricted to America or to Methodism. Many books document the history of revivals since the time of the New Testament. After surveying the global resurgence of Christianity in the 1900s, Mark Shaw boldly argues that revival was the primary delivery system for the resurgence. In fact, according to Shaw, revivals lay behind the substantial penetration of Christianity in

Korea, western Nigeria, India, Uganda, Ghana, Brazil, and the whole of Latin America. He also says that the Chinese house church movement has sparked a global revival among Chinese people. In addition to church growth, he documents four features of revivals: personal liberation, eschatological vision, radical community, and evangelical activism. He defines revivals as charismatic people movements that seek to change their world by translating truth and transferring power. His use of "people movement" connects him to missiology and the Church Growth Movement.[10]

In 1909, James Burns published *Revivals, Their Laws and Leaders*.[11] When one filters the Methodist revival that coincided with the outbreak of the Second Great Awakening in 1800 through Burns' matrix, it becomes clear that his model reflects key aspects of the Methodist situation. According to Burns, the following pattern governs revivals: (1) They come when preparations have been made by the people. The extensive use of spiritual disciplines is an example of how people prepare the way. (2) They come when the times are ripe. This refers to factors like transition, uneasiness, hopelessness with the present situation, discontentment, corruption, backsliding, and a cold languor in the church. (3) This leads to a growing awareness or expectation that something better is coming. People begin to hunger for deliverance or for something to make their lives more bearable. (4) When conditions are right, a messenger appears who speaks God's words with a special charisma or anointing. This leader sums up in him or herself the longings of the times and interprets to the people their inmost needs. He or she has recognition and authority. The leader is the interpreter, not the creator of the movement. God is the force and creator of revival. (5) Usually, the movement starts on the outside of the organized church. Typically, the poor and marginalized are the first who respond to the move of God's Spirit. (6) As the revival spreads, it awakens within people spiritual vitality and new life. It does this by creating within people an overwhelming conviction of sin. This leads to confession and justification. Afterward, the converted rejoice in the awareness of forgiveness and new life. From this new experience proceeds a sense of euphoria. (7) As the joy builds upon itself, it becomes contagious and carries the revival. Love and right living characterize the people who have been transformed. Even after the revival diminishes, the transformed lives of touched individuals continue to witness to its power. (8) In time, the revival enters the church and begins to transform it. At other times, the revival produces a new church. Usually, the organized church is resistant to revival because revival threatens the status quo. (9) Ultimately, the revival is institutionalized and loses its dynamic power. Burns says that it is rare for a revival to last more than twenty years. However, some can last upwards to forty years if the conditions are right and if the people do not destroy them in their attempts to institutionalize them. (10) Finally, a movement in one direction is followed by a movement in an opposite direction. Thus, a revival that goes to one extreme in doctrine or emotion is followed by a counter-movement. This is called the law of recoil.

Based on Asbury's copious descriptions of revival and revival growth as described in this book, one could liken revival to a Holy Spirit shower. A prolonged period of revival would be likened to a rainy season. During a rainy season, it does not rain constantly in any one place even when weather forecasts show that rain is ominous, foreboding, or close at hand. In the same way, in a revival season, a divine downpour is never far off even when it is not happening in a particular location. Furthermore, the early beginnings of the revival season are like the first rains after a long drought in that they soften up the hard ground and allow dormant life to spring forth. That is, the first sprinkles bring new life to the dried up saints and prepare the people for a period of profound spiritual growth that will culminate in a time of great harvest.

Based on the growing season in Palestine and biblical metaphors associated with divine showers, one could speak about the former and latter rains. The former rains would refer to the time when God poured out his Spirit on Pentecost. This was followed by a dry season that was punctuated by occasional revivals and renewal events. The latter rains will be a time of great outpouring. They will precede a time of harvest. Based on this analogy, people should yearn for and seek after revival in the same way that desperate farmers pray for rain when in the midst of a debilitating drought. Asbury did this in the 1790s.

The following quotation from Arthur Wallis' *In the Day of Thy Power* reflects the hearts of those who understand the true nature of revival:

> It was springtime in the year 1938. A boy in middle teens stood in the little schoolroom adjoining Moriah Chapel in the small Welch mining town of Loughor, Glamorganshire. A strange feeling of awe and wonder filled his heart, for this was the very room that witnessed the beginnings of that great outpouring of the Spirit, the Welsh revival of 1904. He listened to his host and guide, himself a convert of that revival, speak of those memorable days when the harden hearts were melted by the presence of the Lord, and when the hills and valleys rang again with the songs of Zion. It was almost too wonderful to be true, but it created questions deep down in his heart for which he could find no answer. If God can achieve such mighty things in times of revival, and if the spiritual labors of fifty years can be surpassed in so many days when the Spirit is poured out, why, he wondered, is the church today so satisfied with the results of normal evangelism? Why are we not more concerned that there should be another great revival? Why do we not pray for it day and night?[12]

Anthony F. C. Wallace articulated an anthropologically informed theory of revitalization that is very similar to Burns' laws of revival in terms of its series of events.[13] His theory has been applied to divergent movements like cargo cults, mass movements, religious revivals, reform movements, the Charismatic movement, African independent churches, and nativistic movements. Wallace labeled British Methodism as a revitalization movement. Mark Shaw discusses and utilizes an adapted version of Wallace's theory in his book.[14]

According to Wallace, human society seeks to maintain a homeostasis. Since societies are organically whole, the chronic stress of its members causes the entire social system to go out of homeostasis. As this happens, the people seek to reduce cultural stress. Individuals in a society maintain a mental image of the society that guides them in their behavior and expectations so that they act in culturally acceptable ways to reduce cultural stress. This mental image is called a mazeway:

> Whenever an individual who is under chronic, physiologically measurable stress, receives repeated information which indicates that his mazeway does not lead to action which reduces the level of stress, he must choose between maintaining his present mazeway and tolerating the stress, or changing the total *Gestalt* of his image of self, society, and culture, of nature and body, and of ways of action. It may also be necessary to make changes in the "real" system in order to bring mazeway and "reality" into congruence. The effort to work a change in mazeway and "real" system together so as to permit more effective stress reduction is the effort at revitalization; and the collaboration of a number of persons in such an effort is called a revitalization movement.[15]

Wallace says that revitalization movements are a normal phenomenon in human history. They are a tool for culture change and renewal. Furthermore, he believes that Christianity originated in a revitalization movement and has been carried forward in history by repeated revitalization movements. The founding of new Christian sects is an example of this. He says, "It can be argued that all organized religions are relics of old revitalization movements, surviving in routinized form in stabilized cultures, and that religious phenomena per se originated in the revitalization process – i.e., in visions of a new way of life by individuals under extreme stress."[16]

Immediately before revitalization, the society passes through a phase of cultural distortion. During this period, an assortment of mazeway alternatives is attempted. Cultural distortion is evidenced by maladaptive behavior, depression, and regressive innovations like alcoholism, extreme passivity, highly ambivalent dependency relationships, intra-group violence, disregard of kinship relationships, increased sexual immorality, and irresponsible behavior by public officials. If the process of cultural deterioration is not reversed, the society can suffer from a self-inflicted ethnocide.

Typically, revitalization comes in the form of a religious movement that performs six major tasks. First, there is a mazeway reformulation. At this point, a guide, prophet, or leader emerges with a vision or new insight. This person embodies the new vision and is identified with it. Second, the leader seeks to preach the revelations to people in an evangelistic way. He or she becomes a prophet. As the leader gathers followers, these assume much of the responsibility for communicating the good word.[17] Third, the new believers are divided into three categories: the prophet, the disciples, and the followers. Many of those who are converted display physical manifestations like hysterical seizures. Others have ecstatic visions. During this phase, the charismatic leader routinizes his or her power so that individuals in a stable social structure can continue the movement. Fourth, the movement will encounter resistance and some internal opposition. This requires adaptation. The adaptation process seeks to minimize the resistance without compromising the vision. Fifth, "as the whole or a controlling portion of the population comes to accept the new religion with its various injunctions, a social revitalization occurs. It is signaled by the reduction of the personal deterioration symptoms of individuals, by extensive cultural changes, and by an enthusiastic embarkation on some organized program of group action."[18] Finally, it becomes established in the culture. When this happens, even those who do not adopt the innovations related to the new revitalization will benefit from its influence in society. Afterward, the revitalization maintains a stabilizing influence in society. Eventually, a new steady stead will emerge.

In most ways the Second Great Awakening qualifies as a revitalization movement. Before 1800, EAM laid a foundation for the Second Great Awakening. After 1800, EAM participated in and gave leadership to the awakening. However, it must be conceded that the revitalization movement that Christianized early America was larger than Methodism. Even still, Methodism was the strongest force in that revitalization process. For many of the same reasons that Burns' revival theory fits EAM, Wallace's revitalization theory also fits.

Additionally, it is also possible to analyze early American Methodist growth in terms of McGavran's "people movement" theory.[19] Originally, the theory described how interrelated people within an Indian caste came to Christ by means of web movements. Later, McGavran and his colleagues used the theory to describe church growth dynamics in other parts of the world. Theologically, the term hinges on how one defines the word *"ethnos"* in the Great Commission's injunction to make disciples of all nations (*ethne*). In the New Testament, the plural form of the word refers to the Gentile nations and is the Greek translation of the Hebrew *ha-goyim*. It may also refer to the nation of Israel (cf. Luke 7:5) or any distinct group. Church Growth defines *ethnos* as a people group or tribe, not a polyglot nation-state (see Chapter One). Hence, the church is required to make disciples of the various people groups. This necessitates a sociologically sophisticated strategy that identifies people groups as it contextualizes the gospel when doing evangelism and church planting. Ideas related to incarnational ministry and cultural relevancy relate to this concept.

A people group may be a "homogeneous unit" within a larger social context. For example, Gypsies in France, Guatemalan workers in the United States, or the Chinese diaspora are examples of homogeneous units. In fact, every modern nation state contains many homogeneous units in which the members intentionally self-identify with each other. However, the grouping does not have to be based on ethnicity. For example, the players on a college football team function as a homogeneous unit when at school. They have a special language and a shared existence that bonds them together even if they come from different social subgroups. Typically, people within a homogeneous unit do not have to cross cultural, linguistic, or class barriers to socialize with each other. Because of this, evangelism flows naturally among them.

In the beginnings of a people movement, a series of small groups of interconnected people come to faith. These small groupings give each other a supportive environment as they bring more of their friends, relatives, and neighbors to faith. At first, the larger community may oppose the new innovation. When the converts achieve a critical mass of believers, new converts can receive Christ without undergoing social dislocation. This lowers social barriers to conversion.

At this point, it becomes acceptable for their friends, relatives, and associates to come to faith in Christ. This accelerates church growth. However, if the people movement is not intentionally taken to other people groups, Christianity will not diffuse into the larger population.

People movement theory may explain why EAM expanded so rapidly among particular groups of people in the various regions. The introduction and growth of Methodism in New England clearly demonstrates the theory. From the literature, it becomes clear that Methodism grew along webs of interconnected people. When Asbury described the typical Methodist in early America, he contrasted the stereotype against other social classes. For example, Methodism did not grow with the worldly rich. Obviously, in the South, slaves formed a homogeneous unit. In other parts, Methodism reached the hoi polloi and spoke the language of the common people. As a class, the Methodists within each of the various regions had a shared self-understanding by which they were socially connected to each other. People brought people to faith. Without a doubt, Methodism spread through web movements of interconnected people.

Garrettson gives an excellent example of the web dynamics of EAM. When explaining the origins of Methodism in Dorset County, Delaware, he describes how Methodism flowed along a chain of interconnected people as it overcame personal prejudice and created a critical mass that allowed people within the social network to convert and remain connected to EAM. According to Garrettson, the Dorset County was hostile to Methodism because most of the inhabitants were united to the Church of England. For that reason, the people were resistant. Finally, the niece to a judge converted. After she endured great ridicule, her sister Polly converted with a few others. Polly brought the sister Catharine to Methodism. Following this, the sister married to Mr. Bassett converted. Her husband also converted. He was a future congressman and governor in Delaware. Afterward, several young lawyers who studied under Mr. Bassett also converted with several other members of their extended families. Later, a sister named Mary evangelized a lawyer by the name of H. A. He sought to prove the Methodists were in error. After coming to them, he was fully converted and determined to make their lot his own. Afterward, the faith spread from those who were converted to those who were connected to those who were converted.[20] This example differs from the typical Methodist web movement in early America because it did not begin with the lower classes. Delaware Methodism grew rapidly and became a center for American Methodism largely because the social stigma associated with Methodism was quickly mitigated following the conversion of noted citizens.

Additional sociological approaches could lead to other useful conclusions. For example, in an article entitled "The Social Movement Dynamics of Modern American Evangelicalism," I examine the historical foundations of American evangelicalism through the lens of collective behavior theories, resource mobilization theory, and political opportunity theory.[21] One theory argues that religious and other social movements are attempts to correct shared grievances and arrive at a better state. The others examine the role of human and/or material resources in the geneses of new movements. Rodney Stark has suggested that a combination of ideas offers a more satisfying understanding of the evolution of social movements. [22]

Final Thought

American Methodism could find inspiration and vision if it looked to the African connection. Like other evangelical churches in that region, African Methodism is surging on the crest of a revival wave. The same is true of the Cuban connection. Its leaders made a collective decision to seek revival and to flow with the outpouring of the Holy Spirit. In the last 20 years, the Cuban Methodist Church has grown in numbers, vitality, and social influence. Would-be ministers have to plant a church before they are considered for an appointment. They define effective ministry in terms of practical and observable ministry outcomes. The plausibility structure on which they have built their revival is contagious. Furthermore, their preachers have become envoys of the revival. The Brazilian connection has also been transformed by revival. In the past century, the Methodist Church in Chile was revitalized through a revival that radically changed the church and the society. However, the leadership of the MEC could not reconcile the revival with its routinized thinking. As such, the renewal movement left the MEC and became the Methodist Pentecostal Church of Chile. On any given Sunday, more people attend their services than attend the services of any other denomination in Chile. In the aftermath of the missed revival, the leaders of the diminished MEC in Chile continued to think that they were the true heirs of the Wesleyan heritage. Sadly, the *Shekinah glory* had departed and they were unaware of it.

United Methodism is at a critical crossroads. Forces within the culture and the denomination are pushing toward secularism. In an effort to remain in homeostasis with a changing society, the denomination is allowing the society to change its core identity. United Methodism no longer reflects the ideals or corporate culture of Wesley or EAM. It has become the establishment. For those who have drunk deeply from the fountain of secularism, this is a good thing. They do not want to be associated with a counter cultural church that seeks to reform the nation and spread scriptural holiness throughout the land. Yet, history proves that the move toward secularism will lead to irrelevancy and decline. EAM transformed the culture before it became routinized in it. United Methodism is the child of a revitalization movement. Incredibly, it has grown to become a mainline denomination that cannot transform anything external to itself.

I suggest that the UMC needs to look backward before it can go forward. It needs to re-examine the ideals and values of those who laid the foundations for the Methodist revivals in England and early America. It needs to ask critical question related to identity and mission. In fact, what makes the UMC Methodist? As United Methodism looks to the past, it may discover a collective vision that can bring unity to the denomination and serve as a springboard for the development of a new Methodism that is true to its evangelical past and culturally relevant. The new vision will build on the past and be tethered to its revivalistic foundations without being locked into pre-modern categories. Furthermore, a shared commitment to kingdom renewal and Methodism's theological heritage can bind liberals and conservatives together in a creative tension that will enable the church to evangelize the masses and bring radical change to the society. One thing is certain; the pathway to social change will not come from embracing secularism. It will come from mass evangelism, church planting, numerical growth, and a collective church witness in word and deed that captures the hopes and aspirations of the unchurched. It will come from revival!

Imagine what would happen if the UMC added a million radical disciples to its rolls. Its voice and presence would be felt in every part of the society. However, if the UMC continues down the path it is treading, it will suffer the same fate as the denominations that dominated the religious landscape before the advent of American Methodism. A dying church does not have much social influence or much of a future. Now is the time to pray for renewal and work for revival.

APPENDIX

The following tables locate the various circuits that are listed in the *Minutes* within state boundaries. On the bottom of each table there is a numerical summary. The numerical progression of the circuits and Methodism within the states may be determined from these tables.

It must be admitted that this has been an inexact process for many reasons. First, the *Minutes* contain mathematical errors in the totals. As such, some of the totals in these tables differ from the totals in the *Minutes* and in other secondary sources that rely upon the *Minutes*.

Second, the *Minutes* frequently omit a circuit from the record for a particular year. When this occurs, Appendix tables attempt to correct the error by averaging the circuit memberships of the bracketing years. For example, in 1795, Wilmington, Delaware, was omitted from the record. The listed memberships for 1794 and 1796 were added together and averaged. The average is listed on the Delaware table for 1795. To indicate that this is a correction to the *Minutes* and an estimation, the averaged number is grayed. This process is only used for hiatuses of one year.

Some omissions are not caused by lost reports or by circuit riders failing to submit a report to conference. When that happens, the *Minutes* duplicate the previous year's membership. On rare occasions an "-" or the words "no report" is inserted. If there is any doubt, the *Minutes* for the previous year are consulted to ensure that a preacher was appointed to the omitted circuit.

No circuit totals were listed in the *Minutes* for 1778 and 1785. The circuit memberships for 1778 were estimated because blanks appear as zeros on linecharts. Zeros skew the charts and give a false impression. Since 1785 comes between two chronological periods, it was omitted from the tables and graphs in this book.

A third problem relates to locating circuits in one state. Circuits are not churches. They encompass a geographical area. Many circuits cross state borders. In his decadal charts John Wigger split the reported membership between the involved states when this happens.[1] Circuits are moving targets that expand and contract on a yearly basis. Knowing which circuits cross state boundaries and how much of the circuit resides in each state is a very difficult task. This book attempts to locate the involved circuit in the state where most of the circuit resides. For example, the Holston circuit was the first to appear in the tri-state area of Virginia, Tennessee, and North Carolina. The Holston River flows between Virginia and Tennessee. However, the most populated area of the circuit existed in Virginia during the 1780s. So the circuit is listed on the Virginia tables.

A fourth problem involved finding circuits that were named after obscure features or ones that used names that are no longer in use. Also, it was difficult to place some circuits because the circuit name appeared in more than one location. For example, the Bridgewater circuit is located in south-central New Hampshire. However, there are Bridgewaters in Vermont, Massachusetts, Connecticut, Maine, and New York. The Tioga circuit is in south-central Pennsylvania where there is a city by that name. However, Tioga County in New York exists on the other side of the border. No circuit was annotated on a state table until it was located on a map and/or referenced in secondary literature. Most circuit locations were verified by multiple sources.

The following procedure was employed when locating circuits. First, an attempt was made to find a reference to the circuit in the *Minutes* for 1796 through 1801. During these years the circuits were listed by state. Lee's *History* was consulted after the *Minutes*. He locates most of the primary circuits through 1809. He does not include all the circuits and he is not always correct in his listings. Also, he misspells many names. He has personal insight because he traveled with Asbury for three years as he itinerated between all the districts. Next, historical atlases were consulted. The following historical atlases were most used: *The Atlas of Early American History*, *The American Heritage Pictorial Atlas of the United States*, and *Adam's Atlas of American History*. If doubt persisted, modern atlases were consulted. Reader's Digest's, *These United States* lists every county, river, municipality, and countless other features. Plus, it has a complete index. This was very helpful because it showed all the different places that a name appears. Fortunately, names remain fairly constant over the years. Special atlases and state maps were also used when needed.[2]

After this, other histories of Methodism were consulted. These include general histories like Emory Bucke's *History of American Methodism* and specific histories like Michael Nickerson's dissertation on New York Methodism. Also, itinerant obituaries included the names and locations of circuits that they served. These are found in the *Minutes* and in histories. When all else failed, the circuit was traced in the *Minutes* to see with which circuits it was most associated.

As Methodism matured, the districts in which circuits were located grew smaller and more specific. For example, the Washataw circuit was never located on a map. It first appeared in the *Minutes* of 1808 and was listed in the Mississippi District. In 1813, the Louisiana District was formed and the Washataw circuit was transferred to it. As such, the Washataw circuit is listed in Louisiana even though it was never located on a map. Unfortunately, some circuits only survived for a few years or changed their names before they could be pinpointed with certainty. When doubt remained after the process was exhausted, the circuit was placed on the most likely state table and circled.

Regrettably, this procedure did not solve problems caused by misspelled names. The *Minutes* spell the circuits like they were pronounced. For example, Opelousas is spelled Appalousa (a type of a horse) and Cache is spelled Cash. Indian and French names are some of the worst. Once a circuit was named, the spelling did not change. Finding misspelled circuits is complicated. One does not know that a circuit is misspelled until one discovers the error. However, one may assume that it is a possibility when the circuit cannot be located by other means. Some circuits only appear to be misspelled because the orthography of the names has been Americanized over the years. It is for this reason that historical atlases were consulted. Usually, misspelled circuits were discovered while this author was studying maps or looking for the location of another circuit. When a misspelled circuit is discovered, the modern spelling is listed in a footnote.

District	1770		1771		1772		1773		1774		1775		1776		1777		1778		1779		1780		1781		1782		1783		1784	
	Black	White	Black	White	Black	White	Black	White	Black	White	Black	White	Black	White	Black	White	Black	White	Black	White	Black	White	Black	White	Black	White	Black	White	Black	White
America	0	0	0	316	0	500	0	0	0	0	0	0	0	0	0	0	0	0	0	0	0	0	0	0	0	0	0	0	0	0
Total for Year	0	0	0	316	0	500	0	0	0	0	0	0	0	0	0	0	0	0	0	0	0	0	0	0	0	0	0	0	0	0
Blacks + Whites	0		316		500		0		0		0		0		0		0		0		0		0		0		0		0	

New York

District	1770		1771		1772		1773		1774		1775		1776		1777		1778		1779		1780		1781		1782		1783		1784	
	Black	White	Black	White	Black	White	Black	White	Black	White	Black	White	Black	White	Black	White	Black	White	Black	White	Black	White	Black	White	Black	White	Black	White	Black	White
New York								180		222		200		132		96														60
Long Island																														24
Total for Year	0	0	0	0	0	0	0	180	0	222	0	200	0	132	0	96	0	0	0	0	0	0	0	0	0	0	0	0	0	84
Blacks + Whites	0		0		0		180		222		200		132		96		0		0		0		0		0		0		84	

New Jersey

District	1770		1771		1772		1773		1774		1775		1776		1777		1778		1779		1780		1781		1782		1783		1784	
	Black	White	Black	White	Black	White	Black	White	Black	White	Black	White	Black	White	Black	White	Black	White	Black	White	Black	White	Black	White	Black	White	Black	White	Black	White
New Jersey								200		257		300		150		60				140		196		512						450
East Jersey																										282		538		
West Jersey																										375		490		513
Total for Year	0	0	0	0	0	0	0	200	0	257	0	300	0	150	0	60	0	0	0	140	0	196	0	512	0	657	0	1028	0	963
Blacks + Whites	0		0		0		200		257		300		150		60		0		140		196		512		657		1028		963	

Pennsylvania

District	1770 Black	1770 White	1771 Black	1771 White	1772 Black	1772 White	1773 Black	1773 White	1774 Black	1774 White	1775 Black	1775 White	1776 Black	1776 White	1777 Black	1777 White	1778 Black	1778 White	1779 Black	1779 White	1780 Black	1780 White	1781 Black	1781 White	1782 Black	1782 White	1783 Black	1783 White	1784 Black	1784 White
Philadelphia								180		204		180		132		96				29		180				281		118		478
Chester										36		74		104		156				60		100		271				326		
Pennsylvania																								90		168		156		50
Little York																										70				
Lancaster																														40
Juniata																														
Total for Year	0	0	0	0	0	0	0	180	0	240	0	254	0	236	0	252	0	0	0	179	0	180	0	361	0	519	0	595	0	568
Blacks +Whites	0		0		0		180		240		254		236		252		0		179		180		361		519		595		568	

Delaware

District	1770 Black	1770 White	1771 Black	1771 White	1772 Black	1772 White	1773 Black	1773 White	1774 Black	1774 White	1775 Black	1775 White	1776 Black	1776 White	1777 Black	1777 White	1778 Black	1778 White	1779 Black	1779 White	1780 Black	1780 White	1781 Black	1781 White	1782 Black	1782 White	1783 Black	1783 White	1784 Black	1784 White
Delaware																						150		1052		1852				
Sussex																				795		260				595				
Dover																												1017		1852
Total for Year	0	0	0	0	0	0	0	0	0	0	0	0	0	0	0	0	0	0	0	795	0	410	0	1052	0	1447	0	1017	0	1852
Blacks +Whites	0		0		0		0		0		0		0		0		0		795		410		1052		1447		1017		1852	

Maryland

District	1770 Black	1770 White	1771 Black	1771 White	1772 Black	1772 White	1773 Black	1773 White	1774 Black	1774 White	1775 Black	1775 White	1776 Black	1776 White	1777 Black	1777 White	1778 Black	1778 White	1779 Black	1779 White	1780 Black	1780 White	1781 Black	1781 White	1782 Black	1782 White	1783 Black	1783 White	1784 Black	1784 White
Maryland								500																						
Baltimore										738		840		900		900				900		880		1000		993		905		830
Frederick										175		336		359		361				430		524		606		491		548		516
Kent										150		253		498		720				493		725		923		610		697		730
Annapolis																120														
Somerset																						s		500		455		250		338
Dorchester																								280		780		751		760
Calvert																								73		305		317		340
Talbot																										660		719		782
Annamessex																												235		260
Caroline																												700		752
Total for Year	0	0	0	0	0	0	0	500	0	1063	0	1429	0	1745	0	2101	0	0	0	1873	0	2129	0	3382	0	4294	0	5122	0	5308
Blacks+Whites	0		0		0		500		1063		1429		1745		2101		0		1873		2129		3382		4294		5122		5308	

Virginia

District	1770 Black	1770 White	1771 Black	1771 White	1772 Black	1772 White	1773 Black	1773 White	1774 Black	1774 White	1775 Black	1775 White	1776 Black	1776 White	1777 Black	1777 White	1778 Black	1778 White	1779 Black	1779 White	1780 Black	1780 White	1781 Black	1781 White	1782 Black	1782 White	1783 Black	1783 White	1784 Black	1784 White
Virginia								100																						
Norfolk										73		125		125												671		417		484
Brunswick										218		800		1611		1360				656		454		477		262		310		317
Fairfax												30		350		330				309		361		301		360				
Hanover														270		262				281		351		351				162		
Pittsylvania													100		50				500		634		600		481		362			
Amelia																620				470		506		506				356		317
Sussex																727				655		620		606		400		540		525
Berkley																				191		205		306		233		165		116
Fluvanna																				300		342		342		320		233		
Mecklenburg (name changed to Lundenburg in '79)																				498		455		350		355		426		293
James City																				77						434				
South Branch																										366				
Isle of Wight																														
Amelia & Buckingham																										200				
Holstein (Holston)																												60		76
Allegheny																												291		240
Old-Town & Cumberland																												50		
Nansemond																														25
Orange																											327		217
Richmond																														168
Portsmouth																														191
Amherst																														290
Total for Year	0	0	0	0	0	0	0	100	0	291	0	955	0	2456	0	3449	0	0	0	3937	0	3928	0	3639	0	4082	0	3699	0	3449
Blacks + Whites	0		0		0		100		291		955		2456		3449		0		3937		3928		3639		4082		3699		3449	

North Carolina

District	1770 Black	1770 White	1771 Black	1771 White	1772 Black	1772 White	1773 Black	1773 White	1774 Black	1774 White	1775 Black	1775 White	1776 Black	1776 White	1777 Black	1777 White	1778 Black	1778 White	1779 Black	1779 White	1780 Black	1780 White	1781 Black	1781 White	1782 Black	1782 White	1783 Black	1783 White	1784 Black	1784 White
North Carolina														683		930														
Roan Oak																				470		480		470		450		400		495
Tar River																				455		455		358		300		332		426
New Hope																				542		455		455		251		183		170
Charlotte																				186										
Yadkin																						21						348		292
Marsh																								50				50		
Edenton																								60						
Yadkin & Pittsylvania																														
Salisbury																										491		30		375
Guilford																												314		318
Bertie																												600		600
Pasquotank (Pasquotank)																												22		
Casewell																														165
Camden & Banks																														350
Wilmington																														80
Halifax																														272
Total for Year	0	0	0	0	0	0	0	0	0	0	0	0	0	683	0	930	0	0	0	1653	0	1411	0	1393	0	1492	0	2279	0	3543
Blacks + Whites	0		0		0		0		0		0		683		930		0		1653		1411		1393		1492		2279		3543	

South Carolina

District	1770 Black	1770 White	1771 Black	1771 White	1772 Black	1772 White	1773 Black	1773 White	1774 Black	1774 White	1775 Black	1775 White	1776 Black	1776 White	1777 Black	1777 White	1778 Black	1778 White	1779 Black	1779 White	1780 Black	1780 White	1781 Black	1781 White	1782 Black	1782 White	1783 Black	1783 White	1784 Black	1784 White
Pee Dee																														99
Total for Year	0	0	0	0	0	0	0	0	0	0	0	0	0	0	0	0	0	0	0	0	0	0	0	0	0	0	0	0	0	99
Blacks + Whites	0		0		0		0		0		0		0		0		0		0		0		0		0		0		99	

Maryland

District	1786 Black	1786 White	1787 Black	1787 White	1788 Black	1788 White	1789 Black	1789 White	1790 Black	1790 White	1791 Black	1791 White	1792 Black	1792 White	1793 Black	1793 White	1794 Black	1794 White	1795 Black	1795 White	1796 Black	1796 White	1797 Black	1797 White	1798 Black	1798 White	1799 Black	1799 White
Frederick	32	390	55	445	91	749	56	322	88	470	93	480	100	500	74	422	90	365	104	377	45	270	36	250	48	256	41	219
Calvert	316	295	550	443	842	505	909	943	1170	811	1029	760	1200	700	923	732	1102	682	924	602	924	602	880	500	737	500	825	451
Baltimore	111	655	96	756	269	950	218	719	80	973	207	944	200	950	144	915	123	695	91	777	90	593	122	507	115	500	129	471
Kent	490	523	604	607	760	840	637	616	411	750	430	520	472	395	462	523	467	372	443	346	468	334	372	259	372	259	278	265
Talbot	332	632	524	1077	524	1077	608	1006	532	794	610	740	343	400	330	635	330	635	266	571	309	481	320	508	261	381	347	458
Dorchester	130	589	135	594	264	721	347	685	403	780	459	785	390	643	431	534	431	534	406	533	634	726	627	697	538	727	515	627
Somerset	50	170	56	223	60	500	48	400	84	522	99	546	95	615	87	563	87	553	109	536	89	485	98	447	129	446	116	434
Annamessex	33	317	43	343	57	347	70	135	46	300	51	325	75	337	85	345	85	345	109	307	105	295	106	225	115	204	115	204
Northampton	9	151	22	178	46	211	84	360	159	525	203	563	248	600	249	616	249	616	277	579								
Caroline	158	657	268	616	275	730	229	705	350	937	318	970	271	799	236	446	236	446	237	648	174	473	148	461	185	465	194	474
Cecil							252	257	332	362	340	418	290	416	321	434	321	434	298	433	200	424	176	354	211	357	223	351
Annapolis					70	60	141	128	165	122	223	106	243	170	243	170	80	120	80	120	82	68	145	68	59	68	92	62
Montgomery							103	648	339	771	347	637	350	650	362	728	340	685	392	578	284	505	254	510	252	421	227	423
Harfort							10	451	192	748	181	633	181	630	178	532	218	519	210	433	118	332	28	327	128	310	93	270
Severn									360	665	411	734	450	900	598	928												
Baltimore Town & Point									151	892																		
Baltimore City											181	430	190	450	207	440	207	440	181	457	91	457	264	466	286	505	327	631
Fell's Point											42	108	42	120	37	95	35	96					37	79	33	102		
Pomonkey (River)													37	112														
Prince George														40	225	65	205	110	222	125	240	140	520	148	541	140	620	141
Queen Ann's													416	532	467	372	467	573	504	529	533	775	573	669	447	729	447	572
Frederick Town															24	24												
Federal																												
Total for Year	1661	4379	2453	5282	3258	6693	3752	7375	4962	10425	5522	9759	5593	9959	5683	9510	5749	8952	5523	11464	4910	12406	5096	6982	4950	6885	5079	6568
Blacks + Whites	6040		7735		9951		11127		15407		15281		15552		15193		11701				12406		12078		11835		11647	

Virginia

District	1786 Black	1786 White	1787 Black	1787 White	1788 Black	1788 White	1789 Black	1789 White	1790 Black	1790 White	1791 Black	1791 White	1792 Black	1792 White	1793 Black	1793 White	1794 Black	1794 White	1795 Black	1795 White	1796 Black	1796 White	1797 Black	1797 White	1798 Black	1798 White	1799 Black	1799 White
Portsmouth	26	330	57	391	259	390	473	480	693	949	574	819	557	787	439	729	367	651	537	665	380	610	327	550	327	550	251	527
Sussex	72	415	93	496	407	1204	508	1300	145	690	206	606	168	565	206	448	1069	1285	240	850	130	644	101	642	194	639	125	459
Brunswick	59	305	59	407	355	1249	315	1102	266	676	200	627	233	677	151	653	216	586	131	520	197	500	150	379	156	399	194	456
Amelia	30	382	51	573	117	630	154	754	158	740	132	651	139	645	139	645	103	545	63	433	41	396	60	347	49	365	46	346
Mecklenburg	37	392	76	828	159	950	117	692	30	480	25	478	32	479	139	479											29	163
Bedford	16	524	25	252	34	373	20	221	150	370	89	303	43	499	102	474	41	345	72	441	69	366	111	389	111	409	111	409
Orange	75	374	3	337	16	394	71	616	109	527	54	530	138	540	62	520	74	642	61	567	61	567	35	435	35	438	24	367
Williamsburg	11	157	5	217	5	230	50	274	155	536	194	473	234	490	241	589	121	423	110	390	97	385						
Alleghany	13	360	17	736	17	417	21	499	21	314	23	351	20	360	20	382	14	285	14	285	7	280	16	264			81	257
Berkley	26	140	26	203	36	285	36	325	115	743	192	1204	95	350	68	57	72	526	72	530	78	430	61	417	76	397	57	417
Fairfax		260		270	8	350	76	474	115	775	111	657	114	675	50	520	50	540	61	363	62	347	52	335	57	337	47	328
Lancaster	114		155	400	130	500	244	630	300	713	210	586	210	586	261	590	130	552	111	436	123	288	123	288	107	259	66	230
Holstein	250		1	449	3	360	9	411	14	450	6	140	13	211	13	271	13	257	15	269		272				245	11	247
Greenbrier				100	5	210	5	222	3	204			2	118	5	202	7	107	7	154	6	172	5	245	6	185	5	154
Amherst			7	100	17	139					130	335	123	345	66	343	10	341	66	288	63	287	90	325	90	365	106	389
Buckingham			10	67	12	222																						
NewRiver					8	372	6	299	15	308	15	320	17	278	15	184	13	255	9	190	13	127	6	94	11	113	2	118
Bath					10	309			40	324	41	315	41	320	22	326	22	290	17	286	13	283	13	231				
Gloucester					56	541	62	657	100	918	62	620	74	658	63	677	81	715	67	677	71	546	125	945	125	1000	93	995
Clarksburg						115	2	130	4	265	4	300		267	3	307	4	334	3	340	2	346		200				118
Ohio					4	353	2	306		260	4	350	6	364	9	362	1	221		316		411	5	288	1	286	12	415
Rockingham						60	5	79	48	287	46	335	46	350	46	350	33	364	31	400	49	337	24	304	24	304	32	286
Hanover						220	131	497	180	717	121	640	138	520	62	477	81	532	78	465	66	338			67	385	67	385
Botetourt								40		115	5	211	15	221	30	470	30	470	20	387	8	336	2	300	12	300	13	300
Cumberland							10	394	34	351	37	385	37	384	43	415	38	399	35	382	40	445	34	392	34	392	22	325
Surry									244	677	705	770	800	831	955	811												
Greensville									300	776	363	720	219	735	347	665	360	878	336	841	230	682	254	970	254	970	292	711
Russell											5	79	2	115	4	125	4	145	5	130	7	130	9		9	133	11	117
Franklin											27	287	68	567	92	566	86	511	73	489	67	390	58	353	58	353	52	346
Essex											20	248																
Stafford											19	258	20	300	45	309	42	324	38	278	14	215	21	230	19	220	18	297
Randolph											2	30		36														
CowPasture													3	36	8	48	8	50	8	50								
Frederick														700	126	485												
Winchester													90		28	55	111	451	111	460	133	403	123	354	118	366	106	304

Virginia, continued

District	1786 Black	1786 White	1787 Black	1787 White	1788 Black	1788 White	1789 Black	1789 White	1790 Black	1790 White	1791 Black	1791 White	1792 Black	1792 White	1793 Black	1793 White	1794 Black	1794 White	1795 Black	1795 White	1796 Black	1796 White	1797 Black	1797 White	1798 Black	1798 White	1799 Black	1799 White
Alexandria															40	58	40	60	40	60	47	73	45	65	45	65	51	62
Norfolk & Portsmouth															159	109			129	93	105	91	129	93	129	93	120	125
Leesburg																	12	55										
Pendleton																	3	67	3	72	10	87	5	106	5	112	4	117
Norfolk																	64	119										
Petersburg																	28	52										
Richmond & Manchester																	4	23			301	537	296	476	265	412	219	375
Northhampton																							95	639	95	650		
Hanover & Williamsburg																							23	390				
Holstein & Russell																									22	424	26	292
Allegheny & Bath																												
Total for Year	370	4064	585	5846	1778	9864	2353	10542	3297	13225	3685	13604	3697	14102	3967	11291	3502	13401	2613	12207	2558	11021	2484	11046	2437	10971	2312	10520
Blacks +Whites	4434		6431		11642		12895		16522		17289		17709		15158		16903		14720		13579		13530		13408		12832	

North Carolina

District	1786 Black	1786 White	1787 Black	1787 White	1788 Black	1788 White	1789 Black	1789 White	1790 Black	1790 White	1791 Black	1791 White	1792 Black	1792 White	1793 Black	1793 White	1794 Black	1794 White	1795 Black	1795 White	1796 Black	1796 White	1797 Black	1797 White	1798 Black	1798 White	1799 Black	1799 White
Salsbury		327	24	394	19	350	27	480	29	438	24	519	40	565	31	565	21	543	28	550	14	560	33	700	32	678	10	496
Yadkin	11	426	20	517	20	500	7	345	8	296	25	401	14	439					14	505	34	645	32	434	32	434	20	459
Guilford	10	400	15	409	22	406	22	410	25	430	36	420	57	613	57	613	51	631	24	504	34	503	39	625	39	640	21	710
Halifax	14	324	22	403	23	417	54	470			8	93												374				
NewHope	3	192	30	291	30	450	31	527	74	415	108	510	145	678	57	735	102	666	111	559	65	470	80	566	106	566	119	601
Tar River	42	607	50	680	87	318	131	878	220	1100	152	655	116	627	60	610	103	570	72	504	32	506	106			325		
NewRiver	72	500	80	495	265	660	420	730	492	1019	466	1160													76			
Roan Oak		474	129	419	218	641	321	758	413	834	362	536	459	573	544	538	423	464	375	524	264	447	337	426	337	426		335
Caswell		163	6	207	12	300	43	351	44	469	31	508	75	517	75	517	58	477	58	500	25	362	50	430	59	432	312	465
Bertie	58	405	50	386	60	330	20	510	97	634	120	650	163	598	176	615	176	615	150	520	113	466	155	422	155	422	57	401
Camden & Banks		257	34	370																							129	
Blanden			30			35		34		167	57	232	64	403	72	480	55	480	22	375	42	386	104	436	143	462	200	450
Camden					39	413	85	424	218	585	229	585	278	539	347	555	304	480	140	378	230	388	247	255	318	278	351	311
Anson							23	561	50	495	56	150	40	241	40	211	36	249	36	300	36	300	36	320				
Lincoln									4	165	12	429	39	453														
Pamlico											50	374	59	346	104	415	92	488	83	370	82	363	27	279	19	210	12	222
Contentney											48	293	105	407	96	360	74	316	44	290	53	250	35	181	31	163	50	160
Banks											30	408	4	174	4	174	16	203		185	22	148	10	102				
Trent															13	174	13	174	337	596	171	389	337	596				
Goshen													520	78	337	587	327	597	51	345	17	390	3	235	3	235	235	
Matamuskeet															52	366	34	355	37	160	45	170	12	111				
Scopeliong (Scopeliong?)													47	64	42	156	39	198										
Swanino													10	67	23	175												
Yadkin & Swanino																70			10	226	10	348	9	263	9	263	8	273
Banks & Matamuskeet																	12	702										
HowRiver																									22	213	22	213
Newbern																											65	308
																								296		296	243	280
Total for Year	210	4065	490	4571	795	4820	1194	6478	1735	7068	1814	7923	2235	8223	2397	7746	1923	8035	1605	7391	1289	7091	2049	7051	1778	6043	1632	5919
Blacks + Whites	4275		5061		5615		7662		8803		9737		10458		10063		9958		8996		8380		9100		7821		7551	

South Carolina

District	1786 Black	1786 White	1787 Black	1787 White	1788 Black	1788 White	1789 Black	1789 White	1790 Black	1790 White	1791 Black	1791 White	1792 Black	1792 White	1793 Black	1793 White	1794 Black	1794 White	1795 Black	1795 White	1796 Black	1796 White	1797 Black	1797 White	1798 Black	1798 White	1799 Black	1799 White
Charleston	23	35	53	34	65	50	69	52	77	51	119	66	82	48	69	50	220	60	260	65	305	76	409	69	421	77	420	74
Santee		75	12	178	20	225	63	420	93	334	126	354	150	300	158	163	149	254	153	187			75	220				
Pee Dee	10	285	33	790	50	885																						
Broad River	10	200	19	403	29	460	18	411	95	400	95	450	86	500	78	541	68	435	57	398	55	410	62	526	58	501	48	590
Edisto			4	240	25	340	25	340	121	530	121	550	163	538	115	474	100	452	112	442	60	412	89	438	114	373	110	525
Cainhoy					24	36	12	27																				
Saluda					11	230	11	231	5	250	5	300	6	266			23	333	30	330	16	292	32	450	50	509	50	509
Waxsaws						20																						
Great Pee Dee							39	369	43	274	49	317	53	260	28	256	127	291	186	276	98	242	60	201	52	229	52	189
Little Pee Dee							20	589	33	737	55	785	33	700	31	589	91	500	91	500	62	720	5	300				
Cherokee							10	78	8	194	10	372	11	453	13	528		204										
Bush River									10	149	15	200	12	76			7	245	4	339	3	314	4	262	7	322	23	348
George Town									11	43	55	46	100	49	80	52	103	53	86	15	70	6	115	8	180	7	181	7
Kingston											84	115											38	233				
Catawba											20	220	22	229	4	163	5	180	7	158			22	200	32	358	27	342
Union												120	24	236	24	236	57	483	39	376	35	334						
Saldua & Bush River															30	555												
Black Swamp																	120											
Santee & Catawba																					16	292			253	463	211	467
Little Pee Dee & Anson																									64	873	74	779
Total for Year	43	595	121	1645	224	2246	267	2517	496	2962	754	3896	742	3665	850	3607	950	3610	995	3086	720	3098	911	2907	1131	3712	1196	3830
Blacks +Whites	638		1766		2470		2784		3458		4650		4397		4457		4560		4081		3818		3818		4843		5026	

Georgia

District	1786 Black	1786 White	1787 Black	1787 White	1788 Black	1788 White	1789 Black	1789 White	1790 Black	1790 White	1791 Black	1791 White	1792 Black	1792 White	1793 Black	1793 White	1794 Black	1794 White	1795 Black	1795 White	1796 Black	1796 White	1797 Black	1797 White	1798 Black	1798 White	1799 Black	1799 White
Georgia		78		430																								
Burke						82	4	297	20	554	43	572		430	10	420			31	523	3	292					22	290
Richmond					22	345	30	545	29	543	72	501	85	590	111	650	111	650	63	500	62	434					115	548
Washington					71	707	148	900	132	807	114	621	91	332	118	518	129	389	113	334	81	302	73	379	75	400	78	451
Augusta								87																				
Savannah Cir.									3	206	4	323		106		104											1	29
Elbert													25	86														
Oconee													21	220	18	202												
Burke & Oconee																	31	523										
Burke & Richmond																							75	643	127	708		
Total for Year	0	78	20	430	93	1134	182	1829	184	2110	233	2017	222	1664	257	1894	270	1662	207	1657	146	1028	148	1022	202	1108	216	1318
Blacks + Whites	78		450		1227		2011		2294		2250		2086		2151		1932		1864		1174		1170		1310		1534	

Kentucky

District	1786 Black	1786 White	1787 Black	1787 White	1788 Black	1788 White	1789 Black	1789 White	1790 Black	1790 White	1791 Black	1791 White	1792 Black	1792 White	1793 Black	1793 White	1794 Black	1794 White	1795 Black	1795 White	1796 Black	1796 White	1797 Black	1797 White	1798 Black	1798 White	1799 Black	1799 White
Kentucky				90																								
Lexington					10	200	21	402	32	424	37	543	41	562	30	401	20	410	16	355	20	300	14	274	16	249	19	284
Danville					50	220	30	410	26	322	28	520	44	597	20	548	19	447	31	470	36	437	16	409	13	296	21	299
Madison									8	212																		
Limestone										66	6	137	7	149	8	242	6	374	10	430	9	323	8	416	12	428	13	363
Salt River											23	259	27	381	24	340	8	350	12	269	10	226	5	226				
Hinkstone															4	281	5	270	7	356	3	380	1	325		342		342
Shelby																							13	90				
Salt River & Shelby																									10	235	11	286
Total for Year	0	0	0	90	60	420	51	812	66	1024	94	1459	119	1689	86	1812	58	1851	76	1880	84	1666	57	1740	51	1550	64	1574
Blacks + Whites	0		90		480		863		1090		1553		1808		1898		1909		1956		1750		1797		1601		1638	

Tennessee

District	1786		1787		1788		1789		1790		1791		1792		1793		1794		1795		1796		1797		1798		1799	
	Black	White	Black	White	Black	White	Black	White	Black	White	Black	White	Black	White	Black	White	Black	White	Black	White	Black	White	Black	White	Black	White
Cumberland					4	59		225	41	241	67	349	57	370	50	270	30	400	47	230	30	190	26	201	34	206	30	216
Green											3	340	8	266	9	345	7	300	15	300	13	313	16	333	18	322	21	364
Total for Year	0	0	0	0	4	59	0	225	41	241	70	689	65	636	59	615	37	700	62	530	43	503	42	534	52	528	51	580
Blacks +Whites	0		0		63		225		282		759		701		674		737		592		546		576		580		631	

Ohio

District	1786		1787		1788		1789		1790		1791		1792		1793		1794		1795		1796		1797		1798		1799	
	Black	White	Black	White	Black	White	Black	White	Black	White	Black	White	Black	White	Black	White	Black	White	Black	White	Black	White	Black	White	Black	White	Black	White
Miami																											1	98
Total for Year	0	0	0	0	0	0	0	0	0	0	0	0	0	0	0	0	0	0	0	0	0	0	0	0	0	0	1	98
Blacks +Whites	0		0		0		0		0		0		0		0		0		0		0		0		0		99	

Delaware

District	1786		1787		1788		1789		1790		1791		1792		1793		1794		1795		1796		1797		1798		1799	
	Black	White	Black	White	Black	White	Black	White	Black	White	Black	White	Black	White	Black	White	Black	White	Black	White	Black	White	Black	White	Black	White	Black	White
Dover	158	690	209	654	209	669	227	509	350	889	396	1022	477	941	507	930	507	930	564	861	493	783	480	697	538	762	538	762
Wilmington							19	43	20	40	48	93	41	83	55	82	55	90	37	65	30	40	37	61	48	69	46	73
Milford									236	879	226	720	310	846	319	781	319	781	319	800	298	594	306	703	353	720	316	680
Total for Year	158	690	209	654	209	669	246	552	606	1808	670	1835	828	1870	881	1793	881	1801	920	1726	811	1417	823	1461	939	1551	900	1515
Blacks +Whites	848		863		878		798		2414		2505		2698		2674		2682		2646		2228		2284		2490		2415	

New Jersey

District	1786		1787		1788		1789		1790		1791		1792		1793		1794		1795		1796		1797		1798		1799	
	Black	White	Black	White	Black	White	Black	White	Black	White	Black	White	Black	White	Black	White	Black	White	Black	White	Black	White	Black	White	Black	White	Black	White
West Jersey		492	8	567																								
East Jersey		365		465																								
Trenton		352		372		526	8	527	33	429	32	420	33	390	41	465	8	156	13	158	16	154	12	162	16	156	13	157
Newark		50																										
Elizabethtown				240		220	13	216	16	237	12	321	3	190	8	226	12	199			5	260	8	210	11	242	7	201
Flanders					3	555	2	281	7	322	8	304		268	12	310	3	258	3	288	4	275	4	222	3	233	4	215
Salem					24	704	24	680	21	933		464	23	554	22	502	94	586	23	512	27	476	42	452	55	450	57	504
Burlington									12	353	13	374	47	507	25	397	15	383	22	356	28	354	28	359	26	532	30	569
Bethel											2	403	3	457	9	433	11	404	13	386	8	340	24	646	29	690	27	741
Freehold																	24	453	25	453	17	397	17	397	23	360	29	328
Elizabethtown & Staten Island																			10	270								
Total for Year	0	1259	8	1644	41	2005	47	1704	89	2274	72	2286	109	2366	117	2333	177	2439	109	2423	105	2246	135	2438	153	2663	167	2725
Blacks + Whites	1259		1642		2046		1751		2363		2358		2475		2450		2616		2532		2351		2573		2826		2892	

Pennsylvania

District	1786 Black	1786 White	1787 Black	1787 White	1788 Black	1788 White	1789 Black	1789 White	1790 Black	1790 White	1791 Black	1791 White	1792 Black	1792 White	1793 Black	1793 White	1794 Black	1794 White	1795 Black	1795 White	1796 Black	1796 White	1797 Black	1797 White	1798 Black	1798 White	1799 Black	1799 White
Redstone		523		756		290		290	6	334	7	360	10	361	9	325	7	278	6	296	5	315	6	313	6	328	8	298
Philadelphia		498		513	17	270	17	256	24	215	36	254	31	297	20	354	60	301	121	311	151	363	163	380	184	397	211	411
Little York		136				108		151	5	190	5	195	5	200		156						13						
Little York & Juniata				136																								
Huntington						59	4	185	4	190	2	200	2	215	2	165	2	184	1	212	1	233		242		203		202
Chester						372	4	344	9	317	15	429	3	367	19	379	19	200	52	186	31	132	6	318				
Bristol						32	2	51	7	53	6	111	6	162	6	194	6	211	7	166	5	162	8	145	8	155	66	137
Pittsburg										97		136		156		151	1	150		174		198		212		182		204
Wyoming												100		106		100		163		174		221		181		181		170
Northumberland														250	1	170	1	310	3	310	1	260	2	264	1	231		229
Tioga														71		70		118		137		138		110		127		181
Little York & Carlisle																	7	276										
Washington																	6	222										
Lancaster																	4	256	2	233	6	239	6	250	11	241	8	204
Carlisle																			8	250	50	162						
Strasburg																							7	485	7	535	5	519
Greerfield																												
Chester & Strasburg																									7	384	11	435
Total for Year	0	1157	0	1405	17	1161	27	1277	55	1451	71	1785	57	2265	57	2064	113	2694	200	2449	380	2796	188	2900	224	2964	309	3000
Blacks + Whites		1157		1405		1178		1304		1451		1856		2242		2121		2807		2649		2796		3098		3188		3309

New York

District	1786 Black	1786 White	1787 Black	1787 White	1788 Black	1788 White	1789 Black	1789 White	1790 Black	1790 White	1791 Black	1791 White	1792 Black	1792 White	1793 Black	1793 White	1794 Black	1794 White	1795 Black	1795 White	1796 Black	1796 White	1797 Black	1797 White	1798 Black	1798 White	1799 Black	1799 White
New York	28	178	40	235	54	276	78	399	102	522	112	524	130	511	154	639	125	575	155	600	145	641	141	740	147	753	172	646
Long Island	8	116	7	160	9	230	9	215	9	288	17	255	23	266	21	271	34	250	31	226	19	280	25	325	23	358	38	408
NewRochelle					3	522	6	725		774	16	661	11	390		375	11	364			18	375	18	520			12	426
Dutchess						10	3	200	5	405	6	473	7	546	7	381	10	406	7	405	6	391	10	384	10	343	6	318
Columbia							1	60	3	379	3	253	3	226		230	2	251	1	291		243	1	257	1	114	1	224
Cambridge								154		300		260		316		440		412		421		326		400		612		680
Coeyman's Patent								10																				
Newburgh							4	257	8	324	7	412	6	394	4	397	13	430	13	336	6	357	5	378	4	300	6	316
Albany									3	264	4	242		261	6	388	5	475		369	9	328	5	379	8	406	5	560
Saratoga												100		182		270		160		241		246		241	1	311		409
Otsego												80		207		296		140										
Croton													7	318	6	278		283									11	274
StatenIsland													3	77		77		70										
Herkimer															8	142	2	182				301		378		465		482
Delaware																		290		325	6	314	6	344		425		439
Seneca Lake																		81		133		215		243		272		265
Brooklyn																			12	23	15	24	27	23	29	52	25	48
Herkimer & Otsego																				299								
NewRochelle & Croton																			7	647								
AlbanyCity																									22	670		40
Mohawk																												118
Oneida																												28
Total for Year	36	324	47	395	66	1038	101	2020	130	3236	165	3256	90	3693	206	4184	212	4369	226	4336	281	4041	238	4612	245	5081	276	5681
Blacks + Whites		360		442		1104		2121		3366		3421		3883		4390		4581		4542		4259		4850		5326		5957

Connecticut

District	1786		1787		1788		1789		1790		1791		1792		1793		1794		1795		1796		1797		1798		1799	
	Black	White	Black	White	Black	White	Black	White	Black	White	Black	White	Black	White	Black	White	Black	White	Black	White	Black	White	Black	White	Black	White	Black	White
Fairfield										105		173		220		241		220										
Litchfield									1	66		130	1	428		184		195	2	200		231	3	227	4	262	4	297
New Haven										9																		
Middlefields												62																
Hartford												28		195		341												
New Brittain												130																
Middle Town														124	2	170		187	3	173		170	1	184	1	226	2	220
New London																50		219	5	212	6	197	8	211	5	300	10	300
Tolland																		334		263	2	122	2	195	1	216	1	220
Pomfret																				169		180	1	178	1	167	1	167
Redding																				235		142		191		262		276
Total for Year	0	0	0	0	0	0	0	0	1	180	0	523	1	967	2	986	0	1155	10	1252	8	1042	15	1201	22	1433	17	1480
Blacks + Whites	0		0		0		0		181		523		968		988		1155		1262		1050		1201		1455		1497	

Massachusetts

District	1786 Black	1786 White	1787 Black	1787 White	1788 Black	1788 White	1789 Black	1789 White	1790 Black	1790 White	1791 Black	1791 White	1792 Black	1792 White	1793 Black	1793 White	1794 Black	1794 White	1795 Black	1795 White	1796 Black	1796 White	1797 Black	1797 White	1798 Black	1798 White	1799 Black	1799 White
Stockbridge												30																
Lynn												58		115		116		119		131		111		112		107		97
Boston														15		41	4	45	2	40	2	63	8	71	9	77	11	63
Needham														34		50		76		83		84		102		128		136
Pittsfield														224		330		305		311		250		172		248		421
Granville																90		118		165		247	1	316	1	356		319
Marblehead																				32		22		20		20		30
Province Town																				30		45		65	1	166		167
Sandwich																								47		68		71
Martha's Vineyard																										13		24
Merrimack																												70
Total for Year	0	0	0	0	0	0	0	0	0	0	0	88	0	391	0	677	4	723	2	785	2	822	8	905	11	1183	11	1398
Blacks + Whites	0		0		0		0		0		88		391		677		727		787		824		913		1194		1409	

Rhode Island

District	1786		1787		1788		1789		1790		1791		1792		1793		1794		1795		1796		1797		1798		1799	
	Black	White	Black	White	Black	White	Black	White	Black	White	Black	White	Black	White	Black	White	Black	White	Black	White	Black	White	Black	White	Black	White	Black	White
Greenwich																16		30		54		59		42		47		73
Warren																58		127		154		161	2	133	1	114	1	122
Total for Year	0	0	0	0	0	0	0	0	0	0	0	0	0	0	0	74	0	157	0	208	0	220	2	175	1	161	1	195
Blacks + Whites	0		0		0		0		0		0		0		74		157		208		220		177		162		196	

Maine

District	1786		1787		1788		1789		1790		1791		1792		1793		1794		1795		1796		1797		1798		1799	
	Black	White	Black	White	Black	White	Black	White	Black	White	Black	White	Black	White	Black	White	Black	White	Black	White	Black	White	Black	White	Black	White	Black	White
Portland																				36		80		175		165		222
Readfield																				232		204		300		303		300
Bath																								31				
Penobscot																						73		110		263		207
Bath & Union																										100		119
Kennebeck																										105		196
Pleasant River																												73
Total for Year	0	0	0	0	0	0	0	0	0	0	0	0	0	0	0	0	0	0	0	268	0	357	0	616	0	936	0	1117
Blacks + Whites	0		0		0		0		0		0		0		0		0		268		357		616		936		1117	

New Hampshire

District	1786		1787		1788		1789		1790		1791		1792		1793		1794		1795		1796		1797		1798		1799	
	Black	White	Black	White	Black	White	Black	White	Black	White	Black	White	Black	White	Black	White	Black	White	Black	White	Black	White	Black	White	Black	White	Black	White
Chesterfield																						68		92		122		131
Total for Year	0	0	0	0	0	0	0	0	0	0	0	0	0	0	0	0	0	0	0	0	0	68	0	92	0	122	0	131
Blacks +Whites	0		0		0		0		0		0		0		0		0		0		68		92		122		131	

Vermont

District	1786		1787		1788		1789		1790		1791		1792		1793		1794		1795		1796		1797		1798		1799	
	Black	White	Black	White	Black	White	Black	White	Black	White	Black	White	Black	White	Black	White	Black	White	Black	White	Black	White	Black	White	Black	White	Black	White
Essex																												110
Vergennes																									1	85	1	273
Vershire																										100		165
Whitingham																												55
Total for Year	0	0	0	0	0	0	0	0	0	0	0	0	0	0	0	0	0	0	0	0	0	0	0	0	1	285	1	603
Blacks +Whites	0		0		0		0		0		0		0		0		0		0		0		0		286		604	

Canada

District	1786		1787		1788		1789		1790		1791		1792		1793		1794		1795		1796		1797		1798		1799	
	Black	White	Black	White	Black	White	Black	White	Black	White	Black	White	Black	White	Black	White	Black	White	Black	White	Black	White	Black	White	Black	White
Nova Scotia	0	510																		100						
Cataraqui														165												
Oswegotchie																90		1100	1	152	1	139	2	206	2	206		300
Bay Quintie															4	255				265	1	269	1	446	1	446	3	409
Province of Canada, Lower Circuit																	2	116										
Midland Cir.																		216		50								
Passamaquaddy																				64		64		140		154		154
Niagara																			1	64								
Total for Year	0	510	0	0	0	0	0	0	0	0	0	730	0	165	4	345	2	1432	2	631	2	472	3	792	3	806	3	863
Blacks + Whites	510		0		0		0		0		730		165		349		1434		633		474		795		809		866	

Maryland

District	1800 Black	1800 White	1801 Black	1801 White	1802 Black	1802 White	1803 Black	1803 White	1804 Black	1804 White	1805 Black	1805 White	1806 Black	1806 White	1807 Black	1807 White	1808 Black	1808 White	1809 Black	1809 White	1810 Black	1810 White	1811 Black	1811 White	1812 Black	1812 White
Annamessex	113	173	208	294	260	163	410	389	400	340	464	415	549	742	572	768	628	798	598	780	670	846	685	855	684	812
Annapolis	197	62	256	140	207	133	241	103	230	144	209	96	233	100	201	107	222	106	232	100	254	115	276	148	252	148
Baltimore Cir	78	408	110	468	233	1081	443	1275	272	1120	209	1006	267	1063	158	584	121	536	186	602	191	638	210	706	234	725
Washington City													25	61	32	70	44	94	51	101	46	113	42	88	54	91
Calvert	811	399	922	384	1182	430	1459	593	1623	834	1678	853	1664	757	1644	900	1460	813	1438	744	1553	750	1457	741	1517	740
Caroline	188	477	226	546	220	658	436	1068	376	1054	292	811	400	971	604	1491	318	1147	361	1134	359	998	321	905	337	384
Coecil	322	525	378	591	460	787	668	968	683	913	464	562	493	584	511	615	449	653	535	810	459	760	435	747	338	689
Dorchester	553	680	600	700	592	657	527	659	664	709	827	1040	1198	1481	1304	1569	561	824	498	826	547	861	526	817	540	811
Federal	337	414	362	491	496	521	665	575	559	571	613	654	565	661												
Frederick	49	223	190	445	224	520	211	648	185	650	183	658	205	595	259	622	287	604	308	639	284	553	316	674	368	839
Hartford	93	270	161	477	224	556	277	576	305	625	293	656	370	781	318	583	306	615	362	578	551	643	273	536	266	556
Kent	379	295	394	373	424	390			452	356	478	304	455	275	559	420	535	401	559	639	620	617	599	611	473	559
Montgomery	247	370	417	697	584	778	640	736	583	621	608	625	568	632	534	631	567	575	580	576			624	578	552	546
Prince George's	680	153	747	159	857	162	981	181	1086	239	906	265	1038	235	1068	266	950	310							722	330
Queen Ann's	565	496	453	566	460	630	797	815	647	1001	680	1042	707	943	707	943	663	879	817	882	817	821	726	801	723	776
Somerset	137	483	356	983	416	985	349	1003	435	995	509	1010	510	1049	538	1129	621	1224	532	1007	531	978	485	866	445	813
Talbot	393	433	596	504	912	1139	1004	1413	926	1281	849	1150	844	1109	962	1236	963	1137	862	1111	916	1019	859	967	805	869
Baltimore Town City	304	576	360	747	432	814	482	852	684	1173	702	1205			640	1068	637	1115	700	1137	750	1170	800	1238	868	1528
Fell's Point City	48	112	52	66	93	249	123	264							138	277	144	286	144	286	150	300	191	359	204	403
George-Town			37	58									92	110	81	51	107	169	109	96	97	92	118	200	120	190
St. Martin's					487	726	507	807	604	886	687	977	568	906	708	1064	459	78							387	442
George-Town & Washington City					39	72	47	109	94	205	137	173														
Chester-Town & Kent							407	347																		
Frederick-Town									45	52	47	65	49	50	47	45									80	59
Baltimore City & Fell's Point													755	1154												
Chester-Town											62	94	57	80												
Severn															612	663	505	640	513	544	601	501	629	494	637	487
Fell's Point Cir															203	700	205	707	231	668	150		91		204	
St. Mary's																	550	49								
Snow-Hill																	297	553							323	545
Cambridge																	766	925	843	843	756	844	677	717	672	687
Prince George & St. Mary's																			848	352	799	386	625	336		
St. Martin's & Snow-Hill																			691	1138	740	150	710	1050		

Maryland, continued

District	1800		1801		1802		1803		1804		1805		1806		1807		1808		1809		1810		1811		1812	
	Black	White	Black	White	Black	White	Black	White	Black	White	Black	White	Black	White	Black	White	Black	White	Black	White	Black	White	Black	White	Black	White
Great Falls																					226	676	225	680	243	655
Frederick & Frederick-Town																					336	618				
Total for Year	5497	6549	6815	8779	8802	11451	10674	13381	10653	13769	10897	13851	11642	14339	12403	15904	12765	15878	11835	15685	12253	15549	11809	15137	11844	14692
Blacks +Whites	12046		15594		20253		24055		24422		24748		25981		28307		28643		27520		27802		26946		26536	

Virginia

District	1800 Black	1800 White	1801 Black	1801 White	1802 Black	1802 White	1803 Black	1803 White	1804 Black	1804 White	1805 Black	1805 White	1806 Black	1806 White	1807 Black	1807 White	1808 Black	1808 White	1809 Black	1809 White	1810 Black	1810 White	1811 Black	1811 White	1812 Black	1812 White
Alexandria	55	64	54	60	61	72	170	315	200	250	133	84	211	80	148	170	205	133	184	280	133	278	160	254	88	252
Allegheny & Bath	19	283	21	327																						
Amelia	37	445	73	500	70	515	45	460	40	470	40	490	55	594	59	588	58	674	42	827	47	836	45	806	55	750
Amherst	110	400	23	318	93	308	108	469	12	514	125	765	157	864	158	777	155	704	173	901	129	582	51	551	103	502
Bedford	147	440	125	412	108	423	80	427	85	452	267	744	267	795	267	795	228	479	209	473	225	496	186	510	103	455
Berkley	52	417	125	618	66	387	69	436	105	602	65	569	94	515	91	520	106	523	92	528	100	700	117	705	125	773
Bottatourt	39	197	38	159	40	254	64	247	47	350	83	358	98	422	89	376	117	501	98	425	99	514	111	506	99	456
Brunswick	177	413	222	447	173	353	131	406	472	527	175	545	156	550	129	526	117	467	117	453	171	486	163	489	153	475
Clarksburg	4	401	6	514	9	602	5	785	13	791	19	766	28	700			87									
Cumberland	22	300	20	293	13	256	13	255	15	252	33	521	10	572	22	639	55	707	55	744	49	319	11	318	11	288
Fairfax	47	300	48	282	52	261	95	441	172	647	143	619	50	600	133	618	172	648	228	746	269	803	184	330	229	337
Franklin	23	409	27	324	38	317	63	380	75	401	94	464	93	424	96	451	88	467	88	473	75	394	76	423	81	430
Gloucester	93	966	70	838	67	805	44	760	50	1000	46	873	49	910	88	1065	63	1004	95	1021	58	854	50	1057	53	1157
Greenville & Mecklenburg	363	865	363	767	337	793																				
Hanover	49	255	80	318	13	188	68	316					120	419	130	500	90	420	137	439	115	487	129	516	134	482
Holstein	22	385	22	385	175	286	15	683	52	780	44	755	32	639	52	600	56	624	80	653	20	364	30	410	40	541
Lancaster	149	266	149	266	134	286	134	289	135	326	156	335	131	386	132	554	135	710	137	627	131	618	139	632	80	632
Little Kanawha	60	3		47																						
New River	21	118	21	118	27	117	43	286	55	299	49	339	37	296	36	380	40	346	31	319	32	273	42	390	46	430
Norfolk & Portsmouth	155	143	55	150	129	137					265	390														
Northhampton	275	335	325	535	458	587	589	796	242	340																
Ohio	10	311	17	504	17	329	13	335	546	810	25	420	26	478	28	478	25	459	33	470	37	500	36	515	50	584
Orange	24	367	29	452	29	452	13	408	20	424	33	505	31	633	92	658	78	708	58	688	58	434	56	424	109	422
Pendleton	4	99	5	150	7	100	5	171	7	342	12	385	11	368	25	361	70	333	60	330	15	315	16	257	8	310
Portsmouth Cir	206	503	299	550	330	570	306	636	375	650																
Richmond	22	28	15	55	16	49	8	42	21	42	37	79	43	90					49	112	45	145	47	192		256
Rockingham	27	293	20	259	20	260	72	545	107	682	102	850	134	760			108	577	113	561	117	575	121	589	64	711
Russell	21	118	21	118	18	151																				
Stafford	28	255	21	270	21	253	21	206	19	222	9	294	32	306	43	300	45	371	63	343			38	315	40	335
Sussex	146	463	117	430	156	445	192	610	231	650	139	636	100	596	100	646	109	644	220	677	318	816	288	776	90	732
Williamsburg	74	327	57	257			64	236							107	736	113	783		610	58	456	73	623	75	675
Winchester	104	285	115	282	128	280	129	338	209	685	220	508	214	545	112	509	134	537	137	569	131	510	188	530	48	101
Greenbrier	6	348	7	357	8	356	7	400	36	607	41	873	20	544	37	511	38	460	34	589	25	400	27	344	27	331
Hanover & Williamsburg									118	519	118	519														
Allegheny					136	642			14	347	26	428	78	823	84	818	93	724	73	635	112	750	118	755	100	671

Virginia, continued

District	1800 Black	1800 White	1801 Black	1801 White	1802 Black	1802 White	1803 Black	1803 White	1804 Black	1804 White	1805 Black	1805 White	1806 Black	1806 White	1807 Black	1807 White	1808 Black	1808 White	1809 Black	1809 White	1810 Black	1810 White	1811 Black	1811 White	1812 Black	1812 White
Clinch																									79	888
Greensville							276	620	30	745	300	724	380	808	418	746	428	698	410	625	458	648	392	611	501	748
Mecklenburg							58	174	38	165	40	224	41	229	50	280	53	373	73	406	72	402	83	399	84	392
Norfolk							109	240					136	292	152	281	134	202	156	212	203	243	208	235	98	235
Portsmouth							118	106					119	201	139	134	132	146	126	130	132	143	143	118	148	117
Fredericksburg							12	67	10	52													5	63	6	47
Monongahela																							18	790	18	746
Green Mtns. (From Mount in Rockingham Co.)															30	656	20	553	20	576	22	730				548
Staunton															88	209	63	177	53	183	115	548	118	508	109	180
Randolph															6	180	8	278	8	269	76	195	72	84	79	180
Accomack											462	751			672	1238	501	916	589	926	571	857	538	770	534	775
Monroe													15	290	15	324	12	388	15	366	15	400	15	285	15	304
Petersburg											18	37	19	46	18	67	32	57	35	63	60	100	72	95	75	87
Suffolk											348	878	225	805	366	1065	620	1160	592	1265	577	1309	505	1360	455	1196
Giandott (Guyandot)												65			5	50	3	136	3	164		60	6	87	8	163
RockyMount											25						14	164	18	202	27	224	14	246	24	250
Buckingham																					49	329	50	317	38	305
Stafford & Fredericksburgh																					52	366		366		
Little Kanawha																					5	376	5	382	5	340
Saltville (changed to Abingdon)																							35	258	41	295
Loudon																							81	483	82	474
East Wheeling																								187		249
Lynchburg																									54	153
Leading Creek																						100				
Stephensburg (Stevens City)																									145	428
Total for Year	2631	10859	2693	11354	2807	10954	3328	18813	3669	19687	3831	17813	4100	19057	4637	20075	4722	19973	4889	20545	5131	20943	4982	21743	5097	22346
Blacks +Whites	13390		14047		13761		17141		19687		2644		23157		24712		24695		25434		26074		26725		27443	

North Carolina

District	1900 Black	1900 White	1901 Black	1901 White	1902 Black	1902 White	1903 Black	1903 White	1904 Black	1904 White	1905 Black	1905 White	1906 Black	1906 White	1907 Black	1907 White	1908 Black	1908 White	1909 Black	1909 White	1910 Black	1910 White	1911 Black	1911 White	1912 Black	1912 White
Banks: Mattamuskeet	22	213	22	213	5	453	14	105	13	125	4	137	8	159	21	311	93	473	91	541	243	592	137	599	235	627
Bertie	138	371	131	331	201	360	130	368	134	388	156	479	215	590	251	620	258	620	236	634	135	970	174	542	163	428
Bladen	111	730	130	653	217	543	413	633	511	722	22	1031	430	1301	375	1322	108	281	267	625	105	602	406	621	524	741
Camden	506	412	500	373	500	365	500	365	305	312	309	315	434	531	430	533	410	583	352	522	353	472	86	509	102	569
Caswell	120	515	120	520	59	465	123	621	118	599	118	568	86	525	58	534	54	525	82	495	51	850				
Trent																			514	1140	745					
Conferinny	39	137	13	126	11	102	10	111	5	105																
Goshen	3	235	3	235	3	235	11	176	69	251																
Gulford	39	685	39	541	25	615	70	961	62	899	33	687	65	678	36	702	75	789	80	802	68	747	66	752	60	661
Haw River	69	244	44	270	52	288	109	298	61	359	130	341	157	397	153	435	85	243	115	254	123	313	115	397	129	393
Newbern	243	280	243	280	242	308	109	259	387	278	250	30	390	30	512	102	580	201	450	157	365	135	250	121	447	100
Pamlico	23	173					9	131	60	177	27	191	13	158	30	350	49	352	53	360	42	353	123	541	27	332
Roan-Oak	287	222					330	405	467	471	202	596	330	530	528	692	505	702	488	556	347	522	378	602	417	579
Salisbury	23	471	17	417	32	367	32	437	30	427	15	405	26	459	24	495	29	512	33	622	42	626	38	682	22	698
Swanino	8	226	1	100			1	147	1	258	11	300														
Tar River	126	491	43	447	72	497	31	500	76	582	83	737	115	696	316	973	161	653	214	626	221	601	226	617	241	713
Wilmington	231	48	360	60	376	56	478	54	300	24	405	22	330	26	356	34	294	30	279	36	617	53	640	61	704	94
Yadkin	20	459	16	409	16	441	16	541	28	555	31	697	104	731	100	723	39	248	69	249	65	345	50	340	49	308
Morganton			7	144	15	220	13	373	72	382	32	409	33	370	23	275	17	307	21	312	25	315	29	344	19	323
Pamlico & Roan Oak					273	410																				
Trent, Goshen & Conferinny			278								125	700														
Lincoln											48	267							92	460	95	585	117	542	120	652
Buncombe													13	207	13	227	14	310	4	292	7	223	22	328	15	373
Lincoln & Catawba													131	768	115	775	14	225								
Trent & Goshen													380	821	738	1126	759	1323								
Rocky River & Montgomery													115	706												
Rocky River															108	331	70	348	76	356	48	375	91	572	111	611
Montgomery															74	623	74	623	47	503	55	544	55	578	61	583
Brunswick																	340	752	313	697	468	757	399	677	380	682
Catawba																	124	498	164	546						
Iredell																	63	560	63	604	62	639	49	663	29	576
Raleigh																	69	443	52	431	97	502	103	541	166	437
Edenton																			9	9	60	15	52	39	140	70
Straits																			9		40	321				

North Carolina, continued

District	1800 Black	1800 White	1801 Black	1801 White	1802 Black	1802 White	1803 Black	1803 White	1804 Black	1804 White	1805 Black	1805 White	1806 Black	1806 White	1807 Black	1807 White	1808 Black	1808 White	1809 Black	1809 White	1810 Black	1810 White	1811 Black	1811 White	1812 Black	1812 White
Neuse																			83	199	53	211	72	176	53	167
Banks & Islands																					69	276				
South Side of Neuse																					85	241				
Fayetteville																					87	110	120	125	112	130
Mattamuskeet																					16	200				
Mattamuskeet, Banks & Islands																							70	282	82	408
Beaufort																							591	533	492	541
New River																							350	496	160	416
Black River																							98	230	112	122
Washington																									28	24
Raleigh City																									44	32
Total for Year	2061	5942	2027	5529	2100	5818	2370	6540	2769	6911	2017	7882	3401	9693	4261	11173	4324	11601	4248	12008	4683	11895	5067	12510	5294	12393
Blacks + Whites	8003		7556		7918		8910		9683		9899		13094		15434		15925		16256		16378		17577		17459	

South Carolina

District	1800 Black	1800 White	1801 Black	1801 White	1802 Black	1802 White	1803 Black	1803 White	1804 Black	1804 White	1805 Black	1805 White	1806 Black	1806 White	1807 Black	1807 White	1808 Black	1808 White	1809 Black	1809 White	1810 Black	1810 White	1811 Black	1811 White	1812 Black	1812 White
Broad River	62	604	90	525	70	533	97	894																		
Bush River	31	328											46	435	46	435	46	435	56	458	89	512	157	810	135	837
Charleston	440	60	428	54	432	57	679	69	700	65	903	62	1000	62	749	80	1115	122	1650	150	1308	145	2223	226	3128	282
Edisto	126	572									177	756			74	400	53	560	114	678	188	793	219	786	215	845
Georgetown	223	10	287	15			402	58	513	76	565	105									774	44	772	68	816	85
Great Pee-dee	64	212	64	311			28	335	32	373	40	442									294	486	384	733	374	750
Little Pee-dee & Anson	68	603	107	759	75	809	80	1023	156	1441	273	1179														
Santee & Catawba	239	470	206	474	186	479	195	700	397	769	478	838														
Saluda	30	461	29	332	32	411	39	515	40	500	42	511														
Cherokee		79																								
Bush River & Cherokee			15	270																						
Orangeburg & Edisto			64	544	114	582	111	712	196	794																
Bush River & Keewee					36	430	43	732	56	810	25	353														
Gr. Pee-dee & Georgetown					444	265							674	587	745	835	707	655	741	440						
Eadsee									111	886	113	917	119	890	87	904	128	902	153	889	129	706	156	571	156	729
Cypress															100	600	142	822	224	855	326	1006	447	975	597	1190
Columbia									55		4	70	20	89	111	137	103	12	16	52	104	117	121	143	188	134
Sandy River									20	300																
Orangeburg											17	406														
Ready River													34	442	34	442	68	600	56	529	51	524	31	500	53	511
Keewee													30	432	18	440	56	440	26	455	36	531	23	573	21	544
Edisto & Cypress													174	806												
Congaree (Congaree)																					101	446	113	504	158	592
Santee													376	241	517	360	561	406	698	575	1038	667	1052	738	889	708
Little Pee-dee													135	883	97	958	107	783	49	867	77	844	61	700	121	781
Wateree													20		111		103		16		94	565	121	557	188	611
Black Swamp																					94		153		188	96
Camden																									55	93
Union	48	421	65	493	77	500	70	533	69	584	10	370	9	348	9	348	15	392	31	503	37	556	49	636	54	698
Total for Year	1331	3820	1455	3777	1496	4089	1747	5571	2300	6653	2647	6009	2617	5195	2590	5939	3131	6229	3827	6551	5246	7922	5971	8520	7676	9489
Blacks + Whites	5151		5232		5585		7318		8953		8656		7812		8529		9360		10378		13168		14491		17165	

Georgia

District	1800 Black	1800 White	1801 Black	1801 White	1802 Black	1802 White	1803 Black	1803 White	1804 Black	1804 White	1805 Black	1805 White	1806 Black	1806 White	1807 Black	1807 White	1808 Black	1808 White	1809 Black	1809 White	1810 Black	1810 White	1811 Black	1811 White	1812 Black	1812 White
Augusta	9	61	9	61	13	67	20	61	14	72	17	80	17	100	13	62	19	81	16	80			19	64	29	75
Burke	36	297	34	290																						
Richmond	115	548	81	475																						
Washington	92	497	78	536											40	376	78	515	59	415	34	341	74	359
Oconee			61		95	252	333	677	290	832	300	905														
St. Mary's			14		1	12		20	7	100	10	198	17	125	14	102	4	110	56	233	21	68	24	124	6	45
Appalachee					5	210	24	324		599	49	848	52	646	58	745	72	743	148	326	259	1238			161	949
Ogeechee					1	101	2	110	5	277	61	419														
Little River					113	664	132	894	144	938	121	962	131	870	129	906	130	864	153	904	250	1222	236	754	229	772
Broad River					123	788	139	966	122	871	108	809	129	768	138	789	141	827	170	949	192	1036	178	1034	225	1111
Sparta													295	938	326	907	366	987	288	917	295	786	320	727	321	661
Louisville													78	645	56	536	81	558	121	529			77	507	115	606
Milledgeville Cir															14	111	28	265	49	509	108	576	132	657	144	691
Savannah																	7	5	7	4			7	9	2	3
Oakmulgie (Ocuigie)																					5	129	19	265	38	332
Ohoopee																					27	131	20	156	34	150
Alcovi																					44	486	97	756	97	770
Augusta, Louisville & Savannah																					149	594				
Appalachee & Jackson																							180	1002		
Warren																							154	617		
Sattilla																									8	20
Warren & Warrenton																									136	825
Milledgville																									32	106
Total for Year	252	1403	202	1437	361	2094	650	3052	582	3689	666	4221	719	4092	748	4158	888	4816	1086	5966	1409	6681	1497	7013	1652	7575
Blacks +Whites	1655		1639		2455		3702		4271		4887		4811		4906		5704		7052		8090		8510		9227	

Kentucky

District	1800 Black	1800 White	1801 Black	1801 White	1802 Black	1802 White	1803 Black	1803 White	1804 Black	1804 White	1805 Black	1805 White	1806 Black	1806 White	1807 Black	1807 White	1808 Black	1808 White	1809 Black	1809 White	1810 Black	1810 White	1811 Black	1811 White	1812 Black	1812 White
Danville	67	339	74	526	108	714	81	850	53	637	51	614	49	685	36	652	33	662	65	624	44	654	97	800	80	884
Hinkstone	4	283	4	314	4	345	12	458	30	500	27	527	25	565	19	603	51	674	56	698	53	700	103	760	85	845
Lexington	15	273	26	304	38	336	53	356	36	415	68	636	44	711	70	746	81	613	24	624	66	818	48	552	70	733
Limestone	20	417	19	470	18	523	18	702	28	940	37	1023	13	967	20	1186	90	1168	78	1128	58	500	26	539	65	522
Salt River	2	147							7	284									80	380	9	35	9	364	11	351
Shelby	7	167							22	545									65	514	78	600	88	808	103	797
Salt River & Shelby			12	416	15	518	24	851			30	871	43	852	40	895	61	800	23	550	20	571	30	603	26	544
Barren								115		224		309	3	345	12	328	12	380			33	484	30	542	31	613
Green River																					4	111	4	119	4	116
Cumberland																		45		74						
Livingston									2	101	5	180	9	263	13	334	19	384	24	325	39	388	45	458	52	573
Wayne									8	292	27	392	27	453	19	461	26	581	31	758	19	394	17	442	19	425
Red River									20	269	47	450	27	500	28	456	22	514	89	352		364	58	384	99	478
Lexington Town											30	47											8	53		
Hartford											15	305	15	300	16	303	16	320	17	387	9	210	22	352	62	481
Licking														172	7	194	8	176	17	96	11	242	20	242	20	331
Dixon													6						50	441	85	687	95	730	71	712
Fleming																					26	692	22	613	25	620
Henderson																					13	147	10	184	10	165
Eagle Creek																							14	69		
Sandy River																								64	13	284
Goose Creek (in Louisville off of the Ohio River)																									43	759
Total for Year	115	1626	135	2030	183	2436	186	3332	204	4227	337	5334	261	5816	280	6658	418	6322	619	7041	569	7890	736	8678	893	10263
Blacks +Whites	1741		2165		2619		3518		4431		5671		6077		6938		6740		7660		8449		9414		11156	

Tennessee

District	1800 Black	1800 White	1801 Black	1801 White	1802 Black	1802 White	1803 Black	1803 White	1804 Black	1804 White	1805 Black	1805 White	1806 Black	1806 White	1807 Black	1807 White	1808 Black	1808 White	1809 Black	1809 White	1810 Black	1810 White	1811 Black	1811 White	1812 Black	1812 White
Cumberland		247	18	417	39	588																				
Green	22	434	26	517	30	601																				
Nollichukie							35	659	31	636	22	627	29	514	22	576	22	491	22	491	18	449	7	430	17	456
French-Broad							24	683	14	648	12	642	19	478	16	554	19	600	16	694	31	442	30	599	49	910
Nashville/Red River							106	742																		
Nashville									87	637	119	603	97	697	118	677	137	851	104	949	133	982	133	1229	150	1500
Roaring River											21	237	29	288	24	386	41	460	56	499	49	419	44	497	61	658
Powell's Valley												70	1	145	4	195	3	153	11	239	26	239	27	370	37	468
Carter's Valley														4	10	209	11	214	9	211	19	206	16	190	7	190
Duck River																			5	150	12	237	16	401	40	400
Elk River																			5	121	29	196	61	289	55	570
Watauga																					31	170				
Tennessee Valley																					6	375	30	420	21	330
Richland																									7	153
Total for Year	22	681	44	934	69	1189	165	2084	132	1921	174	2265	175	2126	194	2587	233	2769	228	3394	354	3715	364	4415	344	4635
Blacks +Whites	703		978		1258		2249		2123		2439		2301		2781		3002		3622		4069		4779		4979	

Ohio

District	1800 Black	1800 White	1801 Black	1801 White	1802 Black	1802 White	1803 Black	1803 White	1804 Black	1804 White	1805 Black	1805 White	1806 Black	1806 White	1807 Black	1807 White	1808 Black	1808 White	1809 Black	1809 White	1810 Black	1810 White	1811 Black	1811 White	1812 Black	1812 White
Miami	1	98		151		200		411	5	501																
Scioto	1	157	1	202	1	267		354	10	406		474	18	582	5	752	1	911	2	1280	4	744	4	907	4	907
Muskingum & Hockhockin				109											10	662	15	916		685						
West Wheeling					1	265	1	394	2	500	1	548	5	730	8	857	4	819	4	819	4	806	5	1005	5	1150
Muskingum & Little Kanawha (WVA)					3	150																				
Deerfield							4	106	5	163	3	185	1	210	4	270	4	286	4	286	4					
Hockhockin										15		30														
Mad River										100		258	1	410	2	671	2	549	5	765	3	818		767		
Miami & Mad River															1	332	1	531	3	636		826	9	969		641
Licking											12	722	4	879			2	361								
Fairfield																			5	427	6	579	4	422	8	454
Deer Creek																			14	514	17	784	24	801	21	103
Wills Creek																				125		201	4	324	11	466
Cincinnati																					3	818	5	945	5	812
White Oak																					1	766	1	1047		1073
Marietta																						149	4	365		386
Knox																							2	358	3	515
Letart Falls																							1	196	3	207
Tuskarawas (Tuscarawas)																										
Hartford																								79		142
Union																							3	334		
Enon																										690
Pickaway																										306
Delaware																									8	761
Trumbull																										345
																									1	444
Total for Year	2	255	1	462	5	882	5	1268	22	1686	16	2217	29	2811	30	3644	29	4373	41	5537	38	6491	66	8593	69	9402
Blacks + Whites	257		463		887		1273		1708		2233		2840		3674		4402		5578		6529		8659		9471	

Mississippi

District	1800 Black	1800 White	1801 Black	1801 White	1802 Black	1802 White	1803 Black	1803 White	1804 Black	1804 White	1805 Black	1805 White	1806 Black	1806 White	1807 Black	1807 White	1808 Black	1808 White	1809 Black	1809 White	1810 Black	1810 White	1811 Black	1811 White	1812 Black	1812 White
Natchez		60		80		100	2	85	2	100	62	74	72	132	58	94	47	117	52	65	52	65	70	110	49	137
Wilkenson															1	70		80	9	93	5	77	8	110	13	58
Claiborne															33	102	33	98	40	91	40	91	41	97	48	101
Amit (Amite)																									19	151
Total for Year	0	60	0	80	0	100	2	85	2	100	62	74	72	132	92	266	80	295	101	249	97	233	119	317	129	447
Blacks +Whites	60		80		100		87		102		136		204		358		375		350		330		436		576	

Illinois

District	1800 Black	1800 White	1801 Black	1801 White	1802 Black	1802 White	1803 Black	1803 White	1804 Black	1804 White	1805 Black	1805 White	1806 Black	1806 White	1807 Black	1807 White	1808 Black	1808 White	1809 Black	1809 White	1810 Black	1810 White	1811 Black	1811 White	1812 Black	1812 White
Illinois												67		120		110	2	218	3	272		354		341		411
Maessack (Maessac)																										5
Cash Creek (Cache)																										71
Total for Year	0	0	0	0	0	0	0	0	0	0	0	67	0	120	0	110	2	218	3	272	0	354	0	356	0	482
Blacks +Whites	0		0		0		0		0		67		120		110		220		275		354		356		482	

Louisiana

District	1800		1801		1802		1803		1804		1805		1806		1807		1808		1809		1810		1811		1812	
	Black	White	Black	White	Black	White	Black	White	Black	White	Black	White	Black	White	Black	White	Black	White	Black	White	Black	White	Black	White	Black	White
Orleans Territory																								43		
Appalousa (Opelousas)																17										
Washataw & Appalousa																		40		30		30		30		
Rapids (Rapides)																										20
Washataw																										12
Martinville																							7		7	34
Total for Year	0	0	0	0	0	0	0	0	0	0	0	0	0	0	0	17	0	40	0	30	0	30	0	73	7	66
Blacks + Whites	0		0		0		0		0		0		0		17		40		30		30		73		73	

Indiana

District	1800		1801		1802		1803		1804		1805		1806		1807		1808		1809		1810		1811		1812	
	Black	White	Black	White	Black	White	Black	White	Black	White	Black	White	Black	White	Black	White	Black	White	Black	White	Black	White	Black	White	Black	White
White Water															67		1	165	3	349	5	479	5	633		567
Silver Creek																				188	1	234	2	395	6	375
Vincennes																					1	42	3	122	3	170
Total for Year	0	0	0	0	0	0	0	0	0	0	0	0	0	0	0	67	1	165	3	537	7	755	10	1150	9	1112
Blacks + Whites	0		0		0		0		0		0		0		67		166		540		762		1160		1121	

Missouri

District	1800 Black	1800 White	1801 Black	1801 White	1802 Black	1802 White	1803 Black	1803 White	1804 Black	1804 White	1805 Black	1805 White	1806 Black	1806 White	1807 Black	1807 White	1808 Black	1808 White	1809 Black	1809 White	1810 Black	1810 White	1811 Black	1811 White	1812 Black	1812 White
Maramack (Meramec)																	6	44	3	49		354	21	149		147
Missourie (Missouri)																		56		109		102	4	137	4	172
Cold Water																				39		75	7	80	7	83
Cape Girardeau (Girardeau)																					2	52		130		76
New Madrid																								30		27
Total for Year	0	0	0	0	0	0	0	0	0	0	0	0	0	0	0	0	6	100	3	197	2	583	32	496	7	505
Blacks +Whites	0		0		0		0		0		0		0		0		106		200		585		528		512	

Alabama

District	1800 Black	1800 White	1801 Black	1801 White	1802 Black	1802 White	1803 Black	1803 White	1804 Black	1804 White	1805 Black	1805 White	1806 Black	1806 White	1807 Black	1807 White	1808 Black	1808 White	1809 Black	1809 White	1810 Black	1810 White	1811 Black	1811 White	1812 Black	1812 White
Flint																					4	175	12	276	9	339
Tombeckbee (Tombigee)																					15	71	14	120	14	126
Total for Year	0	0	0	0	0	0	0	0	0	0	0	0	0	0	0	0	0	0	0	0	19	246	26	396	23	465
Blacks +Whites	0		0		0		0		0		0		0		0		0		0		265		422		488	

Michigan

District	1800 Black	1800 White	1801 Black	1801 White	1802 Black	1802 White	1803 Black	1803 White	1804 Black	1804 White	1805 Black	1805 White	1806 Black	1806 White	1807 Black	1807 White	1808 Black	1808 White	1809 Black	1809 White	1810 Black	1810 White	1811 Black	1811 White	1812 Black	1812 White
Detroit																						78	4	130	4	130
Total for Year	0	0	0	0	0	0	0	0	0	0	0	0	0	0	0	0	0	0	0	0	0	78	4	130	4	130
Blacks +Whites	0		0		0		0		0		0		0		0		0		0		78		134		134	

Delaware

District	1800 Black	1800 White	1801 Black	1801 White	1802 Black	1802 White	1803 Black	1803 White	1804 Black	1804 White	1805 Black	1805 White	1806 Black	1806 White	1807 Black	1807 White	1808 Black	1808 White	1809 Black	1809 White	1810 Black	1810 White	1811 Black	1811 White	1812 Black	1812 White
Dover	439	717	855	1308	824	1407	852	1486	818	1248	496	677	746	940	730	1133	654	1049	595	965	691	889	465	776	471	787
Milford	381	822	507	1211			465	1173	365	920	341	861	374	1045	426	1351	414	1071	339	960	356	800	351	756	366	702
Wilmington	47	87	85	157	117	125	98	113							96	112	104	99	145	126	134	132	137	137	178	112
Broadkiln & Milford					709	2107																				
Lewistowne (Lewes)							479	1327	403	1172	448	987	404	1007	475	1122	428	990	397	917	351	774	331	755	372	904
Duck Creek											586	669														
Smyrna													663	753	675	988	681	935	746	927	691	856	650	940	648	897
Total for Year	867	1626	1447	2676	1650	3639	1894	4099	1586	3340	1871	3194	2187	3745	2402	4706	2281	4144	2222	3895	2223	3451	1934	3364	2035	3422
Blacks+Whites	2493		4123		5289		5993		4926		5065		5932		7108		6425		6117		5674		5298		5457	

Pennsylvania

District	1800 Black	1800 White	1801 Black	1801 White	1802 Black	1802 White	1803 Black	1803 White	1804 Black	1804 White	1805 Black	1805 White	1806 Black	1806 White	1807 Black	1807 White	1808 Black	1808 White	1809 Black	1809 White	1810 Black	1810 White	1811 Black	1811 White	1812 Black	1812 White
Bristol	7	196	12	208	12	208	17	215	15	222	15	222	24	225	29	244	34	266	60	327	100	431	94	375	94	495
Carlisle	6	213	12	327	33	440	39	564	39	564	45	511	55	527	60	575	59	535	51	536	54	576	46	606	44	525
Chester & Strasburg	10	402	20	470	32	504	39	575																		
Huntingdon	4	215	1	213		417	1	587		260		271	1	398		395	3	398		174	1	357		298		313
Northumberland		244		215		175	2	251	3	430	2	400	5	518	1	342	1	430		532		586		622	1	588
Pittsburgh	8	470	7	462	7	582	7	521	14	601		308		312	2	379		395	10	405	16	412	18	508	20	147
Philadelphia	257	407	448	707	456	721	522	773	647	821	738	950	711	1078	792	1378	874	1503	826	595	933	1544	1061	1629	1340	1708
Redstone	8	375	8	355	9	306	8	371	13	528	21	555	17	531	22	622	19	666	13	660	17	525	32	620	33	847
Tioga		202		136		185		150		362		362		356		276	2	322	2	341		393	4	443	2	484
Wyoming		193		191	3	315		300		446		476		523		440		551		360		363		377	1	404
Erie				37		65		109		168		349				647		665		646		706		501		585
Shenango						119		130		236		206	1	277	1	309		275		282		283		306		436
Academy						102																				
Lancaster																					37	459	52	456	45	481
Dauphin						97	2	121	4	123	12	256	49	382	53	374	47	359	37	396	5	313	5	338	4	360
Lycoming															8	522	10	530	14	553	14	557	2	428	2	472
Chester									140	728	143	622	102	592	65	524	82	611	83	700	103	421	101	558	125	689
Lyttleton									5	413	4	413	2	453	3	392	5	392	2	406		323	42	348	48	325
Juniatta										40		50	3	105	4	123		155		362		154	3	150	3	170
Bald Eagle															7	192										
Greenfield												517	3	521	2	645	3	572	3	467	4	520	8	584	9	564
Erie & Deerfield OH														555				18		67		42		65		
Antalany Auckwhick (Aughwick)																		159	3	172	3	198	3	192	3	181
Bedford Mishannon (Moshannon)																	2		3		2	71	1	116		96
Northampton																							3	42	6	40
Connellsville																								179		
Northampton & Antalany																									10	640
Lancaster																									6	146
																										8
Total for Year	300	2887	508	3321	552	4236	637	4667	880	5942	980	6473	974	7353	1049	8379	1138	8802	1109	8981	1289	9234	1473	9741	1796	10704
Blacks + Whites	3187		3829		4788		5304		6822		7453		8327		9428		9940		10090		10523		11214		12500	

New Jersey

District	1800		1801		1802		1803		1804		1805		1806		1807		1808		1809		1810		1811		1812	
	Black	White	Black	White	Black	White	Black	White	Black	White	Black	White	Black	White	Black	White	Black	White	Black	White	Black	White	Black	White	Black	White
Bethel	30	736	24	704	24	822																				
Burlington	29	623	33	667	45	833	56	862	62	951	61	875	56	819	48	823	51	931	32	941	41	925	32	866	31	290
Elizabeth Town	5	252	11	265	17	490	31	550	21	502	22	455	22	487	15	499	13	577	22	656						
Flanders		235	1	220	6	369	6	544	8	503	7	571														
Freehold	31	316	28	336	29	339	26	391	32	418	31	380	55	365	27	303	30	411	53	762	78	866	53	786	63	736
Salem	63	494	61	584	80	823	81	785	81	764	79	850	111	884	152	1255	150	712	159	746	165	890	202	825	200	930
Trenton	14	201	14	191	12	226	47	258	63	350	68	325	59	362	65	352	76	410	93	445	80	475	78	488	45	212
Cape-May							3	47	5	85	5	93														
Gloucester						50	65	711	71	646	76	630	76	644	75	930	70	890	90	952	92	982	23	938	25	1106
Asbury													5	599	4	550	3	606	3	567	7	644	8	775	11	494
Cumberland																	11	700	11	700	13	811	36	913	45	949
Elizabeth Town & Staten Island																										
Camden																					26	713	37	729		304
Sussex																							76	111	86	587
Essex																									11	381
Bergen																									13	395
NewBrunswick																									27	190
NewMills																									30	857
																									33	
Total for Year	173	2857	172	2967	213	3952	315	4118	343	4298	349	4179	384	4150	386	4172	404	5297	463	5769	525	6314	545	6434	620	7471
Blacks + Whites	3030		3169		4165		4463		4562		4528		4544		5098		5701		6232		6839		6979		8091	

New York

District	1800 Black	1800 White	1801 Black	1801 White	1802 Black	1802 White	1803 Black	1803 White	1804 Black	1804 White	1805 Black	1805 White	1806 Black	1806 White	1807 Black	1807 White	1808 Black	1808 White	1809 Black	1809 White	1810 Black	1810 White	1811 Black	1811 White	1812 Black	1812 White
Albany City	40		8	46	6	57	5	66	5	73	4	81	4	90	16	85	17	91	15	108	13	101	13	116	15	137
Albany Cir	4	704	6	540	9	740	12	775	19	908	4	674	4	628	12	632	11	755	11	782	5	688	6	604	8	507
Brooklyn	20	34	28	36	29	42	29	42	31	42	30	44	42	94	71	154	85	168	93	152	85	170	73	133	70	140
Cambridge	2	701	2	510	3	523	1	364	2	377		398	1	367		420		486	1	647	1	672	12	656	10	646
Chenango		227	2	329		320		425		395		470		386		414		419		455		383		560		412
Columbia	1	113	1	121																						
Delaware		380	1	549	1	418		451	2	513	2	586	1	568	1	583	3	702	4	670	4	688	3	652	4	701
Dutchess	11	310	15	321			14	398	13	393	16	480	21	736	31	839	40	1077	32	1034	29	956	21	496	24	530
Harkimer		294		371		431	4	441	1	210	1	277	1	264	1	317	1	275	1	490		421	2	430	2	370
Long Island	30	360	45	366	50	368	39	494	38	400	50	439	87	538	95	615	76	637	93	670	84	779				
Mohawk		242		280		130																				
Newburgh		351	10	407	12	409	19	446			10	474	19	540	16	584	14	612	6	425	4	450	4	434	4	461
New Rochelle & Croton	16	728	14	736	26	837	29	911																		
New York	131	645	150	685	211	726	248	747	268	750	240	700	365	691	392	1071	424	1330	469	1531	490	1710	530	1924	540	2054
Oneida & Cayuga		209		270																						
Plattsburgh		107		247		325		350		451		468		449		416		404	2	576	3	615	4	496	2	488
Saratoga		444	2	465	2	580	3	535		323	4	363	2	340	3	300	4	310	8	324	5	455	4	478	2	489
Seneca		221		270	5	282	10	354	7	209		322	1	209	2	223		228	1	267	1	361	2	479	3	600
Unadilla				103		125																				
Ulster				98	8	422	5	438	3	410	4	364		337		411		511	5	564	4	464		433	5	446
Western						185		322		249		281	2	258		350	1	300		262	1	343	1	276	1	253
Oneida						92																				
Cayuga					10	270	10	344	9	369	10	446	8	342	6	350	7	400	8	419	8	400	8	432	8	420
Dutchess & Columbia					12	432																				
Otsego (Oswego)								393		297		338		359		374		447	2	430	3	478	3	494	3	490
Westmoreland								152	1	461	1	437	2	440		520		472	7	507	6	601	6	634	11	620
Chatham																	7	704	19	578	6	541	6	547	19	600
Croton										454		420	1	573	20	590	15	652	19	588	21	579	22	511	56	543
New Rochelle									13	460	13	425	30	538	60	650	75	800	62	535	74	510	63	490	2	464
Black River										95		219	1	245		256		465	1	579	1	610				620
Montgomery																		444		378	2	492	3	547	3	544
Lyons										393		325	10	217	3	228	3	314	2	422	10	511	10	641	11	812
Newburgh & Haverstraw									21	573																
Pompey										174		246		388		490	4	501	2	476	15	487	12	513	3	554
Ontario										206		223	4	253	15	343	18	470	2	639	10	670	12	687	12	685

New York, continued

District	1800		1801		1802		1803		1804		1805		1806		1807		1808		1809		1810		1811		1812	
	Black	White	Black	White	Black	White	Black	White	Black	White	Black	White	Black	White	Black	White	Black	White	Black	White	Black	White	Black	White
Haverstraw											10	145	20	204		306	19	314	25	370	28	265	24	331		
Canestio (Canisteo)																										
New Lebanon																199	2	193	2	198		222		225	2	230
Lebanon									2	660																
Schenectady											1	507	1	507	3	69										
Scipio																	9	178	4	248	6	452	7	507	2	370
Holland Purchase (NW corner)													214		200	1	400	1	374	1	417	1	404			456
Courtlandt																		50		90		260		365		663
New Windsor																			6	582	19	602	19	560	22	310
Canaan																			10	56	13	523	8	503	9	584
Staten Island																				218		248		273		126
Suffolk																									14	261
Jamaica																							7	326		
Rhinebeck																							99	530	104	618
Thurman																							10	476	8	497
Malone																								177		172
St. Lawrence																								61		85
Mexico																								84		144
Ticonderoga																							2	430	1	320
Suffolk & Sag-Harbour																								68		141
																								6	243
Total for Year	215	6140	284	6750	384	7764	428	8448	438	9845	407	10152	625	11254	752	12926	836	15048	886	17001	937	18116	982	19593	984	20242
Blacks + Whites	6355		7034		8148		8876		10283		10559		11879		13678		15884		17887		19053		20575		21226	

Connecticut

District	1800 Black	1800 White	1801 Black	1801 White	1802 Black	1802 White	1803 Black	1803 White	1804 Black	1804 White	1805 Black	1805 White	1806 Black	1806 White	1807 Black	1807 White	1808 Black	1808 White	1809 Black	1809 White	1810 Black	1810 White	1811 Black	1811 White	1812 Black	1812 White
Litchfield	1	314		281	1	307	1	340	2	278	2	309	2	342	3	408	4	435	4	464	1	399	1	455	1	491
Middletown	4	252	2	278	1	314	3	307	5	250	4	261	4	260	4	293	10	326	20	381	17	397	24	466	12	445
New London	13	327			16	338	15	365	15	384	17	365	20	361	20	354	19	354	19	521	17	632	14	619	15	555
Pomfret	1	181				251		248	1	211	1	206		193		190	1	218	1	240		209		213		215
Redding		227		191	1	227		307		437			1	449	2	407	2	479	6	567	5	667	7	709	6	740
Tolland	1	245	4	292	2	200	1	172		242		231		262		299	2	275		294	2	388	3	375	2	349
New London & Pomfret			18	501																					12	41
New Haven																										
Redding & South Brittain											1	456	1	50												
South Brittain																										
Total for Year	25	1646	24	1543	21	1637	20	1739	23	1802	25	1828	29	1917	29	1951	38	2087	50	2467	42	2692	49	2837	48	2836
Blacks +Whites	1571		1567		1658		1759		1825		1853		1946		1980		2125		2517		2734		2886		2884	

Massachusetts

District	1800 Black	1800 White	1801 Black	1801 White	1802 Black	1802 White	1803 Black	1803 White	1804 Black	1804 White	1805 Black	1805 White	1806 Black	1806 White	1807 Black	1807 White	1808 Black	1808 White	1809 Black	1809 White	1810 Black	1810 White	1811 Black	1811 White	1812 Black	1812 White
Boston	6	66	10	65	6	60	7	179	20	159	23	228	23	236	20	229	30	310	24	313	24	306	24	361	23	264
Granville		300		410		234		340	1	294		150		226		374		368		381	3	352	5	323	2	317
Lynn		94		89		82		121		126		139		170		170		170		119		245		246		230
Marblehead		26		26		36		58		53			1	77	1	84		81		96		112		112		114
Martha's Vineyard																								73		100
Merrimack		65		62		46																				
Needham		153		136		155		143	2	143		139		150		147		165		210	1	264		247	1	249
Nantucket		65		80		84	2	92	2	90	3	114	2	128	4	124	4	124	8	158	8	146	9	150	12	292
Pittsfield		602	2	598	4	639	2	609				223	2	353	6	672	6	762	5	647	7	618	8	566	3	445
Province Town		137		127		127		100		100		117	1	117												
Sandwich		63		60		60		66		50		69		90		87		107	7	134						
Adams					1	268		265		265																150
Wilbraham						105																				
Northfield														31		47										
Norton								176						252												
Salisbury								48									1	97		93						
Ashburnham								231	1	43	2	204	2	227	2	241	2	227	2	260		265		270	2	273
Salisbury & Kingston										224		50		60												
Marblehead & Ipswich											1	54														
Buckland																24		86		118		120		126		134
Scituate														21		105		34		51						47
Salisbury & Salem															1	125					1	279				
Harwich																129										
Poplin																		140		141		158		184		80
Norton & Easton																80		80		95		111		97		
Poplin & Salem																		164		348				243		248
New Bedford																		30		50		50		49		50
Falmouth																				62				106		100
Salisbury, Poplin & Salem																					1					
Sandwich & Scituate																					6	176		158		
Somerset																						57				
Salisbury & Greenland																								213		165
Easton & Mansfield																										133
Somerset, Warren & Newport																										113
Wellfleet & Truro																										96
Total for Year	6	1571	12	1853	11	1896	11	2428	26	1597	29	1487	31	2138	34	2638	43	2965	46	3272	50	3257	46	3504	43	3600
Blacks +Whites	1577		1865		1907		2439		1623		1516		2169		2672		3008		3318		3307		3550		3643	

Rhode Island

District	1800 Black	1800 White	1801 Black	1801 White	1802 Black	1802 White	1803 Black	1803 White	1804 Black	1804 White	1805 Black	1805 White	1806 Black	1806 White	1807 Black	1807 White	1808 Black	1808 White	1809 Black	1809 White	1810 Black	1810 White	1811 Black	1811 White	1812 Black	1812 White
Greenwich		43		43																						
Rhode Island	2	52	2	52														60	2	77						
Warren	1	129	1	129											1	36		40							
One Circuit					6	306																				
Providence							4	129	5	294																
Bristol										84						104	104		80							
Providence & R.I											2	298		36		34		96								
Bristol, Somerset & Warren												125		106									2	211		
Newport																18		19		26		55				
Bristol & Somerset																144										107
East Greenwich																87		90		97	2	114	2	154	2	
Portsmouth Cir.																				220		260		72		
Providence & Smithfield																				141		90		138		281
Bristol & Warren																						112				
Bristol & Portsmouth																									12	292
New Market & Portsmouth																										87
Total for Year	3	224	3	224	6	306	4	129	5	378	2	423	0	172	0	387	1	405	2	681	2	731	4	575	14	767
Blacks +Whites		227		227		312		133		383		425		172		387		406		683		733		579		781

Maine

District	1800 Black	1800 White	1801 Black	1801 White	1802 Black	1802 White	1803 Black	1803 White	1804 Black	1804 White	1805 Black	1805 White	1806 Black	1806 White	1807 Black	1807 White	1808 Black	1808 White	1809 Black	1809 White	1810 Black	1810 White	1811 Black	1811 White	1812 Black	1812 White
Bath & Union		173		197																						
Norridgwock		166		188		170		205		204		187		224		190		185		226		130	1	125	1	135
Penobscot		218		207		232		294		400		375		297								72		83		95
Portland		230		249								51	1	63	1	112	2	140	2	169	3	169	3	159	2	168
Readfield		310		394		327		364		361		155		221		179		224		221		200		209		205
Union River		105		109		98		99		112		111		99		70		70		67						
Bethel				52		50		50		46		115		117		108		108		84		87				109
Falmouth						89		179		262		99		213		267		211		291		201		240		233
Poland						101		109		121		111		116		123		185		183		203		203		166
Hallowell						100		107		150	2	161	2	187	2	115	2	117		117		152		153		150
Bath						28		29																		
Union						69		111		153		206		211		205		205		227		269		239		231
Bristol								200		188		155		149		185		183		203		205		236		234
Livermore														304		347		295		288		288		259		226
Bowdoinham									1			129	1	211	1	100	1	202								
Scarborough										74		73		85		86		184		181		182		184		122
Durham																101		118	1	327		292	1	311		298
Vesselborough																76		68		100		166		140		156
Orrington																114		182		200		318		305		301
Hamden																180		183		206		310		300		295
Palmira (Palmyra)																			1	39						
George-Town																				55		56		59		53
Boothbay																				12		21		39		33
Industry																						224		250		237
Total for Year	0	197	0	1386	0	1414	0	1747	1	2101	1	2399	4	2497	4	2558	5	2780	4	3146	3	3495	5	3543	3	3447
Blacks + Whites		197		1386		1414		1747		2102		2400		2501		2562		2785		3150		3498		3548		3450

New Hampshire

District	1800 Black	1800 White	1801 Black	1801 White	1802 Black	1802 White	1803 Black	1803 White	1804 Black	1804 White	1805 Black	1805 White	1806 Black	1806 White	1807 Black	1807 White	1808 Black	1808 White	1809 Black	1809 White	1810 Black	1810 White	1811 Black	1811 White	1812 Black	1812 White
Chesterfield		145	2	226		205																				
Hawke		26		45		38		68		74		90														
Hanover			1	58		268		272				99		180		159		142								
Landaff		53		192		164				136		382		290		313		293		295		274		404		446
Landaff & Wentworth								250																		
Dorchester										165				89												
Sandown										203																
Hanover & Grantham																										220
Tuftenborough												37		47		89		125		205		229				
Grantham & Unity												176		221												
Centre-Harbour														141		52		136		172		205		246		
Loudon														74												
Grantham																238		202		178		221		256	1	244
Pembroke																72		72		123		130		168		166
Conway																35		62		74		71		72		91
Bridgewater								54			1	93		95		93		94		98		205				287
Northfield																		42								
Canaan										57										155		170				
Rochester																				34		36				
Canaan & Bridgewater																								337		
Tuftenborough & Rochester																								326		204
Sandwich																										91
Norway Plains																										
Total for Year	0	224	3	521	0	665	0	644	0	635	1	877	0	1137	0	151	0	1168	0	1334	0	1541	0	1799	1	1749
Blacks+Whites		224		524		665		644		635		878		1137		151		1168		1334		1541		1799		1750

Vermont

District	1800 Black	1800 White	1801 Black	1801 White	1802 Black	1802 White	1803 Black	1803 White	1804 Black	1804 White	1805 Black	1805 White	1806 Black	1806 White	1807 Black	1807 White	1808 Black	1808 White	1809 Black	1809 White	1810 Black	1810 White	1811 Black	1811 White	1812 Black	1812 White
Essex		247																								
Vergennes	1	342	1	172		187		227	3	268		240		240	3	323										210
Vershire		270		354		395	2	473		230		224		193		149		165		202		248		230		510
Wethersfield		64	2	232	2	196								360		327		365		340	1	416	2	416		410
Whitingham		92		119		200	2	286	2	296		333	1	335	1	387	1	376	1	375	1	365	1	387		
Brandon			2	263	2	290	2	295		351		388		360		395	1	431	1	558	1	644		408	1	596
Barnard				40		161		238		245		306		277				327		349		380		360		
Fletcher			1	401	2	418	1	382		402		467		530		450		421	6	450	6	467		518		569
Lunenburg						58		124		210		221		186		152		226		167		180	1	210		215
Athens						132				171		152		149		140		144		170		196		201		
Woodstock						63		148																		188
Charlotte																										
Wethersfield & Woodstock								350		384		380					3	303	3	323	6	454		396	3	333
Barre									2	337		306		346		342		347		312		335		318		309
Stanstead										18					2	124	1	119	3	102	2	129	4	196	4	234
Danville								40		73		130		132		140		114	2	134	1	169	1	274		273
Rochester														69												
Grand Isle								152		108		89		176		181		199		211		324		274		261
Durham																291		307		264		319		335		335
Barnard & Rochester																362										
Pownal																					4	502	7	550	6	628
Middlebury																				277				60		60
Manchester																								130		
Barnard & White River																										400
Total for Year	1	1015	6	1601	6	2110	5	2715	7	3093	0	3296	1	3353	6	3763	5	3844	10	4234	22	5148	16	5263	14	5521
Blacks + Whites		1016		1607		2116		2720		3100		3296		3354		3769		3849		4244		5170		5279		5535

NOTES

Introduction

1. Even though the bishop and the cabinet set the appointments, God directs the process. A non-United Methodist might sneer at this. However, UM pastors have learned to "flow" with the Spirit. This is the Methodist way.

2. See C. Peter Wagner's *Our Kind of People* (Atlanta, GA: John Knox Press, 1979) in which he explains and evaluates the homogenous unit principle in church growth.

3. "On September 11, 1991, at 7:00 a.m., an estimated one million students gathered at school flagpoles all over the country. . . . Some sang, some read Scripture, but most importantly, they prayed. . . . They prayed for their schools, for their friends, for their leaders, and for their country. Since 1991, See You at the Pole™ has grown to God-sized proportions" (http://syatp.com/?option=com_content&view=article&id=4&Ite%20mid=5 [accessed August 1, 2012]).

4. See William Payne, "The Case for Scouting Evangelism," *UM Men* 8 (Summer 2005), 25-27.

Chapter 1

1. J. L. Sooy pastored the Tabernacle Methodist Episcopal Church at Camden, New Jersey. In 1888, the *New York Times* described him as "one of the most talented ministers in the New Jersey Conference" (http://query.nytimes.com/mem/archive-free/pdf?res=F20712FA3A5C10738DDDA90994DC405B8884F0D3 [accessed August 1, 2012]).

2. Anthony Atwood, *Causes for the Marvelous (Former) Success of Methodism* (Zarephath, NJ: Pillar of Fire Publisher, 1884), v. In 1784, there were 15,071 Methodists. In 1884, there were 2,906,691 Methodists on the combined rolls of the MEC, the MEC South and the Methodist Protestant Church (Methodist Church Council on World Service and Finance Department of Research, *Methodist Fact Book* [Evanston, IN: Department of Research and Statistics, 1960], 192). That equals 190-fold growth or 19,033 percent growth. The estimated population for America in 1780 was 2,781,000. The population of the United States in 1860 was 31,443,321. That equals an 11-fold growth or 1,130 percent growth. See U.S. Bureau of the Census, *Historical Statistics of the United States 1789-1945*. Washington, DC: Government Printing Office, 1949:25.

3. Roger Finke and Rodney Stark, "Turning Pews into People: Estimating 19th Century Church Membership," *Journal for the Scientific Study of Religion* 25, no. 2 (1986): 180-192; "How the Upstart Sects Won America: 1776-1850." *Journal for the Scientific Study of Religion* 28, no. 1 (1989): 27-44; and *The Churching of America: Winners and Loser in Our Religious Economy* (New Brunswick, NJ: Rutgers University Press, 1992). Also, see Kenneth Scott Latourette, *A History of the Expansion of Christianity: The Great Century in Europe and the United States of America A.D.1800-A.D. 1914*. 2nd ed. (New York: Harper and Brother's Publishing, 1941), 4:341.

4. Francis Asbury, *The Journal and Letters of Francis Asbury*, ed. Elmer Clark, J. Manning Potts, and Jacob S. Payton, vol. 3 (Nashville, TN: Abingdon, 1958), 96; hereinafter cited as *Asbury's Journal*, 1, 2 or 3.

5. Regardless of the exact number of participants, the membership requirements of the MEC excluded most participants from the annual membership summaries including children of members and adults who attended events but were not on the rolls.

6. *Asbury's Journal*, 3:162. From the limited perspective of the Northern District of New York, Freeborn Garrettson describes the distinction between members and hearers in 1790. He states that 2,000 had joined the society, a 1,000 were truly born of the Spirit, and more than 8,000 participated on a regular basis. His ratio of members to hearers was 1:4. See Freeborn Garrettson, *American Methodist Pioneer: The Life and Journals of the Rev. Freeborn Garrettson, 1772-1827*, ed. Robert Simpson (Rutland, VT: Academy Books, 1984), 143. The revival areas of the South had a larger members to hearers ratio.

7. Southern Methodism suffered a drastic downturn in membership in the mid-1790s. That helps to explain why Asbury's comparison is less than Coke's.

8. Robert E. Coleman, *Nothing to Do but Save Souls* (Wilmore, KY: Evangel Publishing House, 1990), 18-19.

9. The assumption cannot be substantiated since rigorous membership requirements lessened over time. During the tenure of Bishop Asbury, Methodist preachers emphasized strict discipline and only issued class tickets to those who maintained the standards. At times, this led to institutional conflict. The democratization of Methodism, growing institutionalism, the phenomenon of the camp meeting, and the mitigation of the class meeting contributed to a reduction in membership standards. It is possible that Methodist membership growth following 1812 was aided by a lessening of the 1:11 membership to participant ratio that existed in the late 1790s.

10. Following 1800, immigration and the annexation of new territories favored Roman Catholicism. Immigration patterns began to switch from Northern Europe to Southern Europe, and the western frontier was loosely occupied by Spanish and French Roman Catholics.

11. Experts note three kinds of church growth: biological, when a person is born into a Christian home and is confirmed into the faith; transfer, when a Christian moves and affiliates with a new local church; and conversion, when a non-Christian is brought into a saving relationship with Christ and affiliates with a local church. Transfer growth reaffiliates a Christian who has become unaffiliated with a local church. Biological and conversion growth relate to conversion and discipleship.

12. Fink and Stark, "Turning Pews into People," 180-192.

13. See Nathan Hatch's Americanization theory in *The Democratization of American Christianity* (New Haven, CT: Yale University Press, 1989).

14. In early American Methodism the system was the same for all regions. The *Disciplines* and the leadership required uniformity. Conferences enforced uniformity. Before the creation of six annual conferences in 1796, Asbury moved the circuit riders from one region to another on a regular basis.

15. For the purposes of this work, the South includes Maryland, Virginia, North Carolina, South Carolina, and Georgia. The western portions of the Southern states extended into the frontier. This work does not count Kentucky and Tennessee with the Southern region because they responded to a separate set of contextual factors in the 1790, e.g., rapid population growth, Indian problems, land scandals, unsettled conditions, frontier politics, lawlessness, and the like.

16. William Price Payne, "Without a Parallel: Reasons for the Expansion of Early American Methodism (1767 through 1812)," (PhD diss., Asbury Theological Seminary, Ann Arbor, MI: UMI, 2001), 406ff. Frontier membership (Kentucky and Tennessee) followed a similar pattern. It posted gains from 1790 through 1794, and then declined through 1798. Afterward, the early tremors of the great revival caused membership to soar.

17. Dean Hoge and David Roozen, *Understanding Church Growth and Decline: 1950-1978* (Nashville, TN: Abingdon Press, 1979); David Roozen and C. Kirk Hadaway, *Church and Denominational Growth* (Nashville, TN: Abingdon Press, 1993); and

Roozen and Hadaway, *Rerouting the Protestant Mainstream* (Nashville, TN: Abingdon Press, 1995).

18. This author has argued for the inclusion of regional settings. See Payne, "Without a Parallel," 352, 380-381.

19. See Ed Silvoso, *Prayer Evangelism* (Regal Books, Ventura, CA, 2000). The effectiveness of evangelistic outreach programs has been dramatically increased when preceded by concerted prayer evangelism. Often, advance teams of prayer warriors travel to a targeted community, map out the spiritual landscape, and engage in cosmic level spiritual warfare months before the evangelist arrives. It is believed that "the god of this world has blinded the minds of those who do not believe" (2 Cor. 4:4 NIV). The advance teams attempt to neutralize negative spiritual factors that impede evangelism and decrease the receptivity of the people to the gospel.

20. Kenneth Inskeep, "A Short History of Church Growth Research" in *Church and Denominational Growth*, ed. David Roozen and C. Kirk Hadaway (Nashville, TN: Abingdon Press, 1993), 135.

21. Roozen and Hadaway, *Rerouting the Protestant Mainstream*, 14.

22. Inskeep, "Short History of Church Growth Research," 135.

23. See George Hunter's *Church for the Unchurched* (Nashville, TN: Abingdon, 1996); *The Celtic Way of Evangelism* (2000); *Radical Outreach: Recovery of Apostolic Ministry and Evangelism* (2003); and *The Apostolic Congregation, Church Growth for a New Generation* (2009).

24. David Roozen, "Denominations Grow as Individuals Join Congregations" in *Church and Denominational Growth*, ed. David Roozen and C. Kirk Hadaway (Nashville, TN: Abingdon Press, 1993), 23.

25. See, Dean Kelley, *Why Conservative Churches Are Growing* (1972; repr., Macon, GA: Mercer University Press, 1986).

26. Payne, "Without a Parallel," 314-318.

27. Recently, the Hartford Institute reversed its emphasis on the determinative nature of contextual factors. In a report released on December 19, 2011 David Roozen states, "Location, Location, Location used to be the kind way that researchers described the extent to which the growth or decline of American congregations was captive to the demographic changes going on in their immediate neighborhoods. Congregations cannot totally ignore what is going on in their context, but the clear message of *FACTs on Growth: 2010* is that in today's world, growth and decline are primarily dependent upon a congregation's internal culture, program and leadership, and therefore a congregation's own ability to change and adapt." See http://faithcommunitiestoday.org/facts-growth-2010 (accessed August 1, 2012).

28. Some have suggested that membership decline pointed to a positive spiritual attribute related to the faithfulness of the denomination as it confronted the various social problems of the 1970s. Accordingly, prophetic ministry and a kingdom agenda are theological ideas that describe why numerical growth can never be an overriding concern. Small is good when small is caused by a faithful witness against a prevailing evil. As a denomination grows large, it compromises core values to the extent that it appeals to a larger community. The Church Growth discipline counters this belief by means of its teaching on "fog," "remnant theology," and the quality verses quantity debate.

29. Kelley, *Conservative Churches*. Kelley did not approve of the book title. Conservative churches do not grow because they are conservative. They grow because they have strong corporate cultures, are evangelistic, and are culturally relevant.

30. C. Peter Wagner, "Church Growth Research: the Paradigm and Its Implications" in *Understanding Church Growth and Decline 1950-1978*, ed. Dean Hoge and David Roozen (Nashville, TN: Abingdon, 1979), 276.

31. C. Peter Wagner "Church Growth Movement" in *Evangelical Dictionary of World Missions,* ed. A. Scott Moreau (Grand Rapids, MI: Baker Books, 2000), 199-200.

32. See Donald McGavran, *Understanding Church Growth.* ed., C. Peter Wagner. 3rd ed. Grand Rapids, MI: Eerdmans, 1990.

33. In order to understand the protocol, I recommend that the reader procure *The Church Growth Survey Handbook* by Bob Waymire and C. Peter Wagner. The book is out of print. One Challenge International owns the copyright. In the past, it has made a PDF copy of the book available to those who request it. The contact info is OC INTERNATIONAL, PO Box 36900, Colorado Springs, CO 80936, 719-592-9292 ext 123, or marciabalyeat@oci.org.

34. For a good discussion of the homogeneous unit principle, see http://www.lasanne.org/en/documents/global-analysis/en/documents/lops/71-lop-1.html (accessed August 1, 2012). According to the 1978 Lausanne Movement's Pasadena Consultation, the homogenous unit principle is about being culturally relevant. "What we have been specially concerned to discuss is the relation of HUs to the evangelistic task laid upon the Church by the Great Commission of our Lord, and the propriety of using them as a means to world evangelization. Dr. McGavran's well-known statement is that 'people like to become Christians without crossing racial, linguistic or class barriers.' That is, the barriers to the acceptance of the gospel are often more sociological than theological; people reject the gospel not because they think it is false but because it strikes them as alien. They imagine that in order to become Christians they must renounce their own culture, lose their own identity, and betray their own people. Therefore, in order to reach them, not only should the evangelist be able to identify with them, and they with the evangelist; not only must the gospel be contextualized in such a way that it communicates with them; but the church into which they are invited must itself belong to their culture sufficiently for them to feel at home in it. It is when these conditions are fulfilled that men and women are won to Jesus Christ, and subsequently that churches grow."

35. Wesley summarizes the marks of a Methodist as an internal process of transformation by saying that a Methodist loves God with all his being, loves neighbor as self, is full of God's joy as he rejoices in the Holy Spirit at all times, gives thanks in all things, prays without ceasing, is pure in heart, seeks God's will above his own, manifests the fruit of the Spirit, keeps the commandments of God, does all things for the glory of God, lives a circumspect life, is ever mindful of the coming judgment, and is not conformed to the world. See "The Character of a Methodist" in Wesley, *Works* 8:339-347 and "The Witness of the Spirit" in Wesley, *Works* 5:111-123.

36. For an excellent discussion on this, see Wesley's letter to Freeborn Garrettson on November 30, 1786 in Wesley, *Works* 13:71-72.

37. Luke Keefer, "John Wesley: Disciple of Early Christianity," *Wesleyan Theological Journal* 19, no.1. (Spring 1984). http://wesley.nnu.edu/fileadmin/importedsite/wesleyjournal/1984-wtj-19-1.pdf (accessed August 1, 2012).

38. Ibid.

39. Wesley, *Works* 8:248-268.

Chapter 2

1. C. Peter Wagner wrote *Your Church Can Grow: Seven Vital Signs of a Healthy Church* (Ventura, CA: Gospel Light Publications, 1984). The book examines the vital signs and diseases associated with church growth and decline. The use of medical terminology reflects an organic understanding of church.

2. Donald McGavran, *Church Growth in Jamaica: A Preview of Things to Come in Many Lands* (Lucknow, India: Lucknow Publishing House, 1962).

Chapter 3

1. Methodist Episcopal Church, *Minutes of the Annual Conferences Annually Held in America from 1773 to 1813 Inclusive* (Nashville, TN: Daniel Hitt and Thomas Ware for the Methodist Conexion in the United States, 1813).

2. This chapter anticipates state boundaries as it plots circuits. For example, Kentucky was a part of Virginia until 1792. However, this chapter locates circuits in Kentucky as early as 1787.

3. Wesleyan Methodist Church, vol. 1 of *Minutes of the Methodists Conferences*. Originally titled *Minutes of the Several Conversations between the Reverend Mr. Wesley and Others from the Year 1744, to the Year 1780* (London, Eng., Mason, 1862).

4. Manning Potts, "Methodism in Colonial America," vol. 1 in *The History of American Methodism*, gen. ed. Emory Stevens Bucke (Nashville, TN: Abington, 1964), 74-95.

5. Jesse Lee, *A Short History of the Methodists in the United States of America Beginning in 1766 and Continued till 1809* (Baltimore, MD: Magill and Clime, 1810), 28.

6. William Warren Sweet, *Virginia Methodism: A History* (Richmond, VA: Whittet and Shepperson, 1955), 46.

7. Robert Williams came to America without income. He intended to earn his living by selling Wesley's books. The American conference in 1773 prohibited him from printing additional books.

8. Joseph Pilmoor, *The Journal of Joseph Pilmore, Methodist Itinerant for the Years August 1, 1769 to January 2, 1774*, ed. Frederick Maser and Howard Maag (Philadelphia, PA: Message Publishing Co., 1969), 25. Most primary sources use Pilmoor instead of Pilmore. Wesley refers to him as "Pillmoor." This book uses Pilmoor.

9. The minutes from the August conference do not appoint the missionaries to America in 1769 even though the conference dispatched them as missionaries to America. The only reference to them appears in question 13. "We have a pressing call from our brethren in New York . . . to come over and help them. Who is willing to go? Answer: Richard Boardman and Joseph Pilmoor." They were appointed to the Dales and Wales respectively in 1768 and to America in 1770. It appears that they did not receive an appointment for 1769.

10. The Wesleyan *Minutes* contain the following summaries for America: 1774—2,204*; 1775—3,148; 1776—3,148*; 1778—6,968*; 1784—14,988. Those with an asterisk are different from the numbers in the American *Minutes*.

11. Robert Coleman, "Factors in the Expansion of the Methodist Episcopal Church 1784 to 1812," (PhD diss., University of Iowa, Ann Arbor, MI: UMI, 1954), 514.

12. The discrete graphs that constitute Figure 2.1 illustrate the membership change in individual states better than the regional line-graphs in Figure 2.2. Regional line-graphs flatten out the trend lines of small membership states when a regional line-graph depicts a large and a small membership on the same figure. However, Figure 3.2 shows the overall membership pattern for the regions better than the discrete graphs in Figure 2.1. The following example demonstrates the difference between the individual graphs and the regionally based graphs. If one state contains 20,000 Methodists and another state contains 10,000, the regionally based graph will be scaled for 20,000. As such, a 1,000 member variation in the state with 10,000 members will appear twice as pronounced on the individual graph that is scaled to 10,000 than it does on the regionally based graph that is scaled to 20,000.

13. Lee, *Short History*, 59.

14. William Williams, "The Delmarva Peninsula as a Case Study, 1769-1820," *Perspectives on American Methodism, Interpretive Essays*, ed. Russell Richey, Kenneth Rowe, and Jean Miller Schmidt (Nashville, TN: Kingswood Books, 1993) 31-45; Russell

Richey, *Early American Methodism* (Bloomington, IN: Indiana University Press, 1991); and Russell Richey, "The Chesapeake Coloration of American Methodism," in *Methodism and the Shaping of American Culture 1760-1860* (Wilmore, KY: Wesleyan/Holiness Studies Center of Asbury Theological Seminary, 1994).

15. Lee, *Short History*, 74.

16. The American *Minutes* listed circuits within state boundaries in 1796. Before that, they were haphazardly listed.

17. Wade Crawford Barclay, *Early American Methodism, 1769-1844; Missionary Motivation and Expansion* vol. 1 of *History of Methodist Missions* (New York: The Board of Missions and Church Extension of the Methodist Church, 1949), 71.

18. The 1785 conference was a called conference. The 1785 conferences were scheduled for April 30th, May 8th, and June15th. The 1785 Christmas Conference began on December 27, 1784. At this "general" conference, the assembled preachers formed themselves into the Methodist Episcopal Church.

19. In the antebellum South, a large plantation kept over fifty slaves. Many kept over a hundred slaves. Since Methodist members were not allowed to keep slaves during much of this period, the itinerants had to work hard to gain access to slaves because the owners did not like the Methodists or feared slave revolts. This problem was particularly acute in South Carolina. Methodism's antislavery rhetoric added to the problem. See Robert William Foge and Stanley L. Engerman, *Time on the Cross: The Economics of American Negro Slavery* (Boston, MA: Little, Brown and Co., 1974).

20. Chapter Six contains a detailed analysis of slave membership.

21. Table 2-3 indicates that New York had a 7.1 population density in 1790. That is misleading because the coastal region of New York was densely populated. For example, New York City had a population of 32,305. However, upstate New York was sparsely populated. In 1790, there were 20 cities in the United States with populations over 3,000. All of them existed on or near the Atlantic coast. French New Orleans had a population of 5,338. Lester J. Cappon, ed., *The Atlas of Early American History* (Princeton, NJ: Princeton University Press, 1976), 97.

22. The Holston circuit first appeared in 1783, thirteen years before Tennessee became a state. At that time, the Tennessee border was not fixed. It was a part of "the State of Franklin." The three forks of the Holston River are in southwest Virginia and have their confluence just over the border in Kingsport, Tennessee. The Holston River ends at the French Broad River to form the Tennessee River near present day Knoxville. Cappon placed the Holston circuit in the northeast corner of Tennessee by Kingsport (*Atlas of Early American History,* 71). Isaac Martin listed Holston in Tennessee with the following description, "The increase which occurred in 1802 was largely in East Tennessee, where there were three circuits: Holston, Nolichucky and French Broad. The Holston circuit covered what are now the counties of Sullivan, Hawkins and Grainger . . . in the two Virginia circuits, Clinch and New River . . ." (*History of Methodism in Holston Conference* [Nashville, TN: The Methodist Historical Society of Holston Conference 1945], 21). That would give Tennessee three circuits during this period and one circuit in the first period. According to John B. M'Ferrin, the Holston circuit included "that part of Tennessee lying on the head-waters of the Holston River: it likewise embraced that portion of Virginia lying on the head-waters of the Kanawha or New River. Mr. Lambert's work, therefore, was in South-western Virginia and East Tennessee" (*History of Methodism in Tennessee*, Vol. 1. [Nashville, TN: The Publishing House of the ME Church, South, 1888], 28). Wallace Smeltzer says that the Holston Circuit was planted on the headwaters of the Tennessee in 1783 (*Bishop Francis Asbury, Field Marshal of the Lord* [Denver, CO: Eastwood Printing and Publishing Co., 1982], 73). By headwaters, it is assumed he meant the Powell, Clinch, and Holston Rivers that flow from Virginia to form the Tennessee River. Because circuits moved from an established area to a new

area, it is logical to assume that the Holston circuit began in Virginia. Lawrence Sherwood made a very insightful remark on this subject. "As we attempt to see these cells of Methodism—the circuits—grow, we are hampered by names. . . . Many of the early circuit names came from streams; the original circuits located on these streams continued to carry the name into larger areas as the circuit grows. Thus, Holston refers to the region of southwestern Virginia and eastern Tennessee; however, we must follow the example of our forefathers in not pressing for too definite a description of what a name means in detail" ("Growth and Spread, 1785-1804," vol. 1 in *The History of American Methodism*, gen. ed. Emory Stevens Bucke [Nashville, TN: Abingdon, 1964], 368).

This work lists Holston with Virginia because the 1796 through 1801 *Minutes* locate it there and Jesse Lee reaffirmed that location (Lee, *Short History*, 82). When the Holston circuit was established, it covered an area that included parts of Virginia and Tennessee. As it was worked, the area and original circuit were divided into the above mentioned circuits. Typically, new circuits in the West started off very large. They were divided into smaller circuits as they were cultivated and as the population increased. Incidentally, the Kentucky circuit that appeared in 1787 also included Tennessee west of the Cumberland Mountains.

23. Before statehood in 1820, Maine was a part of Massachusetts.

24. Richey argues that Delaware and Maryland belong together and that they both should be categorized as "South." "The demographic, social and cultural realities that Methodism encountered in Delmarva peninsula closely resemble those . . . for Virginia" (*Early American Methodism*, 115).

25. The expansion of slavery into the new frontier became a major issue. Before 1787, slavery was permitted in all parts of the U.S. except Pennsylvania and the New England States. The Northwest Ordinance of 1787 banned slavery in the territories west of the Ohio River. New York became a free state in 1799. Ohio followed in 1802. New Jersey acquiesced in 1804.

26. Blacks were in the new states and territories and played a role in the expansion of Methodism. In the following quote from 1803, John Young illustrates this point: "We traveled about twenty miles on . . . Fishing creek [KY]. . . . There was a Methodist society in the neighborhood, the preacher . . . a colored man, by the name of Jacob. . . . Every member of the society had been awakened under his preaching" (Barclay, *Methodist Missions* 1:149). The man may have been a local preacher or a layman who preached. The MEC ordained its first Black deacon in 1799.

Chapter 4

1. For a historical account of the origin and function of societies, classes, and bands, see Wesley's "A Plain Account of the People Called Methodists" (Wesley, *Works* 8:248-268). He gives the explicit rules for each following his "Plain Account" (Wesley, *Works* 8:269-274). Jesse Lee cites them as being applicable to American Methodism (Lee, *Short History*, 29-36). Obviously, there were other levels of organization related to leadership and temporal functions in EAM. Exhorters, lay preachers, and located circuit riders provided leadership to the societies and gave pastoral care to the people in the absence of the circuit riders. Trustees and stewards managed the temporal needs of the society. Stewards controlled the money and paid the bills to include the preachers' salary. Trustees maintained chapels and church property.

2. The term "discipline" was first used to describe rules and regulation in 1787. In that year Coke and Asbury produced *A Form of Discipline for the Ministers, Preachers, and Members of the Methodist Episcopal Church in America*. The title related to the forming conference in 1784. In the words of the bishops, the new discipline "method-

ized" the material in a more acceptable and easy manner. See the revised edition of Robert Emory's *History of the Discipline of the Methodist Episcopal Church*, New York: Carlton and Porter, 1856), 87-88.

3. For more information on this, see James D. Lynn's "The Concept of the Ministry in the Methodist Episcopal Church, 1784-1844," (PhD diss., Princeton Theological Seminary, Ann Arbor, MI:UMI, 1973), 28-79.

4. Pilmoor, *Journal*, 29.

5. *Asbury's Journal*, 1:283.

6. Ibid., 1:311.

7. Raymond Cowan captured the tension in Methodist discipline as it related to rules and spiritual growth. "The inward life provided the motivation; one's behavior was its expression; and the rules provided formal structure to the group who shared those common elements. While the structure thus created could provide a matrix within which the divine-human encounter could occur more easily, [Wesley] did not believe that spiritual life could be generated by subscribing to rules. Maintaining an awareness of that sequence and keeping attention focused on the life rather than the institutional structure was a long and difficult, and ultimately a losing, battle" (Raymond P. Cowan, "The Arminian Alternative: The Rise of the Methodist Episcopal Church, 1765-1850," [PhD diss., University of Iowa, Ann Arbor, MI: UMI, 1991], 101).

8. Arthur Bruce Moss, "Methodism in Colonial America," vol. 1 in *The History of American Methodism*, gen. ed. Emory Stevens Bucke (Nashville, TN: Abingdon, 1964), 117. "Individual membership tickets (sometimes called 'love-feast tickets') were issued to certify members in good standing. These credentials were necessary for admission to the meetings and services restricted to society members. The ticket bore the name of the member, the date of issuance, and the personal endorsement of the preacher in charge. The tickets were renewed quarterly."

9. For a detailed explanation of the organization and function of American classes, see John Atkinson's *The Class Leader. His Work and How to Do it: With Illustrations of Principles, Needs, Methods, and Results* (New York: Nelson & Phillips, 1875).

10. MEC, *The Doctrines and Disciplines of the Methodist Episcopal Church in America with Explanatory Notes by Thomas Coke and Francis Asbury*. Facsimile Edition. ed. Frederick Norwood (Evanston, IN: Academy Books, 1979), 67.

11. Michael George Nickerson, "Sermons, Systems, and Strategies: The Geographic Expansion into New York State, 1788-1810," (PhD diss., Syracuse University. Ann Arbor, MI: UMI, 1988), 108.

12. Barclay, *Methodist History*, 1:71. For a good summary of the organization of colonial Methodism, see Moss' commentary on the structure of colonial Methodism (Moss, "Methodism in Colonial America," 115-120).

13. George Hunter, *The Apostolic Congregation: Church Growth Reconceived for a New Generation* (Nashville, TN: Abingdon, 2009), 5-27.

14. Ibid., 13.

15. Local preachers did not itinerate. Many were ordained. Located preachers were circuit riders who stopped itinerating. Usually, they stopped because they got married or became too frail to ride the circuit. Located preachers kept their ordination but forfeited their conference membership. Local preachers did not have a conference membership.

16. For a detailed analysis of this process, see John Caldwell's "The Methodist Organization of the United States, 1784-1844: An Historical Geography of the Methodist Episcopal Church from Its Formation to Its Division," (PhD diss., University of Oklahoma, Ann Arbor, MI: UMI, 1982); and Michael Nickerson's "Sermons, Systems, and Strategies," 1988).

17. Garrettson, *American Methodist Pioneer*, 54.

18. For more information on this, see Cowan, "The Arminian Alternative."

19. Garrettson, *American Methodist Pioneer*, 135.

20. Lee, *Short History*, 223. At a Virginia conference in 1786, "A proposal was made for preachers to go to Georgia, and if any one felt freedom to offer themselves as missionaries for that service." In 1785, two Methodists were sent as missionaries to Nova Scotia. "At the close of the revolutionary war, some of the Methodists had gone to Nova Scotia and settled in the British province, and were longing and praying for labourers to be sent into that part of the Lord's vineyard" (Lee, *Short History*, 111).

21. Lee, *Short History*, 121.

22. Thomas Coke, *The Journal of Dr. Thomas Coke*. ed. John Vickers (Nashville, TN: Kingswood Books, 2005), 57.

23. *Asbury's Journal*, 1:407.

24. On the frontier, the distinction between society and class often blurred because of the low population density.

25. Lee, *Short History*, 135. "The circuit that was formerly called Augusta was divided, and the lower part was now called Richmond, and the upper part Washington."

26. Ibid.

Chapter 5

1. During this period, the colonies existed as separate entities. They were linked together by a common experience and a shared relationship with Great Britain. As the war approached, they were united in a common cause. Even so, each colony guarded its individual identity. During this period, the colonies related to each other like a confederation of independent states. To a certain extent, EAM reflected the national mindset leading up to the Christmas Conference in 1784.

2. Richard Morris, ed., *Encyclopedia of American History* (New York, Harper, 1953), 442.

3. Cappon, *Atlas*, 22-23.

4. Cappon, *Atlas*, 23.

5. German, Dutch, Swedish and French immigration was also widespread but not a significant factor in Methodist growth or decline. Methodism worked with English-speaking populations at this time.

6. Finke and Stark, "Turning Pews into People," 1986; "How the Upstart Sects Won America," 1989; and "The Churching of America," 1992.

7. Pilmoor said that Webb's preaching bore the seal of God's approval even though it was incorrect and highly irregular. Charles Wesley called Webb a loving enthusiast.

8. W. H. Daniels, *The Illustrated History of Methodism in Great Britain and America* (New York: Methodist Book Concern and Phillips & Hunt, 1880), 407.

9. Moss, Methodism in Colonial America, 104.

10. *Asbury's Journal*, 1:60.

11. Ibid., 1:133.

12. Ibid., 1:151 and 180. Asbury's journal is filled with unfavorable remarks about Rankin (cf. *Asbury's Journal*, 1:132, 140, 145, 146, 151, and 180). Asbury reports that Strawbridge and Rodda shared his negative opinion of Rankin.

13. The *Minutes* call this conference "Conversations between the Preachers in Connexion [sic] with The Reverend Mr. John Wesley." The language follows the terminology used in England. Asbury referred to it as a "General Conference" (*Asbury's Journal*, 1:85).

14. *Asbury's Journal*, 1:86.

15. Lee's *History* does not match what the American *Minutes* or Asbury stated (*Asbury's Journal*, 1:85). "Ought not the doctrine and discipline of the Methodists, as con-

tained in the English minutes to be the rule of our conduct . . ." (Lee, *Short History,* 46). It assumed that the rules were in line with scripture and that they accurately reflected biblical standards. This became a point of contention during later controversy.

16. On Nov. 14, 1772, a great multitude came to hear Pilmoor preach in Portsmouth, Virginia. After giving an altar call of sorts, he read the Rules of the Society and required adherence to them in order to join the society. Only 27 affiliated. (Pilmoor, *Journal,* 162.)

17. Thomas Taylor, "Rev. and Very Dear Sir," New York, April 11, 1768, quoted in Nathan Bangs, *A History of the Methodist Episcopal Church,* 12th ed. vol. 1 (New York: Carlton & Porter, 1860), 55-56.

18. *Asbury's Journal,* 1:41.

19. Ibid., 1:28, 31, 35, 46, 75, 84, 86, 117, 118, 127, 146, 160, 161, and 165.

20. Ibid., 1:31.

21. Ibid., 1:28.

22. Ibid., 1:165.

23. Ibid., 1:86.

24. Ibid., 1:146-147.

25. Ibid., 1:28.

26. Ibid., 1:84.

27. According to Barclay, "One of the great services rendered by the British missionaries in America consisted in regularizing the Methodist Societies: they gave American Methodism a pattern of growth that determined the form of its future development. They brought connectionalism into widely separated beginnings. The purely local character of the Societies at New York and in Maryland ended with the coming of Robert Williams, John King, and Francis Asbury. Wesley had no other thought or expectation than that Methodism in America would develop in accordance with the blueprint he had wrought out in Great Britain: the itinerancy, a closely knit system of Classes, Bands, and Societies, with a highly centralized authoritative administration functioning through Annual Conferences composed exclusively of preachers–the complete cellular structure existing within the Church of England. Conditions of origin and environment in the colonies, so different from those in England, during the first few years threatened to prevent the development of this pattern. Thanks to the faithful, zealous work of Wesley's missionaries. . . . Without them the Societies in New York and in Maryland within a few years would have been absorbed by the previously existing, environing forms of American Protestantism" (Barclay, *Early American Methodism 1769-1844, To Reform the Nation.* vol. 2 of *History of Methodist Missions* [New York: The Board of Missions and Church Extensions of the Methodist Church], 50-51.

Robert Williams was more than a local preacher who came to America with Wesley's consent. Goss states, "Thus the place usually assigned Mr. Williams in history, of being a mere local preacher, of coming to this country of his own accord, and succeeding Boardman and Pilmoor, does him great injustice. He was the first regular Methodist itinerant to this country" (C. C. Goss, Statistical History of the First Century of American Methodism with a Summary of the Origin and Present Operations of Other Denominations [New York: Carton & Porter, 1866], 39). Before coming to America, he was a member of the Irish Conference. In 1769, Wesley gave Williams a permit to preach in America, though he was not appointed to America. He landed in Norfolk in 1769. Immediately upon disembarking he began to preach. On October 1, 1769, he handed out a love feast ticket in New York before the other missionaries arrived. Later, he returned to Norfolk with William Watters in 1772. Soon, they met up with Pilmoor who traveled through that area. On November 14, 1772, Pilmoor formed a society of 27 persons in Portsmouth. A few days later he began a society in Norfolk with 26 people. None of this was associated with Strawbridge. Afterward, he continued his preaching tour to the south and left the fledgling work to Williams and Watters. By 1773, Williams was laboring with Devereux

Jarratt in that great revival that consumed south-central Virginia and the adjacent portions of North Carolina. William Sweet gives a full account of this in *Virginia Methodism*, 51-59. Also, Joseph Wakeley fills in many details in his *Lost Chapters Recovered from the Early History of American Methodism* (1858; repr., Danvers, MA: General Books LLC, 2009), 107-110.

28. Lee, *Short History*, 25.
29. Barclay, *Methodist Missions*, 1:23.
30. Daniels, *Illustrated History*, 377.
31. Ibid., 378.
32. Moss, "Methodism in Colonial America," 112.
33. Daniels, *Illustrated History*, 424.
34. MEC, *Minutes* (1813), 5.
35. *Asbury's Journal*, 1:11.
36. However, he did drive home the rule that was made with particular reference to the Mid-Atlantic societies. "The old Methodist doctrine and discipline shall be enforced and maintained amongst all our societies in America. No person shall be admitted, more than once or twice, to our love feasts or society meetings, without becoming a member. Any preacher who acts otherwise, cannot be retained amongst us as a fellow-labourer in the vineyard" (*Asbury's Journal*, 1:85).
37. *Asbury's Journal*, 1:60.
38. "The Ministerial Office," in Wesley, *Works* 7:273-281.
39. Wesley said that the New Testament term επίσκοπος (episcopos) does not imply a third order of ordained ministry. Rather, in the early church, a bishop was a pastor.
40. Abel Stevens, *History of the Methodist Episcopal Church in United States of America*. Vol 1. (New York, NY: Carlton & Porter, 1866). http://wesley.nnu.edu/wesleyctr/books/0201-0300/stevens/0216-112.htm (accessed August 1, 2012).
41. Barclay, *Methodist Missions*, 2:22.
42. Ibid., 22-23.
43. *Asbury's Journal*, 1:10.
44. Ibid.
45. Ibid., 1:16.
46. Ibid., 1:14.
47. For the complete text of this letter, see Bangs, *A History of the MEC*, 52-59.
48. Ibid., 52-58.
49. See Wesley, *Works* 13:367. Additionally, on August 1, 1769, Wesley says, "We have a pressing call from our brethren at New York, who have built a preaching-house, to come over and help them." He expounds on this in his journal entry for that day (Wesley, *Works* 3:374). Also, he expands on the basic text in his *Short History of the People Called Methodists* (Wesley, *Works* 13:367-368). When this quotation is compared to the quotations in the Wesleyan *Minutes* and his journal, one will notice that a section is added that references Philadelphia and the immigration of Methodists from Europe. The *Short History of the People Called Methodist* was written in 1781. At the time of the Conference in Leeds (1769), Wesley did not know about the work in Philadelphia. His information was taken from a letter that he received from Thomas Taylor (T. T.) from New York in which T. T. explains the situation in New York and asks for preachers. Wesley did not find out about the work in Philadelphia until Pilmoor sent him a letter about it on his arrival to the colonies. Captain Webb organized that society.
50. John Lednum, *A History of the Rise of Methodism* (Philadelphia: John Lednum, 1862), 32. Lednum gave some inadvertent insight into Embury's abilities. He said that "he did not possess a scintillating genius" and "Such abilities as he possessed as a preacher would not attract a congregation at this day in New York."

51. Ironically, soon after the missionary preachers arrived, Embury disappeared from the scene. He moved to Camden, New York, where he organized a small society (Potts, "Methodism in Colonial America," 78). Barbara Heck and her family accompanied him there along with Peter Switzer, Mr. Ashton, and others from the New York society (Ledum, *Rise of Methodism*). In 1774, they relocated to Canada (Daniels, *Illustrated History*, 383). Perhaps they were Loyalists.

52. In 1772, Asbury complained, "Was much distressed on account of so few preachers well qualified for the work, and so many who are forward to preach without due qualifications" (*Asbury's Journal*, 1:92).

53. Lee, *Short History*, 39-40.

54. John Atkinson, *Memorials of Methodism in New Jersey*. 2nd ed. (Philadelphia: Perkinpine and Higgins, 1860), 65-66. "As New Jersey lies between these two cities [New York and Philadelphia], and its upper territory is close adjacent to the former, and its southern to the latter city, it is to be presumed that those earnest pioneers of Methodism would not long prosecute their mission without carrying their message of mercy to its inhabitants. Accordingly, we find Captain Webb preaching justification by faith in the town of Burlington as early as the year 1770" (Atkinson, *Memorials*, 28).

55. Moss, "Methodism in Colonial America," 117. He determined the circuits by mapping Asbury's travels. Also the 1776 *Minutes* lists the New Jersey work. However, the above listed circuit boundaries do not account for the fact that New Jersey was listed as its own circuit in the *Minutes*, with two circuit riders appointed to it.

56. Interestingly, the numerical returns in the *Minutes* never distinguish between the New Jersey circuits. During this time, the membership in the state is reported as if it consisted of a single circuit.

57. *Asbury's Journal*, 1:31.

58. Ibid., 1:32.

59. Ibid., 1:137.

60. Ibid., 1:183.

61. Ibid., 1:184.

62. Lee, *Short History*, 42. Wealthy people could come at any time, but were accustomed only to attending worship on the Sabbath. They resisted midweek preaching services.

63. Ibid., 84.

64. Many church growth scholars categorize a general revival as a spiritual factor (cf. McGavran, *Understanding Church Growth*, 6). Since it is difficult to qualify and quantify spiritual factors, this study categorizes general revivals as contextual factors.

65. Wesley Gewehr, *The Great Awakening in Virginia, 1740-1790* (Durham, NC: Duke University Press, 1965), 117. Gewehr shows that the revival among the Baptist stopped in 1775.

66. Robert B. Semple *History of the Rise and Progress of the Baptists in Virginia*, ed. G. W. Beale (1810; repr., Richmond, VA: Pitt and Dickinson, 1894). He traces the history of early Virginia Baptists by local associations and uses their reports to substantiate what he writes.

67. Iain H. Murray, *Revival and Revivalism: The Making and Marring of American Evangelicalism* (Carlisle, PA: The Banner of Truth Trust, 1994), 66-68.

68. For more information on this significant priest, consult Jarratt Devereux, *The Life of the Reverend Devereux Jarratt, Rector of Bath Parish, Dinwiddie County, Virginia, Written by Himself to the Rev. John Coleman* (1806; repr., New York: Amo Press, 1969). The name of Jarratt's parish was Bath, in Dinwiddie County. In December 1790, Virginia created Bath County. Bath County and Bath are in different locations. Bath County was the site of a later revival. See, John Clements, *Flying the Colors: Virginia Facts* (Dallas, TX: Clements Research, 1991); and Michael F. Doran, *Atlas of County Boundary Chang-*

es in Virginia 1634-1895 (San Bernardino, CA: Borgo Press, 1987). Virginia county boundaries changed as the state aged. Most became smaller. Others changed names.

69. Asbury's Journal, 1:207f.
70. Ibid., 1:208.
71. Ibid., 1:209.
72. Ibid.
73. Ibid., 1:207f.
74. Ibid., 1:211 and Lee, *Short History*, 56.
75. Hilde Heun Kagan, *The American Heritage Pictorial Atlas of United States History* (New York: American Heritage Book, 1966), 86.
76. William Payne, "Religious Community in a Cuban Refugee Camp: Bringing Order out of Chaos," in *Missiology 25*, no. 2 (1997):141.
77. For more information of liminality and religion see Ralph H. Turner, *Ritual Process: Structure and Anti-Structure* (Chicago, IL: Aldine, 1969). Many authors have applied this theory to various contexts to show its usefulness as an interpretive model.
78. Some studies on revivalism have attempted to show the correlation between social disruption and the increase of revival. For example, J. Edwin Orr argues that religious apathy, French deism, the unsettled state of society in the years following the Revolutionary War, the changing social conditions of America, the lure of the western frontier, the rugged individualism of the frontiersman, the break-up of family, and alienation from church due to migration were contextual factors that contributed to the great revival of the 1790s (J. Edwin Orr, *The Eager Feet: Evangelical Awakenings, 1790-1830* [Chicago: Moody Press, 1975], 7). Many of the same factors also apply to Virginia and North Carolina during the revival in the 1770s.

Chapter 6

1. This book has not distinguished between north and south in an exact way because the Maryland growth area blurs those categories during this period. It was a border region that existed in the South but had some northern traits. However, the sectional crisis of 1779 and 1780 demonstrated EAM's self-understanding of those terms.
2. *Asbury's Journal*, 1:346.
3. No circuit memberships are listed for 1778 in the *Minutes*. However, appointments to circuits were listed. New Jersey was the only Mid-Atlantic circuit to receive a traveling preacher. Twenty-eight were appointed to southern circuits.
4. They are Baltimore, Frederick, and Calvert in Maryland and Fairfax and Berkley in Virginia. The *Minutes* group the Fairfax and Berkley circuits with the Maryland circuits.
5. Lee, *Short History*, 55.
6. When the Maryland Conference considered the southern mutiny in April 1780, it stipulated that Virginia Methodism "come no farther north than Hanover circuit" (*Asbury's Journal*, 1:347). Hanover is halfway between Fairfax in northeast Virginia and the southern border of Virginia.
7. In order to understand how the war affected demographics and church growth, one needs to document where the fighting occurred. This section is dependent on the *Atlas of Early American History* (Cappon 1976), the *Atlas of American History* (Robert Ferrell [New York: Facts of Life, Inc., 1987]), *The Encyclopedia of American Facts and Dates* (Gordon Carruth and Associates, eds, [New York: Harper & Row Publishers, Inc., 1987]), and Morris' *Encyclopedia of American History* for that information. Also, the United States Military Academy maintains digitized maps of every battle and campaign of the Revolutionary War. They are available at http://www.emersonkent.com/map_

achive/american_ revolution_map.htm (accessed August 1, 2012). Since this summary is a compilation of many sources and is common knowledge, individual references would be cumbersome and distracting.

8. In November 1775, the British governor of Virginia issued a proclamation promising freedom to any slave of a rebel who joined the British cause. About 300 were organized into an "Ethiopian" brigade. In New England, African slaves and freedmen fought on the side of the Patriots. Approximately, 5,000 African Americans fought during the Revolutionary War. See http://www.nps.gov/revwar/about_the_revolution/african_americans.html (accessed August 1, 2012).

9. *Asbury's Journal*, 1:181.
10. Lee, *Short History*, 62.
11. Garrettson, *American Methodist Pioneer*, 68.
12. Bangs, *A History of the MEC*, 118.
13. *Asbury's Journal*, 1:183.
14. Ibid., 1:184.
15. Bangs, *A History of MEC*, 118-119.
16. Lee, *Short History*, 62.
17. Ibid., 63.
18. Garrettson, *American Methodist Pioneer*, 64.
19. *Asbury's Journal*, 1:346.
20. In the 1777 *Minutes*, Spraggs was appointed to Frederick, Maryland. After 1777, Spraggs disappeared from the *Minutes*. On March 9, 1778, Asbury notes that Spraggs worked the upper circuit. Evidently, he was in hiding with Asbury in Delaware. On the 10th, he and George Shadford departed Delaware. Shadford returned to England. Nothing more is heard of Spraggs until 1783.
21. Wakeley, *Lost Chapters*, 577.
22. Ibid., 275.
23. "Most of the Churches in the city being closed or converted into barracks, must have greatly increased the congregation at the Methodist preaching-house and this vastly increased their public collections. This is the only way I can account for their magnitude. They were much larger during the war than before or after" (Wakeley, *Lost Chapters*, 287).
24. According to Abel Stevens, Spraggs received $300 per year while in New York City, the largest salary of any Methodist preacher during that era. Plus, he did not have to itinerate. He enjoyed a parsonage, prestige, and a settled pastorate. All of this spoiled him. Afterward, the prospect of being a poor itinerant no longer appealed to him. That is why he became an Episcopal rector. See Stevens, *History of the Methodist Episcopal Church in the United States of America*, 420. Also see http://anglicanhistory.org/usa/seabury/ordinations1882.html (accessed August 1, 2012). The record shows that Bishop Seabury ordained Spraggs at Trinity Church in the City of New Haven on Sept 16, 1785.
25. Coen G. Pierson, "Methodism and the Revolution," vol. 1 in *The History of American Methodism*. gen. ed. Emory Stevens Bucke (Nashville, TN: Abingdon, 1964), 183.
26. Even though Maryland did not see actual combat, it was affected by the war. While in Baltimore in March 1776, Asbury reported that the people were greatly alarmed by the report of a man-of-war being near. Many of them were moving out of town (*Asbury's Journal*, 1:179). Six days later he reported that the ship was in the river. Some moved off to avoid fighting, while others began to bear arms (Ibid., 1:186). On August 24, 1777, Asbury said that many left Annapolis (Ibid., 1:245).
27. Lee, *Short History*, 60.
28. The Norfolk circuit reappeared in the 1783 *Minutes*. James Morris was appointed to it. However, it disappeared from the *Minutes* before the 1784 conference. No member-

ship was reported. The MEC attempted to establish other circuits in the Norfolk area. The Isle of Wright was formed in 1782 and reported 366 members in 1783. In the following year, it disappeared from the *Minutes*. At that time, Nansemond appeared in the *Minutes*. It reported 327 members in 1783 and 215 members in 1784.

29. *Asbury's Journal*, 1:302.
30. Lee, *Short History*, 68.
31. Ibid., 77.
32. *Asbury's Journal*, 1:408.
33. Ibid., 1:385.
34. Ibid., 1:387.
35. Lee, *Short History*, 74.
36. Ibid., 77.
37. Ibid., 78.
38. Ibid., 82.
39. *Asbury's Journal*, 1:354 and 1:368.
40. Lee, *Short History*, 84.
41. Ibid., 84-85.
42. Ibid., 85.
43. Ibid., 89. It can be deduced that the above quotations refer to the Virginia growth area for several reasons. First, the Eastern Shore growth area continued to grow in every year except 1780. Plus, it did not have a frontier or thinly settled areas. Second, the Maryland growth area actually declined from 1782 to 1784. It lost 366 members and one preacher. Third, the Mid-Atlantic grew from 1778 through 1783 and it had a growing frontier in Pennsylvania. However, it only increased by one circuit from 1782 to 1784.

Chapter 7

1. For a summary of Baptist persecution in Virginia, see Semple's *History of the Rise and Progress of the Baptists in Virginia.*
2. Gewehr, *Great Awakening in Virginia,* 137. "From the religious standpoint, the principal reason for the check in the Baptist movement was due to the fact that another strongly evangelical group became heir to the revival."
3. Sweet, *Virginia Methodism*, 119-137.
4. Sandra Rennie, "Virginia's Baptist Persecution, 1765-1778," vol. 12 in *The Journal of Religious History,* no. 1 (June 1982): 48-61.
5. Gewehr, *Great Awakening in Virginia.*
6. *Asbury's Journal,* 1:236.
7. Ibid., 1:267.
8. Ibid., 1:335.
9. Garrettson, *American Methodist Pioneer*, 100.
10. *Asbury's Journal*, 1:301, 316-317.
11. Ibid., 1:308.
12. Lee, *Short History,* 74-75.
13. *Asbury's Journal,* 1:340.
14. Ibid., 1:318. Caroline County is in on the Eastern Shore of Maryland. It should not be confused with the Caroline county in Virginia.
15. Ibid., 1:340. Many early American Methodist preachers demonstrated a persecution complex. Asbury is an example. Repeatedly, he noted that bad things happened to those who persecute Methodists. He believed that God judged on the Methodist behalf. The following Asbury quotation illustrates this: "I do not recollect an instance of one

preacher that has been thus treated, that something distressing has not followed his persecutors; it may not be for the preacher's holiness, but rather the cause of God which the Eternal vindicates" (Ibid., 1:404). Garrettson also believed that God was on the side of the Methodists. In April 1779, a sheriff came to arrest him. He told the sheriff that if he touched him he would be touching the Lord's anointed. The sheriff was afraid to arrest him (*American Methodist Pioneer*, 78). In July, another sheriff met him and intended to put him in jail. Garrettson told him, "I am going on the Lord's errand, and if you have power, here I am, take me; but remember, that the God against whom you are fighting, who made yonder sun is just now looking down upon you; and I know not but that he will crush you to the earth if you persist in fighting so furiously against him. . . . The consequences of you stopping me in this manner will be rueful" (89). The sheriff quickly relented. Six months later, while being carried to jail, Garrettson recounted a story to the "keeper of the peace." He reminded him of the judge in Talbot County who sentenced itinerant Joseph Hartley to jail. Asbury mentions the same episode (cf. *Asbury Journal*, 1:316). Because of his wicked deed, God struck him in his sleep. Before he died, he sent for the Methodist preacher, begged forgiveness, and asked him to do his funeral. Also, he told his family to follow the Methodists. Then he died. After relating the story, Garrettson told the justice to "think seriously of what you have done, and prepare to meet God." At that moment a rogue flash of lightning struck. Immediately, the justice and all his escorts fled and he was left alone to ponder the situation (*American Methodist Pioneer*, 96-97).

16. Lee, *Short History*, 77.

17. Jeffrey Williams, *Religion and Violence in Early American Methodism: Taking the Kingdom by Force* (Bloomington, IN: Indiana University Press, 2010), 188 n 65.

18. According to Jeffrey Williams, "American Methodists who would not participate in or condone the Revolution rejected Wesley's conflation of the Christian religious battle with armed political conflict. American Methodists refused to read the political conflict through the lens of their battles against evil. American Methodists constructed an inverse relationship between the two forms of warfare. They emphasized that their participation in the battle leading to spiritual liberty left them with little interest in the military struggle for liberty's political correlate. These Methodists insisted that war distracted them from their greater battle for salvation" (*Religion and Violence*, 42).

19. *Asbury's Journal*, 3:29-30. Asbury said that sickness and a high rate of mortality contributed to the growth of Methodism in the New Jersey area during this time. It made people more concerned with their need for religion and it countered the apathy caused by peace with England and prosperity (Ibid., 3:30).

20. Ibid., 3:31.

21. Ibid., 3:31.

22. *Asbury's Journal*, 1:344.

23. Ibid., 1:372.

24. Ibid., 1:379.

25. Ibid., 1:344.

26. Ibid., 1:393.

27. Ibid., 1:458.

28. Ibid., 1:4:71.

29. Garrettson, *American Methodist Pioneer*, 138. The quotation continues, "[She] earnestly prayed to the Lord to shew [sic] her his will. One night after she had thus prayed, she went to bed, and not long after her eyes were closed in sleep, she thought she saw our dear Lord with his arms extended and an infant presented to baptism. Some time after this, in the state of Vermont, she had an opportunity of hearing the Methodists, who, she immediately perceived, preached the same doctrine which the Lord had taught her; and she had never before met with a people with whom she could join."

30. David Benedict, *A General History of the Baptist Denomination in America, and Other Parts of the World* (London: Lincoln & Edmands, 1813). http://www.reformedreader.org/history/benedict/baptistdenomination/overview.htm (accessed August 1, 2012).

31. William Warburton was bishop of Gloucester. In 1762 he published his *Doctrine of Grace* (Farmington Hills, MI: GaleEcco Print Edition, 2010) directed against John Wesley's views (*Asbury's Journal*, 1:340n).

32. *Asbury's Journal*, 3:28.
33. *Asbury's Journal*, 1:322.
34. Ibid., 1:437.
35. Ibid., 1:356.
36. Lee, *Short History*, 83.
37. *Asbury's Journal*, 1:362.
38. Ibid., 1:443.
39. Ibid., 1:302.
40. See *Asbury's Journal*, 1:334-336 for more examples of "funeral evangelism."

Chapter 8

1. MEC, *Minutes* (1813), 20. In 1779, the northern conference voted that Asbury should be the general assistant in America. His authority was limited to "Hearing every preacher for and against what is in debate, the right of determination shall rest with him according to the Minutes" (Ibid., 20). In 1782, the conference unanimously chose Asbury to act according to Wesley's original appointment, and preside over the American conferences and the whole work (Ibid., 37). It was not until December 1783 that a letter from Wesley designated Asbury to that position. All the preachers were directed to submit to his authority (*Asbury's Journal*, 1:450).

2. Russell Richey, Kenneth Rowe, and Jean Schmidt, *The Methodist Experience in America: A Sourcebook*. vol. 2 (Nashville, TN: Abingdon Press, 2000), 64. This source includes the minutes from the southern conference.

3. For a helpful discussion on this, see Jorgen Thaarup's "Three Types of Authority within the Leadership of the United Methodist Church" (London, UK: The Europe Methodist Council Committee on Theology Meeting in London, January 2004). http://www.metodistkyrkan.se/utbildningen/pdf/2009_Authority.pdf (accessed August 1, 2012).

4. J. J. Prats and the Historical Marker Database. *The "Regular" Methodist Conference* (Springfield, VA, 2009). http://www.hmdb.org/marker.asp?marker=16917 (accessed August 1, 2012).

5. Lee, *Short History*, 69-70. James O'Kelly, one of the participants in the conference and the father of Republican Methodism, states that the inspiration and leader for the ordination movement was John Dinkins. According to O'Kelly, Dinkins determined that a Presbyterian form of government was the biblical form. He contended that John Wesley argued for this. James O'Kelly, *The Author's Apology for Protesting Against the Methodist Episcopal Government* (Richmond, VA: John Dixon, 1798).

6. *Asbury's Journal*, 1:350.
7. Ibid., 1:441.
8. For a good discussion on this, see Frederick Norwood, *The Story of American Methodism*. (Nashville, TN: Abingdon, 1974), 90-93.
9. MEC, *Minutes* (1813), 25. Immediately following the unification, Asbury took the slavery cause to the South. While in Virginia in June 1780 he wrote, "I spoke to some select friends about slave-keeping but they could not bear it: this I know, God will plead the cause of the oppressed, though it gives offense to say so here. O Lord, banish the

infernal spirit of slavery from thy dear Zion" (*Asbury's Journal,* 1:355). Later he invited a black man to preach to a white congregation. He said that they listened with attention. After the 1783 conference in Virginia, Asbury reported that all agreed in the spirit of African liberty (*Asbury's Journal,* 1:441).

10. Lee, *Short History,* 72. In 1785, while at conference in North Carolina, Coke spoke out strongly against slavery and agitated some of the people there. Lee rebuked Coke for his harsh words. Afterward, Coke objected to Lee's character (*Asbury's Journal,* 1:487n).

11. *Asbury's Journal,* 1:414-415.
12. Ibid., 1:425.
13. Lee, *Short History,* 57.
14. MEC, *Minutes* (1813), 47.
15. *Asbury's Journal,* 1:380 "Rode that evening . . . where a watch-night was held by brothers Finney, Bailey, and Foster. I spoke to our brethren upon a firm and lasting union; it was opposed. . . . It began to be a doubt with me whether I should leave Virginia until conference." None of the above mentioned preachers appear on the pledge list (MEC, *Minutes* [1813], 28).
16. *Asbury's Journal,* 1:424.
17. Ibid., 1:425.
18. Lee, *Short History,* 73.
19. *Asbury's Journal,* 1:300 and 1:423.
20. Their names are listed in *Asbury's Journal,* 1:381.
21. Wesley sent a letter that put Asbury in charge. All the preachers were directed to submit to his authority (*Asbury's Journal,* 1:450 and 460).
22. For a detailed account of Glendinning's visions, his struggles with Satan, and his conflict with Asbury, see Jeffrey Williams, *Religion and Violence in Early American Methodism,* 84-87.
23. *Asbury's Journal,* 1:355.
24. Ibid., 1:418.
25. MEC, *Minutes* (1813), 37.
26. *Asbury's Journal,* 1:319.
27. Ibid., 1:341.
28. Ibid., 1:345.
29. Ibid., 1:342.
30. Ibid., 1:470.
31. Ibid., 1:352.

Chapter 9

1. Barclay, *Methodist Missions,* 2:74.
2. Thomas Umbel, "The Making of an American Denomination: Methodism in the New England Religious Culture, 1790-1860," (PhD diss., Johns Hopkins University, Ann Arbor, MI: UMI, 1991).
3. Wesley, *Works* 8:251-252.
4. According to Wesley, the distinction in function occurred as a product of corruption and natural evolution. The distinction dates back to the time of Constantine (Wesley, *Works* 7:273-281). A bishop was the pastor of a local, independent congregation that was in communion with all other churches of Christ. In the New Testament period, they were under the authority of the apostles in a loose way. The Church at Jerusalem and the Council of Jerusalem illustrate this.
5. Wesley, *Works* 8:252.

6. When Coke arrived, he spoke to John Dickens about Wesley's letter and his plan. According to Coke (*Journal*, 37), Dickens highly approved of it and wanted Coke to publish it because the preachers most earnestly longed for it. Coke says that Dickens pressed him to make it public because Wesley had determined the point, and therefore it was not to be investigated, but complied with. Dickens participated in the Fluvanna Conference and pushed for the ordination of the itinerants without Wesley's approval. Since the plan ratified the action of the Fluvanna Conference, Dickens greatly favored it and would want it published. Coke was the one who argued that the Christmas Conference had to obey the order.

7. MEC, *Minutes* (1813), 51.

8. This quote was altered from the original text. The earliest editions of the 1785 *Discipline* did not contain the word bishop. They read, "We will form ourselves into an Episcopal Church, under the direction of Superintendents, Elders, Deacons, and Helpers, according to the forms of ordination annexed to our Liturgy, and the form of discipline set forth in these Minutes" (MEC, *The General Minutes of the Conferences* [1786], 323). At the Christmas Conference, Coke argued that a superintendent was a functional bishop. His many sermons at the conference referred to the office of bishop. It is likely that many people began to call Asbury and Coke bishop at that time. However, neither the Christmas Conference nor Wesley designated Coke and Asbury as bishops.

While revising the *Discipline* in 1787, Coke and Asbury changed the word superintendent to bishop. Section IV was called "On the constituting of Bishops, and their Duty" (MEC, *The General Minutes of the Conferences.* [1787], 6). This became a point of contention. According to Lee, "In the course of this year [1787], Mr. Asbury reprinted the general minutes [i.e., the *Discipline*]; but in a different form from what they were in before. . . . The third question in the second section, and the answer, read thus. Q. Is there any other business to be done in conference? A. The electing and ordaining of Bishops, Elders and Deacons. This was the first time that our Superintendents ever gave themselves the title *Bishops* in the minutes. They changed the title themselves without the consent of the conference; and at the next conference they asked the preachers if the word *Bishop* might stand in the minutes; seeing that is was a scripture name, and the meaning of the word *Bishop*, was the same with that of *Superintendent*" (Lee, *Short History*, 128).

It was not Wesley's desire that Asbury and Coke be bishops. He preferred "general superintendent" because the term "bishop" was packed with a historical, ecclesiastical, and theological bias that Wesley rejected. In a letter to Asbury in 1788, Wesley wrote, "How dare you suffer yourself to be called Bishop? I shudder, I start at the very thought! Men may call me a knave or a fool, a rascal, a scoundrel, and I am content; but they shall never by my consent call me Bishop! For my sake, for God's sake, for Christ's sake put a full end to this!" (*Asbury's Journal*, 3:65).

9. Emory, *History of the Discipline*, 23-25 and John Tigert, *The Making of Methodism: Studies in the Genesis of Institutions* (Nashville, TN: Publishing House of MEC South, 1898), 93.

10. Emory's *History of the Discipline*, 22-77 contains a copy of the 1785 *Discipline*.

11. MEC, *Form of Discipline* (1787), 13.

12. Ibid., 35.

13. MEC, *Form of Discipline* (1786), 324.

14. Ibid., 324.

15. MEC, *Form of Discipline* (1787), 21.

16. Ibid., 23.

17. Ibid.

18. Ibid., 40.

19. *Asbury's Journal*, 1:481.

20. Williams, "Delmarva Peninsula," 33.

21. Barclay, *Methodist Missions,* 1:124.
22. Coleman, "Factors in Expansion," 83.
23. *Asbury's Journal,* 2:56 and 58.
24. *Asbury's Journal,* 1:481.
25. MEC, *Form of Discipline* (1786), 336.
26. *Asbury's Journal,* 1:461.
27. *Asbury's Journal,* 1:495.

Chapter 10

1. Over three-fourths of Americans were from English-speaking origins in 1790 (Morris, *Encyclopedia,* 445).
2. Martin Gilbert, *American History Atlas* (1968; repr., London: Weidenfield and Nicolson, 1985), 30.
3. U.S. Bureau of the Census, *Historical Statistics,* 25.
4. Ibid., 13.
5. Ibid., 11, 12; Gilbert, *American History Atlas,* 30; and Cappon, *Atlas,* 67.
6. The facts come from a population density map for 1790 in Cappon's *Atlas,* 65.
7. U.S. Bureau of the Census, *Historical Statistics,* 12.
8. Cappon, *Atlas,* 102.
9. For census data for 1790 through 1810, see https://www.census.gov/history/www/reference/maps/centers_of_population.html (accessed August 1, 2012). The 1790 data differs from Cappon's table.
10. See www.census.gov/dmd/www/resapport/states/kentucky.pdf (accessed August 1, 2012).
11. The terms emigrate and immigrate are easily confused. One emigrates from a location and immigrates to a location. Migration refers to relocating from one place to another.
12. Samuel S. Hill Jr., *The South and the North in American Religion* (Athens, GA: University of Georgia, 1980), 36.
13. Coleman, "Factors in the Expansion," 146.
14. *Asbury's Journal,* 1:514.
15. Ibid., 1:515.
16. Lee, *Short History,* 120.
17. *Asbury's Journal,* 1:567.
18. Ibid., 1:593n.
19. See William Williams, *The Garden of American Methodism: The Delmarva Peninsula 1769-1820* (Wilmington, DE: Scholarly Resources Inc., 1984), and *Asbury's Journal,* 2:11.
20. *Asbury's Journal,* 2:214.
21. Ibid., 2:160.
22. Ibid., 2:280.
23. Cappon, *Atlas,* 97.
24. Morris, *Encyclopedia,* 508.
25. Ibid.
26. Bangs, *A History of MEC,* 1:79.
27. Morris, *Encyclopedia,* 111.
28. David Ramsay, *Ramsay's History of South Carolina* (Newberry, SC: W. J. Duffie, 1858), 235-238.
29. Morris, *Encyclopedia,* 508 and Ramsay, *South Carolina,* 240.

30. Ramsay, *South Carolina,* 249. The cotton gin is a machine that removes seeds from cotton fibers. Versions of the cotton gin reached America from India in the 1740s. In 1793, Eli Whitney's cotton gin became widely used in America. Its larger gins could process fifty times more cotton in a day than fifty people working by hand. This made cotton a cash crop.

31. *Asbury's Journal,* 1: 612.

32. *Asbury's Journal,* 2:77, 2:81, and 2:175.

33. *Asbury's Journal,* 1:581

34. Ibid., 1:608.

35. *Asbury's Journal,* 2:75.

36. The relationship between a lack of institutional funding and the number of traveling preachers in EAM is very complicated. In addition to money, a cluster of other factors determined the numerical strength of the traveling preachers, e.g., internal politics, illness, family issues, ineffective training, epidemics, personality conflicts, burn-out, disappointing appointments, and death. In 1790, Asbury wrote, "The work of God in our view has suffered for want of labourers, many sick, disabled, dispirited and dead" (*Asbury's Journal,* 2:90).

37. MEC, *Minutes* (1813), 76.

38. In 1786, a yearly collection of £182 was raised to help pay the deficiency. Another £54 was raised to support missionaries (MEC, *Minutes* [1813], 61).

39. MEC, *Form of Discipline* (1787), 40-41.

40. MEC, *Minutes* (1813), 68.

41. Ibid., 71.

42. Ibid., 96.

43. *Asbury's Journal,* 1:631.

44. MEC, *The General Conferences of the Methodist Episcopal Church from 1792 to 1896* (Cincinnati, OH: Curts and Jennings, 1900), 14.

45. Ibid., 15-16.

46. *Asbury's Journal,* 3:130.

47. Ibid., 2:109.

48. MEC, *Journals of the Annual Conference of the Methodist Episcopal Church, 1796-1836.* vol. 1 (New York: Carlton and Phillips, 1855), 20-22.

49. *Asbury's Journal,* 2:92.

50. MEC, *Journals from 1796-1836,* 22.

51. Lee, *Short History,* 250.

52. Ibid., 263.

53. MEC, *Minutes* (1813), 50-238.

54. *Asbury's Journal,* 2:176.

55. MEC, *Journals from 1796-1836,* 34-38.

56. Ibid., 46.

57. *Asbury's Journal,* 3:144.

58. *Asbury's Journal,* 2:474.

59. Ibid., 2:160.

60. MEC, *The Doctrines and Disciplines,* 1979, 79.

61. Morris, *Encyclopedia,* 111; William Sweet, *The Story of Religion in America* (1950; repr., Grand Rapids, MI: Baker Book House, 1973); and Mark Lloyd, "A Rhetorical Analysis of the Preaching of Bishop Francis Asbury," (PhD diss., Michigan State University, Ann Arbor, MI: UMI, 1976).

62. Kagan, *American Heritage,* 117.

63. "The Federalist Papers, considered a political classic and the definitive statement on the principles underlying the United States constitution, appear on the surface the

product of two minds in complete concord about the subject at hand. Indeed, the ratification of the constitution was a goal of absolute importance to both authors, which is why Hamilton called for Madison's help on the project; and why Madison agreed to do it. Both ambitious and brilliant, equally knowledgeable on a wide variety of subjects, Hamilton and Madison sparked immediately when they met in the continental congress in 1783. They agreed that the confederation government was ineffective and were dedicated to creating a system which would solidify the union and make the United States a viable and great nation. On an intellectual level they were perfectly matched; politically, however, they were diametrically opposed. The issue on which they differed was to become the most divisive in American politics: states' rights" (Lisa Marie DeCarolis, "A Biography of Alexander Hamilton [1755-1804]," *From Revolution to Reconstruction - an .HTML project*. [The University of Georgia, 1994]) http://www.let.rug.nl/usa/B/hamilton/hamil22.htm (accessed August 1, 2012).

64. Morris, *Encyclopedia*, 123 and 406.
65. Ibid., 126-127.
66. Ibid., 146-147.
67. By vote of the House of Representatives, Jefferson became President because he and fellow Anti-Federalist, Aaron Burr each had 72 electoral college votes. Jefferson won on the 36th ballot. Adams received 65 electoral college votes. Before the 12th Amendment, each person in the electoral college voted for two people. The tie happened because Jefferson and Burr ran together and continued to receive a vote from the same electors.
68. Morris, *Encyclopedia*, 124.
69. Barclay, *Methodist Missions*, 2:19. Ironically, Hamilton came from a poor family in the West Indies. For all practical purposes, his father abandoned the family when he was young and his mother died when he was 12. He was dependent on the largess of his mother's family. Because of his exceptional abilities, his aunts saved up enough money to send him to King's College (Columbia) in New York.
70. Morris, *Encyclopedia*, 123-124.
71. Barclay, *Methodist Missions*, 2:19.
72. Morris, *Encyclopedia*, 122-123.
73. Ibid., 123.
74. *Asbury's Journal*, 2:45.
75. Ibid. 46.

Chapter 11

1. *Asbury's Journal*, 1:560. The Sussex Circuit grew by 1,203 members from 1787 to 1778.
2. The Surry circuit continued to grow. By 1793, the black membership equaled 955 and outnumbered the white membership. In 1794, the Surry and Sussex circuits were reunited. After the reunion, the black membership withered away. Notwithstanding that decrease, numerical growth continued in Virginia through 1794. By that time, 23 new circuits were added. The new circuits accounted for 9,458 of the 18,186 members in the state.
3. Lee, *Short History*, 129-130.
4. Ibid., 130-131.
5. Ibid., 131-132.
6. Ibid., 133-134.
7. Ibid., 139.

8. *Asbury's Journal*, 1:608.
9. *Asbury's Journal*, 2:247-248.
10. Lee, *Short History*, 146-147.
11. *Asbury's Journal*, 2:76.
12. Lee, *Short History*, 271.
13. Ibid., 273.
14. *Asbury's Journal*, 2: 247-248.
15. Ibid., 2:235.
16. Ibid., 2:250.
17. Ibid., 2:257. Evidently, many of the converted came from New England. Asbury calls them "the sons of the Puritans." Since the Puritan descendants in New England worked to oppose Methodism, Asbury found it ironic that the Puritan migrants blessed the Methodists for their new religion.
18. This point is confusing because circuits were listed in two ways in the *Minutes*. First, membership summaries were listed for every circuit. Second, each itinerant was appointed to a named circuit for the next year. A comparison of the two lists shows that some circuits that received an appointment did not file a membership summary for the following year.
19. *Asbury's Journal*, 2:76.
20. MEC, *Form of Discipline* (1787), 26-27.
21. MEC, *The Doctrines and Disciplines* (1979), 52. "The objection brought by some, that many of the most useful preachers are taken out of the circuits for this purpose [to serve as a presiding elder], whole preaching-talents are thereby lost to the connection."
22. *Asbury's Journal*, 3:164. "Methodism is Union all over; Union in exchange of preachers; Union and exchange of sentiment; Union and exchange of interests; we must draw resources from center to circumference."

Chapter 12

1. Edwin Gaustad, *A Documentary History of Religion in America*, 2nd ed. (Grand Rapids, MI: Eerdmans, 1993), 297. In a personal letter to Adams, Jefferson wrote, "If by *religion*, we are to understand *Sectarian dogmas*, in which no two of them agree, then your explanation on that hypothesis is just, 'that this world would be the best of all possible worlds, if there were no religion in it.' But if the moral precepts, innate in man, and made a part of his physical condition, as necessary for social being, if the sublime doctrines of philanthropism, and deism taught us by Jesus of Nazareth in which all agree, constitute true religion, then, without it, this would be 'something not fit to be named, even indeed a Hell.'"
2. John C. Miller, *The Federalist Era, 1789-1801* (New York, Harper and Row, 1960).
3. Orr, *Eager Feet*, 7. "[Jefferson] was bitterly anticlerical, accusing the clergy or priesthood of selfishness, greed, stupidity, bigotry, dishonesty and the corrupting of the Gospel and pure religion. . . . Their theologians he calls 'crazy theologists' and accuses them of causing the divisions of mankind into sects by their corrupting of natural religion and the pure precepts of Jesus with their 'casuistries'" (John Orr, *English Deism: Its Roots and Its Fruits* [Grand Rapids: MI: Eerdmans Publishing Company, 1934], 214).
4. Sweet, *Religion in America*, 190.
5. Ramsay, *South Carolina*, 240.
6. Barclay, *Methodist Missions*, 2:20.

7. Orr, *Eager Feet,* 7. Besides the influence of the French Republicanism, Orr also mentioned seven other factors that contributed to American apathy – the unsettled state of society following the Revolutionary War, the self-assertive feelings which accompanied independence, the changing social conditions, the lure of the western frontier, the rugged individualism of the frontiersman, and the break-up of family and church relationships due to emigration.
8. Ibid.
9. Miller, *Federalist Era,* (1960).
10. *Asbury's Journal,* 2:256n.
11. Kagan, *American Heritage,* 125.
12. William A. Withington, *Kentucky in Maps* (Lexington, KY: Franklin Geographical Society, 1980), 53.
13. Ramsay, *South Carolina,* 242.
14. Ibid., 242-243.
15. Ibid., 243.
16. Robert Molloy, *Charleston, A Gracious Heritage* (New York: D. Appleton-Century Company, 1947), 82-83.
17. Ibid., 83.
18. *Asbury's Journal,* 1:564.
19. *Asbury's Journal,* 2:40.
20. Ibid., 2:41.
21. Ibid., 2:117.
22. Ibid., 2:116.
23. Ibid., 2:39.
24. Ibid., 2:41.
25. Ibid., 2:78.
26. Ibid., 2:117.
27. Richard Peters, ed., *Public Statutes at Large of the United States of America from the Organization of the Government in 1789, to March 3, 1845.* vol. VIII (Boston: Charles Little and James Brown, 1846), 116-132. Originally published as *Treaty of Amity, Commerce, and Navigation between His Britannic Majesty and the United States of America, by Their President, with the Advice and Consent of their Senate* in 1795.
28. Morris, *Encyclopedia,* 128.
29. Molloy, *Charleston,* 83.
30. Ramsay, *South Carolina,* 240-241.
31. Lee, *Short History,* 126.
32. The conference was willing that Garrettson be set aside for the episcopacy and dispatched to Nova Scotia provided he did not return to America and assume an episcopal relationship in the American connection. About this, Garrettson states, "It was the desire of Mr. Wesley and others, that I should be set apart for the superintendency of the work in Nova Scotia – my mind was divided – man is a fallible creature – In the end I concluded not to leave the states; for thousands in this country are dear to me" (*American Methodist Pioneer,* 133).
33. Lee, *Short History,* 127.
34. Ibid., 126.
35. *Asbury's Journal,* 1:538 and 3:50-51.
36. Lee, *Short History,* 125.
37. *Asbury's Journal,* 3:54.
38. In 1798, O'Kelly claimed the following: "After those days, Francis took with him a few chosen men, and in a clandestine manner expelled John, whose sir-name was Wesley, from the Methodist Episcopal Church. The fourteen preachers were utter strangers to the things that had happened for a reason; till it began to be whispered abroad, and we

then discovered W__'s name was blotted out of the book. This confirmed the report. This cruel act was thought by [Coke] to hasten the death of dear Wesley" (O'Kelly, *Apology*, 12). Other sources do not corroborate O'Kelly's claim. He was not a friend of England or the English Church. His *Apology* against the MEC's episcopal form of government demonstrates this.

39. This is a redacted version of the letter. "There is not a man in the world so obnoxious to the American politicians as our dear old Daddy, but no matter, we must treat him with all the respect we can and that is due to him. . . . We may form a friendly treaty with England, and new model our government to look more like monarchy and aristocracy. Still there will be a jealousy. . . . My real sentiments are union but no subordination, connexion but no subjection. I am sure that no man or number of men in England can direct either the head or the body here unless he or they should possess divine powers, be omnipotent, omniscient and omnipresent. That one thousand preachers traveling and local; and thirty thousand people would submit to a man they never have nor can see, his advice they will follow as far as they judge it right. For our old, old Daddy to appoint conferences when and where he was pleased, to appoint a joint superintendent with me, were strokes of power we did not understand. He told me he would not ask the preachers' consent as to whom he should appoint. What security was left for them, whether he should be a wise man or a fool, a good or a bad man? Who was to remove him but he that appointed him? . . . I believe [Rankin] has got the ear of old Daddy too. He sometimes prates against me with malicious words because I was bold to stay when he like a coward ran away, not only through fear, but hope of gaining preferment in the church or state. . . . When a Continental Captain and other great men informed me Mr. Wesley had written so and so, I told them I wished he had not so written, and I knew not that he had written such books, but be that matter as it would brother Wesley was in England and I was in America. He thought it his duty to support that, and I my duty to support this Government, and altho' I had respected his religious creed, I did not think myself obliged to adopt his political creed. . . . We enjoy real liberty here, no denomination hath any preeminence over another, and I hope never will have. I wish we may all stand on equal ground" (*Asbury's Journal*, 3:62-64).

40. Before the gathering, he notified Whatcoat and told him to meet him for the purpose of being ordained a bishop. Asbury intended to obey Wesley until the conference voted to the contrary.

41. *Asbury's Journal*, 1:745.

42. *Asbury's Journal*, 3:53.

Chapter 13

1. Lee, *Short History*, 149.
2. Ibid., 149-155.
3. "As I sat the table, I opened my mouth and spake after this manner; this council I fear will brake (*sic*.) our union, and not preserve it: One district may receive what another may reject, *etc*. Francis jogged my elbow, and I ceased speaking" (O'Kelly, *Apology*, 15).
4. MEC, *The Doctrines and Disciplines* (1979), 51-52. O'Kelly's commentary on the encountered sheds additional light on it. He stated, "In observing the contents, we discovered a new constitution of a very despotic nature. Nine men could act [the minimum quorum of the Council] as the legislative, but the Bishop had the negative on the Council for time to come" (O'Kelly, *Apology*, 18). O'Kelly continues, "Brother, you know our infant state, grant us one year to consider the matter coming before us. Or, if your refuse this, take away your negative. And if you refuse, I shall as a duty I owe to the Church use mine influence" (Ibid., 18-19).

5. *Asbury's Journal*, 1:620. O'Kelly states that Asbury wrote him back in this manner: "Thy letter greatly alarmed me! But pray, who boldly demands my negative? My negative is my own. I never have received such a check from any preacher in America" (O'Kelly, *Apology*, 19).

6. Ibid., 1:642. As a leading apologist of the Methodist Protestant Church, Drinkhouse, shares much of O'Kelly's criticism. Like O'Kelly, he imbibed the rhetoric of Republicanism. The following quotation reflects the politically tinctured nature of the opposition's sentiment: "Asbury himself, blind to his assumptions of power, thought of nothing, perhaps, but the prudential advantages of [holding many conferences each year]; it saved travel, time, and expense to the preachers, and it rid him of the trouble of the concentration when they were sure to assert their Christian manhood at times, and criticize the methods of their believed but not infallible chief. It was much easier to assign them to their posts besides, a few days' talk together and he read them out, his saddle horse nearby, which he incontinently mounted and was off before even complaint could reach his years, and then at Baltimore the whole Plan of Appointments was finally settled by him and published in the minutes. These preachers – some of whom in person, or in that their fathers, were in the Revolutionary struggle for liberty, which meant the overthrow of the principle, which England had endeavored to fasten upon the colonies (of Passive obedience and Non-resistance) – could not but contrast their new-found freedom in the State with the absolute subjection to the will of one man in the Church, so the murmur, if low, was deep and full of meaning" (Edward Drinkhouse, *History of Methodist Reform, Synoptical of General Methodism, 1703-1899*. vol. 1 [Baltimore, MD: The Board of Publication of the Methodist Protestant Church, 1899], 366-367).

7. "In the evening, the preachers desired my advice on the matter which was to be laid before them on the morrow. I answered them after this manner; Brethren, you know my mind on the subject, and my sorrows have I not hid from you. I judge it best that you assemble yourselves together this night, with prayer: but I will not be with you. Consider it as the cause of your God; divest yourselves of fear of man; give your voice in the fear of God, to the best of your judgment. And it was so, they followed my counsel, and we all met the next morning before the president, in number about twenty-one; if I remember right. The president proposed it as above observed, and we all (except two) with one voice rejected it altogether. Then answered Francis and said, 'ye have all spoken out of one month.' Henceforth, 'ye are all out of the union.' Then, as one in distress, he gathered up his papers; so ended the conference without prayer" (O'Kelly, *Apology*, 22). Note that O'Kelly refers to Asbury as "the president" instead of the bishop.

8. O'Kelly, *Apology*, 23.

9. *Asbury's Journal*, 1:644.

10. James W. May, "From Revival Movement to Denomination: A Re-Examination of the Beginnings of Methodism," (PhD diss., 1962; repr. Columbia University, 1978), 242.

11. *Asbury's Journal*, 1:649.

12. *Asbury's Journal*, 3:99n.

13. Ibid.

14. Ibid., 3:95-96.

15. *Asbury's Journal*, 1:667-668. "I prepared a letter of information for Thomas, who was expected at the Charleston Conference. He came according to expectation, he received my letter, and pleaded my cause in the conference; withstood Francis to the face; condemned his conduct; and (he) being the senior, had a general meeting appointed [general conference] according to our request" (O'Kelly, *Apology*, 29).

16. Coke, *Journal*, 157n.

17. Lee, *Short History*, 159.

18. *Asbury's Journal*, 1:687.

19. May, "Beginnings of Methodism," 253.
20. MEC, *Discipline* (1787), 32-37.
21. Jeremiah Burroughs and Richard Baxter, *The Causes, Evils, and Cures, of Heart and Church Divisions: Extracted from the Works of Burroughs and Baxter*. ed. John Dinkins (New York: Carlton & Phillips, 1855 [1792]).
22. Burroughs and Baxter, *The Causes*, 158.
23. Coke, *Journal*, 147.
24. Charles W. Ferguson, *Methodists and the Making of America* (Austin, TX: Eakin Press, 1983), 175-177.
25. *Asbury's Journal*, 1:686. Asbury said that he did not appoint Hammett because he was an unknown foreigner and he did not acknowledge the authority of the American conference. Also, he never attempted to join it (Ibid., 1:707). Wesley had warned about preachers coming from Europe and stated that they must submit to the authority of the conference or the MEC should not employ them.
26. Ibid., 1:647.
27. *Asbury's Journal*, 3:100. Dickins was the book agent. Willis was an itinerant who had traveled with Asbury. Haskins was a located preacher who wanted a seat in the district conference.
28. Ibid., 3:108.
29. "Minority" referred to preachers from Virginia who would not take their appointments. Somehow, Hammett became associated with these disaffected preachers.
30. *Asbury's Journal*, 3:109.
31. *Asbury's Journal*, 1:675.
32. Ferguson, *Methodists*, 177. "Mr. Hammett had sent abroad circular letters, and had been railing against the presiding eldership, &c. I am not surprised that he should find fault with the office – its duties he was man not likely to fulfill: yet had it not been for the power attached to it, how greatly might Mr. Hammett have confused the society in Charleston, and perplexed the preachers in the district!" (*Asbury's Journal*, 1:716-717).
33. Lee, *Short History*, 207.
34. Ibid.,205-209; *Asbury's Journal*, 1:706n.
35. *Asbury's Journal*, 1:752.
36. Ibid., 1:706.
37. Coke, *Journal*, 230-231.
38. Barclay, *Methodist Missions*, 1:126-127.
39. *Asbury's Journal*, 1:712.
40. Ibid., 1:744.
41. *Asbury's Journal*, 2:4.
42. *Asbury's Journal*, 1:669n.
43. *Asbury's Journal*, 2:6.
44. Lee, *Short History*, 177.
45. *Asbury's Journal*, 1:734.
46. Lee, *Short History*, 178.
47. Ibid., 179.
48. O'Kelly, *Apology*, 29-38.
49. *Asbury's Journal*, 3:114.
50. May, "Beginnings of Methodism," 247. This is the entire text. "As to their literature, if we may judge from their publications, there appears no great display of wisdom therein. Their journals are, for the most part, insipid. They are partly filled with violent attacks on personal and public characters – these are no marks of learning. Their kind of discipline may (perhaps) answer better to the north of this, where the British armies were long suffered to plunder the honest patriots. But when they came to exercise their feloni-

ous practices in Virginia, they were sent back in the degraded situation of prisoners; and I hope that British policy will always meet with the like repulse from our Virginians that the British power has done. Your Bishop Asbury has complained in my hearing that he had more trouble in governing the Virginians than all the connection besides. It is not our superior wisdom, nor ignorance, that renders us so ungovernable; but our invariable determination to stand fast in our civil and religious liberties, 'wherein God hath strangely made us free'" (W. E. MacClenny, *Life of Rev. James O'Kelly - Christian Church in the South - Restoration Movement* [Ann Arbor, MI: Cushing-Malloy, 1950]), http://www.piney.com/RmOKXVII.html (accessed August 1, 2012).

51. By 1797, the regional issue became more acute. In the aftermath of the O'Kelly schism and the continuing debate, some talked about dividing the MEC along sectional lines. Asbury opposed this idea. "[Lee] and every man that thinks properly, will find it will never do to divide the North from the South" (*Asbury's Journal*, 3:164). National unity under a strong episcopacy was a guiding vision of Asbury in his administration of the MEC. In this regard, he reflected Federalist thinking.

52. Lee, *Short History*, 203.
53. Ibid., 204.
54. Ibid., 205.
55. Because of rapid migration to the frontier, Kentucky Methodism did not have a numerical decline until 1796. However, starting in 1793, its membership became static. A. H. Redford implicates the O'Kelly schism. "On inquiry, I found that James Haw, who was one of the first preachers that came to Kentucky, had located and settled in Cumberland, and embraced the view of O'Kelly, and by his influence and address had brought over the traveling and every local preacher but one in the country to his views, and considerable dissatisfaction had obtained in many societies (*The History of Methodism in Kentucky*. vol. 1 *From the Landing of James M'Bride in the District, in 1754, to the Conference of 1808* [Nashville, TN: Southern Methodist Publishing House, 1868], 159). One may assume that the controversy was felt in all the sections of Kentucky and Tennessee at this time.

56. Lee, *Short History*, 203.
57. O'Kelly, *Apology*, 47.
58. David Benedict, *A General History of the Baptist*.
59. Lee, *Short History*, 204.
60. *Asbury's Journal*, 2:228.
61. Ibid., 1:752.
62. Lee, *Short History*, 203-205.
63. *Asbury's Journal*, 1:759.
64. Ibid., 2:155-156.
65. Lee, *Short History*, 255.
66. MEC, *The Doctrines and Disciplines* (1979), 34.
67. Ibid., 42.

Chapter 14

1. Redford, *History of Methodism in Kentucky*, 159.
2. See Coleman, "Factors in Expansion," 146-148. Coleman rightly argues that the spirit of French infidelity and the MEC's need to consolidate the revival growth of preceding years also contributed to numerical loss. Also, see Norwood's *The Story of American Methodism*, 127-129. He incorrectly isolates O'Kelly's losses to Virginia.
3. *Asbury's Journal*, 3:81n.

4. J. H. Spencer, *A History of Kentucky Baptists from 1769 to 1885*, vol. 1 (Cincinnati: J. R. Baumes), 1885. An extensive survey of Baptist histories shows that most ignore membership declines. For example, a great many play up the progress through the early 1790s, remain silent about any declines, and continue with the progress following the Second Great Awakening in 1800. This represents triumphalism and institutional hagiography. In fact, the Baptist did have southern declines in the 1790s that paralleled those of the MEC. Robert Semple's *Baptist in Virginia* clearly points to this. Henry Vedder's *A History of the Baptists in the Middle States* (Philadelphia: American Baptist Publication Society, 1898), 336-337, does include a year-by-year membership analysis of the 1790s. However, it does not list any southern states to include Maryland. According to it, only Delaware declined in the 1790s. Methodism in Delaware also declined from 1794 through 1797. *The Baptist History Homepage* contains over 50 full-text histories. See http://baptisthistoryhomepage.com/ (accessed August 1, 2012).

5. Semple, *Baptists in Virginia*, 232.
6. Ibid., 124.
7. Ibid., 232.
8. Ibid., 258.
9. Ibid., 385.
10. Coleman, "Factors in Expansion," 82-83.
11. *Asbury's Journal*, 3:81n.
12. MEC, *Minutes* (1813), 25.
13. Ibid., 41.
14. Ibid., 47.
15. Barclay, *Methodist Missions*, 2:72.
16. Richard Cameron, "The New Church Takes Root," vol. 1 in *The History of American Methodism*, gen. ed. Emory Stevens Bucke (Nashville, TN: Abingdon, 1964), 253
17. Barclay, *Methodist Missions*, 2:74.
18. Lee, *Short History*, 120.
19. Hill, *South and the North*, 80.
20. Cameron, "The New Church Takes Root," 254.
21. *Asbury's Journal*, 1:488.
22. Barclay, *Methodist Missions*, 2:73.
23. *Asbury's Journal*, 1:489 and Coke, *Journal*, 63.
24. Ibid., 1:498.
25. *Asbury's Journal*, 3:82n.
26. Ibid.
27. Coke, *Journal*, 65.
28. Barclay, *Methodist Missions*, 1:109.
29. Cameron, "The New Church Takes Root," 255.
30. MEC, *Journals from 1796-1836*, (1855), 22.
31. Ibid.
32. Ibid., 37-41.
33. *Asbury's Journal*, 1:582.
34. Ibid.
35. Ibid., 1:615.
36. Ibid., 1:620.
37. *Asbury's Journal*, 2:8.
38. Ibid., 2:46.
39. Ibid., 2:51.
40. Ibid., 2:65.
41. Ibid., 2:62.
42. Ibid., 2:109.

43. Ibid., 2:144.
44. Ibid., 2:7.
45. Ibid., 2:151.
46. *Asbury's Journal*, 3:160.
47. *Asbury's Journal*, 2:143.
48. Ibid., 2:155-156.
49. Ibid., 2:156.
50. Ibid., 2:272.
51. Ferguson, *Methodists*, 206-207.
52. *Asbury's Journal*, 2:281.
53. Ibid., 2:266.
54. Lee, *Short History*, 270.
55. Ibid.
56. Ibid., 270-271.
57. *Asbury's Journal*, 2:129.
58. U.S. Bureau of the Census, *Historical Statistics*, 11-12.
59. Morris, *Encyclopedia*, 508; Ramsay, *South Carolina*, 240.
60. Ramsay, *South Carolina*, 249.
61. Doris Elisabett Andrews, "Popular Religion and the Revolution in the Middle Atlantic Ports: The Rise of the Methodists, 1770-1800," (PhD diss., University of Pennsylvania, Ann Arbor, MI: UMI, 1986), 269-317.
62. Andrews, "Rise of the Methodists," 301.
63. *Asbury's Journal*, 1:497.
64. Ibid., 1:651.
65. Ibid., 1:748.
66. *Asbury's Journal*, 2:280.
67. Ibid., 2:117.
68. Ibid., 2:122.
69. *Asbury's Journal*, 1:540.
70. Ibid., 1:723.
71. Ibid.
72. Ibid.,1:607.
73. *Asbury's Journal*, 2:41.
74. Ibid., 2:241.
75. *Asbury's Journal*, 1:601.
76. MEC, *Form of Discipline* (1788), 35.
77. Andrews, "Rise of the Methodists," 316.
78. Barclay, *Methodist Missions*, 1:126-127.
79. *Asbury's Journal*, 2:242.
80. Preachers no longer had to account for gifts before receiving their pay. The annual salary increased from $64 to $84. Each circuit had to build a parsonage and to furnish it with heavy furniture. If a country circuit could not afford to buy land and build a parsonage, it had to rent a house when a married preacher was assigned to it. Finally, the general conference authorized itinerants a 15 to 25 percent cut on all the books they sold through the Book Concern. The cut represented their share of the profits and it served as an incentive for them to sell more books. MEC, *Journals from 1796-1836*, 34–46.
81. *Asbury's Journal*, 3:144.
82. MEC, *Minutes* (1813), 143.
83. Redford, *History of Methodism in Kentucky*, 248ff.
84. Ibid., 254.

Chapter 15

1. Freeborn Garrettson and the famous Black Harry (Harry Hoosier) preached in Connecticut and the eastern sections of Massachusetts at the same time as Lee. They preached to large crowds in Sharon, Farmington, and Hartford. However, they did not remain in New England or begin a lasting work. At this time, Garrettson was the presiding elder of the district directly west of Connecticut. His duties allowed him to reach into new areas for the MEC. See Garrettson, *American Methodist Pioneer*, 141-144.

2. Garrettson, *American Methodist Pioneer*, 142.

3. George Claude Baker Jr., *An Introduction to the History of Early New England Methodism, 1789-1839* (Durham, NC: Duke University Press, 1941), 5-6.

4. The *Minutes* incorrectly list the city as Standford (MEC, *Minutes* [1813], 83). Lee's History is the primary source for the early history of Methodism in New England. His account is corroborated by the MEC *Minutes*. However, the *History of Stamford, Connecticut* argues that Samuel Talbot or Peter Moriarty founded the Stamford MEC in 1788. Lee came after them. One served the Dutchess (sic) circuit and the other the New Rochelle circuit in eastern New York. See Rev. E. B. Huntington, *History of Stamford, Connecticut, from its Settlement in 1641, to the Present Time* (Stamford, CT: Steam Press of Wm. W. Gillespie & Co., 1868), 328-329.

5. Lee, *Short History*, 165

6. Ibid., 214.

7. Contrary to what the Methodist sources say, Richard Shiels argues that Congregational New England was in revival during the 1790s. He states, "The resuscitation of Congregationalism began in the last decade of the eighteen century. Edward Dorr Griffin, the Congregational pastor in Farmington, Connecticut, identified 1792 as the year in which 'an unbroken series of revival' began in New England" ("The Methodist Invasion of Congregational New England" in *Methodism and the Shaping of American Culture*, ed. Nathan Hatch and John Wigger [Nashville, TN: Kingswood Books, 2001], 261). Shiels also argues that Methodism helped to spark the Congregational resurgence in several ways. First, many who were converted through Methodist preaching joined the Congregational churches. Second, Methodists stirred the Congregation preachers to action. Third, the Congregational preachers copied the style and practices of the Methodists to include small group meetings during the week.

8. *Asbury's Journal*, 3:67.

9. *Asbury's Journal*, 1:676-677.

10. W. A. Chandler, *Great Revivals and the Great Republic* (Nashville, TN: Publishing House of the M. E. Church, South, 1904), 164.

11. Barclay, *Methodist Missions*, 1:104.

12. Ibid., 1:14.

13. Ibid.

14. Ibid.

15. Orr, *Eager Feet*, 8-11; Chandler, *Great Revivals*, 165-172.

16. *Asbury's Journal*, 1:767.

17. Lee, *Short History*, 214.

18. Thomas Umbel, "American Denomination," 184.

19. William Warren Sweet, *Religion in Colonial America* (New York: Charles Scribner's Sons, 1943), 89.

20. Barclay, *Methodist Missions*, 1:132.

21. *Asbury's Journal*, 2:22.

22. See Chapter 5.

23. *Asbury's Journal*, 1:767.

24. Ibid., 2:25.

25. For a fuller explanation, see Payne, "Without a Parallel," 261-263. Jefferson and Anti-Federalism embraced the seven following principles: (1) a democratic agrarian order based on the individual freeholder: (2) a broad diffusion of wealth: (3) relative freedom from industrialism, urbanism, and organized finance: (4) sympathy for debtor interests: (5) distrust of centralized government: (6) belief in the perfectibility of humankind: and (7) confidence in the view that people, acting through representative institutions could be left to govern themselves (Morris, *Encyclopedia of American History*, 123-124).

26. In 1790, Garrettson offers a rationalized critique of Calvinism that is not based on scripture. "Touching unconditional election and reprobation, I never did believe it; and I am persuaded I never shall whilst I retain the use of my reason. What! to suppose that the Judge of the whole earth should unconditionally from eternity, destine part of the human race to eternal flames! If any man can persuade me to believe it, then it will not be a hard matter to make me believe, that he has unconditionally set apart a select number, (whom he calls the elect) for eternal felicity: and of course do what they will, it is impossible for them to lose their election, or as some term it, to fall from grace. . . . I have not conversed with any man, since I have been acquainted with men and things, that could be consistent in supporting such a doctrine. And thus it is, that they so often contradict themselves" (*American Methodist Pioneer*, 143).

27. Umbel, "American Denomination," 181.
28. Ibid., 64.
29. In Baker, *Early New England Methodism*, 27.
30. Ibid., 36-41.
31. Ibid., 16.
32. Ibid., 17-18.
33. Barclay, *Methodist Missions*, 1:137.
34. Umbel, "American Denomination," ix.
35. Baker, *Early New England Methodism*, 48.
36. Barclay, *Methodist Missions*, 2:23.
37. Umbel, "American Denomination," 160.
38. "It seems well authenticated that the Anti-Federalist party, the Republicans, included most of the Methodists. One itinerant of this period wrote: 'The great mass, if not the entire, of the Methodist Church and her adherents were Republicans.' This was true, of course, not only in New England, but also in the country at large, and most especially among those who removed to the West. In his Connecticut in Transition, Purcell writes that the republican rise to control [in 1800] was the result of its appeal to 'the laboring element' and to religious discontent. He explains: 'All dissenters [in New England], save Episcopalians, could be described as Republicans by 1803.' . . . The Methodists joined the democratic forces who were fighting for equalitarianism as well as religious liberty" (Baker, *Early New England Methodism*, 47-48).
39. Umbel, "American Denomination," 100.
40. *Asbury's Journal*, 1:678.
41. Ibid., 1:684.
42. Lee, *Short History*, 165.
43. Ibid., 166-167.
44. *Asbury's Journal*, 2:57.
45. Lee, *Short History*, 198.
46. Ibid., 165.
47. *Asbury's Journal*, 1:685.
48. Lee, *Short History*, 166.
49. James Mudge, *History of the New England Conference of the Methodist Episcopal Church, 1796-1910* (Boston, MA: The New England Conference, 1910), 35. "Monday, November 29th, [Lee] received a letter from Benjamin Johnson, of Lynn, inviting

him there. Mr. Johnson . . . had heard Methodist preaching some twenty years before on his business trips, and was glad to improve this opportunity of hearing it again."

50. Lee, *Short History,* 165-166.
51. Barclay, *Methodist Missions,* 1:133n.
52. Ibid., 135n. According to Mudge, there was a providential preparation for Methodism in Lynn. "The great dissatisfaction which existed in the Congregational church with their pastor, who had just been dismissed, combined with a long succession of church divisions and trials . . . left them in a condition to welcome almost any change, especially one which gave promise of evangelical earnestness and religious warmth" (Mudge, *New England Conference,* 37n).
53. *Asbury's Journal,* 1:767n.
54. *Asbury's Journal,* 2:21.
55. Ibid., 2:67.
56. Lee, *Short History,* 199.
57. *Asbury's Journal,* 1:765.
58. Finke and Stark, *Winners and Losers,* 278.
59. See *Asbury's Journal,* 1:766n.
60. Ibid. "The secret of the matter was, that many in that congregation would have been kind to us, but meeting with Mr. Wilson, coming from Ireland (once a travelling preacher), he settled with them: their convenience suited his interest. But the people can hear us in the school house; and if any are awakened, they will join the Church over the bridge" (*Asbury's Journal,* 1:765).
61. Lee, *Short History,* 291.
62. Scott Maters, *The Jesse Lee Project* . (Chesterfield, NH: Asbury UMC), http://jesseleeproject.org/about-jesse-lee/ (accessed August 1, 2012).
63. Lee, *Short History,* 164-165.

Chapter 16

1. See Kelley, *Conservative Churches.*
2. Ibid., xxv.
3. Ibid., 17-34. For more detailed information on these issues, see William Payne, "The Social Movement Dynamics of Modern American Evangelicalism," *Ashland Theological Journal* 35 (2004): 37-54.
4. According to an updated version of Kelley's theory, successful churches are strict churches whose traditional religion preserves high tension with the environment and demands the sort of single-minded sacrifices from members that discourages participation in other groups and militates against free riders. Typically, participants in liberal churches are less committed to the church because liberal churches do not satisfy a set of psychological needs related to ultimate meaning. The church is one of many good organizations that compete for their time and presence. On the other hand, conservative churches do not compete with the Peace Corps, environmentalism, or the ACLU. They sell salvation and focus on a narrow spectrum of ultimate meaning. This limits their competition to other evangelical churches, new religious movements, cults, and world religions. Thus, they can attract a more dedicated following and make higher demands on their members. See N. J. Demerath, "Church Victory and Organizational Defeat in the Paradoxical Decline of Liberal Protestantism," *Journal for the Scientific Study of Religion* 34, no. 4 (1995): 458-469.
5. High expectation is another way of expressing the term "strict." A strict church has high expectation for its membership and it makes demands upon it. One should dis-

tinguish between sect and cult when reading Kelley. From a sociological perspective, the two are similar. One person's cult is another's strong sect. In the end, theology and societal attitudes distinguish between the two.

6. Kelley, *Conservative Churches*, 58.
7. Coleman, "Factors in Expansion," 286-288 and 293.
8. *Asbury's Journal*, 2:96.
9. Ibid., 1:211.
10. Lee, *Short History*, 134.
11. Kelley, *Conservative Churches*, 78-79.
12. Ibid., 80.
13. Ibid.
14. *Asbury's Journal*, 1:322.
15. Ibid., 3:87.
16. H. K. Carroll, *The Francis Asbury Centenary Volume* (Cincinnati: The Methodist Book Concern, 1916), 81.
17. Kelley, *Conservative Churches*, 95.
18. Ibid., 93.
19. H. Reinhold Niebuhr wrote *The Social Sources of Denominationalism* (Cleveland and New York: The World Publishing Company, 1929). Robert Coleman wrote "Factors in the Expansion." James W. May wrote "From Revival Movement to Denomination: A Re-examination of the Beginnings of American Methodism." James D. Lynn wrote "The Concept of the Ministry." Umbel wrote "American Denomination." Also, Roger Finke and Rodney Stark have written extensively on the subject. *The Churching of America* is widely read. Others also have written on this subject. Recently, theories related to secularization have become popular and have supplanted the sect-to-church theory in many quarters. A fierce debate raged between the theorists. Sharon Hanson has outlined the debate and the facts related to it in "The Secularisation Thesis: Talking at Cross Purposes," in *The Journal of Contemporary Religion* 12, no. 2 (1997), 159-171. Finke and Stark have argued against the secularization of religion theory by saying that the levels of religiosity in America have not declined. Others expand the meaning of secularization to include the idea of institutional authority and the centrality of organized religion. Based on this approach, the influence of religion has declined.
20. Niebuhr, *Social Sources*, 17-18.
21. Ibid. 18.
22. Ibid., 18-19.
23. Ibid., 19-20.
24. Ibid., 170-178.
25. Ibid., 171.
26. Ibid., 175.
27. Ibid., 173.
28. Ibid., 175.
29. See Hatch, *Democratization of American Christianity*.
30. Cowan, "The Arminian Alternative," 3.
31. Finke and Stark, *The Churching of America*, 163.
32. Umbel, "American Denomination," xii.

Chapter 17

1. Finke and Stark, *The Churching of America*, 73.
2. George Hunter, *To Spread the Power: Church Growth in the Wesleyan Spirit* (Nashville, TN: Abingdon Press, 1987).

3. Ibid., 109-144.
4. U.S. Bureau of the Census. *Nation's Population One-Third Minority.* http://www.census.gov/newsroom/releases/archives/population/cb06-72.html (accessed August 1, 2012).
5. Roozen and Hadaway, *Rerouting the Protestant Mainstream*, 35.
6. C. Peter Wagner's *Strategies for Churches: Tools for Effective Evangelism and Missions* (Ventura, CA: Regal Books, 1987).
7. McGavran, *Understanding Church Growth*, 17.
8. Sentinel Group, "International Fellowship of Transformation Partners." (Right Brain Media). http://www.glowtorch.org/tabid/2531/Default.aspx (accessed August 1, 2012).
9. For more information on this subject refer to Alistair Petrie's *Releasing Heaven on Earth: God's Principles for Restoring the Land* (Grand Rapids, MI: Chosen Books, 2000) and Charles Kraft's *The Rules of Engagement: Understanding the Principles that Govern the Spiritual Battles in Our Lives* (Colorado Springs, CO: Wagner Publications, 2000).
10. Mark Shaw, *Global Awakening: How 20th-Century Revivals Triggered a Christian Revolution* (Downers Grove, IL: IVP Academic), 2010. Also, interested persons should review Richard Riss, *A Survey of 20th-Century Revival Movements in North America* (Peabody, MA: Hendrickson Publishers), 1988 and Collin Hansen and John Woodbridge, *A God-Sized Vision: Revival Stories that Stretch and Stir* (Grand Rapids, MI: Zondervan), 2010. Riss carefully documents the vast number of revivals that have happened in various parts of North America since the outbreak of Pentecostalism. Additionally, he reviews the foundations to the century of American revivals by looking at precursors to them in America and Wales. More recently, Collin Hansen and John Woodbridge document the origins of the revival spirit in America and in other parts of the world and also offer biblical and theological criteria by which to study and name a revival. In the last chapter of their book, they identify and summarize six revival traits. One of the most influential books on revival and church renewal was written by Richard Lovelace. His book reviews every conceivable aspect of the topic. See *Dynamics of Spiritual Life: An Evangelical Theology of Renewal* (Downers Grove, IL: IVP, 1979).
11. James Burns, *Revivals, Their Laws and Leaders* (London, Hodder and Stoughton, 1900).
12. Arthur Wallis, *In the Day of Thy Power* (Fort Washington, PA: CLC Publications, 1956), 17.
13. Anthony F. C. Wallace, "Revitalization Movements." In *Reader in Comparative Religion, An Anthropological Approach*, ed. William A. Lessa and Evon Z. Vogt, 3rd ed. (New York: Harper and Row, 1972), 503-512.
14. According to Shaw, normal life gradually gives way to a problem stage. In the problem stage, the old ways do not work. This causes a paradigm shift. New leaders with new messages emerge. They produce new movements. As the movements gain speed, problems arise. The conflict from within and resistance from without can derail the new movement. If it survives, it will have a transforming influence (*Global Awakening*, 24-27).
15. Wallace, "Revitalization Movements," 505.
16. Ibid., 506.
17. Ibid., 508.
18. Ibid., 509.
19. According to McGavran, "A people movement results from the joint decision of a number of individuals all from the same people group, which enables them to become Christians without social dislocation, while remaining in full contact with their non-Christian relatives, thus enabling other segments of that people group, across the years,

after suitable instruction, to come to similar decisions and form Christian churches made up exclusively of members of that people." McGavran, *Understanding Church Growth*, 223.

20. Garrettson, *American Methodist Pioneer*, 94.
21. Payne, "Social Movement Dynamics," 37-54.
22. Rodney Stark, *Sociology* 6th ed. (Belmont, CA: Wadsworth Publishing Company, 1996), 642.

Appendix

1. John Wigger, "Taking Heaven by Storm: Enthusiasm and Early American Methodism, 1770-1820," (PhD diss., University of Notre Dame, Ann Arbor, MI: UMI, 1994), 347-350.
2. Most circuit locations were verified by multiple sources. Two helpful web based tools are MIT's Geographic Nameserver at http://stuff.mit.edu/ cgi/geo (accessed August 1, 2012) and the U.S. Census' Gazetteer: 2010, 2000, and 1990 at http://www.census.gov/geo/maps-data/data/gazetteer.html (accessed August 1, 2012). These will locate any geographic feature (e.g., river, bridge, park, dock, school, and church) in all the places that the name occurs within the United States. Also, an online Rand McNally atlas from 1895 has a search capability that shows where every city was located at that time. See "The New 11 x 14 Atlas of the World" at http://www.livgenmi.com/ 1895/ (accessed August 1, 2012).

BIBLIOGRAPHY

Andrews, Doris Elisabett. "Popular Religion and the Revolution in the Middle Atlantic Ports: The Rise of the Methodists, 1770-1800." PhD dissertation, University of Pennsylvania, 1986.

Asbury, Francis. *The Journal and Letters of Francis Asbury*, Edited by Elmer T. Clark, J. Manning Potts, and Jacob S. Payton. 3 Vols. Nashville, TN: Abingdon. 1958.

Atkinson, John. *Memorials of Methodism in New Jersey*. 2nd ed. Philadelphia: Perkinpine and Higgins, 1860.

_____. *The Class Leader. His Work and How to Do it: With Illustrations of Principles, Needs, Methods, and Results*. New York: Nelson & Phillips, 1875.

Atwood, Anthony. *Causes for the Marvelous (Former) Success of Methodism*. Zarephath, NJ: Pillar of Fire Publisher, 1884.

Baker, George Claude, Jr. *An Introduction to the History of Early New England Methodism, 1789-1839*. Durham, NC: Duke University Press, 1941.

Bangs, Nathan. *A History of the Methodist Episcopal Church*. 4 Vols. 12th ed. New York: Carlton & Porter, 1860.

Barclay, Wade Crawford. *History of Methodist Missions*. Vol. 1, *Missionary Motivations and Expansion*. New York: The Board of Missions and Church Extension of the Methodist Church, 1949.

_____. *History of Methodist Missions*. Vol. 2, *To Reform the Nation*. New York: The Board of Missions and Church Extension of the Methodist Church, 1950.

Benedict, David. *A General History of the Baptist Denomination in America, and Other Parts of the World.* London: Lincoln & Edmands, 1813. Accessed August 1, 2012, http://www.reformedreader.org/history/benedict/baptistdenomination/overview.htm.

Bucke, Emory Stevens, Gen. ed. *The History of American Methodism.* 3 Vols. Nashville: Abingdon Press, 1964.

Burns, James. *Revivals, Their Laws and Leaders.* London, Hodder and Stoughton, 1900.

Burroughs, Jeremiah and Richard Baxter. *The Causes, Evils, and Cures, of Heart and Church Divisions: Extracted from the Works of Burroughs and Baxter.* Edited by John Dinkins. New York: Carlton & Phillips, 1855 [1792].

Caldwell, John. "The Methodist Organization of the United States, 1784-1844: An Historical Geography of the Methodist Episcopal Church from Its Formation to Its Division." PhD dissertation, University of Oklahoma, 1982.

Cameron, Richard M. "The New Church Takes Root." Vol. 1 in *The History of American Methodism.* Edited by Emory Stevens Bucke, 241-290. Nashville, TN: Abingdon, 1964.

Cappon, Lester J., ed. *The Atlas of Early American History.* Princeton, NJ: Princeton University Press, 1976.

Carroll, H. K. *The Francis Asbury Centenary Volume.* Cincinnati: The Methodist Book Concern, 1916.

Carruth, Gordon and Associates, eds, *The Encyclopedia of American Facts and Dates.* New York: Harper & Row Publishers, Inc., 1987.

Chandler, W. A. *Great Revivals and the Great Republic.* Nashville, TN: Publishing House of the M. E. Church, South, 1904.

Clements, John. *Flying the Colors: Virginia Facts.* Dallas, TX: Clements Research, 1991.

Coke, Thomas. *The Journal of Dr. Thomas Coke.* Edited by John Vickers. Nashville, TN: Kingswood Books, 2005.

Coleman, Robert E. "Factors in the Expansion of the Methodist Episcopal Church 1784 to 1812." PhD dissertation, University of Iowa, 1954.

_____. *Nothing to Do but Save Souls.* Wilmore, KY: Evangel Publishing House, 1990.

Cowan, Raymond P. "The Arminian Alternative: The Rise of the Methodist Episcopal Church. 1765-1850." PhD dissertation, University of Iowa, 1991.

Daniels, W. H. *The Illustrated History of Methodism in Great Britain and America.* New York: Methodist Book Concern and Phillips & Hunt, 1880.

DeCarolis, Lisa Marie. "A Biography of Alexander Hamilton (1755-1804)," *From Revolution to Reconstruction - an .HTML project*. The University of Georgia, 1994. Accessed August 1, 2012. http://www.let.rug.nl/usa/B/ hamilton/hamil22.htm.

Demerath, N. J. "Church Victory and Organizational Defeat in the Paradoxical Decline of Liberal Protestantism." *Journal for the Scientific Study of Religion* 34, no. 4 (1995): 458-469.

Devereux, Jarrett. *The Life of the Reverend Devereux Jarratt, Rector of Bath Parish, Dinwiddie County, Virginia, Written by Himself to the Rev. John Coleman*. 1806. Reprint. New York: Amo Press, 1969.

Doran, Michael F. *Atlas of County Boundary Changes in Virginia 1634-1895*. San Bernardino, CA: Borgo Press, 1987.

Drinkhouse, Edward J. *History of Methodist Reform: Synoptical of General Methodism 1703 to 1898*. Vol. 1. Baltimore, MD: The Board of Publication of the Methodist Protestant Church 1899.

Emory, Robert. *History of the Discipline of the Methodist Episcopal Church*. Rev. ed. New York: Carlton and Porter, 1856.

Ferguson, Charles W. *Methodists and the Making of America*. Austin, TX: Eakin Press, 1983.

Ferrell, Robert, *Atlas of American History*. New York: Facts of Life, Inc., 1987.

Finke, Roger, and Rodney Stark. "Turning Pews into People: Estimating 19th Century Church Membership." *Journal for the Scientific Study of Religion 25*, no. 2 (1986): 180-192.

_____. "How the Upstart Sects Won America: 1776-1850. *Journal for the Scientific Study of Religion 28*, no. 1 (1989): 27-44.

_____. *The Churching of America: Winners and Losers in Our Religious Economy*. New Brunswick, NJ: Rutgers University Press, 1992.

Foge, Robert William and Stanley L. Engerman. *Time on the Cross: The Economics of American Negro Slavery*. Boston, MA: Little, Brown and Co., 1974.

Foster, Ellsworth D. ed., *The American Educator,* Vol. 8. Chicago, IL: Ralph Durham Company, 1921.

Garrettson, Freeborn. *American Methodist Pioneer: The Life and Journals of the Rev. Freeborn Garrettson, 1772-1827*. Edited by Robert Simpson. Rutland, VT: Academy Books, 1984.

Gaustad, Edwin. *A Documentary History of Religion in America*. 2nd ed. Grand Rapids, MI: Eerdmans, 1993.

Gewehr, Wesley. *The Great Awakening in Virginia, 1740-1790*. Durham, NC: Duke University Press, 1965.

Gilbert, Martin. *American History Atlas.* 1968. Reprint. London: Weidenfield and Nicolson, 1985.

Goss, C. C. *Statistical History of the First Century of American Methodism with a Summary of the Origin and Present Operations of Other Denominations.* New York: Carton & Porter, 1866.

Hansen, Collin and John Woodbridge. *A God-Sized Vision: Revival Stories that Stretch and Stir.* Grand Rapids, MI: Zondervan, 2010.

Hanson, Sharon. "The Secularisation Thesis: Talking at Cross Purposes," in *The Journal of Contemporary Religion* 12, no. 2 (1997): 159-171.

Hatch, Nathan. *The Democratization of American Christianity.* New Haven, CT: Yale University Press, 1989.

Hill, Samuel S. Jr. *The South and the North in American Religion.* Athens, GA: University of Georgia, 1980.

Hoge, Dean, and David Roozen. *Understanding Church Growth and Decline*: 1950-1978. Nashville, TN: Abingdon Press, 1979.

Hunter, George G. *To Spread the Power: Church Growth in the Wesleyan Sprit.* Nashville, TN: Abingdon Press, 1987.

_____. *Church for the Unchurched.* Nashville, TN: Abingdon, 1996.

_____. *The Celtic Way of Evangelism.* Nashville, TN: Abingdon, 2000.

_____. *Radical Outreach: Recovery of Apostolic Ministry and Evangelism.* Nashville, TN: Abingdon, 2003.

_____. *The Apostolic Congregation, Church Growth for a New Generation.* Nashville, TN: Abingdon, 2009.

Huntington, Rev. E. B. *History of Stamford, Connecticut, from its Settlement in 1641, to the Present Time.* Stamford, CT: Steam Press of Wm. W. Gillespie & Co., 1868.

Inskeep, Kenneth. "A Short History of Church Growth Research." In *Church and Denominational Growth*, Edited by David Roozen and C. Kirk Hadaway. Nashville, TN: Abingdon Press, 1993.

John Leland Baptist College. *Baptist History Homepage.* Georgetown, KY. Accessed August 1, 2012, http://baptisthistoryhomepage.com/.

Kagan, Hilde Heun. *The American Heritage Pictorial Atlas of United States History.* New York: American Heritage Book, 1966.

Keefer, Luke. "John Wesley: Disciple of Early Christianity." *Wesleyan Theological Journal 19, no. 1* (Spring1984). Accessed August 1, 2012 http://wesley.nnu.edu/fileadmin/imported_site/wesleyjournal/1984-wtj-19-1.pdf

Kelley, Dean. *Why Conservative Churches Are Growing* 1972. Reprint. Macon, GA: Mercer University Press, 1986.

Kraft, Charles. *The Rules of Engagement: Understanding the Principles that Govern the Spiritual Battles in Our Lives*. Colorado Springs, CO: Wagner Publications, 2000.

Latourette, Kenneth Scott. *A History of the Expansion of Christianity: The Great Century in Europe and the United States of America A.D. 1800-A.D. 1914*. 2nd ed. Vol. 4. New York: Harper and Brother's Publishing, 1941.

Lausanne Committee for World Evangelizaiton. The Pasadena Consultation - Homogeneous Unit Principle. Lausanne Occasional Paper 1. 1978. Accessed August 1, 2012, http:// www.lausanne.org/en/ documents/global-analysis/en/documents/lops/71-lop-1.html.

Lednum, John. *A History of the Rise of Methodism*. Philadelphia: John Lednum, 1862.

Lee, Jesse. *A Short History of the Methodists in the United States of America Beginning in 1766 and Continued till 1809*. Baltimore, MD: Magill and Clime, 1810.

Lloyd, Mark Brooks. "A Rhetorical Analysis of the Preaching of Bishop Francis Asbury." PhD dissertation, Michigan State University, 1976.

Lovelace, Richard. *Dynamics of Spiritual Life: An Evangelical Theology of Renewal*. Downers Grove, IL: IVP, 1979.

Lynn, James D. "The Concept of the Ministry in the Methodist Episcopal Church, 1784-1844." PhD dissertation, Princeton Theological Seminary, 1973.

M'Ferrin, John B. *History of Methodism in Tennessee*. Vol. 1. Nashville, TN: The Publishing House of the ME Church, South, 1888.

MacClenny, W. E., *Life of Rev. James O'Kelly - Christian Church in the South - Restoration Movement*. Ann Arbor, MI: Cushing-Malloy, 1950. Accessed August 1, 2012, http://www. piney.com/RmOKXVII.html.

Martin, Isaac. *History of Methodism in Holston Conference*. Nashville, TN: The Methodist Historical Society of Holston Conference, 1945.

Martisk, Kenneth C. *The Historical Atlas of Political Parties in the United States Congress: 1789-1989*. New York: Macmillan, 1989.

Massachusetts Institute of Technology. Geographic Nameserver. Cambridge, MA. Accessed August 1, 2012, http://stuff.mit.edu/cgi/geo.

Maters, Scott. *The Jesse Lee Project*. Chesterfield, NH: Asbury UMC, Accessed August 1, 2012, http://jesseleeproject.org/about-jesse-lee/.

May, James W. "From Revival Movement to Denomination: A Re-Examination of the Beginnings of Methodism." PhD dissertation, 1962. Reprint. Columbia University, 1978.

McGavran, Donald. *Church Growth in Jamaica: A Preview of Things to Come in Many Lands.* Lucknow, India: Lucknow Publishing House, 1962.

_____. *Understanding Church Growth.* Edited by Peter Wagner. 3rd ed. Grand Rapids, MI: Eerdmans, 1990.

Methodist Church Council on World Service and Finance Department of Research, *Methodist Fact Book.* Evanston, IN: Department of Research and Statistics, 1960

Methodist Episcopal Church. *The General Minutes of the Conferences of the Methodist Episcopal Church in America Forming the Constitution of Said Church.* London: Frys and Couchman, 1786.

_____. *Form of Discipline for the Ministers, Preachers, and Members of the Methodist Episcopal Church in America. Considered and Approved at a Conference Held at Baltimore, in the State of Maryland, on Monday the 27th of December, 1784: in which The Reverend Thomas Coke, L.L.D. and the Revered Francis Asbury, Presided.* New York, W. Ross, 1787.

_____. *Form of Discipline for the Ministers, Preachers, and Members of the Methodist Episcopal Church in America. Considered and Approved at a Conference Held at Baltimore, in the State of Maryland, on Monday the 27th of December, 1784: in which The Reverend Thomas Coke, L.L.D. and the Revered Francis Asbury, Presided.* Elizabeth Town: Shepard Kolloc, 1788.

_____. *Minutes of the Annual Conferences Annually Held in America from 1773 to 1813 Inclusive.* Nashville, TN: Daniel Hitt and Thomas Ware for the Methodist Conexion in the United States, 1813.

_____. *Journals of the Annual Conference of the Methodist Episcopal Church, 1796-1836.* Vol. 1. New York: Carlton and Phillips, 1855.

_____. *The General Conferences of the Methodist Episcopal Church from 1792 to 1896.* Cincinnati, OH: Curts and Jennings, 1900.

_____. *The Doctrines and Disciplines of the Methodist Episcopal Church in America with Explanatory Notes by Thomas Coke and Francis Asbury.* Facsimile Edition. Frederick Norwood, ed. Evanston, IN: Academy Books, [1798]1979.

Miller, John C. *The Federalist Era, 1789-1801.* New York, Harper & Row, 1960.

Molloy, Robert. *Charleston, A Gracious Heritage.* New York: D. Appleton-Century Company, 1947.

Morris, Richard, ed. *Encyclopedia of American History.* New York: Harper, 1953.

Moss, Arthur Bruce. "Methodism in Colonial America." Vol. 1 in *The History of American Methodism*. Edited by Emory Stevens Bucke, 95-144. Nashville, TN: Abingdon, 1964.
Mudge, James. *History of the New England Conference of the Methodist Episcopal Church, 1796-1910*. Boston, MA: The New England Conference, 1910.
Murray, Iain H. *Revival and Revivalism: The Making and Marring of American Evangelicalism*. Carlisle, PA: The Banner of Truth Trust, 1994.
Nickerson, Michael George. "Sermons, Systems, and Strategies: The Geographic Expansion into New York State. 1788-1810." PhD dissertation, Syracuse University, 1988.
Niebuhr, H. Reinhold. *The Social Sources of Denominationalism*. Cleveland and New York: The World Publishing Company, 1929.
Norwood, Frederick. *The Story of American Methodism*. Nashville, TN: Abingdon, 1974.
O'Kelly, James. *The Author's Apology for Protesting Against the Methodist Episcopal Government*. Richmond, VA: John Dixon, 1798. (Note: original book anonymous.)
Orr, J. Edwin. *The Eager Feet: Evangelical Awakenings, 1790-1830*. Chicago: Moody Press, 1975.
Orr, John. *English Deism: Its Roots and Its Fruits*. Grand Rapids: MI: Eerdmans Publishing Company, 1934.
Payne, William Price. "Religious Community in a Cuban Refugee Camp: Bringing Order out of Chaos," in *Missiology 25*, no. 2 (1997):141-154.
_____. "Without a Parallel: Reasons for the Expansion of Early American Methodism (1767 through 1812)." PhD dissertation, Asbury Theological Seminary, 2001.
_____. "The Social Movement Dynamics of Modern American Evangelicalism," *Ashland Theological Journal*, no. 35 (2004): 37-54.
_____. "The Case for Scouting Evangelism." *UM Men 8* (Summer 2005): 25-27.
Peters, Richard, ed. *Public Statutes at Large of the United States of America from the Organization of the Government in 1789, to March 3, 1845*. Vol. VIII. Boston: Charles Little and James Brown, 1846.
Petrie, Alistair. *Releasing Heaven on Earth: God's Principles for Restoring the Land*. Grand Rapids, MI: Chosen Books, 2000.
Pierson, Coen G. "Methodism and the Revolution." Vol. 1 in *The History of American Methodism*. Edited by Emory Stevens Bucke, 145-184. Nashville, TN: Abingdon, 1964.

Pilmoor, Joseph. *The Journal of Joseph Pilmore, Methodist Itinerant for the Years August 1, 1769 to January 2, 1774.* Edited by Frederick Maser and Howard Maag. Philadelphia, PA: Message, 1969.

Potts, Manning. "Methodism in Colonial America." Vol. 1 in *The History of American Methodism.* Edited by Emory Stevens Bucke, 74-95. Nashville, TN: Abington, 1964.

Prats, J. J. and the Historical Marker Database. *The "Regular" Methodist Conference.* Springfield, VA, 2009. Accessed August 1, 2012, http://www.hmdb.org/marker.asp?marker =16917.

Project Canterbury. *A Reprint in full of the Registry of Ordinations by Bishops Seabury and Jarvis, as Published in the Journal of A.D. 1882, by Order of the Convention,* 1882. Transcribed by Richard Mammana. Accessed August 1, 2012, http://anglicanhistory.org/usa/seabury/ordinations1882.html.

Ramsay, David. *Ramsay's History of South Carolina.* Newberry, SC: W. J. Duffie, 1858.

Rand McNally. *The New 11 x 14 Atlas of the World.* 1895. Accessed August 1, 2012, http://www.livgenmi.com/ 1895/.

Redford, A.H. *The History of Methodism in Kentucky.* Vol. 1. *From the Landing of James M'Bride in the District, in 1754, to the Conference of 1808.* Nashville, TN: Southern Methodist Publishing House, 1868.

Rennie, Sandra. "Virginia's Baptist Persecution, 1765-1778." Vol. 12 in *The Journal of Religious History,* no. 1 (1982): 48-61.

Richey, Russell. *Early American Methodism.* Bloomington, IN: Indiana University Press, 1991.

_____. "The Chesapeake Coloration of American Methodism." In *Methodism and the Shaping of American Culture 1760-1860.* Wilmore, KY: Wesleyan/Holiness Studies Center of Asbury Theological Seminary, 1994.

Richey, Russel, Rowe, Kenneth, and Schmidt, Jean, eds. *The Methodist Experience in America: A Sourcebook.* Vol. 2. Nashville, TN: Abingdon Press, 2000.

Riss, Richard *A Survey of 20th-Century Revival Movements in North America.* Peabody, MA: Hendrickson Publishers, 1988.

Roozen, David. "Denominations Grow as Individuals Join Congregations" in *Church and Denominational Growth,* Edited by David Roozen and C. Kirk Hadaway. Nashville, TN: Abingdon Press, 1993.

Roozen, David, and Kirk C. Hadaway. *Church and Denominational Growth.* Nashville, TN: Abingdon Press, 1993.

_____. *Rerouting the Protestant Mainstream.* Nashville, TN: Abingdon Press, 1995.

Semple, Robert B. *History of the Rise and Progress of the Baptists in Virginia*. Edited by G. W. Beale. 1810. Reprint. Richmond, VA: Pitt and Dickinson, 1894.

Sentinel Group. "International Fellowship of Transformation Partners." Right Brain Media. Accessed August 1, 2012 http://www.glowtorch.org/tabid/2531/Default.aspx.

Shaw, Mark. *Global Awakening: How 20th-Century Revivals Triggered a Christian Revolution*. Downers Grove, IL: IVP Academic, 2010.

Sherwood, Lawrence. "Growth and Spread, 1785-1804." Vol. 1 in *The History of American Methodism*. Edited by Emory Stevens Bucke, 360-418. Nashville, TN: Abingdon, 1964.

Shiels, Richard D. "The Methodist Invasion of New England." In *Methodism and the Shaping of American Culture 1760-1860*. Wilmore, KY: Wesleyan/Holiness Studies Center of Asbury Theological Seminary, 1994.

────── . "The Methodist Invasion of Congregational New England." In *Methodism and the Shaping of American Culture*. Edited by Nathan Hatch and John Wigger. Nashville, TN: Kingswood Books, 2001.

Silvoso, Ed. *Prayer Evangelism*. Ventura, CA: Regal Books, 2000.

Smeltzer, Wallace Guy. *Bishop Francis Asbury: Field Marshal of the Lord*. Denver, CO: Eastwood Printing and Publishing Company, 1982.

Spencer, J. H., *A History of Kentucky Baptists from 1769 to 1885*. Vol. 1. Cincinnati: J. R. Baumes, 1885.

Stark, Rodney, *Sociology*. 6th ed. Belmont, CA: Wadsworth Publishing Company, 1996.

Stevens, Abel. *History of the Methodist Episcopal Church in United States of America*. Vol. 1 of *The Planting of American Methodism*. New York, NY: Carlton & Porter, 1866. Accessed August 1, 2012, http://wesley.nnu.edu/wesleyctr/books/0201-0300/stevens/0216-112.htm.

Sweet, William Warren. *Religion in Colonial America*. New York: Charles Scribner's Sons, 1943.

────── . *Virginia Methodism: A History*. Richmond, VA: Whittet and Shepperson, 1955.

────── . *The Story of Religion in America*. Reprint. Grand Rapids, MI: Barber Book House, 1973.

Taylor, Thomas. "Rev. and Very Dear Sir," New York, April 11, 1768, quoted in Nathan Bangs, Vol. 1 of *A History of the Methodist Episcopal Church*. New York: Carlton & Porter, 1860.

Thaarup, Jorgen. "Three Types of Authority within the Leadership of the United Methodist Church." London, UK: The Europe Methodist Council Committee on Theology Meeting in London. January 2004. Accessed August 1, 2012, http://www.metodistkyrkan.se/utbildningen/pdf/2009_Authority.pdf.

Tigert, John. *The Making of Methodism: Studies in the Genesis of Institutions*. Nashville, TN: Publishing House of MEC South, 1898.

Turner, Ralph H. *Ritual Process: Structure and Anti-Structure*. Chicago, IL: Aldine, 1969.

Umbel, Thomas. "The Making of An American Denomination: Methodism in the New England Religious Culture, 1790-1860." PhD dissertation, Johns Hopkins University, 1991.

U.S. Bureau of the Census, *Historical Statistics of the United States, 1789-1945*. Washington, DC: Government Printing Office, 1949.

———. *Centers of Populations*. Accessed August 1, 2012, https://www.census.gov/history/www/reference/maps/centers_of_population.html.

———. *Census of Population and Housing, 1790*. Accessed August 1, 2012, http://www.census.gov/prod/www/abs/decennial/1790.html.

———. *Gazetteer: 2010, 2000, and 1990*. Accessed August 1 2012, http://www.census.gov/geo/maps-data/data/gazetteer.html.

———. *Nation's Population One-Third Minority*. Accessed August 1, 2012, http://www.census.gov/newsroom/releases/archives/population/cb06-72.html.

———. *Resident Population and Apportionment of the U.S. House of Representatives for Kentucky, 1789-2000*. Accessed August 1, 2012, http://www.census.gov/dmd/www/resapport/states/kentucky.pdf.

U.S. Military Academy. *Historical Map of the American Colonies: Population Density 1775*. Accessed on August 1, 2012, http://www.emersonkent.com/map_archive/american_colonies_population.htm.

Vedder, Henry. *A History of the Baptists in the Middle States*. Philadelphia: American Baptist Publication Society, 1898.

Wagner, Peter C. "Church Growth Research: the Paradigm and Its Implications" in *Understanding Church Growth and Decline 1950-1978*, Edited by Dean Hoge and David Roozen. Nashville, TN: Abingdon, 1979.

———. *Our Kind of People*. Atlanta, GA: John Knox Press, 1979.

———. *Strategies for Churches: Tools for Effective Evangelism and Missions*. Ventura, CA: Regal Books, 1987.

———. *Your Church Can Grow: Seven Vital Signs of a Healthy Church*. Ventura, CA: Gospel Light Publications, 1984.

Wagner, Peter C.
_____. "Church Growth Movement." In *Evangelical Dictionary of World Missions.* Edited by A. Scott Moreau. Grand Rapids, MI: Baker Books, 2000, 199-200.

Wakeley. Joseph. *Lost Chapters Recovered from the Early History of American Methodism.* 1858. Reprint. Danvers, MA: General Books LLC, 2009.

Wallace, Anthony F. C. "Revitalization Movements." In *Reader in Comparative Religion, An Anthropological Approach.* Edited by William A. Lessa and Evon Z. Vogt, 3rd ed. New York: Harper and Row, 1972, 503-512.

Wallis, Arthur. *In the Day of Thy Power.* Fort Washington, PA: CLC Publications, 1956.

Warburton, William. *Doctrine of Grace.* Farmington Hills, MI: GaleEcco Print Edition, 2010.

Waymire, Bob and C. Peter Wagner. *The Church Growth Survey Handbook.* 3rd ed. Santa Clara, CA: Global Church Growth, 1983.

Wesley, John. "A Plain Account of the People Called Methodists," Vol. VIII in *The Works of John Wesley.* 3rd ed. Edited by Thomas Jackson. 248-268. Grand Rapids, MI: Baker, 1991.

_____. "A Short History of the People Called Methodists." Vol. XIII in *The Works of John Wesley.* 3rd ed. Edited by Thomas Jackson. 303-381. Grand Rapids, MI: Baker, 1991.

_____. John Wesley to Freeborn Garrettson, November 30, 1786. Vol. XIII in *The Works of John Wesley,* 3rd ed. Edited by Thomas Jackson. 71-72. Grand Rapids, MI: Baker, 1991.

_____. "The Character of a Methodist." Vol. VIII in *The Works of John Wesley.* 3rd ed. Edited by Thomas Jackson. 339-347. Grand Rapids, MI: Baker, 1991.

_____. "The Ministerial Office." Vol. VII in *The Works of John Wesley.* 3rd ed. Edited by Thomas Jackson. 273-281. Grand Rapids, MI: Baker, 1991.

_____. "The Witness of the Spirit." Vol. V in *The Works of John Wesley.* 3rd ed. Edited by Thomas Jackson. 111-123. Grand Rapids, MI: Baker, 1991.

Wesleyan Methodist Church. Vol. 1 of *Minutes of the Methodists Conferences.* Originally titled *Minutes of the Several Conversations between the Reverend Mr. Wesley and Others from the Year 1744, to the Year 1780.* London, Eng: Mason, 1862.

Wigger, John. "Taking Heaven by Storm: Enthusiasm and Early American Methodism, 1770-1820." PhD dissertation, University of Notre Dame, 1994.

Williams, Jeffery. *Religion and Violence in Early American Methodism: Taking the Kingdom by Force*. Bloomington, IN: Indiana University Press, 2010.

Williams, William. *The Garden of American Methodism: The Delmarva Peninsula 1769-1820*. Wilmington, DE: Scholarly Resources Inc., 1984.

_____. "The Delmarva Peninsula as a Case Study, 1769-1820." In *Perspectives on American Methodism, Interpretive Essays*, Edited by Russell Richey, Kenneth Rowe, and Jean Miller Schmidt. Nashville, TN: Kingswood Books, 1993.

Withington, William A. *Kentucky in Maps*. Lexington, KY: Franklin Geographical Society, 1980.

Index

A

Abbott, David and Benjamin, 95
Adams, John, 132, 153, 326, 327
African American, xii, 31, 37, 54, 99, 182, 185, 189, 224, 318
Albany, NY, 60, 81, 119, 199
Allen, Beverly, 167
Allen, Richard, 185
Amelia Circuit in VA, 141, 143, 179
American Methodism, 1, 2, 4, 13, 21, 25, 53, 54, 56, 59, 60, 61, 63, 67, 68, 70, 79, 85, 101, 103, 104, 110-116, 124, 140, 154, 155, 157, 158, 160, 161, 162, 186, 199, 227, 230, 233, 237, 245, 247, 253-255, 257, 311, 314
Anglican, 73, 95, 98, 106, 110, 111, 114, 115, 148, 154, 180, 207; Anglican Church, 92, 108, 114, 115, 148, 207, 229; Anglican priest, 73, 93, 106, 111, 115, 154, 180, 207
Anti-Federalism, 110, 132, 133, 147-153, 167, 212, 335
Anti-Federalist, 131-135, 147, 150, 152, 153, 234, 235, 326, 336
antinomianism, 97, 203, 209
apostolic, 4, 8, 13, 14, 54, 55, 67, 105, 172, 193, 211, 225, 242, 244, 307, 312; Apostolic Church, 17, 217, 240
Arminian, 177, 200, 202, 210, 312, 338; Wesleyan-Arminian, 56; *Arminian Magazine*, 96, 202; Arminianism, 4, 110
Asbury, Frances (Bishop), xiv, 2, 3, 13, 25, 51, 52, 57, 60-63, 66, 69, 70, 72, 77, 78, 82-85, 87, 88, 93-116, 118, 122, 124-131, 135, 140-43, 145, 151, 152, 154-173, 177-184, 186-195, 197, 199, 200, 202, 204, 205, 207, 208, 212-217, 226-228, 230, 234, 235, 250, 253, 257, 306, 311, 313, 314, 318-323, 325, 327, 339-332
Asplund, Joh, 170
autocratic, 60, 104, 107, 113, 155, 157, 216, 235

B

Baltimore, 17, 22, 25, 60, 63, 67, 77, 107, 119, 120, 154, 163, 179, 182, 194, 201, 213, 217, 218, 317, 318, 330; Baltimore Circuit, 66, 103, 165; Baltimore Conference, 126, 142, 143, 158, 165, 178, 181; Balitimore-Town, 141, 142, 165
bands, 11, 51, 53, 145
Bangs, Nathan, 83, 84, 231, 315
Baptism, 116
Baptist, 3, 9, 46, 73, 91, 92, 96-98, 114, 115, 121, 176-178, 183, 195, 196, 204, 206, 216, 218, 234, 241, 245, 246, 316, 319, 333; Baptitst Church, 176
Barclay, Wade, 26, 68, 114, 133, 149, 166, 179, 203, 204, 207, 212, 215
Baxter, Richard, 163, 191
Benedict, David, 97, 170
Bible, xi, xii, 51, 172, 217, 247
biological growth, 3, 242
bishop, 54, 55, 102, 111, 112, 115, 152, 155, 156, 159-165, 168, 170, 172, 173, 177, 185, 186, 242, 311, 315, 322, 323, 329, 331

353

Boardman, Richard, 22, 62, 68, 309, 314
Book Concern, 5, 84, 107, 127, 130, 163, 172
Boston, MA, 57, 60, 97, 118, 119, 199, 201, 203, 206, 213, 214, 217, 218
bridging growth, 55
Brunswick, 24, 73, 77, 81, 87, 194, 307; Brunswick revival, 25, 87; Brunswick Circuit, 25, 78, 140, 141
Burr, Aaron, 132, 153, 326

C

Calvinism, 46, 96, 97, 177, 200, 203-205, 209, 210, 212, 336; Calvinistic, 115, 177, 202, 210
camp meeting, 4, 21, 109, 144, 306
Canada, 17, 42, 81, 86, 315
Census, U.S. Bureau of, 2, 3, 31, 117, 120, 121, 244; Census of 1790, 117
Chandler, W. A., 203
Charleston, SC, 60, 80, 81, 86, 120, 150, 151-153, 158, 164-167, 182, 184, 185, 188, 190-192, 226, 331; Circuit, 165, 172
Christian, 1, 4, 9, 10, 16, 170, 180, 203, 223, 224, 225, 245, 247, 248, 251, 306, 319, 330, 339, 340
Christmas Conference, 21, 54, 97, 110-118, 154, 158, 178, 207, 229, 309, 314
church growth, ix, xiv, 6, 7, 9, 10-15, 18, 19, 21, 55, 114, 140, 144, 186, 194, 222, 238, 240, 241, 247-249, 252, 253, 305, 306, 308, 316, 317; Church Growth Movement, 10, 12, 54, 249; church growth study, 19, 232, 240
Church of England, 73, 111, 253, 314
Cincinnati, OH, 118, 120
circuit rider, xiii, 4, 13, 17, 51, 52, 54-58, 62, 67, 72, 88, 93, 95, 99, 105, 107, 112, 122, 125, 158, 159, 193, 196, 217, 227-229, 231, 241-243, 248, 256, 306, 311, 312, 316
circuit system, 4, 12, 98, 228, 234
class, 11, 13, 17, 51-55, 58, 64-66, 70, 92, 100, 115, 123, 131, 145, 151, 189, 211, 218, 224, 226, 227, 234, 240, 253, 311-314; class leader, 57, 140, 229, 244; class meeting, 51, 57, 226, 306; class ticket, 52, 306
clergy, 13, 112, 115, 147, 163, 207, 210, 211, 212, 222, 236, 237; professional clergy, 233, 234, 241, 244; Anglican/Episcopalian Clergy, 93, 95, 98, 108
Coke, Thomas (Bishop), 2, 3, 13, 57, 110-113, 125, 130, 154, 155-157, 159, 162-169, 178-181, 186, 215, 226, 311, 322, 323
Cokesbury College, 124, 125
Coleman, Robert, 3, 23, 115, 121, 122, 175, 177, 227
Congregational, 3, 4, 201, 337, 337; Congregational Church, 47, 204, 208, 214, 215, 217
Connecticut, 31, 33, 43, 45-47, 86, 123, 126, 172, 191, 200, 201, 203, 205-208, 213, 214, 236, 257
connection, xiv, 2, 8, 22, 66, 67, 69, 102, 105, 109, 110, 111, 116, 128, 133, 149, 151, 155-159, 161, 163, 166-173, 178, 193, 213, 233, 242, 243, 247, 254, 329, 328, 331; connexion, 156, 171, 184; connectional, 8, 161
conservative, 9, 15, 212, 222-225, 241
contextual factors, 7-10, 12, 19, 21, 70-72, 74, 78, 80, 109, 110, 148, 153, 196, 205, 212, 216, 222, 232, 236, 239-241, 245, 306, 307, 316, 317
conversion growth, 4, 15, 18, 306
Council, the, 2, 3, 110, 157-163, 167-169, 173, 222, 230, 305, 321, 322, 329
course of study, the, 210, 244
Cowan, Raymond, 312

D

deacon, 54, 111, 185, 285, 311
Deism, 147-149, 197, 203, 204, 210, 245; deistic, 147, 148, 203, 317, 327
Delaware, 23-26, 29, 31, 37, 43, 62, 71, 78, 80, 81, 83, 84, 93, 94, 97, 101, 104, 106, 108, 118, 119, 122, 143, 172, 178, 213, 253, 256, 311, 318, 333
Delmarva, 25, 26, 29, 77, 78, 82, 86, 104, 114, 122, 178, 182, 309, 311, 323, 323
democratic, 47, 115, 132, 133, 149, 163, 164, 177, 204, 207-209, 212, 227, 235, 335, 336; democratic gospel, 148; democratic theology, 4, 98
denominations, 4, 6-10, 12, 15, 52, 55, 60, 74, 86, 91, 95, 96, 177, 197, 208, 212, 224, 233, 241, 244-246, 255, 307, 314
Dickins, John, 85, 107, 165, 168, 331
discipleship, vii, xiv, 4, 11, 114, 194, 237, 306
discipline, 4, 5, 10, 11, 51, 52, 55, 62, 63-68, 70, 72, 96, 107, 110, 127, 163, 165, 176, 192, 226, 227, 229, 234, 241; the Discipline, 51, 53, 112, 113, 116, 118, 125, 131, 145, 160, 163, 172, 178-181, 185, 226, 312, 323
dissenters, 64, 93, 96, 200, 206, 207, 212, 336
district conference, 122, 158-162, 331
divine election, 132, 202, 203
division method, 56, 58
doctrine, 4, 63, 95, 107, 134, 149, 177, 192, 209, 210, 227, 234, 249, 315, 320
dream/dreams, 107, 186, 200, 207, 320
Dromgoole, Edward, 95, 107

E

Early Methodism, 11, 55, 113
Eastern Shore, 25, 78, 87, 91, 94, 95, 98, 106, 122, 141, 142, 143, 177, 213, 321
ecclesiology, 11, 111
economic depression, 123, 124
Edisto, SC, 143, 164, 167
elder, 54, 111, 112, 124, 145, 159-161, 165, 168, 172, 335
election, political, 132, 147, 177; church elections, 173, 185, 235
elite, the, 9, 133, 172, 192, 233, 237
emancipation, 151, 179, 180, 182; (See manumission)
Embury, Philip, 22, 59, 62, 64, 69, 315
emigration, 86, 121, 122, 196, 243, 245, 247, 327
England, xiv, 22, 69, 74, 123, 132, 152, 154, 156, 190, 207, 254, 313, 314, 318, 320, 329, 330
episcopacy, 110, 112, 113, 148, 158, 161, 162, 165, 168, 173, 178, 328, 332
Episcopal, 1, 4, 5, 15, 65, 86, 98, 101, 155, 167, 173, 242, 332; Episcopal Church, 15, 67, 102, 107, 108, 112, 150; Protestant Episcopal Church, 2, 162
evangelical, xiv, 4, 9, 15, 73, 98, 99, 115, 147, 149, 216, 222-225, 237, 245-247, 249, 254, 319, 337
evangelism, vii, ix, xii-xiv, 4, 6, 7, 9, 11, 12, 47, 56, 67, 73, 91, 113, 114, 127, 140, 186, 188, 195, 203, 204, 209, 222, 224, 225, 237, 240, 241-245, 247, 248, 250, 252, 255, 307, 321; evangelization, xi, xiv, 4, 10, 19, 54, 186, 234, 240, 246
evangelist, 56, 66, 67, 242, 307, 308
exhorter, 12, 97, 228, 229, 244
expansion growth, 54
extension growth, 54

F

fairs, 72, 230
federalism, 133, 149, 245
Federalist Papers, 325
Finke, Roger, 4, 221, 237, 241, 246
Finney, Charles, 74
Florida, 31, 245
Fluvanna, VA, 92, 101-104, 106, 157, 158; Fluvanna crisis, 92, 157, 168; Fluvanna Conference, 102, 106, 110, 161, 177, 322
France, 132, 149, 151-153, 197, 245, 252
French Republicanism, 148, 151, 327
French Revolution, 132, 147-149, 151, 152, 307
frontier, 5, 10, 17, 31, 32, 40-42, 45, 48, 72, 80, 89, 109, 118-122, 125, 126, 132, 134, 138, 140, 144, 149, 170, 175,193, 196, 200, 219, 234, 237, 306, 311, 313, 317, 319, 327, 332; Frontier Thesis 236; frontier states, 31, 32, 40, 45; fronteir region, 40, 57, 158; New England frontier, 47, 110, 119, 204, 235, 236; Southern frontier, 98, 109, 112, 118, 119, 131, 150, 178; Western fronteir, 57, 190, 236

G

Garrettson, Freeborn, 56, 65, 83, 85, 95, 97, 102, 106, 107, 197, 199, 200, 253, 306, 320, 335, 336; persecuted, 93-94, 320; declined episcopacy, 154, 155, 328
Gatch, Philip, 65, 95, 101, 107
General Assistant, 54, 67, 106, 321; Thomas Rankin, 63; Frances Asbury, 101-104
General Conference, 15, 127, 128, 130, 143, 154, 163, 164, 167, 169, 172, 173, 181-185, 193, 241, 313; **1792**, 127, 167, 168; **1796**, 127, 128, 181, 183; **1800**; 130, 143, 182, 184, 193, 336; **2012**, 27, 128
gentry, 9, 92, 131, 150, 191, 193, 239
Georgia, 30-32, 40, 45, 57, 58, 70, 81, 87, 96, 98, 118, 122, 137, 138, 144, 149, 158, 164, 166, 167, 171, 187, 196, 232, 306, 313
Gewehr, Wesley, 92
Glendinning, William, 95, 107, 322
government, 11, 88, 110, 112, 115, 131-134, 149, 150, 154-156, 159-165, 168, 169, 171-173, 177, 178, 197, 210, 228, 234, 248, 329, 326, 336
governor, 153, 319, 320; Delaware, 94, 253; North Carolina, 179
Great Britain, 132, 149, 315, 314
Great Commission, 16, 17, 100, 239, 252, 308
growth center, 77-80, 82, 91, 95

H

Hadaway, Kirk, 241, 246
Hagerty, Jogn, 65
Haggard, Rice, 168, 171
Hamilton, Alexander, 131-134, 152, 325, 326
Hammett, William, 154, 164-167, 172, 173, 175, 193, 195, 217, 331
Hartford, CT, 7, 119, 143, 200, 201, 307, 334
Hartford Seminary Foundation, 6, 9, 10, 307; Hartford study/typology, 7, 222, 232, 240, 241, 247, 307
Hartley, Joseph, 93, 95, 320
Hatch, Nathan, 236, 246
Hispanic, xii-xiv, 244, 245
holiness, 4, 97, 107, 113, 115, 134, 202, 205, 239, 244, 247, 254, 320
Holston, River and Circuit, 79, 256, 310, 311
homogeneous, 54, 118, 308; homogeneous congregation, 7; homogeneous unit, 10, 252, 253,

310; homogeneity, 8, 49
Hosier, Harry (Black), 99, 335
House of Representatives, U.S., 132, 326
Hunter, George G. III, xiv, 8, 55, 242

I

immigrant, xiv, 3, 22, 54, 60, 61, 86, 100, 206, 236, 244, 245
immigration, 6, 60, 86, 109, 170, 243, 244, 246, 306, 312, 315
Indian, 31, 42, 82, 131, 196, 252, 257, 306; See Native Americans
institutional factors, 4-8, 10, 34, 70, 74, 77, 82, 86, 110, 117, 145, 169, 173, 196, 205, 212, 214, 216, 222, 232, 236, 239, 240, 241
internal growth, 54
Ireland, 65, 69
Ireland, John, 92
Irish, 60; Irish connection 22, 217, 314

J

Jacobins, 147, 151
jail, 85, 93, 94, 167, 320
Jarratt, Devereux, 73, 74, 92, 98, 102, 107, 180, 314, 316
Jay, John, 131
Jay's Treaty, 152
Jefferson, Thomas, 92, 132-134, 147-150, 152, 153, 177, 189, 209, 212, 336, 337

K

Keefer, Luke, 11
Kelley, Dean, 9, 10, 221, 222, 224, 226, 228-232, 238, 307, 337
Kentucky, 31, 32, 40-42, 45, 57, 118, 120, 126, 141, 144, 150, 167, 170, 172, 175, 176, 196, 306, 309, 311, 328, 332, 334
King, John, 22, 62, 70

L

Lafayette, Marquis de (General) 149, 150
Lancaster, PA, 78, 82, 119
lay preachers, 22, 57, 72, 233, 311
Lee, Jesse, 23, 25, 32, 57, 58, 72, 77, 78, 83, 84, 87-89, 94, 99, 102, 104, 105, 107, 121, 122, 128, 129, 140-143, 155, 158-160, 163, 165, 169-171, 179-182, 185, 186, 199, 201, 204, 207, 210, 212-218, 226, 228, 257, 311, 322, 335
Lexington, KY, 80, 118, 120, 328
liberalism, 8, 222-225
Local church, 242
local preacher, 4, 22, 50, 55, 57, 62, 65, 67, 72, 85, 97, 99, 101, 102, 103, 105, 106, 110, 121, 140, 145, 167, 170-173, 175, 177-181, 184, 186, 192-196, 204, 227, 228, 230, 242, 311, 314, 332
located preacher, 103, 122, 129, 331
love feast, 11, 63, 64, 86, 226, 314, 315
Loyalists, 72, 80, 86, 315 (see Tories)
Lutheran Church, 15
Lynn, MA, 57, 201, 204, 212, 337; Lynn Society, 208, 214, 215

M

Madison, James, 131-133, 148, 325
Magaw, Samuel Rev. Dr., 98, 108
Maine, 31, 32, 42, 43, 45, 47, 118, 172, 201, 202, 204, 206, 215, 257, 311
mainline church, 9, 15, 222-225, 235, 246
Mann, John, 85, 86
manumission, 104, 178; (See emancipation)
manumit, 106
marriage, 182, 193, 242; marriage fee, 127, 130; Thomas Coke's marriage 130
married preachers, 124-126, 193, 211

358 Index

Maryland, 22-26, 29-31, 37-39, 43-45, 48, 56, 59, 65, 66, 77-79, 82, 86, 87, 91-95, 98, 104, 106, 117, 119, 121, 122, 132, 133, 137-139, 141-144, 158, 165, 166, 172, 175-178, 182, 186-188, 190, 194, 195, 213, 226, 306, 311, 314, 317-319, 333

Massachusetts, 3, 31, 32, 42, 43, 45-47, 57, 75, 118, 121, 123, 124, 172, 199, 201, 204, 205-208, 213, 217, 236, 257, 311, 314

McGavran, Donald, 10, 19, 247, 252, 308, 316, 339

McRoberts, Archibald, 73

Methodist Church, 2, 3, 115, 182, 186, 254; Methodist leaders, 8, 86, 134, 205; Methodist membership, 2, 5, 22-26, 28-30, 32, 33, 35, 37, 38, 39-46, 48, 62, 71, 79, 108, 120, 121, 147, 194, 237, 242, 306

Michigan, 42, 325

Mid-Atlantic, 5, 24, 26, 29, 32, 37, 43, 44, 47, 48, 57, 62-64, 68-72, 77, 78, 80, 82, 85-87, 98, 104, 109, 118-121, 132, 190, 204, 228, 245, 315, 317, 319

missionary, xii, xiii, 3, 11, 16, 22, 42, 52, 56, 57-60, 62-70, 72, 74, 83, 84, 92, 95, 100, 103, 110, 111, 115, 130, 138, 144, 164, 166, 172, 177, 193, 199, 201, 202, 204, 205, 212, 216, 226-244, 309, 312, 314, 325

missionary method, 56, 57, 243

N

Natchez, MS, 17, 42, 57, 122
Native Americans, 54, 81, 82, 197
Newport, RI, 81
New England, 5, 8, 31-34, 42, 43, 45-48, 57, 81, 97, 109, 110, 118-123, 131, 132, 134, 138, 158, 173, 192, 193, 196, 199-221, 226, 231, 235-237, 245, 253, 311, 317, 322, 327, 334-337

New Hampshire, 31, 32, 43, 45, 47, 118, 123, 201, 202, 206, 257
New Haven, CT, 86, 119, 201, 205, 206, 306, 318
New Jersey, 23-27, 29, 31, 37, 43, 62, 67, 70-72, 77, 78, 80-85, 98, 106, 118, 119, 172, 178, 199, 305, 311, 316, 317, 320
New Light movements, 222
New Orleans, LA, 7, 120, 310
New York, 24, 27, 29, 31, 37, 43, 52, 54, 56, 57, 62-64, 68-71, 75, 77, 80, 81, 84-86, 117-119, 126, 132, 133, 158, 165, 172, 185, 191, 199, 214, 257, 309-312, 314-316, 326, 335; New York City, 22, 60, 80-82, 85, 310, 314, 315, 318; New York Society 52, 62, 63, 70, 85, 86, 314, 315
Newport, RI, 81, 119
Niebuhr, Reinhold, 221, 233-235, 237
Norfolk, VA, 60, 70, 80, 86, 87, 118, 120, 314, 318
North Carolina, 10, 23-26, 29-31, 38, 39, 44, 45, 48, 73-75, 77, 78, 81, 88, 96-98, 102, 118, 122, 134, 135, 137-139, 143, 144, 149, 158, 166, 170, 172, 175, 176, 179, 183, 187, 256, 306, 314, 317, 321
Nova Scotia, Canada, 57, 86, 154, 314, 328

O

O'Kelly, James, 84, 92, 101, 112, 154-178, 180, 187, 190, 193, 195, 196, 207, 215, 230, 321, 329-332; O'Kelly and the Council, 157-160; O'Kelly's schism/revolt, 107, 110, 111, 154, 160, 161, 167; O'Kelly and the 1792 General Conference, 163, 168, 169; O'Kelly and the Republican Methodist Church, 169, 170; O'Kelly's *Apology*, 160, 161, 170;

Oaths of Allegiance or state oaths, 84, 85, 92-95, 106
Ohio, 31, 40-42, 45, 120, 126, 131, 313
Orr, J. Edwin, 148, 149, 327
Owings, Richard, 65, 103

P

Paine, Thomas, 148-151, 245
parachurch, 223, 241
pastor, 7, 14, 47, 55, 62, 67, 102, 115, 164, 215, 236, 242, 315, 322, 335, 337
Pennsylvania, 22-24, 26, 27, 29, 31, 37, 43, 62, 65, 67, 71, 75, 77, 78, 80-82, 96, 106, 117, 119, 120, 122, 132, 134, 172, 178, 257, 311, 319, 334
Pentecost, 143, 250; Day of Pentecost, 15; Pentecostal, 222, 246; Pentecostal Church, 254
Persecution, 200, 226, 229; of Baptists, 86, 91, 92, 319; of Methodists, 93-95, 106, 152, 205, 226, 319
Philadelphia, 22, 60, 62-64, 67, 69-72, 81-85, 98, 117, 119, 164, 165, 185, 190, 315
Pilmoor, Joseph, 22, 62-64, 70, 309, 312-315
Pinckney, Charles, 153
poor, the, 9, 92, 124, 126, 128, 134, 183, 185, 189-193, 195, 209, 211, 235, 249, 318, 326
poverty, 68, 124-127, 196
pragmatism, 11, 12
Presbyterian, 4, 96, 102, 168, 321; Presbyterian Church, 3; New Light Presbyterian, 73; presbytery, 101, 102, 111
presiding elder, 54, 56, 84, 92, 110, 112, 127, 145, 156, 159-161, 165, 167, 168, 173, 199, 233, 327, 331, 335
priest, 67, 73, 86, 92, 98, 102, 107, 112, 115, 147, 183, 207, 224, 229, 244, 314; priestcraft, 208

Primitive Methodist Church, 165
prison, 85, 92-94, 123
prisoner, 71, 88
Providence, 119, 216, 217
Puritan, 203, 204, 206, 207, 327

Q

Quaker, 46, 64, 96, 104, 184, 206, 216, 230

R

Ramsey, David, 150
Rankin, Thomas, 63, 64, 66, 72, 101, 102, 103, 111, 313, 329
Reed, Nelson, 101, 165
Religion, xii, 148, 191, 317, 320, 327, 337, 338
renewal, 18, 96, 115, 153, 202, 221, 223, 224, 226, 250, 251, 254, 255, 339
repent, 16, 52, 162, 210, 218, 240; repentance, 4, 16, 113, 248
republican, 110, 113, 134, 149, 153, 156, 166, 169, 171-173, 177, 192, 207, 211, 234, 235; republicanism, 110, 147-150, 153, 154, 157, 162, 189, 193, 207, 209, 245, 336
Republican Methodist Church, 169, 170
revitalization movement, 250-252, 254
revitalization theory, 252
revival, xi, xiii, 18, 24, 25, 48, 55, 59, 72-75, 77, 78, 87, 89, 91, 93, 96, 105, 109, 139-145, 167, 176, 177, 194, 212, 217, 228, 232, 245, 247-250, 252, 254, 255, 306, 314, 316-319, 329, 332, 335, 338, 339; revivalism, 5, 74, 75, 212, 248, 316, 319; revivalistic, 255
Revolutionary War, 41, 59, 80, 82, 104, 114, 123, 124, 134, 149, 234, 317, 318, 327
Rhode Island, 31, 32, 42, 43, 45, 46,

81, 123, 172, 201, 204, 206, 212, 216, 232
Richmond, VA, 77, 120, 315
Rodda, Richard, 83, 313
Roman Catholic, 3, 4, 306; Roman Catholic Church, 244, 246
Roozen, David, 241, 246
Ruff, Daniel, 67, 95
rules, 12, 15, 52, 62-66, 104-106, 108, 160, 171, 172, 178-181, 186, 195, 226, 227, 231, 311, 313

S

sacraments, 54, 55, 65-67, 70, 96, 101-103, 105, 108, 111, 114, 115, 161, 179, 229, 233
salary, 126, 127, 130, 196
sanctification, 4, 209, 210
Savannah, GA, 40, 60, 70, 81, 86, 87, 118, 120, 144, 166, 172, 232
schism, 111, 163, 165, 166, 168, 170, 178, 215, 232, 332
Scripture, 12, 163, 305
Seabury, Samuel (Bishop), 86, 318
Second Great Awakening, 21, 34, 48, 109, 203, 245, 249, 252, 332
sectarian, 222, 234
sect-to-church theory, 221, 233, 237, 238
secularism, 9, 15, 223, 245, 246, 254, 255
Semple, Robert, 176
Senate, U.S., 123, 132, 328
Shadford, George, 74, 85, 318
Shays, Daniel, 123
Shays' Rebellion, 131
slave, 10, 39, 60, 65, 72, 80, 104-106, 109, 117, 124, 148-152, 166, 167, 171, 178-190, 192, 195, 253, 310, 317, 321
slavery, 104, 105, 109, 135, 166, 178, 179-189, 195, 196, 239, 311, 321
Smeltzer, Guy W., 51, 310
society, 11, 22, 25, 39, 51-54, 56-58, 62-67, 69, 71-73, 85-89, 92, 94, 98, 99, 104, 113, 121, 122, 126, 131, 135, 141-143, 148-150, 154, 164-166, 170, 179, 181-183, 185, 186, 188, 190-192, 194, 195, 201, 205, 206, 208, 210-215, 217, 218, 221, 222, 225-227, 234, 242, 246, 250-252, 254, 255, 311-317, 331
Sooy, J. L., 2, 4, 6, 305
South Carolina, 29-32, 38-40, 44, 57, 58, 75, 96, 98, 117, 118, 122, 137, 138, 144, 149-151, 153, 164, 166, 167, 171, 176, 182, 184, 185, 187, 191, 306, 310, 324, 327, 328, 334
spiritual factors, 6, 247, 248, 306, 316
Spraggs, Samuel, 85, 86, 318
standing order, the, 123, 207, 208, 210, 211, 212
Stark, Rodney, 4, 221, 237, 241, 246, 254, 338
steward, 107, 182, 227, 311
Strawbridge, Robert, 22, 59, 61, 65-70, 73, 77, 78, 102, 103, 106, 107, 122, 177, 313, 314
Sussex Circuit in VA, 26, 73, 140, 141, 326
Sweet, William, 91, 205, 314

T

Tennessee, 31, 32, 40, 45, 118, 126, 144, 150, 172, 196, 256, 306, 310, 311, 332
rich, the, 124, 131, 133, 151, 189, 191, 247
Tories, 72, 80, 81, 83, 86, 92-95; (See Loyalists)
transfer growth, 3, 18
trustee, 83, 182, 190, 244

U

Umbel, William, 205, 209, 212, 237
UMC, ix, xiv, 15, 222, 243, 244, 245, 246, 247, 254, 255

Unitarians, 203, 204, 210
Universalists, 46, 96, 203, 204, 210; Universalism, 204

V

vanguard method, 56, 57
Vasey, Thomas, 111, 154
Vermont, 31, 32, 37, 42, 43, 45, 47, 118, 123, 201, 202, 257, 320
Virginia, 22-26, 29-31, 37-39, 44-48, 50, 57, 58, 62, 65, 66, 70, 72-75, 77, 78, 82, 84, 86-89, 91, 92, 96, 98-102, 104-106, 108, 115, 117-119, 121, 122, 137-140, 143, 144, 148-158, 160, 161, 169-172, 175-185, 187, 191, 194-196, 215, 226, 228, 245, 256, 306, 309-314, 316-322, 326, 331-333

W

Wagner, C. Peter, 6, 10, 247, 307, 307, 308, 339
Wakeley, J. B., 85, 86, 314, 318
Wallace, Anthony F. C., 250-252
Washington, 2, 3, 31, 80, 81, 87, 119, 120, 132, 134, 152, 180, 339
Washington, DC, 2, 3, 31, 119, 120
Watters, William, 65, 95, 102
Webb, Thomas (Captain), 22, 59, 62, 69, 70, 313, 315, 316
Weber, Max, 221
Wesley, John, vii, 9, 11, 12, 22, 51, 52, 54, 55, 59-74, 82-86, 95, 96, 101-104, 106, 107, 110-113, 116, 125, 151, 154-157, 161-166, 190, 199, 205, 209, 210, 230, 235, 244, 254; *Calm Address*, 83; Wesley's order of salvation, 11, 51, 209, 226; Wesley's rules; 62-64; Wesley's authority, 63, 68, 154, 162; Wesley's books, 311; Wesley's guidance, 95, 112; Wesley's missionaries, 22, 59, 63, 65, 68, 70, 74, 83, 314; Wesley's assistants, 63-65, 321; Wesley's letters, 64, 107, 110-112, 154, 308, 322; Wesley's expulsion from American *Minutes*, 156, 162; ragmatism, 11, 12; Tory, 95; *The Ministerial Office*, 67; created an American Methodist church, 110-112; Wesley Chapel, 85-86; Wesley's death, 162.
Whatcoat, Richard (Bishop), 111, 154, 155, 329
Whiskey Insurrection, 134
White, Thomas (Judge), 25, 93, 101
White, William (Bishop), 2
Whitefield, George, 73, 199
William Williams, 25, 309, 324
Williams, Robert, 22, 70, 73, 309, 314
Wren, William, 95

X

XYZ Affair, 149, 150, 153

Y

Yearly conference, 172

www.ingramcontent.com/pod-product-compliance
Lightning Source LLC
Chambersburg PA
CBHW021115300426
44113CB00006B/160